ROMANS

ABINGDON NEW TESTAMENT COMMENTARIES

ROMANS

LEANDER E. KECK

Abingdon Press
Nashville

ABINGDON NEW TESTAMENT COMMENTARIES:
ROMANS

Copyright © 2005 by Abingdon Press

This book is printed on acid-free paper.

Library of Congress Cataloging-in-Publication Data

Keck, Leander E.
    Romans / Leander E. Keck.
        p. cm. — (Abingdon New Testament commentaries)
    Includes bibliographical references.
    ISBN 0-687-05705-1 (alk. paper)
    1. Bible. N.T. Romans—Commentaries. I. Title. II. Series.

    BS2665.53.K43 2005
    227'.107—dc22

                                                            2005008999

05 06 07 08 09 10 11 12 13 14—10 9 8 7 6 5 4 3 2 1
MANUFACTURED IN THE UNITED STATES OF AMERICA

For

Paul S. Minear:

teacher, colleague, friend

CONTENTS

FOREWORD

The *Abingdon New Testament Commentaries* series provides compact, critical commentaries on the writings of the New Testament. These commentaries are written with special attention to the needs and interests of theological students, but they will also be useful for students in upper-level college or university settings, as well as for pastors and other church leaders. In addition to providing basic information about the New Testament texts and insights into their meanings, these commentaries are intended to exemplify the tasks and procedures of careful, critical biblical exegesis.

The authors who have contributed to this series come from a wide range of ecclesiastical affiliations and confessional stances. All are seasoned, respected scholars and experienced classroom teachers. They take full account of the most important current scholarship and secondary literature, but do not attempt to summarize that literature or engage in technical academic debate.

Their fundamental concern is to analyze the literary, socio-historical, theological, and ethical dimensions of the biblical texts themselves. Although all of the commentaries in this series have been written on the basis of the Greek texts, the authors do not presuppose any knowledge of the biblical languages on the part of the reader. When some awareness of the grammatical, syntactical, or philological issue is necessary for an adequate understanding of a particular text, they explain the matter clearly and concisely.

The introduction of each volume ordinarily includes subdivisions dealing with the *key issues* addressed and/or raised by the New Testament writing under consideration; its *literary genre, structure, and character;* its *occasion and situational context,* including its wider social, historical, and religious contexts; and its *theological and ethical significance* within these several contexts.

In each volume, the *commentary* is organized according to literary units rather than verse by verse. Generally, each of these units is the subject of three types of analysis. First, the *literary analysis* attends to the unit's genre, most important stylistic features, and overall structure. Second, the *exegetical analysis* considers the aim and leading ideas of the unit, deals with any especially important textual variants, and discusses the meanings of important words, phrases, and images. It also takes note of the particular historical and social situations of the writer and original readers, and of the wider cultural and religious contexts of the book as a whole. Finally, the *theological and ethical analysis* discusses the theological and ethical matters with which the unit deals or to which it points, focusing on the theological and ethical significance of the text within its original setting.

Each volume also includes a *select bibliography,* thereby providing guidance to other major commentaries and important scholarly works, and a brief *subject index.* The New Revised Standard Version of the Bible is the principal translation of reference for the series, but the authors draw on all of the major modern English versions, and when necessary provide their own original translations of difficult terms or phrases.

The fundamental aim of this series will have been attained if readers are assisted, not only to understand more about the origins, character, and meaning of the New Testament writings, but also to enter into their own informed and critical engagement with the texts themselves.

Victor Paul Furnish
General Editor

PREFACE

A preface, though written last, is meant to be read first, for it gives the author the opportunity to comment on the completed work by disclosing some aspect of one's relationship to it. This, then, is the place to acknowledge that the subject matter of Romans has drawn me into an ongoing engagement with Paul.

Nonetheless, understanding this letter has not grown easier. Grasping it as a whole—both its content and its purposes—is more challenging than understanding its parts, though they too resist facile explanations. The task is never finished. So I must acknowledge also that publishing this commentary requires a measure of audacity—though not as much as was required of Paul in writing this troublesome letter in the first place. Indeed, the longer I have lived and worked with this text, the more evident his boldness has become.

He had the audacity to claim that what God had achieved in the death and resurrection of Jesus overcomes both the human dilemma in the face of God's impartiality and the human condition (being subject to the power of sin and its accomplice, death). That same achievement, Paul also argues, discloses the parity of Jew and Gentile in both plight and redemption, yet avoids dissolving the particularity of Israel's indestructible election. In the effort to convey Paul's audacity, I have reached for that dimension of the God-reality that his assertions assume—namely, God's otherness, expressed as God's freedom, the unstated theme of Romans. Paul's audacity in writing Romans, then, reflects his effort to grasp the audacity of God. The commentary reflects my effort to grasp the audacity of Paul.

The commentator's task is to help the reader of Romans understand the apostle's bold thinking distilled in the text. While some will read it in Greek, for most it is the Englished Paul they meet. Consequently, this commentary attends to the English versions commonly used, for they too—like all translations—are interpretations. With the Anglophone user in mind, I also decided—with some reluctance—to restrict references to secondary literature in English. (Users with competence in French or German will find ample references in the commentaries by Cranfield, Dunn, Fitzmyer, and Moo.) Given the focus on the text, my engagement with the work of predecessors and peers usually goes unnoted, though my indebtedness to them is deep.

Some debts must, however, be recorded, especially because often they were incurred through ongoing conversations about Paul and his letter to the Romans. I am particularly grateful for what I have learned in this way from Paul Achtemeier, Victor Paul Furnish, Paul W. Meyer, and above all from J. Louis Martyn. Lou has been a cherished friend for over half a century; during the last fifteen years he has also been a neighbor. He graciously read drafts of this commentary and invariably asked penetrating questions that drove me back to the text. While our occasional disagreements are always instructive, it is for his steadfast encouragement that I am most grateful.

This commentary is dedicated to Paul S. Minear, whose course in Romans at Andover Newton Theological School in 1952 first energized my study of this letter, and whose own audacity in interpreting the New Testament continues to stimulate my own efforts to understand this remarkable part of the Christian Bible.

Bethany, Connecticut, August 2004

LIST OF ABBREVIATIONS

1 Apol.	Justin, *First Apology*
1QH^a	*Thanksgiving Hymns^a*
1QpHab	*Pesher Habakkuk*
1QS	*Rule of the Community*
2 Bar.	*2 Baruch (Syriac Apocalypse)*
AB	Anchor Bible
ABD	*Anchor Bible Dictionary*
Abr.	Philo, *On the Life of Abraham*
ad loc.	*ad locum* (at the place)
alt.	alternate translation
Ant.	Josephus, *Jewish Antiquities*
ANTC	Abingdon New Testament Commentaries
AT	Author's translation
AV	Authorized Version (King James Version)
BDAG	W. Bauer, F. W. Danker, W. F. Arndt, and F. W. Gingrich, *Greek-English Lexicon of the New Testament*
Bib	*Biblica*
CBET	Contributions to Biblical Exegesis and Theology
CBQ	*Catholic Biblical Quarterly*
CBQMS	Catholic Biblical Quarterly Monograph Series
CD	Cairo Genizah copy of the *Damascus Document*
CEV	Contemporary English Version
Conf.	Philo, *On the Confusion of Tongues*
Congr.	Philo, *On the Preliminary Studies*
Contempl.	Philo, *On the Contemplative Life*
Decal.	Philo, *On the Decalogue*
Diogn.	*Diognetus*

HDR	Harvard Dissertations in Religion
Her.	Philo, *Who Is the Heir?*
Hist. eccl.	Eusebius, *Ecclesiastical History*
IB	*Interpreter's Bible*
IBC	Interpretation: A Bible Commentary for Preaching and Teaching
IBS	*Irish Biblical Studies*
ICC	International Critical Commentary
Interp	*Interpretation*
JAAR	*Journal of the American Academy of Religion*
JBL	*Journal of Biblical Literature*
JR	*Journal of Religion*
JSNTSup	Journal for the Study of the New Testament: Supplement Series
Jub.	*Jubilees*
L.A.B.	Pseudo-Philo, *Liber antiquitatum biblicarum*
Leg.	Philo, *Allegorical Interpretation*
Let. Aris.	*Letter of Aristeas*
lit.	literally
LXX	Septuagint
Mart. Pol.	*Martyrdom of Polycarp*
MNTC	Moffatt New Testament Commentary
Moffatt	The New Testament in the Moffatt Translation
Mos.	Philo, *On the Life of Moses*
NASB	New American Standard Bible
NCB	New Century Bible
NEB	New English Bible
NIB	*New Interpreter's Bible*
NICNT	New International Commentary on the New Testament
NIV	New International Version
NJB	New Jerusalem Bible
NovT	*Novum Testamentum*
NRSV	New Revised Standard Version
NTS	*New Testament Studies*
Pss. Sol.	*Psalms of Solomon*
REB	Revised English Bible

RSV	Revised Standard Version
SBLDS	Society of Biblical Literature Dissertation Series
SBT	Studies in Biblical Theology
SD	Studies and Documents
sg.	singular
SNTSMS	Society for New Testament Studies Monograph Series
Somn.	Philo, *On Dreams*
SP	Sacra Pagina
Spec. Leg.	Philo, *On the Special Laws*
s.v.	*sub verbo* (under the word)
T. Benj.	*Testament of Benjamin*
T. Gad	*Testament of Gad*
T. Jos.	*Testament of Joseph*
T. Reu.	*Testament of Reuben*
TPINTC	TPI New Testament Commentaries
WBC	Word Biblical Commentary
WUNT	Wissenschaftliche Untersuchungen zum Neuen Testament
ZNW	*Zeitschrift für die neutestamentliche Wissenschaft*

INTRODUCTION

Like widely differing siblings raised by the same parents, each letter produced by Paul has its own distinguishing character. For the historically minded critic, each letter's unique traits provide important clues for detecting the circumstances in which Paul wrote it as well as what he hoped to achieve with it. Scholars assume that by examining the content of the letter (the "answer"), they can infer the readers' situation that Paul is addressing (the "question")—a method sometimes called "mirror reading." In the case of Romans, however, both the particular traits and the overall content are so unusual that scholars continue to debate why Paul wrote precisely *this* letter and what he hoped to achieve by it in *Rome* (see, e.g., Wedderburn 1988 and the essays in Donfried 1991). The place to begin, however, is not with the sundry "solutions" to the problems presented by the letter, but with the phenomenon of Romans itself. This introduction has three parts: (a) a brief overview of Romans as a literary phenomenon, identifying its salient features and the issues they raise for understanding the letter; (b) a discussion of efforts to locate the historical context of Romans; and (c) a brief orientation to the theology of Romans. (Those not already familiar with Romans are urged to read the entire letter first.)

THE PHENOMENON OF ROMANS

Romans in the New Testament

The only Romans we have is part of the New Testament; while Romans was expected to stand on its own feet when first read in Rome, no manuscript containing only Romans exists. Moreover, its location in the New Testament is deliberate: It follows Acts, which ends by reporting Paul's arrival in Rome. Placing Romans here subtly invites one to infer that the substance of Paul's proclamation in Rome of "the kingdom of God and teaching about the Lord Jesus Christ" (Acts 28:31) is to be found in the letter that follows immediately. Yet Acts does not imply that the letter had arrived in Rome before he did (as he had expected it would). In fact, Acts does not mention any of Paul's letters. Though Romans was not his first letter, it now heads the list of his letters because the church came to regard it as his most important writing and made it the introduction to the whole collection of thirteen letters claiming Paul as their author. Consequently, the location of the letter has the effect of minimizing the importance of the letter's first readers (indeed, several Greek manuscripts actually lack the references to Rome in 1:7, 15). We do not read the letter as its first recipients did, for it comes to us already interpreted by its placement. So then, the more we read Romans only in light of its (alleged) original setting, and as a single letter from Paul to believers in Rome, the more we "undo" the phenomenon of Romans in the New Testament. Recognizing this does not invalidate historical exegesis, but expands its horizon by reminding us if the early church had not canonized this letter we would not be reading it at all. The New Testament Romans is the only Romans that exists.

Moreover, because Romans is part of the New Testament, we can compare it with the other letters ascribed to Paul, as well as with what Acts reports about his message and mission. But the first readers of Romans had only this letter from him; they could compare it only with what they may have heard about him. While this commentary does from time to time compare Romans with what Paul had said before, it concentrates on Romans itself; what Paul says *in this text* should not be conflated with—nor inflated into—what he *thought* comprehensively, though it is essential to understand that as well.

Discourse as Letter

As a literary phenomenon Romans is a letter, but with one significant distinguishing feature: It begins and ends like a letter (1:1-

15; 15:14–16:27) but its core reads like a discourse. Moreover, unlike Paul's other letters, this core contains scant references to the readers—understandable, since he had not yet been to Rome. Whereas Paul was known to his other letters' readers, in Romans he presents himself to readers who for the most part did not yet know him. But if so, why does this self-presentation turn into a long discourse (1:16–15:13), most of which is a theological argument? Further, neither the discourse nor the epistolary framework refers to the other (except for 15:15); each can be read independently of the other. What, then, accounts for the fact that Romans not only combines them but also does so by putting the discourse within the letter?

Some explanations point to the situation in which Paul wrote the letter. In 15:22-32, he discloses that he is on his way to Jerusalem with funds collected for poor believers there. He is aware that this trip might endanger his life because he will face fierce opposition when he gets there. Did he, then, compose this letter as his "last will and testament" (so Bornkamm 1963)? Or did he send to Rome the speech he would make to defend his gospel to hostile believers in Jerusalem (so Jervell 1971)? Or did Paul create it in light of his plan to go to Spain after coming to Rome (15:24, 28-29, see below)? If so, the content of the discourse part of Romans is significant for understanding Paul's reasons for announcing his plan for Spain. Unfortunately, however, he does not explain exactly why he is determined to go there. Or is the letter itself the explanation? Although each of these— Jerusalem, Spain, Rome—is on Paul's mind when he wrote, none of these factors accounts for the way Romans is put together.

In any case, to account for Romans one must understand it as a whole. It cannot be understood piecemeal, for it is more than the sum of its parts. Moreover, the more one tries to grasp it as a whole, the more evident it becomes that how one understands one part affects how everything else is understood. The need to grasp Romans as a whole shows why reading it in light of ancient letter-writing conventions, important as that is, does not suffice, because doing so illumines the epistolary framework but not the "body" of the letter, the discourse part. To understand the text as a whole, therefore, some scholars have begun to read it in light of ancient rhetoric. The move to rhetoric makes sense; after all, Romans was written to be *heard* by assembled believers, not studied silently in private. Moreover, since rhetoric—broadly understood—concerns the art of persuasion, reading Romans as a speech should disclose what Paul expected to achieve when it was heard, and so account—at least partly—for its composition and content.

Given Aristotle's classification of the types of speeches—judicial (used in courts to adjudicate a past event), deliberative (used in assemblies to decide a future action), and demonstrative (epideictic, used in various settings "to enhance knowledge, understanding or belief, often through praise or blame, whether of persons, things or values," as Kennedy [2001, 45] put it)—Romans is clearly epideictic (so Wuellner 1976, 134, 139). But what sort of epideictic, and for what purpose does it enhance "knowledge, understanding or belief"? Rhetorical analysis of Romans has not, unfortunately, been particularly successful in answering these questions, though noting Paul's use of rhetorical devices and modes of argument is often illuminating. For example, Jewett (1982) called Romans an "ambassadorial letter" in which Paul introduces himself as Christ's emissary before giving a "rationale for his forthcoming visit." But this classification, like identifying parts of the letter in rhetorical terms (exordium, narration, proofs, peroration), does little more than paste a rhetorical label on the letter. Not helpful either is the proposal that Romans is a *logos protreptikos,* a discourse then used by philosophers to "win converts . . . to a particular way of life" (Aune 1991). Would Paul send such a text to persons whose faith is already well known (1:8) and which he lauds (15:14)?

Recently, Philip Esler combined attention to "the rhetorical situation" with diverse sociological studies, especially of group identity, to account for Romans without marginalizing its theology. A "rhetorical situation" has three components: "some disorder in social relationships marked by urgency," an audience whose behavior can be modified, and various "constraints" (such as persons, events, interests, or values) that can interfere with the desired modification (Esler 2003, 16). Relying heavily on the epistolary framework, Esler proposes that the social disorder Paul deals with is the strained relations between Judeans (his word for "Jews") and Greeks in the Roman house churches, and so Paul emphasizes their new common ingroup identity as participants in the Christ-movement. Seen sociologically, in asserting his leadership Paul becomes an "entrepreneur of identity" by demonstrating that he is an exemplar of the new identity in Christ. If one agrees that the conflict in Rome was essentially ethnic, Esler not only accounts for the phenomenon in a fresh way, but also allows one to visualize the impact of Paul's theology on real people with real prejudices.

The literary phenomenon of Romans—a discourse within a letter—invites us to look more closely at both the epistolary framework and the discourse, bearing in mind that together they constitute one text. It is not Paul who calls attention to the seams where they join, but scholars. Only for the sake of convenience, then, will they be discussed separately.

The Structure of the Discourse

The discourse part of Romans juxtaposes three distinct sections, each with its own theme: 1:16–8:39 (an exposition of the gospel and Christian existence); 9:1–11:36 (a discussion of Israel and the nations in God's purpose); and 12:1–15:13 (various exhortations, followed by an extended counsel focused on one issue, religiously sanctioned observances). Whereas the second section begins abruptly, without indicating how it is related to the first, the third section begins with a "therefore" at 12:1, thereby inviting the reader to discern how the following exhortations flow from what Paul had written about Israel and the nations in chapters 9–11, and about the gospel in chapters 1–8.

In the *first* section (1:16–8:39), Paul's rhetorical skill appears initially in the composition of the dramatic indictment of human wickedness (1:18-32), then in his use of the diatribe style (beginning with 2:1–3:8), in which the speaker and an imagined interlocutor have brief exchanges in order to advance the argument (Paul controls both sides of the "conversation"; see Stowers 1994).

This section has two distinct major units, consisting of 1:16–5:11 (some say 4:25) and 5:12–8:39, each with its own characteristic mode of argument (for a discussion of the way Paul's reasoning affects the structure of Romans, see Boers 1994, chap. 3). The word "righteousness," pivotal in 1:16–5:11, virtually disappears from the second unit; also, quotations from scripture, frequent in 1:16–5:11, are suddenly rare in 5:12–8:39 but reappear even more frequently in the next section (chaps. 9–11). So impressed was Scroggs (1975) by these (and other) differences that he argued that chapters 1–4 and 9–11 probably are "the actual text of a sermon Paul had preached," whereas chapters 5–8 were once a homily on the Christian life that Paul embedded in the other sermon—a shrewd but unpersuasive proposal. In fact, adopting it does not explain the phenomenon but simply restates the question it generates: Why would Paul have interrupted his sermon with chapters 5–8? Putting a homily on the Christian life after chapter 11 would have created a much smoother transition to the moral exhortations in chapters 12–15.

One distinguishing feature of the *second* section (chaps. 9–11) is Paul's disclosure of his intensely personal stake in the subject matter—God's way with Israel and the Gentiles, especially in light of Israel's special relation to God (9:1-5). The letter had opened with Paul asserting his identity as an apostle with a mission to Gentiles; not a word was said there about a mission to Jews or his ethnic identity. Not until the discussion of Abraham in chapter 4 does it become explicit that Paul is a Jew. Now, however, he opens the tightly argued chapters 9–11 by disclosing his intense agony over the problem created by the Jews' refusal of the gospel about their own messiah (9:1-5). Later, Paul even adduces himself—a Christian Jew—as evidence that God has not rejected "his people" (11:1). Assuming that the "I" in chapter 7 is primarily rhetorical, nowhere else in Romans is Paul himself such an explicit factor in the argument.

The important distinguishing feature of chapters 9–11, of course, is the content. None of Paul's other letters contain anything comparable, though the problem that generated these chapters had been discussed briefly in 2 Cor 3 and Rom 2:28–3:8.

Some (e.g., Stendahl 1976, 4) have regarded these chapters as the high point of the letter and the key to the whole. In any case, the interpretation of these chapters has generated more intense debate than any other part of the letter, especially because Paul's argument moves toward the assertion that "all Israel will be saved" (11:26). Since Romans is part of the church's scripture, that statement is important not only for understanding what Paul may have had in mind *then,* but also for what it implies about the church's relation to Judaism *today.*

The *third* section, like the first, has two distinct large units, 12:1–13:14 (Paul's exhortations about various matters) and 14:1–15:13 (focused on one issue—the meaning of religious practices). Distinctive about the first is Paul's counsel to "be subject to the governing authorities" (13:1-7), which has no parallel in his other letters. Distinctive about the second is its similarity with 1 Cor 8–10. Consequently, Karris (1974) argued that Rom 14:1–15:13 is a generalized restatement of the earlier exhortation, not evidence of a live issue in Rome. Others (like Esler 2003; Sampley 1995; Donfried 1991, 102-25) see in these chapters the very live issues that prompted Paul to write the letter and to say what he did. Minear (1971), in fact, identified those passages in the letter that Paul addressed to specific groups in the Roman dispute. The more difficult it is to account for Romans by looking at Paul's own situation (see above, p. 21), the more scholars have looked to chapters 14–15 and what follows—the concluding part of the epistolary framework that begins at 15:14—for information about the recipients that might explain the letter.

Features of the Epistolary Frame (1:1-15; 15:14–16:27)

Two passages in 1:1-15 are noteworthy. (a) Into a customary letter-opening, Paul inserts a christologically centered statement of the gospel (vv. 2-4). The only other time Paul interrupts the salutation this way is in Gal 1:1-2, which signals that his status as apostle is an issue to be dealt with. In Romans, it is the insertion's Jewish cast (Christ as a descendant of David) that makes it remarkable because Paul goes on to refer to the letter's recipients as Gentiles who fall within the scope of his mission. Is there something about the recipients that prompts him to begin in precisely this way? Assuming that the recipients were familiar with letter-writing conventions, did they ask the same question?

(b) Paul says he does not preach the gospel (to win people to the faith) where it has been proclaimed already (15:20). But in 1:15 he is eager "to proclaim the gospel to you also who are in Rome," implying that he intends to bring them his version of the gospel (presumably found in the first section of the discourse, 1:16–8:39), even though he is grateful that the readers' faith is already "proclaimed throughout the world" (v. 8). Why, then, does Paul want to bring them the gospel in order to "reap some harvest [karpos, often a metaphor for conversions] among you" (1:13)? Klein (1969), noting the word "church" does not appear before 16:1, claimed that Paul does not regard the Christian community in Rome as a bona fide church because it was not founded by an apostle (hence not by Peter), and that Paul's preaching will meet this deficit. Even if this proposal is unpersuasive, it prompts one to ask two questions: Just what sort of "harvest" did Paul hope to reap in Rome? and What role did he expect this letter to play in it? Was the letter the planted seed whose results Paul expected to harvest on arrival?

In 15:14-32, Paul writes more fully about his travel plans than in 1:10-15. Now he reveals that he regards his anticipated arrival in Rome as a stopover, for his eye is really on a new mission in Spain (15:23-24), for which, he subtly suggests, he would welcome the Romans' support ("sent on by you"). Whereas in 1:13 he explained why his desired trip to Rome had "been prevented" (he does not say by whom or what), now he explains why his journey is delayed again: he must take the offering to Jerusalem (15:25-28). While he gives a rationale for this gift from Gentile churches, he mentions neither the meeting in Jerusalem when he agreed to collect these funds (Gal 2:7-10), nor his efforts to complete the undertaking (1 Cor 16:1-4; 2 Cor 8 and 9); nor does he explain just what he expected to accomplish in Jerusalem. Instead, he reveals his apprehension about what might happen to him in Jerusalem and asks the readers to join him in praying for a positive outcome so that he will arrive in Rome "with joy."

Virtually all of the unusual features of chapter 16 have proven significant for understanding Romans—its author, its content, its first readers, and its use in the early church. Although Manson (1962b) argued that Paul attached chapter 16 to a copy of Romans sent to Ephesus, Gamble (1977) showed that from the start this chapter was part of the letter sent to Rome (for a contrary view, see Peterson 1991). Only if chapter 16 was always part of the letter can one mine it for information about Christians in Rome, as well as infer that Paul was sufficiently informed about their problems to address them in 14:1–15:13.

The first unusual feature appears at the outset—the little "letter of introduction" for Phoebe (16:1-2), a significant figure in the church at Cenchreae, the port near Corinth from which Paul probably expected to embark for Jerusalem. Such letters were widely used, but Paul incorporates one only in Romans—probably because it was Phoebe who carried the letter to Rome and read it to the assembled believers. In doing so, she functioned as Paul's surrogate voice.

Especially remarkable are the many greetings, first from Paul (16:3-16), then from others (16:21-23). Except for Galatians, such greetings are found in all of Paul's other letters, but only in Romans—sent to believers, most of whom he does not yet know— does he greet twenty-five individuals by name (plus one not named) as well as several groups of unspecified size. Frequently, he also discloses his high estimate of these individuals' significance in the spread of the gospel—an indication that he had known these people in conjunction with his own mission before they went to Rome (see Lampe 1991). He appears to send greeting to everyone he can think of, as if to demonstrate that among the yet-unknown believers in Rome he has these distinguished friends. If Paul is aware that he has been misinterpreted, perhaps also in Rome (see 3:8), perhaps he expects his friends to vouch for him.

Among the distinguishing features of chapter 16 is the abrupt warning in verses 17-20, which stands between Paul's own greetings and those sent by others. There is no evidence that Paul wrote this paragraph with his own hand, as there is in 1 Cor 16:21-24 and Gal 6:11-18. Moreover, except for 3:8, already noted, nothing else in Romans anticipates this kind of warning. Many, including this commentary, regard it as someone's addition to the letter.

Finally, Rom 16:25-27 exposes the problem of the text of Romans, for some manuscripts do not include it, while others put it after 14:23 or 15:33. Sometimes it is followed by verse 24, which is lacking in other manuscripts (recent translations put this verse in a footnote). Indeed, the text of Romans appears in six forms:

> 1:1–14:23 + 15:1–16:23 + 16:25-27
> 1:1–14:23 + 16:25-27 + 15:1–16:23, 25-27
> 1:1–14:23 + 16:25-27 + 15:1–16:24
> 1:1–14:23 + 15:1–16:24
> 1:1–14:23 + 16:24-27
> 1:1–14:23 + 16:25-27 + 16:1-23

Of these, this commentary (like NRSV) uses the first form of the text. Since the data are found elsewhere (e.g., Gamble 1977; Fitzmyer 1993; Moo 1996), here it suffices to state what the evidence indicates: By omitting the chapters devoted to local matters in Rome, as well as the personal greetings, Romans was made less parochial and more pertinent to all Christians—consistent with its placement in the canon at the head of Paul's letters.

Some scholars are convinced that it was not only the end of Romans that was modified but the body of the letter as well (see Walker 2001, chap. 8), sometimes by adding an occasional phrase or sentence, but especially by inserting large blocks of material. John O'Neill (1975), for example, labeled the following as additions: 1:18–2:29; 3:9-20; 5:12-21; 7:14-15; 10:6*b*–11:32; 12:1–15:13; 16:16*b*-20, 14-27. This proposal, despite many astute observations, is driven largely by the conviction that Paul's theological reasoning was simple, straightforward, and less dialectical than what we now find in Romans. Relieving Paul of the responsibility for these passages, most of them difficult, does yield a simpler line of thought. But was it Paul's? Romans was subjected to surgery before. In the second century, Marcion did the same thing with Paul's letters generally, and provided a similar explanation: After Paul was off the scene, others (for Marcion, Christian

Jews who had opposed Paul) distorted what he had written by adding passages; Marcion too "recovered" the original text by deleting the alleged additions. While arguments for major excisions are unconvincing, especially since no manuscripts lack the alleged additions, Romans may well contain occasional short additions to the text. The commentary will call attention to such passages. (An outline of the letter as a whole is displayed in the table of contents.)

THE HISTORICAL CONTEXT

Significant Clues

For recent efforts to reconstruct the circumstances in Rome that prompted Paul to write this letter, no passage has been exploited more often than 16:3-4, Paul's greetings to Prisca and Aquila, mentioned also in Acts where she is called Priscilla. According to Acts 18:1-3, when Paul came to know them in Corinth, they were among the Jewish refugees whom Claudius had expelled recently from Rome; subsequently, they accompanied him to Ephesus (Acts 18:18, 24-26). When Paul wrote 1 Corinthians (from Ephesus), they were still there, as 1 Cor 16:19 shows. Now they are back in Rome, presumably because after Nero's accession to power in 54 CE, Claudius's decree (commonly dated in 49 CE, though not without difficulty; see Achtemeier 1997; Esler 2003, 98-102; Lampe 2003a, 14-15) was no longer in effect. The second-century Roman historian Suetonius reports that Claudius had expelled Jews because they "constantly made disturbances at the instigation of Chrestus *(impulsore chresto),*" often regarded as a garbled reference to conflicts over the messiahship of Jesus (*Lives of the Caesars,* "Claudius," 25).

By combining the evidence from Suetonius, Acts, and Rom 16, scholars (following Wiefel 1970) have advanced a reconstruction that has influenced the interpretation of Romans at many levels. Stated simply, Christianity in Rome began among Jews (for details, see Lampe 2003a); the resulting conflicts within the Jewish community prompted Claudius to expel them (not "all" of them, as in Acts 18:2, however). In their absence, Christianity became predominantly Gentile, perhaps primarily among those who had been "God-fearers" (Gentiles attracted to Judaism but not converts to it). When the Christian Jews returned (along with other Jews), they found themselves marginalized, and often at odds with Gentile believers over Torah-observance, particularly over diet, because Christians customarily shared meals in conjunction with the Lord's Supper. Assuming this reconstruction, it is held that in chapters 14–15 the "weak in faith" are the observant Christian Jews while "the strong" are the Christian Gentiles, perhaps a majority now, who insist that Christians are free to eat anything they wish. Plausible as this reconstruction may be, the fact is that nowhere in Romans does Paul allude to the *return* of Jews, not even of Prisca and Aquila. Nor is it clear that in the controversy the fault line ran simply between Jewish and Gentile Christians, for some non-Jews too had dietary scruples and taboos. The interpretation of Romans in this commentary takes this widely accepted reconstruction not as established fact but as a plausible, though unverifiable, hypothesis. More is at stake here than simple caution about a historical reconstruction based on very limited evidence. No reconstruction of earliest Christianity in Rome accounts adequately for much of the theological argument of the whole letter because it ignores the likelihood that the content of Paul's argument has its own logic and so was not directly his response to what he thought was going on in Rome.

The Letter's Probable Setting and Purpose

First, around 57 CE Paul dictated this letter while at Cenchreae (the port near Corinth, mentioned at 16:1); he was at a pivotal juncture in his mission (see 15:19-23), when taking the fund to Jerusalem would conclude his work in the East and free him for a wholly new venture in the westernmost part of the empire, Spain. Here, where there seem to have been virtually no Jews at the time (so Jewett 1991, 267), he would fully exercise his calling to be "an apostle to the Gentiles" (11:13). For this new undertaking, he hoped to have the support of the westernmost Christians, those in Rome, most of whom were Gentiles themselves.

Second, Paul could not, however, count on their support so long as they were squabbling over dietary observances, which he regarded as evidence that the full import of the gospel had not yet been grasped. Indeed, if a bowdlerized version of his views fueled the dispute, he could not expect the believers in Rome to support the mission of a divisive apostle.

Third, for Paul, the quarrels were a symptom of the deeper problem—the attitude of Christian Gentiles toward Jews, especially non-Christian Jews. Evidently the Jews' widespread refusal of the gospel prompted some Gentile believers to conclude that their salvation through Christ was quite adequate apart from the Jewish people; even more, it was these believers who were thinking that the Jews' No to the gospel implied God's No to the Jews. Unless Paul corrected those misunderstandings, he could not expect them to understand and support his mission in Spain, for he was not going there to propagate a Gentile religion in the name of Jesus, in effect an alternative to Judaism.

Fourth, Paul explained the gospel-meaning of Jesus in a way that emphasized God's way of dealing with the human condition (as he understood it, see below), not with either an alleged Jewish or a Gentile condition. Consequently, the "rhetorical situation" (see above) prompted Paul to write Romans as his theology of mission.

Fifth, to counter the rumor that his emphasis on faith made morality irrelevant (perhaps implied in 3:8), Paul included the moral/ethical counsels in chapters 12–13. These chapters clearly show that for Paul, the gospel of God's righteousness/rectitude and Christian morality (righteousness/rectitude) are inseparable.

Sixth, whatever the extent to which the conflict over dietary observances was an ethnic controversy between Christian Jews and Christian non-Jews, Paul avoided exacerbating the situation by addressing the problem in ethnic terms; instead he cast his counsel in terms consistent with the rest of the letter. Whereas he told the Galatians that in Christ "there is no longer Jew or Greek" (Gal 3:28), now he argues that God's people includes both *as* Jews and Gentiles (Rom 4:9-12). Even if Gal 3:28 lies behind Romans historically, and under the text substantially, it should not be smuggled into the interpretation of Romans. However one views Paul's consistency or lack of it, he was not his own disciple. Romans is a fresh text.

PAUL'S THEOLOGY IN ROMANS

If one is to engage Romans, one must engage its theology, for every line in it is affected by Paul's theological thinking. But does Romans itself *have* a theology? Not if "theology" refers to a comprehensive statement of what Christians believe (or ought to believe), carefully crafted so that the logical relation of all the parts becomes evident as a system of doctrines (see Furnish 1990). Romans does have a theology if one is prepared to let Paul present it in his own way. This discussion does not, however, offer a summary *of it*, but rather a brief orientation *to it*. Instead of presenting a digest of the letter's theology before *one* has read and pondered the text itself, the following observations call attention to certain features that characterize the theology that one meets in the text.

The Character of Paul's Theology in Romans

First of all, the theology in Romans is not comprehensive (the word "cross" does not appear, and the Lord's Supper is not mentioned); rather, this theology is focused by Paul's purposes in writing the letter. Energized by his unprecedented and unrepeatable situation—the moment between a mission in the East and one in the West—he now draws on what he had come to understand during two decades of preaching, teaching, counseling, suffering, and letter-writing; now he explains how the gospel pertains to the overarching purposes of God for humanity (thereby validating his mission). Since Romans is probably Paul's last letter (unless Philippians was written in Rome), this letter expresses his matured theology. Paul's thought was not static (so Furnish 1970). Still, it is difficult to demonstrate how his thought changed ("developed" is not the proper word) over time because each letter's thought addresses the circumstances in Paul's churches. (For differing reconstructions of the stages by which Paul reached the understanding of his vocation in Romans, see Donaldson 1997 and Park 2003.)

Even though Romans is Paul's most sustained theological argument, he is not clarifying concepts (Romans lacks definitions); he is clarifying the import of the Christ-event for the human plight. Here he selects, restates, amplifies, condenses, and emphasizes those aspects of his thought that he believed would show why his message and mission are mandated by God's purposes. The theology in Romans assumes that Paul realized that unless the gospel announcing the Christ-event deals decisively with the *human* condition, there would be little reason to announce to Gentiles what the God worshiped by Jews has achieved in Christ. It is the universality of the particular that drives this theology. At the time, Epicureanism, Stoicism, mystery religions, and incipient Gnosticism also had their own understandings of the human condition and its resolution. Paul's is rooted in biblical and Jewish apocalyptic thought, whose universal scope he appropriated because—as we shall see—it allowed him to include Gentiles in the one salvation wrought by God in the event of Christ. That is why Romans is the first Christian theology of mission.

Understandably, today's readers find the theology in Romans to be quite different from much Christian theology since the modern era began. This theology has been driven by the need to show how the Christian faith is still credible in the post-Enlightenment world. Paul's task was rather to show why the gospel should be believed at all and what difference it makes if one believes it. So he concentrated not on its rationality (its reasonableness) but on its rationale, its inner logic; his thinking is not defensive but assertive. Moreover, since Romans is not a programmatic essay but a letter (a writing substituting for direct speech), its theology addresses the reader with truth claims. Consequently, one can scarcely avoid asking, Is Paul right? And if he is, what difference does it (still) make? Doubtless, the letter generated the same questions when it was first heard in Rome. The basic task of this commentary, however, is not to make Paul's theology credible, but to expose that theology's own distinct intelligibility, so that the reader can engage the apostle's thought and so decide whether, and to what extent, Paul was right.

The Pivotal Event

Paul's theology becomes more intelligible when we read the letter with the grain, as we learn to think with him, proceeding from the same starting point from which his own thought moved. That point of departure was not a "big idea" but a defining event, Jesus Christ, whose significance for Paul pivots on his death and resurrection. Since Romans was written for believers, Paul need not explain the Christ-event itself, for he assumes that they do not need information about it (Keck 1989, 430-60). What he does need to do is spell out its import for the human plight. But if we are to follow his thought, it is essential to understand his view of Jesus' death and resurrection (in Paul's mind, they are distinguishable but not separable; when one is mentioned, the other is implied). Jesus' resurrection was not the absolute starting point, of course; it was the starting point for Paul's rethinking the theology he inherited. Paul's Christian theology is the result of thinking on this side of the Jesus-event. Paul's theology is *ex post facto* theology (Keck 1993, 27-38).

For Paul, Jesus' resurrection is neither a figure of speech nor a miracle—an exception to the rules that by definition confirms the rules; rather it was an event in which God changed the rules, so to speak. How so? Because that event signaled the breakthrough of the New Age into the present Age (see Wright 2003). According to Jewish apocalyptic eschatology in which resurrection belief emerged, the New Age (called "The Age to Come") will bring the definitive alternative to everything that has gone awry in history. This alternative state of affairs is not another stage in history (comparable to the Iron Age following the Bronze Age), but the God-given alternative to what history has become, when everything at last is as it should be. To characterize this understanding of Jesus' resurrection, theologians use the phrase "the eschatological event."

Whereas our problem with Jesus' resurrection (or anyone else's) is usually conceptual (How can we conceive of such a thing?), the pre-Christian Paul's problem was different. As a Pharisee, he already understood and believed what resurrection entailed: the arrival of the New Age. His problem was, Did it really happen to the crucified Jesus? Once he was convinced that it did happen, he no longer lived and thought out of the past and present into the future, but out of the future (the arriving New Age) into the present. His life now had the character of celebration and anticipation, living now by what is not yet fully here but which will be fully here at the coming of the Christ (the parousia, not actually mentioned in Romans), when his victory over sin and death would be completed. The Christian Paul had to make sense of the changed present even though the Age to Come had not yet completely and manifestly replaced This Age. Paul's whole theology is marked by this tension between "the already" and "the not yet." He had not only to think new and different thoughts; he had also to think old thoughts differently. So it is not surprising that following the flow of his thought is often arduous. It was surely arduous for him to work it out.

When in Romans Paul works out the import of the pivotal event for humanity's plight, he declares that in the gospel "the righteousness of God is revealed through faith for faith" (1:17). Since the christologically shaped outline of the gospel that Paul inserted into the salutation (1:2-4, see above) emphasizes Jesus' resurrection, it is necessary to see how Paul relates God's righteousness to that event.

Paul did not rehearse the steps by which he worked out this relationship, but we can surmise how he might have done so, perhaps taking the following steps:

(a) The axiomatic starting point, rooted in the Old Testament, is that God is righteous, that God does right because God is right.

(b) Since the New Age, when everything is right because it has been made right, burst into the present in Jesus' resurrection, the making right of all things (and all people) is now under way because God's rightness is activated definitively. In other words, God's rightness, God's righteousness, God's rectitude rectifies whatever is not right and therefore not rightly related to God. Because making the English word "righteous" into the verb "righteousify" creates an intolerable barbarism, translators turn to the Latin equivalent "just," which can be turned into the verb "justify." In short, "justification" is rectification, the making right what is wrong.

(c) Because as yet there is no unambiguous empirical public evidence that Jesus was resurrected, Paul—and those to whom he announced it—could only believe it or deny it. But if they did believe it, their own wrongness was now being made right when they believed the news of what God had done. They were rectified/justified *by faith,* the appropriate response to this news.

(d) Because by definition the New Age is as universal as This Age, the rectification that occurs in faith must be available to everyone, Gentiles no less than Jews. Indeed, both are rectified through the same undeserved act of God in Jesus. That being the case, their parity in rectification implies also their parity in plight, even though Jews have the law and Gentiles do not.

(e) Since the rectifying God is the One of whom scripture speaks, and who made commitments to Israel, God's undeserved rectification of Jew and Gentile alike must accord with scripture. For Paul it does.

Rectifying everything and everyone, important as it is, does not yet deal with the reason wrongness is universal—for Paul, the inescapable power of sin (resulting in the human dilemma) and its ultimate expression, death (the unavoidable condition). Paul finds the solution in the death/resurrection of Jesus: By participation in this event, one is as freed from sin and death as was Jesus. In short, Paul can find in this event the definitive solution to the human plight precisely because he understands it as the *eschatological event* that has "already" begun, though it has "not yet" been completed. What makes following Paul's thought in Romans so arduous is the relentlessness with which he thinks through the various consequences of what God has achieved in Jesus. (First Cor 15 shows that in Romans Paul did not say everything about the significance of Jesus' resurrection.) Romans has no paragraph in which Paul explains God's righteousness as a concept. Instead, he taps his understanding of God's rectitude in order to illumine something else, especially why no one is rectified by obeying the law (3:19-20) and why the Jews thus far have refused the gospel (10:1-3). Nor does Paul abandon the motif of God's rectitude when he writes of participating in Jesus' death and resurrection (chap. 6); nor is it accidental that the motif returns as his exposition of Christian existence reaches its high point in chapter 8. Even though righteousness terminology does not reappear in chapters 12–15, one would not distort Romans by saying that these chapters sketch the resulting ethos of the rectified.

While God's rectifying rectitude is foundational for Paul's theology in Romans, it is not the only idea on which his arguments rely. For example, he assumes that the God who elected Israel is the Creator who is concerned also for the redemption of creation from death (8:19-23). At times, he appeals also to axiomatic statements in order to warrant a point, such as the conviction that God, being impartial (2:11), is not God of Jews only (3:29-30), or that everyone will face God's judgment (14:10). Above all, what is noteworthy about Paul's theology in Romans is the way the pivotal significance of Jesus' death and resurrection emphasizes the character of God. The theology of Romans is theocentric because it is christomorphic. That is, the understanding of God, which Paul inherited from the Pharisaic Judaism he had once advocated assiduously (Gal 1:14), was reshaped in light of his conviction that God had resurrected the crucified Jesus. For the theology of Romans (as for Paul's theology as a whole), what matters is not what Jesus of Nazareth had done and said in his Galilean ministry, but what God had done in resurrecting him, and thus far only him. If God has done that, then what does that disclose about God that was not known before, and how is this new disclosure related to what was known through scripture, which emphasizes God's commitment to Israel? Such are the questions that propel Paul's theological thinking in this letter.

The Role of Scripture

An important factor in the theology of Romans is Paul's use of scripture, even though his explicit reliance on it is not distributed evenly throughout the letter but is noticeably prominent in chapters 1–4 and 9–11. While his quotations generally follow the wording of the Greek Bible (LXX), from time to time Paul either quotes a peculiar version or, more likely, rewords the text so that it "fits" his point better—as other writers of the day did also. In attending to Paul's use of scripture, it is essential to bear in mind that his Bible was not yet called "Old Testament" (or "First Testament"), for there was no "New Testament." More important, recent studies have called attention to the ways Paul's argument probably was influenced by the biblical text even where it is not actually quoted (see Hays 1989, who studies Paul's use of scripture generally, and Wagner 2002, who analyzes the use of Isaiah in Romans). In the nature of the case, of course, allusions are not always apparent to all readers—probably including those who first heard the letter in Rome. Still, one must reckon with the likelihood that many of the Christian Gentiles in Rome had been God-fearers who had become familiar with the Greek Bible while attending the synagogues before their conversion. In any case, what matters here is recognizing that in using scripture Paul does far more than quote it as a "proof text" that lends authority to an argument made on other grounds. Again and again, the argument itself expresses Paul's reasoning from the text. In other words, especially in Romans, Paul appears as the first biblical theologian in the early church. He not only reads his Bible in light of Christ, but also reads the Christ-event in light of his Bible—not to play one off against the other, but to show their coherence because God is consistent. Because Paul does not read scripture in light of the historical circumstances in which it was written, his interpretive moves often appear arbitrary to those who simply assume that every text must be read in light of its historical context. Following Paul's theologizing by means of scripture may well be as much of a challenge as understanding his ideas.

COMMENTARY

THE MESSENGER AND THE MESSAGE (1:1-15)

This passage is the first half of the epistolary framework that surrounds the discourse part of Romans (the second part begins at 15:14). Here Paul presents himself as the bearer of the Good News of God by stating why the news is good. The unit is composed of two paragraphs. The "grace wish" at the end of verse 7 ends the first, the reference to Paul's desire to preach in Rome (v. 15) rounds out the second. English translations end verse 15 with "Rome," but Paul's Greek sentence ends with "preach the gospel" *(euangelisasthai)*; this allows Paul to segue smoothly into a summary statement of the gospel in verses 16-17. It also helps the hearer follow the thought. Paul often ends a statement with a word that is the springboard for the next point—evidence that he composed the letter with great care.

◊ ◊ ◊ ◊

Salutation (1:1-7)

Even before Phoebe, the presumed courier and reader of the letter (16:1-2), got to verse 15, the first long sentence (vv. 1-7) would have alerted the hearers that something unusual is afoot. According to well-established custom, letters first named the sender, then the recipient; next came the greeting. But before mentioning the recipients, Paul inserts verses 2-6, and then replaces the normal "Greeting!" *(chairein)* with a wish for grace *(charis)* and peace. Phoebe's hearers may have thought this is how Paul always wrote letters, but today's students, having Paul's other letters,

39

know that only in writing to the Galatians did he also modify the salutation (Gal 1:1). They also know why: In that letter Paul defends himself and his gospel from gross distortion, and he signals what is to come by this modification. But the insertion here combines Christology and Paul's vocation, probably because that is on his mind right now. Romans is peculiar also in another detail: Paul writes in his name alone (the "we" in v. 5 is stylistic). Paul's coworker Timothy, cosender in most of his other letters, simply sends greetings (16:21). Romans appears as a personal statement.

In this personal self-presentation, Paul avoids all autobiographical information and instead concentrates on a theological self-interpretation, expressed in three significant phrases. (a) As in Gal 1:10 and Phil 1:1, he says he is Christ's "slave," which English translations consistently replace with "servant" in order to avoid the odious associations with slavery. But "servant" dilutes Paul's meaning, for in slavery the master acquires the person, not just the person's labor. But even though he uses the language of acquired property to speak of himself (and on occasion of others as well, see 1 Cor 6:20; 7:22-23), he sees himself not demeaned thereby but dignified, for the image implies that he is wholly at the disposal of Christ, whom he calls "Lord."

(b) In claiming that he is "a called apostle" he is not saying that he is "called an apostle" (by others) or that he is "called to be an apostle" (as translations have it), as if invited to that status; rather, he is saying that "call" is the means by which he became an apostle. This "call" is neither an invitation nor a summons but God's sovereign action, God's deliberate choice (as in 8:28). Paul neither volunteered to be an apostle, nor did he view himself as the church's apostle. In Gal 1:1 he insists that he did not owe his apostleship to any human agency but, as he explains in verse 15, only to God's revealing his Son to him. In 1 Cor 15:3-9 he speaks of this as the Risen Christ's appearing to him—a disruptive event that he insisted made him as much an apostle as the original disciples. For Paul, God's intervention in his persecuting activity (not mentioned in Romans) shows that his apostleship is a gift of God's grace (Rom 1:5; 1 Cor 15:10).

(c) Being "set apart for the gospel of God" also refers to God's action, for the passive voice (not evident in English) implies that God is the actor. Galatians 1:15 lies behind this phrase also. There Paul wrote that God "set me apart before I was born"—thereby claiming that his apostleship was not the result of historical circumstances but of God's destiny for him, now activated. His language paraphrases that of God's Servant in Isa 49:1 and about Jeremiah (Jer 1:5). In the present, Paul is Christ's slave; in the past he was made "a called apostle," but even before he was born God had selected him. He owes his vocation to God's specific action, not just to God in a general way. Paul was not plagued by "low esteem." He knows who he is, and why he has become who he is. Near the end of the letter he will note that he had written "rather boldly . . . because of the grace given me by God" (15:15). Today's readers too will note his alacrity.

Already in his earliest letter, Paul wrote of "the gospel of God" (1 Thess 2:2, 8, 9). To argue whether "of God" also there means that it is God's gospel, about God, or from God is to engage in sophistry, for all three dimensions are included in Paul's understanding. While he uses "the gospel of Christ" much more frequently, he never writes of "the gospel of Jesus" (Jesus' own message).

The word "gospel" (from the Old English *godspel*, "a good spiel" or message) translates accurately the Greek noun *euangelion*, whose Latin equivalent is retained in the German *Evangelium* and in the French *evangile*. Although the Greek verb *euangelizomai* lies behind "evangelize," New Testament translations use "preach/proclaim the gospel" and render *euangelistēs* (used only three times) as "evangelist," not as "gospeller," the long-abandoned Old and Middle English word. Paul apparently appropriated the verb from the LXX, where it renders the Hebrew word meaning "to announce good news," especially news of God's impending salvation (as in Isa 40:9; [and 52:7, which Paul quotes in 10:15]; 60:6; 61:1). In using this verb to speak of the meaning of Christ, Paul expresses his conviction that what Isaiah had announced had become an event, Jesus Christ. Since Isaiah never uses the noun (and the LXX rarely), Paul probably appropriated it from common Greek usage. He was not, however, the first to use it for a message with religious significance, for a famous inscription (from shortly before the birth of Jesus) announced that "the birthday of the god Augustus was the beginning for the world of good tidings [*euangelia*, plural!] that came by reason of him" (full text with commentary in Boring et al. 1995, 169). Whether Paul used the noun (always in sg.) as a deliberate challenge to Roman imperial propaganda, as claimed by some (e.g., Georgi 1997, 150-51), is not clear, especially in light of Rom 13:1-7 (see comment).

Verses 2-4 outline the content of "the gospel of God." The first thing Paul says about it is that God had "promised it beforehand through his prophets in the holy scriptures concerning his Son" (AT). The importance of this concise clause is hard to exaggerate. Built into it are the following claims: (a) God keeps the promise as documented in scripture. (b) God's prophets were Paul's predecessors in being "set apart" for conveying God's Word. (That is why Paul can appropriate the prophets' self-interpretation to speak of himself.) (c) The gospel cannot be construed as an alternative to scripture, let alone as its abrogation; it must be seen as the means by which God's fidelity to God's own promise is made known. (d) Paul did not read his scriptures (our Old Testament) for "background information," but as precedent (explained in chap. 4) and as promise, here the promise of the gospel. Indeed, here NRSV probably misreads Paul's Greek syntax, for by inserting "the gospel" at the beginning of verse 3, it has Paul begin afresh with "the gospel concerning his Son" (as do many commentators), whereas his sentence reads more naturally as "which he promised in the holy scriptures concerning his Son, who . . ." (so NIV; Hays 2002, 280 n. 18). Paul finds the gospel promised (not predicted) in scripture because he sees in Christ God's enacted faithfulness.

What Paul says about God's Son in verses 3-4 continues to generate far-ranging discussions because the interpretation of these verses has consequences for Paul's Christology generally as well as for its place in the history of early Christology, though tracing those consequences is not the task of this commentary. The pivot on which those discussions turn is the claim that both the parallel structure and the unusual phrasing indicate that Paul is quoting a tradition (formulated in Jewish Christian circles) that he modifies to conform more closely to his own Christology (see, e.g., Jewett 1995, 97-104). Those not persuaded by this hypothesis (e.g., Wright 2002) hold that Paul is simply using traditional phrases. This is certainly a simpler explanation at first glance, but a second look raises the question, Why, in presenting himself and summarizing the gospel, did Paul not mention either the cross or the significance of Jesus for the human condition? Moreover, he uses "spirit of holiness," not his way of referring to the Holy Spirit. Such considerations make it likely that Paul is adopting, and perhaps adapting, a piece of tradition without saying so. What matters here, of course, is understanding the text before us.

The deliberate parallel structure of the two lines implies a contrast between the status of the Son in the first line and the second:

concerning his Son
    who was descended from David   according to the flesh
    who was declared Son of God   in power according to the
                                       spirit of holiness
                                       by resurrection
                                     from the dead
Jesus Christ our Lord. (NRSV, modified)

"Descended from David" alludes to a common Jewish qualification of the Messiah, sometimes distilled in the title "Son of David," based on passages like 1 Sam 7:14. In these two lines, Christ's status is expressed in three types of contrasts: (a) action at pivotal points: descent and declaration; (b) origin: Davidic paternity and divine paternity; (c) modality of existence: "according to the flesh" and "according to the spirit of holiness" (a phrase used only here in the New Testament). The resurrection is clearly the climax.

This overview invites a closer look. (a) If Paul is indeed quoting, then the initial "who" has replaced some other word that had begun the statement. Was it "the Messiah"? "Jesus"? In any case, Paul introduces the statement here with "his Son," in keeping with

8:3, where he writes of God "sending his own Son," and especially with Gal 4:4, "God sent his Son, born of a woman. . . ." In other words, as Paul saw it, God's Son "pre-existed" before he became a human being "according to the flesh" (a few scholars disagree; e.g., Dunn 1980, 33-46). Thus, by first mentioning "his Son," Paul aligned the tradition behind verses 3-4 with Phil 2:6-11 (also regarded widely as a tradition), which begins with pre-existence and ends with post-existence. Since some Jews called the Davidic messianic figure "son of God" (one utterly obedient to God, as in Matt 5:9 [obscured by NRSV's "children of God"]), Paul could easily assimilate that view of "son of God" into his pre-existence Son Christology. As a result, the Christ-event is framed by the Son's arrival on the human scene by becoming a descendant of David and by his departure from it by resurrection, which designated him Son of God.

(b) The precise meaning of the contrast between "according to the flesh" and "according to the spirit of holiness" is not altogether clear. When REB translates the former as "on the human level" and the latter as "on the level of the spirit," it suggests the later doctrine of two simultaneous "natures" of Christ, which NIV makes explicit with "as to his human nature." But Paul is probably talking about the sequence of the Son's status (a terse narrative being implied), not about his "natures." Significant for understanding these lines is the phrase "with power" (v. 4). Because it clearly mars the symmetry of the lines, Paul may have added it to the tradition. But is the phrase used adjectivally or adverbially? Does it qualify "Son of God," implying that as a result of the resurrection the Son had power that the Son as descendant of David did not have? Or does it modify the verb, as in NIV and REB? REB reads "he was proclaimed Son of God by an act of power," and NIV has "was declared with power to be the Son of God." But because "with power" comes after "Son of God" and not after "declared," NRSV is to be preferred. It was the resurrection that designated Christ as "Son of God with power."

(c) Nor is it obvious that "descended" and "declared" are adequate translations. The former renders *genomenou*, from the word that means "happen, occur, come to pass" and sometimes "born" (so here NASB). The text speaks of an *event* (lit., came to pass, occurred), not simply descent or lineage. (Paul shows no awareness of the problem that Matthew addressed: how to combine the Virgin Birth with Davidic descent through Joseph; see Matt 1:16.) This event is contrasted with another: "was declared to be Son of God with power . . . by [or on the basis of] resurrection." Behind this "declared" is the participle of *horizō*, to mark off, define, determine, designate, and hence appoint (as in Acts 10:42; 17:31). Thus the statement asserts that the Son, having occurred from the stock of David, was designated or appointed to a higher status, Son of God with power—power greater than he enjoyed as a historical figure. Now he is "Jesus Christ our Lord" (Paul never uses "Lord" for the pre-existent Son of God).

This remarkable christological statement expresses the identity and significance of the Son by concentrating on his becoming a historical figure and on his being given (by God) a new trans-historical status by resurrection. (For Paul, resurrection is never confused with mere resuscitation; it always entails transformation.) Here, what matters for Christ's identity is his Sonship *before* he became "Son of David" and his *present* Sonship with power because (or since) he was resurrected. Everything between these transitional events (Jesus' ministry) is bypassed; the crucifixion is assumed. This Christology lies at the heart of the good news of God in Romans.

By ending the christological statement with "Jesus Christ *our Lord*," Paul sets up the rest of the paragraph, which makes the common Lordship concrete in what he says about his relation to the Roman believers. He begins by explaining his apostleship ("grace and apostleship" are not two gifts but one, expressed by a *hendiadys*, two words meaning one thing, as in "each and every"). Its goal is "the obedience of faith among all the Gentiles." By adding "for the sake of his name" (viz., Lord), the apostle alludes to his own obedience as Christ's slave and to the readers' status as well. "The obedience of faith" concisely fuses Paul's insistence that faith *is* the obedient response to the gospel with his equal insistence that this faith must be actualized in a new moral life under Christ. Unfortunately, what Paul fused, REB separated: "obedience *and* faith"; RSV has "obedience *to* the faith," as if Paul's aim were to achieve submission to a body of doctrine; here NIV is better: "the obedience that comes from faith." Better yet, "the obedience that *is* faith" (taking "of faith" as explanatory).

Paul deliberately points out that his vocation is "among all the Gentiles" because this includes the letter's recipients who, like Paul, are "called ones who belong to Jesus Christ" (AT). Romans is a word from the called writer to the called readers; Jesus Christ is their common Lord. Verses 5-6 show that Paul sees himself writing to Christian Gentiles, though the Roman house churches surely included believing Jews as well, as the names in chapter 16 show (see comment).

Not until verse 7 does Paul resume the letter-writing convention (sender to recipient), which verses 2-6 interrupted. (A few manuscripts omit "in Rome" here and in v. 15.) The fact that Paul addresses the readers as "God's beloved" instead of "the church," as he does in all his other letters except Philippians, has generated various explanations (e.g., Klein 1969, 29-43, see introduction, p. 26), none of them convincing. The phrase "grace and peace" is formulaic, but its content is pertinent to the situation in Rome, where believers are squabbling; in fact, 15:7 may be regarded as the hortatory application of the "grace wish" in verse 7.

◊ ◊ ◊ ◊

The salutation is at least as provocative today as when Paul dictated it. Woven into this one long sentence are theological perspectives and assertions that are unexpected in a statement designed to outline the gospel as the good news about that Reality called "God." Yet Paul neither trumpets a "new theology" nor informs the readers how to have a more intense "experience" of God. Instead, he announces what God has *done*: kept the promised gospel by resurrecting Jesus from the domain of death. God's deed arcs from the promise made in the past to the promise now kept. Remarkably, here it is not Christ that was promised but the gospel, though the event of Christ is its core content.

Paul and the Romans (1:8-15)

The hearers will have recognized verse 8 as the customary state-ment of thanksgiving (or petition to the deity) found regularly in letters at this point. Careful study of the "thanksgiving para-graph" (found in all of Paul's letters except Galatians, and replaced by a "blessing" in 2 Corinthians) has shown that he regularly adapted this convention by expanding it and phrasing it to signal important themes in the body of the letter. Here, how-ever, Paul devotes only verse 8 to expressing gratitude to God and uses verses 9-15 to explain his travel plans instead.

Just as he writes to "all God's beloved," so he now thanks God for all of them, because their "faith is proclaimed throughout the world"—a hyperbolic way of saying that the whole network of Christian groups knows that there are believers even in Rome. He underscores the truth of what he is about to disclose in verses 9-10 by saying that God is the "witness," not the onlooker but the one who can attest in court that Paul always mentions the recipi-ents in his prayers, asking that God grant his long-standing ("at last") desire to come to Rome. The parenthetical clause ("whom I serve . . . Son") reminds the readers that he is engaged in the service of God. Exactly what he means by saying that he does so "in [or with] my spirit" remains obscure (Cranfield [1975] lists seven pos-sibilities!); not obscure is the allusion that "the gospel of his Son" makes to verses 2-4 (the difference between "the gospel of God" and the "gospel concerning his Son" is simply a matter of accent, not substance). In verses 11-12 Paul states his purpose in Rome: to share an (unspecified) spiritual gift (a *charisma*, a gift bestowed by the Spirit, a "begracement") in order to "strengthen" them—that is, to deepen the faith they already have. Lest this sound patronizing, he corrects himself (rhetorically: an *epanorthōsis*): He really looks forward to *mutual* encouragement, as in REB: "I want us to be encouraged by one another's faith when I am with you, I by yours and you by mine."

In verse 13, he amplifies what he has just said in order to lead up to the declaration in verses 14-15. Only after Paul has written of Christian mutuality (v. 12) does he address the readers as "brothers" (NRSV: "brothers and sisters"); he will do so repeatedly (7:1, 4; 8:12; 11:25; 12:1; 15:14, 30). His use of this term in all of his previous letters is understandable, for they were sent to people he had come to know through his mission. In using it here to address largely yet unknown readers, Paul establishes rapport with them (rhetoricians call this strategy *captatio benevolentiae*, cultivating a favorable response); it also expresses his conviction that those for whom Jesus is Lord are members of a "family" ("fictive kinship," anthropologists call it; see Meeks 1983, 84-89).

The expression "I want you to know" (lit., a double negative: "I do not want you to be ignorant"), used also in 11:25 (as well as 1 Cor 10:1; 12:1; 2 Cor 1:8; 1 Thess 4:13), signals that what follows is important. Here it is the fact that Paul's long-standing desire to come to Rome has been prevented up to now, not what prevented the trip. And even here, the current delay is not explained. He does not blame Satan for frustrating his travel plans, as he had in 1 Thess 2:18. Perhaps 1 Cor 16:8-9 offers a clue; there he wrote that he will remain in Ephesus "for a wide door for effective work has opened to me, and there are many adversaries." If that is the right clue, his trip to Rome was often delayed because he had not yet finished his work. This is generally consistent with what he will say when he returns to the subject in 15:22-29. While Acts reports this intent to go to Rome, it says nothing about repeated delays; it simply says that while in Ephesus, "Paul resolved in the Spirit to go through Macedonia and Achaia, and then to go on to Jerusalem. He said, 'After I have gone there, I must also see Rome'" (Acts 19:21; see Gaventa 2004, *ad loc.*). This way of accounting for Paul's travels bypasses historical factors. In Rom 15:25-26, however, we learn what they were: collecting the funds for the poor believers in Jerusalem and then taking the gift to the Holy City. Acts also reports that in Jerusalem Paul had a vision in which the Lord assured him that he "must bear witness also in Rome" (Acts 23:11).

In verse 13 he writes of wanting some "fruit" (NRSV: "reap some harvest") also in Rome as he had already "among the rest of the Gentiles." To show that this includes all of them, in verse 14 he uses a double contrast: Greeks and barbarians, wise and foolish. "Greeks" is not an ethnic designation but a way of referring to those whose culture is Hellenized in contrast with those not influenced by it, the "barbarians" (originally, those who could not speak Greek). The contrast was well known. (There is no evidence that the "wise" or the "foolish" refers to Jews.) Paul sees himself as a "debtor" because being "a called apostle" entails an obligation to those for whose sake he was "set apart." This obligation explains why he is "eager" to preach the gospel also in Rome (a few manuscripts omit reference to Rome here). By the end of verse 15, Paul has set the stage for the programmatic statement in verses 16-17.

The first fifteen verses, taken together, are a remarkable self-presentation from a battle-scarred apostle with a strong ego. For one thing, by delaying an ampler comment on his vocation as well as his long-range plans until the latter half of the epistolary framework (15:14-33), he in effect allows the discourse part of the letter to serve as his real self-presentation. The readers (apart from Paul's friends greeted in chap. 16) meet the apostle by encountering his thought centered on the gospel of God. Such a mode of self-presentation is a direct reflection of his self-understanding. His public persona coheres with his identity as a person; neither is polished to outshine the other. As a "called apostle" he is the bearer of the message, but what he wants to convey to the readers is not the nature of his "call" but the content of the message. Nowhere in Romans does he leverage the message by tracing it to his personal "religious experience" (as circumstances required him to do in Gal 1:11-17). Rather, Romans precipitates his vocation into an extended theological argument without calling attention to himself—except for one thing: He links being "a called apostle, set apart for the gospel of God" (v. 1) and being a "debtor" eager to bring the gospel to the hearers (vv. 14-15). He is accountable to the God who chose him for the way he meets his obligation to Gentiles (by being their "debtor"); as a result of

God's call, he owes it to them to bring the gospel. In doing so, he does not make them indebted to *him*, but to God's grace—just as he is.

THE MESSAGE FOR THE HUMAN PLIGHT (1:16–8:39)

Romans 1:16–8:39 is the first of the three sections that make up the discourse part of Romans and it discusses "the gospel of God" outlined in 1:2-4. The section is framed by a thematic statement of the gospel (1:16-17) and the concluding celebration of God's invincible love (8:31-39). The exposition of the gospel consists of two differing parts, 1:18–5:11 (some say 4:25) and 5:12–8:30. In the former, the gospel is expressed in the idiom of rectification because the human plight is viewed as a *dilemma*, facing the impartial judgment of God for doing wrong and being wrongly related to God. In the latter, the human plight is viewed as a *condition* or status from which one must be freed; accordingly, here the good news is put in terms of participation in a different status.

The Gospel Stated (1:16-17)

These verses are generally regarded as stating the theme of the whole section. They are crafted with care; understanding them requires careful attention to details, beginning with the opening declaration that Paul is "not ashamed of the gospel." Those who take these words at face value wonder why Paul would insist on this negative point. It is more likely that this is a *litotes* ("the emphatic affirmation of something by denying its opposite"; so Rowe 2001, 128). Paul is really saying, "I am proud of the gospel," or "I have full confidence in the gospel."

◊ ◊ ◊ ◊

Verses 16-17 consist of two sentences, each giving the basis for the previous statement. Moreover, each sentence concludes with a secondary element that sharpens the primary point. In verse 15, Paul is eager to preach the gospel

(16) For the gospel is God's power for salvation for all
who believe,
for the Jew first and also for the Greek.
(17) For in it God's righteousness is being revealed "from
faith" to faith,
just as it is written, "The Righteous One from faith
will live." (AT)

Each line requires careful attention if one is to understand the passage as a whole, as well as its significance in a letter written with mostly Gentiles in mind.

Behind Paul's declaration in verse 16 lies what he had written in 1 Cor 1:18-25. There, to subvert the Corinthians' passion for "wisdom," Paul emphasized the message of the cross as "foolishness to those who are perishing, but to us who are being saved it is *the power of God*." He goes on to say that "Jews demand signs and Greeks desire wisdom, but we proclaim Christ crucified, a stumbling block to Jews and foolishness to Gentiles, but to those who are the called, both Jews and Greeks, Christ *the power of God* and the wisdom of God." But only Romans says it is "for the Jew *first*." The meaning of this "first" is disputed, but Paul will clarify it, beginning with 3:1-8 and especially in chapters 9–11. Here it suffices to note that the "first" may well have puzzled the Christian Gentiles in Rome, as it still puzzles most Christian Gentiles wherever they are.

Neither the boldness nor the significance of Paul's declaration should be missed. In claiming that the gospel *is* God's power, Paul is saying neither that it conveys new information *about* God's power, nor that God *has* power for salvation (that would not have been news, let alone "Good News"), even less that he knows how to release God's power to meet human need or desire (that would have been welcome news but not Good News). Rather, for Paul the gospel *is* God's power because the message itself has the capacity to effect salvation (what "salvation" entails will be spelled out in chaps. 5–8), though only those who believe it know that Paul's assertion is true (in accord with 1 Cor 1:18-25). NRSV's "have faith" does not do justice to Paul's *pisteuonti* ("for those who believe"), for he does not regard "faith" as a thing (a noun) one "has" but as an activity (a verb), ongoing, active trusting or relying on. Paul never explains, probably wisely, just how this trusting is linked to salvation. The initial "for" in verse 17 does, however, explain why the gospel is God's power for salvation.

The gospel is saving power because of what is being revealed (present passive) in it—God's righteousness (not "righteousness *from* God" as NIV has it). Since "righteousness" *(dikaiosynē)* basically means "rightness," Paul implies that when the gospel is believed, God's righteousness/rightness saves because it makes right, rectifies, what is wrong (spelled out in 3:21-31). This being made "right" lies at the heart of what Paul means by "salvation" in 1:16–5:11. Since Paul often uses the passive to refer to God's action without expressly mentioning God, the passive of the verb *apokalyptō* (reveal) implies that God reveals God's rectitude—precisely in (or by means of) the gospel. Taken together, verses 16-17 announce that the gospel is God's power to save because it is the means by which God saves, disclosing God's true character, rectitude/righteousness. The text does not say that the gospel informs people that God is righteous; rather the gospel is the means by which God's rectitude is effective action for salvation. Moreover, by using the present passive, Paul clearly implies that it *is now being revealed* through the gospel. When that occurs, it is God's power for salvation (in accord with 1 Cor 1:18-25, noted above).

Paul might have stopped here. Theologically, that might have sufficed. But he continues, saying *how* this revelation occurs (*ek pisteōs*; NRSV: "through faith") and the *purpose* for which it occurs (*eis pistin,* "for faith"); moreover, he supports this claim by quoting scripture (Hab 2:4): "the Righteous One 'by faith' *[ek pisteōs]* will live" (AT). It is the use of *ek pisteōs* in Hab 2:4 that caught Paul's eye and prompted him to appropriate it in verse 17*a*. As a result, this key passage bristles with problems. (a) What is the meaning of the preposition *ek* (lit., out of) when used with the noun "faith"? Does it mean "through faith," "on the basis of faith," or "from faith"? (b) How does the quotation from Habakkuk support the claim that in the gospel God's rectitude is being revealed "from faith for faith"? (c) In the quotation, does "by faith" *(ek pisteōs)* modify the subject ("the one who is *righteous from faith*") or the verb ("the one who is righteous will *live by faith*")? (d) Who is the righteous one? Is it the Christian believer, as widely assumed?

The appropriate starting point is the quotation of Hab 2:4, which Paul cites also in Gal 3:11. Paul's wording, however, agrees with neither the Hebrew nor the LXX, nor with Heb 10:38 ("my righteous one will live by faith," though manuscripts vary). Habakkuk (6th century BCE) wrestled with the problem of theodicy: Why does God bring on the wicked Chaldeans (Babylonians) to wreak havoc in Judah (Hab 1:5-6)? The answer: Wait for God's envisioned future, which "will surely come, it will not delay." In the meantime,

> Behold, as for the proud one [the Chaldean],
> His soul is not right within him;
> But the righteous will live by his faith. (Hab 2:4, NASB)

Here "faith" renders *emûnâ*, which also means "faithfulness" (REB: "by being faithful"). That is, during this distressful time, the righteous person will live by fidelity to God. According to the LXX, however, "the righteous one will live by *my* [God's] *pistis*" (here, "faithfulness" rather than "faith"). Paul's quotation, however, has neither "by *his* faithfulness" nor "by *my* faithfulness" but simply "by faith/faithfulness" *(ek pisteōs)*. But if Paul understands the righteous one to be the Christian believer, as commonly assumed, why would he not follow the LXX of Hab 2:4 and say that this person lives by God's faithfulness? Moreover, since he uses the quotation to support the claim that God's righteousness is being revealed in the gospel, would he say that a person's faith reveals *God's* righteousness? A different way of reading the text merits consideration.

A strong argument has been advanced that Paul understood the quotation as a messianic promise, kept in the event of Jesus Christ, because Paul read the LXX carefully. Whereas the Hebrew of Hab 2:3-4 urges the faithful to wait for the future even if *it* delays, the LXX speaks of *him*, thereby implying a messianic figure. Moreover, in some Jewish circles "the Righteous One" apparently was used to designate the deliverer and judge of the End Time. Unfortunately, the supporting evidence in *1 En.* 38:2; 53:6 appears in the *Similitudes* (chaps. 37–71), whose pre-Christian date is uncertain because this part of *Enoch* was not found at Qumran. However, in Acts 3:14; 7:52; and 22:14 Christian Jews do refer to Jesus as "the righteous one." (For a fuller discussion, see Hays 1989, 191-215 [summarized in Hays 2002, 273-81]; Hanson 1974, 49-54; and Campbell 1994, 265-85.) Further, quoting Hab 2:3-4 as a messianic promise at the end of verse 17 recalls 1:2, according to which God previously promised the gospel "through his prophets . . . concerning the Son." In short, Paul did not read the quotation anthropologically (referring to believers) but christologically—as a statement about Christ, the Righteous One. *He* will live *ek pisteōs* (from, or on the basis of) faithfulness. And that is the basis for saying that God's righteousness is being revealed in the gospel centered in Christ. At this point, Paul simply makes the assertion; what he means by Christ's faithfulness will be explained in 3:21-31 and 5:12-21. Verse 17 also says that God's righteousness/rectitude is being revealed *ek pisteōs eis pistin* (NRSV: "through faith for faith"). Here "for faith" clearly refers to the purpose of the revelation, namely, the intended result of hearing the gospel, igniting Christian faith.

The initial "For" in verse 17 signals that the entire verse states the basis for saying that the gospel is God's power for all who believe (v. 16). Surprisingly, Paul does not say in *whom* they believe (as he does in 4:24-25) or *what* they believe (as in 10:9). Here the unqualified reference to believing itself reflects Paul's unstated conviction that *pistis/pisteuō* (faith/believe) is the appropriate response to the gospel, whether made by Jew or Greek (= Gentile), for *pistis* is neither a peculiarly Jewish nor a distinctly Gentile act. As Paul sees it, *pistis* is the same remedy for both because both are caught in the same human dilemma ("under sin" he calls it in 3:9), even though Jews are monotheists with the law and Gentiles are polytheists without it. In crafting Romans, Paul's theological task is to explain how the salvation wrought by God through the gospel addresses those dimensions of the human predicament that are common to Jews and Gentiles, and why, accordingly, the same solution (the faith response to the gospel) is adequate for both. Otherwise there would be one salvation for Jews and another for Gentiles. But that would be inconsistent with the oneness of God, as Paul points out in 3:29-30.

It is significant that the dense theology in verses 16-17 appears as the programmatic statement in a letter that has in view primarily Christian Gentile readers in Rome. Paul is not trying to persuade them to believe the gospel; they already do. Nor is he trying to convince them that he is the apostle to the Gentiles, for he assumes he need only remind them of that (1:5, 13-14; 11:13). What he does not assume is that they understand adequately *why* it is important that there be but one salvation for Jews and Gentiles, and what flows from this. As Paul proceeds, he functions as a teacher who explains the gospel of God in a way that puts it on the large screen so that all his hearers can see how their own faith figures in the one grand purpose of God. If they grasp that, perhaps they will welcome him and support his work in Spain where he will continue to do his part to advance God's purpose. That is why Romans is the earliest written Christian theology of mission.

◊ ◊ ◊ ◊

It is not customary to think that God's rectitude is being revealed in the gospel, for it is assumed that God is righteous. Even less common is Paul's central point—that it is the disclosure of God's righteousness in the gospel that gives the message its power for salvation. So if Paul got it right, a gospel that does not disclose God's righteousness is not God's power to save, whatever capacity it may have to produce other results such as a positive disposition toward God. Since these verses only state the theme, we must read on in order to find out what verses 16-17 really mean. In the meantime, something else is worth pondering—Paul's double use of the *present tense*: The gospel *is* God's power for salvation because in/by it God's rectitude *is being* revealed. How does what happened to the dead Jesus on Easter unveil God's rectitude so that the news of that event in the past continues to be God's power to save others, whether Jew or Greek? Whoever wants to think with Paul has to think about that.

God's Rectifying Rectitude (1:18–5:11)

Although Paul has just stated the gospel in terms of God's righteousness/rectitude (vv. 16-17), he does not immediately proceed to explain why God's rectitude is Good News, gospel. Instead, he first discusses the human dilemma, doing so in language that fits the motif of God's rectitude, for the diagnosis must match the cure. So the whole discussion from 1:18–5:11 concerns God's rectifying rectitude, God's making right what is wrong. What makes being wrong such a serious dilemma is being accountable to God for it, especially because God—at least as Paul argues here—does not regard it as something we will outgrow with help. Something has to be *done* about it, something has to *happen* that only God can accomplish; Paul insists that such an event has occurred. But first he explains why the dilemma is so dire: God's wrath is impartial (1:18–3:20).

The Impartiality of God's Wrath (1:18–3:20)

To understand why only God's rectifying rectitude (God's righteousness) transforms the human situation, one must understand the situation properly. That is why Paul's thematic statement of the gospel in verses 16-17 is followed by the sobering exposé of the dilemma. Moreover, since he aims not only to inform but also to persuade, the unit is designed to win the readers' agreement: "Yes, that's the way it is!" Not until that is granted is one ready to hear the "gospel of God" in 3:21–5:11. Because the whole unit concerns only humanity's dilemma, it ignores almost completely the positive human achievements. Even so, it is not a mini-treatise on sin, but an argument leading up to the conclusion in 3:19-20. The argument emphasizes the universality of the human plight; it begins by asserting God's hostility to "*all* ungodliness" (v. 18) and ends by declaring that the *whole world* is "accountable to God." Being accountable is such a perilous situation because no one will be rectified by doing what the law prescribes (3:20). This plight is universal because God is impartial.

The purpose of the unit accounts for its structure. (a) After formulating the human dilemma (1:18-19), (b) Paul first portrays its

Gentile manifestation (1:20-32), then (c) discusses the import for Gentiles and Jews of God's impartial rectitude (2:1-16) before turning to (d) the Jews' unique situation (2:17-29). Next, 3:1-18 (e) discusses the integrity of God's righteous judgment, before (f) the conclusion (3:19-20) indicts everyone, using language that looks ahead to the resolution of the human plight in 3:21–5:11. The restatement of the human dilemma in 3:19-20 forms an *inclusio* (bracket construction) with 1:18. It is essential to keep in view the nature and goal of the argument lest, being distracted by its diverse references to related matters, one requires Paul to address topics he did not need to discuss.

◊ ◊ ◊ ◊

The Human Dilemma: God's Wrath (1:18-19): This opening statement announces that humans' suppression of the truth by their wicked behavior is responsible for God's wrath, now being revealed. God's wrath is not an irrational rage but God's legitimate response to the human abuse of the relation to God. (Nowhere does Paul's argument blame Satan, for that would detract from human accountability.)

Important is the way verses 18-19 are related to verse 17 on the one hand, and to verses 20-32 on the other. The initial "For" in verse 18 signals that it states a warrant for verse 17 (so also at the beginning of vv. 15, 16, 17, 18, 19, 20—showing the argumentative character of the passage). But the transition from verse 17 to verse 18 seems so abrupt, and the following content so unexpected, that Walker (2001) has argued that 1:18–2:29 is an addition to what Paul wrote—a view not accepted here. Others, accepting 1:18–2:29 as Pauline, have suggested that the "For" at the beginning of verse 18 merely signals a transition. By omitting the word "For," NIV and REB imply that Paul begins an unrelated topic. Verse 18 continues the argument by deliberately repeating the *apokalyptetai* ("is being revealed") in verse 17:

God's righteousness   is being revealed (in the gospel).
God's wrath   is being revealed from heaven.

Unfortunately, in both cases NRSV's "is revealed" implies that Paul used the perfect tense (used to express the ongoing result of past action, as in "Christ is raised"). But the present tense is an important element in both assertions, and ties them together. Likewise, the passive in both verses is important, for it implies that God is the one who does the revealing. What, then, is the relation between God's ongoing disclosing of God's righteousness and God's ongoing disclosing of God's wrath?

For one thing, the present tense precludes inferring that God's wrath in the past is now replaced by God's righteousness—popularized in the alleged contrast between the wrathful God of the Old Testament and the loving God of the New. Not precluded by the present tense is the view that God's wrath will be revealed in the future, at the great Judgment, since 2:15-16 actually mentions God's future judging, and 5:9 refers to "the wrath" (of God) from which believers will be saved. Evidently Paul implies that God's wrath in the future will confirm the wrath that is presently being revealed. So one may also infer that the current revelation of God's rectifying righteousness too will be confirmed in the future—a dimension of "justification by faith" not to be overlooked. In other words, in the present God's wrath is already at work, though it is not recognized apart from God's revelatory action. The parallel between verse 17 and verse 18 implies, then, that the revelation of God's rectitude and the revelation of God's wrath are distinguishable but not separable; indeed, it is the former that discloses the latter. Moreover, both the present righteousness and the present wrath lean into the future when they will be completed, for both are seen in light of Paul's apocalyptic eschatology, which understands the present as marked by the inbreaking of the New Age. Paul assumes he need not explain all this.

Except for Eph 5:6 and Col 3:6, Paul uses the phrase "God's wrath" *(orgē theou)* only here; elsewhere in Romans he writes simply of "the wrath" (as in 3:5; 5:9; 9:22; 13:5) or "the day of wrath" (2:5), to which he refers also in 1 Thess 1:9-10. There Paul, reminding readers of their conversion, says they "turned to God from idols, to serve a living and true God, and to wait for his

Son from heaven, whom he raised from the dead—Jesus, who rescues us from the wrath that is coming." Even though he writes Romans for people whom he had not yet taught, he does not explain exactly what he has in mind because—we may infer—rescue from the future wrath was part of common early Christian teaching. God's wrath, a motif rooted in the biblical prophets, was expected also in Jewish apocalyptic thought. The future coming of God's wrath was expected to bring God's definitive, destructive verdict on wicked human behavior, as well as God's approbation of good behavior (as in 2:5-10). In light of 1 Thess 1:10, it is the reality of God's inevitable, legitimate wrath that makes believing the gospel urgent; otherwise, what the gospel announces about the identity and resurrection of God's Son (in vv. 3-4) is noteworthy but not crucial.

Just as the gospel is God's saving power for *all* who believe, so God's wrath is "against *all* human *asebeia* and *adikia*." *Asebeia* is irreverence, disrespect toward the deity and/or sacred institutions; REB's "impiety" is preferable to NRSV's "ungodliness." *Adikia* (the opposite of *dikos*, right, just) is usually rendered "wickedness" but can also mean "injustice." What Paul understands by *asebeia* he will say in verse 25, where he uses the related verb (which the original hearers would catch) *esebasthēsan* (reverenced; NRSV: "worshiped") to accuse Gentiles of idolatry; what he means by *adikia* he will spell out in verses 29-31, where "filled with every kind of wickedness" introduces a list of vices. If for rhetorical reasons *asebeia* and *adikia* are paired because they sound alike *(paronomasia)*, they are joined for substantive reasons too, because the former refers to the wrong attitude toward God and the latter to wrong behavior toward other people. This dual characterization is onerous because by disrespect for God and wicked behavior people "suppress the truth." Truth is the first and primary victim, not because of what they do not know but because of what they do know. The result is especially heinous because the truth that is suppressed (Fitzmyer 1993, "stifled") concerns "what can be known about God" (not "everything that can be known . . . " as in CEV), which "God manifested to them." Humans are accountable for the suppression of truth about God, thus evoking God's wrath which, coming "from heaven," is against *all* who are guilty—for Paul, everyone. That is the *human dilemma*, which, as noted, is to be distinguished from the *human condition*. How the dilemma of facing God's wrath is now being revealed with respect to *Gentiles* Paul outlines in the next unit.

◊ ◊ ◊ ◊

That God's wrath is aimed at disrespect toward God and at wickedness/injustice is hardly a remarkable idea. What *is* noteworthy here is the emphasis on *all*, for it shuts the door against the proclivity to think that God's wrath is directed against "them," the sinful "others," those who have aroused *our* ire because of *their* irreligion and/or wickedness/injustice. Such a mindset is itself a sign that the truth of God is being "stifled."

The Dilemma of the Gentiles (1:20-32): Like a prosecuting attorney in court, Paul aims to show why the Gentiles have no excuse for their immoral behavior, even though they lack the law of Moses. To do so, he must hold them accountable for a gross violation of something so fundamental that it accounts for their current plight; this he finds in the *source* of idolatry. Gentiles can be held accountable only if the worship of the not-God as if it were God is the result of neither fate nor immaturity but of human action. Given Paul's purpose, it is understandable that he shows no appreciation of Gentile religions. Only after he has finished his indictment will he argue that because of God's impartiality Gentiles too can receive God's approbation for their good deeds (2:12-16).

Paul's argument nowhere refers to his Roman readers, most of whom were Gentiles! (In fact, he doesn't even use the word "Gentile" here; he doesn't need to, because the content—the consequences of idolatry—doesn't apply to Jews.) It is highly improbable that 1:18-32 is a "protreptic speech" (one that urges hearers to turn away from one way of life to another; see introduction, p. 22), for the readers have already done so.

Like Hellenistic Jewish writers such as Philo and the author of Wisdom of Solomon (Wis 13–15 is especially significant), Paul traced Gentile immorality to idolatry. Like his predecessors, he was convinced that the human mind can infer the existence of the Creator from the created, the Maker from the made (later called the cosmological argument for the existence of God, somewhat similar to the recent "intelligent design" theory). For example, a third-century BCE text avers that just as the invisible soul governs human activity, so there is a single unseen and unseeable agent that governs the cosmos; indeed, "this is what we must also believe about God, who . . . though he is invisible . . . is seen through his deeds" (Pseudo-Aristotle, *On the Cosmos* 399b, quoted from Boring et al. 1995, 338-39; see also Philo, *Spec. Leg.* 1.32-35). If that is the case, how does one account for polytheist idolatry?

While Paul never quotes Wisdom of Solomon, his understanding is both similar to and dissimilar from its views. Wisdom 13 begins by saying that

> all people who were ignorant of God were foolish by nature;
> and they were unable from the good things that are seen to know
> the one who exists   [an allusion to Exod 3:14],
> nor did they recognize the artisan while paying heed to his works.

However,

> these people are little to be blamed,
> for perhaps they go astray
> while seeking God . . .
> [since] they trust in what they see. (13:6-7)

Yet,

> not even they are to be excused;
> for if they had the power to know so much
> that they could investigate the world,
> how did they fail to find sooner the Lord of these things? (13:8-9)

The answer (chap. 14) relies on the explanation customarily traced to Euhemerus—that the currently worshiped gods once were human heroes whose beautiful representations gradually prompted people to regard them as deities. For Paul, however, idolatry was not traceable to error but to disobedience. But he does agree that "the idea of making idols was the beginning of fornication, / and the invention of them was the corruption of life" (Wis 14:12).

In order to establish Gentile culpability, verses 20-21 begin by explaining the assertion in verse 19 that "what can be known of God is manifest among them, for God has manifested it to them" (AT). It is important to note how this assertion functions in Paul's argument: Convinced that Jesus' resurrection is the eschatological event (see introduction, p. 34), Paul reasoned that there was now one solution to the *human* dilemma, and that this parity in solution implied parity in plight as well. But since one is culpable for not doing what one knows must be done (or doing what must not be done), how can Gentiles who do not have the law of Moses share culpability with Jews who have it? Answer: Just as God disclosed the divine will by giving the law to Jews, so God manifested to humans "what can be known of God," and did so primordially—before there were Jews. Ergo, Gentiles are as accountable for what they did with what God disclosed to them as Jews are for what God disclosed later to them. In the face of God's wrath against *all* wickedness, the Gentiles cannot claim that God treated them unfairly; they too "knew better." To support his argument that Gentiles are not victims of fate but culpable agents of their own undoing, Paul goes on to say that "ever since the creation of the world his eternal power and divine nature [lit., Godhood, *theiotēs*], invisible though they are, have been understood and seen through the things he has made." Gentiles are doubly culpable: They ignore what God manifested to them, and they did not discern God from the created order—though they could have and should have.

According to Paul, what can be known of God by inference from the phenomenal, observable world is that the world is *not* God. The footprint is not the foot that made it. This radical otherness of God, God's true Godhood, is axiomatic for the understanding of God in the entire letter. It comes to expression as God's freedom to rectify the human situation in ways consistent with God's resurrecting Jesus from the dead, an act analogous to

God's creating the world from nothing (4:16-25). Paul calls attention to God's otherness because if this is what the human mind can know of God ever since creation, then even apart from God's particular self-disclosure to Abraham and Moses, Gentiles are "without excuse" (v. 20).

Just as verse 20 clarified verse 19, so verse 21 explains why Gentiles are "without excuse": Despite knowing God (i.e., knowing that God's Godhood radically differentiates God from the phenomenal world), "they did not honor him as God or give thanks to him" (i.e., they were guilty of *asebeia*). Paul refuses to be distracted from his argument by explaining what prompted this refusal or how it actually came about. Nor does he allude to the serpent's role in the disobedience of Eve and Adam, because doing so might have implied that humans are excusable after all. In fact, the story of Adam's "fall" does not shape what Paul says here, as sometimes claimed (e.g., Hooker 1960, 297-306, and Dunn 1988, 1:53, 72; even less persuasive is the claim that the story of Sodom lies behind our passage; so Esler 2003, 149-50). Instead, Paul traces Gentile culpability to their refusal to respect God's Godhood and to be thankful; honoring God as the invisible Other and being grateful are complementary ways by which the Gentiles should have related rightly to God in light of what is known (and knowable) of God. Thus Paul holds Gentiles accountable by tracing their dilemma to their refusal of rudimentary knowledge and worship of God.

Since the subject matter concerns intertwined actions—the creature's response to the Creator's self-manifestation—the refusal affects how each actor relates to the other. The latter half of verse 21 expresses this in a way that sets up the rest of the chapter: "They were made futile [the passive implies that *God* did it] in their reasoning and their senseless heart was made dark" (AT). The futile reasoning is explained in verses 22-23 as idolatry, the darkened heart by the whole discussion that begins at verse 24, where "the lusts of their hearts" picks up verse 21. Paul asserts that the refusal to honor God rightly has consequences for both the reasoning of the mind and the commitments of the heart, the seat of the self's moral will, affections, and bent. The whole self is now distorted. In other words, when God's otherness is not respected, human reasoning about God becomes "futile" precisely when it claims to be sophisticated (as v. 22 says). When one refuses to acknowledge with gratitude one's contingency on the Other, the moral life is bent out of shape as well because the agent is no longer subject to the will of the Other. While this rudimentary narrative explanation of the origin of the Gentiles' plight does not follow the *story line* of Adam's "fall," Paul's explanation rests on the theological reading of that story by locating the plight's origin in disobedience.

According to verses 22-23, the refusal to honor God's real Godhood (and its corollary, the creature's contingency) did not result in agnosticism or in a "secular" life but in a debased religiosity that "exchanged the glory of the immortal God" for images of mortal humans, birds, quadrupeds, and reptiles. In this carefully crafted sentence the absurdity of this development is signaled by its first clause: "claiming to be wise, they were made fools" (AT; again the passive implies that God is the doer; REB's "they have made fools of themselves" is very misleading). This clause precludes inferring that the turn to idolatry was a mistake made in ignorance (as in Wisdom of Solomon); it also implies that idolatry, being an expression of the claim to wisdom, is actually gross self-deception (for a perceptive discussion of self-deception in Paul, see Via 1990, 19-45). When verse 23 speaks of "exchange," it expresses what in fact occurred, not the idolaters' intent (as if they decided to trade or "trade up" deities). The wording depends on Ps 106:20 (which refers to *Israel's* idolatry in making the golden calf): "They exchanged the glory of God / for the image of an ox that eats grass." Paul appropriates this language because it expresses what he sees in idolatry *per se*, wherever it occurs (also in 10:25-26 Paul applies to Gentiles biblical language about Israel). So, taking his cue from the psalmist, Paul expresses the absurdity of idolatry with a double contrast: Instead of glory (the sign of divine reality present), a mere image; instead of the immortal (lit., incorruptible) Creator God, mortal creatures. Though Paul shares the biblical and early Jewish abhorrence of idolatry, he foregoes mocking those who pray to some figure produced in a shop (as in Isa 40:18-20; 44:9-20; Wis 13:10-19; Letter of Jeremiah), for his purpose is to expose the moral consequences of idolatry.

These consequences are spelled out in verses 24-31; verse 32 both rounds out the paragraph and prepares the way for the next topic, God's impartial rectitude (2:1-16). Because the consequences include same-gender sex, verses 24-32 have become more controversial today than they probably were in Paul's day. It is therefore especially crucial to understand what Paul actually says (and does not say), the perspective from which he says it, and why he says these things at all.

The consequences of idolatry in verses 24-32 are not cultic (temple practices) but moral (viz., immoral practices). The composition of the passage is designed to be rhetorically effective, especially when *heard*. First, three times (vv. 24, 26, 28) it declares that in response to idolatry God "handed them over" (NRSV: "gave them up"), each time stating the immoral results. Second, as the passage moves along, the offending idolatry is stated with increasing brevity while the description of the immoral results grows longer and more detailed. Third, the list of vices (vv. 29-31) begins and ends with words that sound the same (rhetorically, the latter is a *homoioteleuton*). In saying "therefore God handed them over" Paul expressly claims that God subjected them to the results of their own actions; they became victims of their own deeds:

v. 24: *eis akatharsian* (to [or into] impurity)
v. 26: *eis pathē atimias* (to dishonorable passion)
v. 28: *eis adokimon noun* (to an unfit or incompetent mind)

Each time, this subjection is then concretized by a passive verb or participle; in verse 24, their bodies are dishonored *(atimazesthai)*; in verse 27 their appetites are inflamed *(exekauthēsan)*; in verse 29 they are filled *(peplērōmenous)* with every wickedness. God's handing them over results in a situation that is contrary to God's will; that is, the consequences of idolatry run their destructive course. Paul regards this process as an act of God because God is not a bystander who merely permits the immoral consequences to develop. God's otherness and Godhood are not suspended by the results of human disobedience but are expressed in them—negatively. What Paul implies here he will formulate as a question in 6:16: "Do you not know that . . . you are slaves to what you obey, whether of sin that leads to death or of obedience [to God] that leads to righteousness?" (AT). In "handing them over," in letting them be enslaved, God did not forfeit sovereignty but exercised it rightfully, since the punished were "without excuse" (v. 20), having "exchanged the truth of God for the lie" (v. 25 [AT], not "a lie" [NRSV] but *the* lie, idolatry). Noteworthy is the way the results of God's action progress from the body (v. 24) to the emotion (v. 26) to the mind (v. 28). Since the offense is always the same, the progression is not causal (as if one result led to the next) but theological and rhetorical: By becoming ever more specific, the text shows that the whole self and its relationships are distorted.

Not to be missed is Paul's comment that God's action occurred "in the desires of their hearts" (v. 24, AT), the locus of the will. Paul does not speak here (as in Gal 5:16) of the "desires of the flesh" but of the heart, the volitional center of the self. Similarly, in Susanna (appended to Daniel in the LXX) Daniel accuses the elders who dishonored the woman: "Desire has perverted your heart" (Sus 56). Paul too implies that the will was seduced by desires *(epithymiai)*. While Paul can occasionally use *epithymia* in a positive sense (Phil 1:22; 1 Thess 2:17), here the word has a negative meaning (NRSV: "lusts"; REB: "vile desires"), in agreement with many writers of the time who saw it as one of the four major kinds of passion (along with grief, fear, and pleasure), all of which can be dangerous. The Gentiles' hearts (not the mind, as in NRSV) cannot resist the power of desire because it has been "darkened" by the refusal to honor the Godhood of God (v. 21).

Paul's emphasis on the malign effect of desire was by no means unusual. Greek antipathy toward *epithymia* grew stronger from the time of Plato onward, who had explained that the immortal part of the soul was placed near the head where it can heed reason in order to subdue desires (*Timaeus* 70A). Plato also had Socrates claim that "the soul secures immunity from desires by following reason" (*Phaedo* 83A). Hellenized Jewish writers could share this perspective easily, for in the LXX the tenth commandment (usually rendered, "You shall not covet") reads, "You shall not desire." The *Apocalypse of Moses* (embedded in the Greek text of *The Life of Adam and Eve*) says, "*epithymia* is the origin of every sin" (19:3). Philo had said it before: "*epithymia* is the fountain of all evils" (*Spec. Leg.* 4.84; Plato's influence is clear). So too, Wis 4:12 observed that "roving *epithymia* perverts the innocent mind." What, then, can be done about this situation?

For the author of 4 Maccabees, reason has a prophylactic constraining power over desire: "None of you can eradicate desire, but reason can ensure that you do not become enslaved to desire" (3:2; Charlesworth 1985, 2:547). What this book emphasizes, however, is one of the four cardinal virtues, temperance (*sōphrosynē*, moderation, prudence, astute practical reasoning): "Temperance is mastery over desires" (1:31). Philo too believed that "it is by *sōphrosynē* that we can heal and cure our desires" (*Leg.* 1.70), though he also recognizes that "desire is never filled up, but continues always thirsty and in want of more" (3.150). The virtuous life is a constant struggle against desire, not acquiescing to its power.

Given this widespread antipathy to desire (see Stowers 2003, 531-34), Paul's *Gentile* readers would not have been surprised by his negative assessment of desire in verse 24, nor would they have known that in 1 Thess 4:3-5 he had regarded uncontrolled desire as a characteristic of Gentiles: "The Gentiles who do not know God" treat their wives with "lustful passion" *(pathei epithymias)*. In fact, nowhere does he say that *Jews* were dominated by passions and desires—understandable, since the tenth commandment prohibited them. Stowers (1994, chap. 2) claims that "self-mastery" (the antidote to desire) was a major issue in Paul's churches, whose members had been God-fearers in the synagogues where they had been taught that obeying the law leads to self-mastery, as Philo pointed out (*Spec. Leg.* 2.61-62). Paul's antidote, however, was the Spirit.

Whereas the first consequence of God's "handing them over" is stated generally as "degrading [*atimazesthai*, lit., dishonoring] of their bodies among themselves" (v. 24), the second amplifies this as "dishonorable passions" *(pathē atimias)*, specified in verses 26-27 as same-gender sex acts by women and men, regarded as "contrary to nature" *(para physin)*. Understanding this phrase is advanced by noting its opposite, "according to nature" *(kata physin)*. Stoics, convinced that the universe is permeated and governed by reason, insisted that one should live rationally, in accord with nature *(kata physin)*. Paul's near contemporary, Epictetus, said that being *kata physin* "is the object which the good and excellent man has ever before him" (*Discourses* 4.5.8), that "whatever is done *kata physin* is rightly done" (1:11:5). Despite many similarities between popular Cynic-Stoic values and Paul's exhortations (see the evidence assembled in Malherbe 1986), his thought is not anchored in such a philosophical, comprehensive view of "nature." (His appeal to what nature "teaches" regarding proper hair length [1 Cor 11:6] shows that what he regards as "natural" is really common practice deemed self-evidently right.) Though he uses the "against nature" argument, his negative view of same-gender sex is probably grounded more in the biblical prohibition (Lev 18:22; 20:13); Paul does not cite it here, however, perhaps because he is making a case for the culpability of the Gentiles who do not have the law.

In verses 26-27 he does not *argue* that same-gender sex acts are wrong; he assumes they are. Nor does he explain what makes them "unnatural," because he also assumes his readers will agree that they are. And that suffices for developing the argument; Paul is not writing an essay on sex ethics. Robin Scroggs noted that "unnatural" was "the most common stereotype" used by writers who rejected homoerotic acts (Scroggs 1983, 60). For example, Musonius Rufus, writing somewhat later than Paul, regarded sex between males as "a monstrous thing and contrary to nature" (quoted from Malherbe 1986, 153). Early Jewish writers also insisted that same-sex intercourse is contrary to nature (the texts are assembled by Gagnon 2002, 159-83). Though same-gender sex was widely practiced, Paul assumed he could count on such antipathy among his readers as he developed his argument (for a useful survey of negative views of same-sex eros, see Schoedel 2000; for a fully documented survey of negative views of female homoeroticism, see Brooten 1996). It is important to bear in mind that Paul's purpose here is not hortatory—he is not trying to dissuade the readers from such practices. Rather, he is using the subject as evidence of the consequences of idolatry. Paul does not reject same-sex intercourse because of its social consequences (e.g., it does not lead to procreation and so has a bad effect on society—something Philo pointed out) but because he regards it as vivid documentation of what exchanging the truth of God for a lie (v. 25) leads to. (He could have expanded the evidence to include incest and sex with animals had such deeds been more common.)

Central to his argument is the theme of "exchange," mentioned three times: the exchange of God's glory for mere images (v. 22), the exchange of the truth of God for the lie of idolatry (v. 25), and now the exchange (v. 26) or abandonment (v. 27) of the natural for the unnatural. His language about same-gender sex instantiates what he has been talking about all along—not what certain individuals do but what happened "generically" when the senseless Gentile heart was "darkened" as a result of idolatry. Being "handed over" to these sexual practices he deems as contrary to nature as idolatry is contrary to the "truth of God" (v. 25, AT). The emphasis on "exchange" might well suggest that he had in view homoerotic sex acts by heterosexual persons; however, Paul does not seem to be thinking of individuals. What he would have said about persons who claim to be naturally homoerotic—if such a modern idea had ever crossed his mind—cannot be inferred readily from his brief discussion here.

The sole description of same-gender sex appears in verse 27, where Paul says that males, "having abandoned the natural use of females, were burned up in their appetites for one another" (AT). Also in 1 Cor 7:9 he used the image of fire for intense, uncontrollable sexual desire: "It is better to marry than to be aflame with passion" (pyrousthai). Philo used the same imagery when he said that the source of adultery is "the love of pleasure," which consumes "like an unquenchable fire all that it touches, leaving nothing wholesome in human life" (*Decal.* 122); earlier he wrote that "all who are rebellious will continue to be burnt . . . by their inward *epithymia*" (*Decal.* 49). Fourth Maccabees 3:17 writes of the "compulsion of the emotions and . . . their flaming goads" (*oistrō n*, frenzied passions). David Fredrickson has shown that this fire imagery made vivid the notion that a person was overwhelmed by erotic passion as an invasive force, not as the externalization of an inner disposition (Fredrickson 2000, 210-11). This accords with Paul's view of what is entailed in being "handed over": One loses control and instead becomes controlled.

Having said (v. 26) that God handed them over to dishonorable passion, in verse 27 Paul goes on to say that the men "wrought the shameless with males" (AT). He does not really speak of shameless *acts* (NRSV) but by using the singular refers to the phenomenon as such. He probably regarded shamelessness as indecency, in accord with Philo's definition: "all those unseemly actions, when the mind uncovers shameful things which it ought to hide from view, and [instead] prides itself on them" (*Leg.* 2.66). Paul continues: They "received in themselves the retribution [*antimisthian*, payback, whether reward or punishment] which was necessary [*edei*] from their error" (AT). Although he does not identify this "retribution," he probably regards the status of being overcome with passion as itself the punishment. On the other hand, if Paul has pederasty in mind (so Scroggs 1983, 69, 116), then what Philo said about the unfortunate effects of pederasty are pertinent. In *Contempl.* 60-62 he says that such "common vulgar love" robs men of courage, creates effeminacy, and makes them a "hybrid of man and woman" *(androgynous)*; it damages the pederast's body, soul, and property (because he neglects it and uses its income to pay his lover). Moreover, because pederasty precludes procreation, it affects population adversely. It also reduces the boy to the status of a girl (mounted in copulation). In any case, when Paul emphasizes the necessity of punishment, he is not referring to future retribution, but to the present state of the inflamed (there is no reason to think he has venereal disease in mind). By calling male same-gender sex an "error" *(planē)*, he is not regarding it as a mistake; rather, given verse 21, he is calling it a deceit, echoing

Wis 12:23-24: Idolaters "went astray on the paths of error" and so "were deceived." NIV's use of "perversion" seems tendentious.

While the many recent studies of sexuality in antiquity have provided valuable information about same-sex practices in Paul's culture, that information must not be allowed to blur the fact that here Paul shows no interest whatever in specifying which particular form of same-gender sex is "unnatural." Given his theological purpose, he had no need to be as specific as the author of the long recension of *2 Enoch*, who reports that Enoch was shown the place of punishment "for those who do not glorify God, who practice on earth the sin which is against nature, which is child corruption in the anus in the manner of Sodom" (10:4-5; a list of vices follows).

Paul's list of vices (vv. 29-31) is presented as signs of God's wrath. He introduces it with a play on words impossible to reproduce in acceptable English: "since they did not see fit *[edokimasan]* to acknowledge God, God handed them over to an *adokimon* mind" (AT; NRSV: "debased mind"). Since something *dokimos* is competent and valued because it has been tested and proven "fit," here what is *adokimos* probably means unfit, not competent to make proper moral judgments, a state that leads to "doing improper things" *(ta mē kathēkonta)*. The distinction between what is proper and improper, common in Stoic thought, was more than an aesthetic judgment, for what was "proper" *(ta kathēkonta)* was also right and a matter of obligation. What is improper is not right even if it is not contrary to nature.

Paul's list of vices begins with the sweeping statement, "They were filled with every kind of wickedness" *(adikia,* unrighteousness/injustice), repeating the word used twice in verse 18. Vice lists appear frequently in the New Testament (e.g., Mark 7:21-22; 1 Cor 6:9-10; 1 Tim 1:9-10; 2 Tim 3:2-5), sometimes paired with lists of virtues, as in Gal 5:19-23 where "the works of the flesh" are contrasted with "the fruit of the Spirit." Such lists were used frequently; Philo provides one with 147 items *(Sac. 32;* for other examples, see Malherbe 1986, 138-41; for a concise survey of such lists, see Fitzgerald 1992, 857-59). The sequence of the vices in verses 29-31 is neither alphabetical nor logical nor psychological but rhetorical: It is designed to have a cumulative effect rhetorically. It is impossible to reproduce this in translation, though in verse 31 NRSV comes close to it: "faithless, heartless, ruthless." Virtually all the vices listed here signify a wrong relationship between people; none pertains to civic affairs. Paul devotes more space to the vices than to homoerotic behavior.

The theme of Gentile culpability returns in the conclusion (v. 32). Just as Gentiles turned to idolatry despite knowing God (vv. 19, 21), so here they do "such things" despite knowing God's *dikaiōma* (NRSV: "decree"; REB: "just decree"; NIV: "righteous decree"; NASB: "the ordinance of God"; perhaps "right order" makes the point better). Unfortunately, Paul does not specify the content of God's *dikaiōma*. Even though Paul says the doers deserve death, it is unlikely that he has in mind Lev 20:13 (which calls for the execution of males engaged in same-gender intercourse) because "such things" seems to include the vices just named, which are not punishable by execution. Moreover, an allusion to Leviticus would imply that the Gentiles did these things despite knowing the law, whereas Paul denies this in 2:14. The point is that the Gentiles are culpable, liable to God's wrath because they know what is right but do not do it. In the flow of Paul's argument, this contradiction between the right that is known and the wrong that is done has the same function as the abandonment of the natural for the unnatural and the "exchange" of the truth of God for the lie. Paul is saying neither that these vices characterize all Gentiles, nor that the Gentiles are bereft of all morality (as 2:14 makes clear); nor is he asserting that the guilty should be executed. Rather, he says that God's wrath *is* already manifested as the immoral consequences of idolatry. Vice, like virtue, is its own reward.

The last clause underlines the moral depravity: Deliberately doing the wrong when the right is known is bad enough, but applauding those who do it is even worse. This comment should, Paul may hope, induce the hearers to respond with revulsion at the sinners and to agree with the argument. If so, he has set up the abrupt transition to the next unit.

◊ ◊ ◊ ◊

When Paul refers to "those who by their wickedness suppress the truth" (v. 18) and then traces this suppression to the refusal to honor God as God, he calls attention to the way truth is vulnerable to morality. Instead of saying that theology influences the moral life (which he assumes), he points out that the moral life shapes theology. Though this emphasis serves his particular argument, Paul's point here should be given its due weight on its own terms, for wicked behavior always suppresses the truth. What we do affects what we know or think we know about God, largely because we rationalize our behavior, especially when it is wrong.

Moreover, as Paul sees it, God is not honored as God when God's otherness (God's invisible power and "Godhood") is not acknowledged. The consequences of this non-acknowledgment are so disastrous because the Reality we call "God" is the ultimate ground of being and value. It is not surprising, then, that the confusion about who God is, and who we are in relation to God, distorts who we think we are and what it is we regard as right. Gross examples of this in history are not hard to find. But finger-pointing at "them" is dangerous; indeed, it is self-indicting, because everyone has "interests" (my own "special interests") in play when speaking of God. Since God is the ground of being and value, this is inevitable. The situation is actually self-reinforcing: who we think God is affects who we think we are and what we do, and who we think we are and what we do shapes who we think God is. Apparently aware of this dilemma, Paul addresses it by arguing that our rectification coincides with a rectified understanding of God. That too is entailed in the meaning of the Christ-event.

God's Impartial Rectitude (2:1-16): The declaration that God's wrath is against *all* human wickedness (1:18) rests on the conviction that God is impartial (2:11; in Gal 2:6 God's impartiality serves a different purpose). This impartiality also warrants the assertion that the gospel is God's power for salvation for *all* who believe, first for the Jew but also for the Greek (1:16). Neither the ubiquity of wickedness nor the universality of salvation effected by God's rectitude, however, dissolves the distinction between Jew and Greek into an undifferentiated "humanity"—at least not for

Paul. But can God's impartiality be squared with the special status of the Jews who have received both the promise of the gospel (1:2) and the law? It can, because from Paul's angle, parity in plight (both Jews and Greeks are "under" sin, 3:9) does not make the *forms* of their accountability identical, though the *fact* of their accountability is the same. God's impartial rectitude holds both accountable for what they *do,* not for who they are (after all, it was God's election of Israel that created the distinction between Jews and non-Jews in the first place). After portraying the dilemma of Gentiles (1:18-32), and before turning to the dilemma of Jews at 2:17, Paul discusses God's impartiality in 2:1-16. (For an analysis of God's impartiality in Romans, see Bassler 1982, 121-70.)

Paul does not implicitly turn to the situation of the Jew in 2:1 (as many still hold); rather, 2:1 clearly continues the indictment of Gentiles in 1:18-32. But it does so from a different perspective, signaled by the change in style: Whereas 1:18-32 *described* the Gentiles, at 2:1 Paul begins *confronting* them, diatribe style, with the inescapable consequences of God's righteous judgment on deeds (words for "judge" or "judgment" appear ten times in 2:1-16). But he also reasons: if God's impartiality punishes evil deeds, then God's impartiality rewards good deeds as well, whether done by Jews or Gentiles. If that is the case on Judgment Day, what difference will it make—if any—that Jews have the law and Gentiles do not? (To understand Paul's argument, it is absolutely essential to bear in mind that for Paul the law was the God-given, normative, unique expression of God's will for the chosen people first of all, not simply the source of customary obligatory practices that differentiate Jews from everyone else.) In 2:1-16 Paul's thought moves quickly and relentlessly as he unfolds the import of God's impartial rectitude for Jew and Gentile. Because he touches many themes briefly, and in verses 5-8 weaves multiple ideas into a single, long period, it is essential to keep in view the argument as a whole, as well as its function—to show the significance of God's impartiality.

In 1:32 Paul had pointed out that those guilty of the vices listed in 1:29-31 even applaud those who do such things. But what about the person who disapproves of these vices? Paul refuses to let such a person off the hook. Suddenly using an *apostrophē* (a turn from the general audience to an exclamation addressed to an individual, real or imagined), he declares, "Therefore, you, O man [generic *anthrōpos*, not *anēr*, male], have no excuse, all of you who pass judgment on someone else" (AT; CEV, ignoring the apostrophe and so losing the power of the rhetoric, produces an insipid translation: "Some of you accuse others of doing wrong"). He does not say, "You should not be judgmental," or "You don't really understand those people." Rather, by saying, "You have no *excuse*," Paul steers the discussion toward the theme of accountability. The person addressed has no excuse because "in passing judgment on someone else" he condemns himself. How so? "Because you, the judge, are doing the very same things" (NRSV). To regard this judge as a Jew who finds Gentile immorality repugnant, as is often claimed, is to miss a significant part of the argument, signaled by the way the passage begins, "You are without excuse, O man"—that is, *anyone* who judges others because he regards himself as an exception. This judge, like those guilty of the vices, too knows God's *dikaiōma* but uses it to extricate himself from the immoral many by passing judgment on *them* while "doing the very same things himself." The word *anapologētos*, "without excuse," clearly recalls its use in 1:20-21, where it refers to Gentile culpability for not honoring the otherness of God. Here, however, it does not matter which of "the very same things" deprives the judge of an excuse. What matters for the argument is that he too is a wrongdoer. When 2:1-16 is read together with 2:17-29 (addressed to the Jew), it becomes clear that "O man" is precisely on target, for both Gentile and Jew are accused of the same thing, though manifested differently, as we will see.

Because NRSV regards verse 2 as a comment of the person addressed in verse 1, it puts verse 2 in quotation marks and inserts "You say," in accord with diatribe style. Thereby the judging person agrees with Paul: God's judgment on "those who do such things" (repeating 1:32) is "in accordance with truth" (i.e., rightly grounded). Indeed, granting that God's judgment is rightful is precisely what makes the situation so self-incriminating, for it leaves no room to protest that God is unfair. Suddenly and surprisingly, knowledge of God does not provide security but its opposite.

In verses 3-4 Paul restates the point and presses it relentlessly, first with the taunt, "Do you think you will escape God's judgment?" then with the accusatory question, "Are you not misreading your whole situation precisely because, despite claiming to know that God judges rightly, you use this knowledge to judge others instead of applying it to yourself, and so repenting?" (AT). As Paul sees it, the judging person assumes that, in escaping God's judgment by passing judgment on others, he sides with God and so will benefit from God's kindness. In other words, by judging others the person tacitly assumes that he is not bad enough to be judged or that God is too good to judge him, or both. But on this assumption the wrongdoing judge really "despises" the amplitude ("riches") of God's kindness, forbearance, and patience, for he is trying to manipulate God's goodness for his own benefit, instead of repenting and *thereby* escaping God's judgment. By not repenting, Paul continues, the judge's "hard and impenitent heart" is making matters worse for himself on the Day of Wrath. In 1:18-32 Paul argued that God's wrath "is being revealed" now in the consequences of idolatry; here he implies that the present activity of the judging person adds to the wrath under which he already stands ("storing up wrath"), and that will be consummated on the day when God's "righteous judgment" *(dikaiokrisia)* will be revealed, fully manifest.

When Paul explains what he means by God's righteous judgment (in vv. 6-11), he begins by quoting the last line of Ps 62:12 (LXX 61:13, changing "you" to "he"): "He will repay each according to his deeds" *(erga,* often rendered as "works"); Prov 24:12 says the same thing. (Oddly, neither NRSV nor REB put the words from the psalm in quotation marks, as does NIV.) Despite the prolix formulation, verses 6-11 have a clear structure based on the line from Ps 62, as well as on the theme that reward and punishment fit good or evil deeds. (To have allowed for deeds that are partly good and partly evil would have muddied Paul's argument.) The chiastic (reverse order) structure of the passage is clear if one omits the words used to characterize each group:

a God will repay each according to his deeds
  b Those who seek immortality will receive eternal life
    c Those who disobey the truth will get wrath and fury
    c′ There will be anguish for everyone who does evil
  b′ There will be glory for everyone who does good
a′ There is no favoritism with God

The characterizing words are important nonetheless. In verse 7 Paul recognizes that some persons do *seek* the right things (glory and honor and immortality; lit., incorruptibility), thereby recognizing that they do not yet possess them; moreover, their quest is marked by "patiently doing good" (NRSV; REB: "by steady persistence in well-doing"). It is the *deeds* of these persons that God will repay with eternal life. In verse 10 Paul interprets eternal life as peace (not absence of conflict but the situation when everything is rightly related to God). In verse 8 he characterizes the evildoers' disobedience by stating first its ground (they live out of selfishness [*ex eritheias*]), then by stating what they do obey—*adikia* (unrighteousness, wickedness), thereby alluding to 1:29 ("filled with every *adikia*") and rephrasing 1:18 as well.

The chiastic structure of the passage implies that the first line ("God will repay each according to his deeds") and the last ("For there is no favoritism with God") complement each other; indeed, the last line states the basis of what the first line introduces. It is because God is impartial that God will repay each person on the basis of *deeds*. Recompense not according to deeds would express favoritism or arbitrariness; the former would imply that God is unfair, the latter that the ultimate arbiter of right and wrong is not dependable. Here, because God's impartiality is axiomatic, Paul need not argue *for* it but can argue *from* it, using it to warrant the assertion about reward according to deeds. God's impartiality is deeply rooted in scripture (e.g., Deut 10:13; Job 34:19; 2 Chr 19:7) and was asserted repeatedly in early Jewish writings (Bassler 1982, 7-119).

But if God's impartiality in the Great Assize means that God will reward/punish everyone—Jew and Greek—on the basis of deeds, why does Paul say this recompense pertains to the Jew *first*?

Would not God's impartiality have been expressed better by saying "to the Jew first and also to the Greek"? The same question can be asked of 1:16, where "for all who believe" is also followed by an assertion of God's impartiality, expressed as God's wrath against "*all* ungodliness" (1:18, AT). Thus what 1:16 and 1:18, taken together, imply is made explicit in 2:9-11—that God is as impartial in saving all who believe as in repaying everyone according to deeds. "The Jew first" does not refer to rank (as if the Jew received either a better salvation or a worse punishment), nor to sequence (as if God saves Jews before saving Gentiles); rather, it is a "logical first," the consequence of Israel's irrevocable election (11:29).

If these observations illumine theologically *why* Paul writes "the Jew first," they do not explain historically *where* he writes it—namely, only in Romans, sent to believers who are mostly Gentiles. Since it appears probable that Christian Gentiles in Rome were beginning to infer that the Jews forfeited their elect status by refusing the gospel, it seems likely that this letter emphasizes "the Jew first" in order to correct such thinking in Rome, and to reassure Christian Jews there that he is not going to Spain because God has written his people off.

Having seemingly dissolved the difference between Jew and Greek by saying that because God is impartial, both will be rewarded or punished for what they have done, in verses 12-16 Paul now clarifies the role of the law—essential for Jewish identity—in the Great Judgment. (This is the first appearance of the word "law" in Romans.) Here, too, the remarkable craftsmanship of this passage should not be missed. The flow of thought is chiastic: Gentile and Jew (v. 12), Jew and Gentile (vv. 13-16).

In verse 12 Paul begins with a maxim-like, rhetorically balanced declaration of the law's function in the Judgment:

[Gentiles] who have sinned	apart from the law
will also perish	apart from the law
[Jews] who have sinned	in [the jurisdiction of] the law
will be condemned	through the law. (AT)

That is, not having the law will not excuse the Gentiles from punishment, nor will having the law protect the Jews, because

God repays deeds. With or without the law, both have sinned (*hēmarton*, first used here), and so are punished, for

> it is not the hearers [*akroatai*] of the law that are righteous [*dikaios*]
> in God's sight
> but doers [*poiētai*] of the law will be declared right [by God]. (AT)

(Here *dikaiothēsontai* is rendered "declared right" rather than "justified" in order to show the connection with *dikaios*, righteous, right.) This emphasis on doing is not peculiar to Paul. In the Mishnah (the oldest part of the Talmud) we find that Rabbi Simeon said, "Not the study [of the law] but the carrying out is the essential thing" (*Abot* 1:17). Closer to Paul is Jas 1:22: "Be doers of the word, and not merely hearers [*akroatai*, also Paul's word] who deceive themselves." The contrast between saying and doing appears also in the Sermon on the Mount, where the disparity has a christological focus (Matt 7:21-23). Paul does not need to argue that verse 13 is true; he simply states it as self-evidently true. Interestingly, he will conclude the whole section by saying that "no human being will be justified [*dikaiothēsetai*] in his sight by deeds prescribed by the law [*ex ergōn nomou*]" (3:20). Whether this contradicts 2:13 will be discussed at 3:29-30. Another matter needs attention just now.

The juxtaposition of verse 12 and verse 13 generates two problems for the Gentiles: (a) though not having the law of Moses, they sinned nonetheless, and so perish in the state in which they sinned—without the law. But if it is the doers of the *law* that will be declared right by God, how can they ever be declared right? Must they cease to be Gentiles by becoming proselytes? (This possibility is left unexplored in Romans, though it lies at the heart of Galatians.) (b) If they did not have the law, how can they have sinned, since "sin is not reckoned when there is no law"? (5:13). To have sinned at all, they must have violated something. Yet they "perish without the law" because they are held accountable for their sins. Verses 14-16 address these questions.

Given what he has said about the Gentiles up to now, one does not expect him to say (a) that the Gentiles who do not have the law (said twice in v. 14) nonetheless do "what the law requires" (lit., "the things of the law"), or (b) that in so doing they *show* (or demonstrate, *endeiknuntai*; *endeixis* means "demonstration," as in 3:25)—not merely imply—that "what the law requires" (lit., "the work of the law") is written in their hearts, or (c) that the phenomenon of conscience indicates this to be the case. Many commentators, alert to the differences between verses 14-16 and 1:18-32, insist that verses 14-16 refer to Christian Gentiles, claiming as well that the law written in the hearts refers to what Jeremiah had written: "I [God] will put my law within them, and I will write it on their hearts" (Jer 31:31-34). This interpretation, however, is unacceptable, for among other reasons, it violates Paul's whole argument, which concerns non-Christian Gentiles. Further, Paul would never say that *Christian* Gentiles "are their own law" (v. 14, REB).

The key to a proper understanding of verses 14-16 is recognizing that these verses, far from abruptly switching to Christian Gentiles, actually continue to speak of non-Christian Gentiles and so carry forward the argument (begun at 1:18) concerning the dilemma of the Gentiles before God—their culpability for God's wrath. Accordingly, verses 14-16 neither ameliorate their situation (by offering a loophole: doing) nor acknowledge exceptions to the portrayal in 1:18-32 (the existence of some good Gentiles proves the rule). Rather, verses 14-16 provide the final evidence that the Gentiles without the law "are without excuse" (1:20; 2:1), even though the phrase is not used here. These verses insist that even without the law of Moses, Gentiles are accountable to a "law," an inner law; moreover, the phenomenon of conscience shows that they acknowledge their accountability.

Following the argument, however, requires that verse 14 be translated precisely. Achtemeier (1985, 45) rightly insists that Paul does *not* say, "When Gentiles, who do not possess the law, do instinctively [lit., by nature, *physei*] what the law requires" (so NRSV, NIV, REB, and many commentators). What he does say is, "When the Gentiles, who *do not possess the law by nature* do the things of the law, they who do not possess the law are the law for themselves" (AT). In other words, *physei* (by nature) does not refer to the basis on which they do what the law requires (logically making knowledge of the law unnecessary!), but to the fact that the law is not their "natural" possession. Not having the law "by nature" underscores the "nevertheless" aspect of their doing the things of the law without it (not the whole law of Moses, but deeds that coincide with what is prescribed in the law; see v. 7).

In verse 14, the initial "When" is essential; one should not replace it with "If," for Paul is not speaking hypothetically or conditionally. Instead, granted that Gentiles (for the argument, it does not matter how many or which Gentiles) do "the things of the law" despite not having it, Paul explores and exploits the meaning of this phenomenon when it occurs. He sees that Gentiles are in fact obeying law, a moral norm of what ought to be done and not be done. They are not without law categorically. Rather, they "experience the transcendent claim of the divine will and thus become, not *the* law or *a* law, but law to themselves" (Käsemann 1980, 64). By focusing on the inner law, the unwritten law ("written" on the heart), and by calling attention to conscience, Paul actually exposes Gentile accountability at its deepest level—awareness of the obligatory, as Käsemann saw. In short, Paul's reasoning here is comparable to that in chapter 1; there he used the "cosmological argument" for the existence of God, not to lay the foundation of "natural theology" on which to erect a biblical doctrine of God, but in order to hold Gentiles accountable for their idolatry and its consequences. Similarly, here he uses the acknowledged Gentile morality not to mitigate their accountability, but to underscore it. Their not having the law by nature neither exempts them from being accountable nor prevents God from rewarding them for doing what is right. While the exact meaning of Paul's reference to conscience is not evident, he apparently means that the present witness of the Gentiles' conscience, whether accusing or exonerating, will come to a head when God will judge their secrets (*not* "secret thoughts," as in NRSV). God will judge the secrets (*ta krypta*, "the hidden things") because the whole self will be judged, including what occurs in the heart that can be seen only by God.

Looking back at 2:1-16 as a whole, what has Paul's argument achieved? He has brought the impartiality of God to bear on the dilemma of the Gentiles in such a way that the non-Jew has no excuse, and so is truly accountable precisely because of what he or she *knows*. Concretely, (a) the knowledge of right and wrong—the basis on which the Gentile judges evildoers—precludes the judging person from thinking that he or she will escape God's judgment, because that judgment will be based on what one does, not on what one knows. "Knowing" makes accountability more devastating for the wrongdoer. (b) Not having the law of Moses is no excuse either, for when Gentiles' deeds coincide with what the law prescribes, the Gentiles themselves show that they heed an unwritten law. (c) Indeed, the fact of conscience shows that they know themselves just as accountable for obeying that law as Jews are accountable for obeying the written law. (d) Despite the difference between Jews and Gentiles, the impartiality of God's judgment levels the field, because in God's court what matters are deeds—even unseen ones—for which everyone is accountable.

The more people understand themselves as members of discrete groups whose identity emphasizes the contrasts with "others," the more important God's impartiality becomes. Groups—be they ethnic, national, socioeconomic, or religious—look to God's impartiality to validate their self-understanding; that is, assuming God to be impartial, they also assume that God recognizes that they are better than the "others," and so deserve their privileges—even if they do not yet have them. Thus appeal to God's impartiality to validate one's own group's identity readily turns God's impartiality into partiality. But according to Paul, since God is truly impartial in assessing deeds, God's very impartiality threatens the assumption that, of course, God is "on our side." If Paul is right, God's impartiality threatens everyone who is in the wrong. If so, then theology gets really serious.

The Dilemma of the Jews (2:17-29): Whereas Gentiles are culpable despite lacking the law (2:1-16), Jews are culpable because they have it (v. 12). Here too, as in 2:1, Paul opens the discussion confrontationally, this time using a special form of the diatribe, *prosōpopoiia* ("speech in character," so Stowers 1994, 16-21, 143-58). With this technique, the speaker depicts an entity or an imagined person, a "type" outfitted with traits selected to advance the argument; here the traits expose the Jew's (not the Jews'!) lack of integrity. In other words, 2:17-29 is *not* Paul's indictment of Judaism as such. Rather, he uses this indictment of the hypocrisy of a particular type of Jew to express the idea that simply being a Jew does not automatically confer privileged status in God's impartial judgment.

Paul alerts the hearers to his purpose by the way he begins the confrontation in verse 17. Instead of "But if you are a Jew . . . ," he writes, "But if you *call yourself* a Jew," thus hinting that the man's self-image does not square with reality. If 1:18-32 was designed to elicit the readers' revulsion, this paragraph is designed to elicit their contempt, for the very things this man uses to distinguish himself from Gentiles actually subvert his proud posture. It is not the man's Jewishness that is at fault, but his construal of it. By the end, what is implied at the outset becomes a flat-out accusation: As a "law breaker" he dishonors God, and so fits what scripture says, "The name of God is blasphemed among the Gentiles because of you" (v. 24). With this quotation, Paul puts the man in essentially the same position as the Gentiles who did not "honor [God] as God" (1:21), even though he is not an idolater. The quotation modifies LXX Isa 52:5, where God says, "Because of you my name is blasphemed continuously among the Gentiles," meaning that Gentiles revile God because conquerors apparently get away with treating God's people Israel shamefully (similarly Ezek 36:20-21). What Paul hears in the quotation, however, is quite different: God's name is "profaned" (REB) among the (idolatrous) Gentiles by the contradiction between this Jew's self-image, projected in the name of God, and reality.

In keeping with the principle that "those who sin in the jurisdiction of the law will be judged by the law" (v. 12, AT), verses 17-20 accent the Jew's relation to the law: He relies on it, he knows God's will in it, and, being instructed "out of the law" (or "by the law," *ek tou nomou*), he knows how to discern what matters. That this man is a Diaspora Jew is implied first by Paul's use of *ta diapheronta* (the things that matter), alluding to the well-known Cynic-Stoic distinction between what matters and what does not (the *adiaphora*), and second by the silence about the Jerusalem temple (still functioning). This man indeed lives "in the law." Consequently, he has convinced himself (oddly, recent translations omit this reflexive pronoun!) that he is in a position to be a guide of the blind, a light for those in the dark, a corrector of the imprudent (*paideutēs aphronōn*), a teacher of the immature (lit., children)—for in the law he has "the embodiment of the true knowledge and of the truth" (AT). Being neither an idolater nor a polytheist, he "boasts in God" (v. 17; REB: "you take pride in your God"; both NRSV and NIV take the phrase to mean pride in election: "your relation to God"). In short, he sees himself as being so enlightened that he has the right to instruct the benighted Gentiles.

In 2:1-11 Paul had confronted the judging Gentile with his hypocrisy, disclosed by his doing the same things for which he faults others, thereby making his situation before God worse. Similarly, Paul now confronts the Jew with his hypocrisy, which results in exactly the opposite of what he expects: instead of God's name being honored, it is blasphemed. Paul drives toward this result with a series of questions that confront the Jew with his own violations of the same law that he advocates to Gentiles: "You who teach others, will you not teach yourself? You who preach, 'Do not steal!' do you steal? You who say, 'Do not commit adultery!' do you commit adultery? You who abhor idols, do you rob temples?" (AT). (An affirmative answer is expected to all these questions.) What Paul has in view with the last question remains opaque; perhaps it is part of a traditional Jewish list of sins, for the same three sins appear in the same sequence in Philo (*Conf.* 163). Paul's point is clear: If the Gentile who condemns himself when judging others for doing what he himself does has no excuse (2:1), neither does this Jew, for he transgresses the law that he boasts about. God shows him no favoritism—not despite his having the law and relying on it, but precisely because he has it and relies on it.

When Paul continues, he suddenly brings up the subject of circumcision (required of Hebrew males; see Gen 17:9-14; for a discussion of this practice in antiquity and its multiple meanings, see Hall 1994, 1025-31). Jews regarded it as the physical sign of their chosenness and of their consequent obedient loyalty to God's law (though they knew that also non-Jews practiced circumcision, albeit for other reasons). Greeks and Romans, however, regarded it as contemptible self-mutilation. In discussing circumcision, then, Paul deals with Jewish identity in the Gentile world as well as in relation to God.

"Circumcision" *(peritomē)* can refer to the act itself (Gal 5:11), to its result (Rom 4:10), or to the person/group on whom the operation was performed ("the circumcision" = the Jews, Rom 3:30). Likewise, *akrobystia* (lit., foreskin, usually rendered "uncircumcision") can refer to the state of not being circumcised (Rom 4:12: *en akrobystia* = while Abraham was in the state of being uncircumcised) or to the non-Jewish person/group (the Gentiles, Rom 3:30). The terminology can also be used metaphorically ("circumcision of the heart" refers to being open to God's will, as in v. 29; this expression occurs frequently in the Old Testament [e.g., Deut 10:16; Jer 4:4; Ezek 44:9], and in postbiblical texts like the *Habakkuk Commentary* [11:13] found at Qumran). While Philo regarded circumcision as a symbol of "the excision of pleasure and all passions," he also insisted that Jews must not think they can have the meaning without the operation, the signified without the signifier (*Migr. Abr.,* 92).

Paul uses *peritomē* and *akrobystia* here because this terminology was rhetorically more effective than simply "Jew and Greek," especially if this language was used derogatorily. *Akrobystia* was not a Gentile self-designation but the Jews' disdainful way of referring to them (as in Acts 11:3, where Christian Jews complain that Peter went to "men having foreskin" [NRSV: "uncircumcised men"]); Gentiles, on the other hand, may well have used *peritomē* to speak contemptuously of Jews. Thus the theological argument in verses 25-29 was freighted with prejudices evoked by these terms (for a discussion of this terminology, see Marcus 1989, 67-81).

In verses 25-29 the discussion of circumcision brings to a head Paul's insistence that God's impartiality implies that all people are repaid according to their deeds (vv. 6-11). In 1 Cor 7:18-19 Paul had insisted that male Christian Gentiles are not to be circumcised nor are Christian Jews to "remove the marks of circumcision" (an operation called epispasm), because "circumcision is nothing, and uncircumcision is nothing; but obeying the commandments of God is everything" (in Gal 6:15, "new creation" is everything, not obeying the commandments, because obedience to the law was precisely at issue). Paul now pursues the logic of 1 Cor 7:18-19: Circumcision "benefits" (*ophelei;* NRSV: "is of value") the Jew if he does what the law says he should do (Paul need not specify how or when it benefits, because what matters for the argument is the idea that it does). But what happens "if you break the law" (lit., "if you are a transgressor *[parabatēs]* of the law," picking up the language of v. 23)? Then "your circumcision has become [perfect tense: it has already become and now is] foreskin"; that is, you might as well not be circumcised because circumcision no longer benefits you. Paul is *not* saying that disobedience terminates the Jew's membership in the covenant community, for disobedience is not apostasy. The point is straightforward: since it is deeds that really matter, what disobedience really terminates is the benefit of circumcision—a relation to God based on obedience. Understandably, when the interlocutor returns at 3:1, he asks, "Then what advantage has the Jew? Or what is the value of circumcision?"

In verse 26 Paul turns the coin over as he speaks now of the uncircumcised Gentile, using a rhetorical question to which the affirmative answer is presumed to be self-evident. If he keeps "the right requirement of the law [*ta dikaiōmata tou nomou,* a phrase used often in Deuteronomy; e.g., LXX Deut 4:14; 6:2; 28:45] will not his *un*circumcision be regarded [by God] as circumcision?" Of course it will, because in God's impartial judgment it is the "doers of the law" who "will be declared righteous" (v. 13, AT). In other words, given the link between circumcision and obedience to God, the disobedience of the Jew undoes the benefit of circumcision, and the Gentile's obedience confers it.

Moreover, at the Judgment the physically uncircumcised law-observer will judge (*krinei;* NRSV: "condemn") the Jewish law-breaker who has the letter (*gramma;* NRSV: "written code") and circumcision (REB paraphrases: "He may be physically uncircumcised, but by fulfilling the law he will pass judgement on you who break it, for all your written code and your circumcision"). Paul's reasoning here recalls that of Jesus when he said that the repenting Ninevites will judge his unrepenting fellow-Jewish contemporaries (Matt 11:20-24).

Clearly, if circumcision can become uncircumcision, and if uncircumcision can be regarded as circumcision (not by an unusually liberal Jew but by God), then it is no longer obvious who is a real Jew. Paul does not evade the issue, but addresses it in verses 28-29, where he takes the reader back to verse 17, which introduced the distinction between *calling oneself a Jew* and *being a Jew.* Now Paul explains who the real Jew is: "not the one who is a Jew in the open *[ho en tō phanerō]* nor whose circumcision in the flesh is in the open, but the person who is a Jew in what is hidden *[en tō kryptō]* and whose circumcision of the heart is in [the realm of] spirit and not in [that of] the letter, and whose praise is not from humans but from God" (AT). Even if it is unclear whether *en pneumati* means "in the realm of human spirit" or "in the domain of the divine Spirit" (NRSV's "spiritual" preserves this ambiguity nicely), the general point is clear enough: The real Jew is not the empirical, phenomenal, ethnic Jew as such, but the obedient person whose circumcision has occurred in the heart, where it is not visible, and whose life is not marked by the contradiction between what is preached to others and what the preacher does (vv. 21-23). Because this contradiction may not be visible to the observer (stealing, adultery, and temple-robbing are not public acts), the one who calls himself a Jew may indeed be praised by humans who do not know of the disparity between word and deed, but the real Jew will be praised by God who judges "the hidden things" (v. 16, AT). (This possibility does not preclude the disparity being observed, and so leading to the blasphemy of God's name.)

To regard verses 28-29 as "Paul's critique of his own native religion" because "it puts too much stress on the outward" (so Dunn

1988, 1:124) is to misunderstand the passage profoundly, for Paul is not talking about "Judaism" at all; rather, he is thinking through, unflinchingly, the consequences of God's judging everyone impartially, on the basis of what they have done. Far from being a critique of Judaism, Paul's argument is actually an expression of Judaism's conviction about God's impartiality.

◊ ◊ ◊ ◊

More than any other New Testament writer, Paul thought through, relentlessly, the implications of God's impartiality—understandably, because theologically the impartiality of God is an important aspect of the radical otherness of God. Moreover, what distinguishes Paul's thinking here—what makes it remarkable, if not unique—is the way he probes the theme. On the one hand, he keeps his eye on the distinction between Gentile and Jew instead of talking about a generic "humanity," while on the other hand, he reaches for what is constitutive of the human dilemma in light of God's impartial judgment—culpability for misusing the knowledge of God. Since Gentile and Jew, each in his own way, is guilty of this offense, it is not surprising that in the next unit Paul will say that "all, both Jews and Greeks, are under the power of sin" (3:9), and in the following section he will declare that "there is no distinction, since all have sinned and fall short of the glory of God" (3:22-23, restated at 10:12).

Accordingly, then, it is not surprising either that the portrayals of the Gentile who judges (2:1-16) and the Jew who is arrogant with his knowledge of God (2:17-29) are in some ways similar even though differing in other ways because the Jew has the law but the Gentile does not. In keeping with "there is no distinction," the following similarities are worth noting: (a) Both the Gentile "judge" and the Jewish "teacher" do what each rejects (compare 2:1-2 and 2:21-22); (b) like the Gentile who thinks he can escape God's judgment (2:3), so the Jew does not teach himself what he teaches others (2:21) because he assumes he does not need to; (c) like the Gentile whose refusal to repent is a sign of despising God's goodness (2:4), so the Jew's behavior causes God's name to be blasphemed (2:23); (d) each in his own way instantiates what scripture says (compare

v. 6 and v. 24); (e) finally, because God's impartial judgment concerns deeds, the status of each is reversible: The Gentile who does "the works of the law" will be regarded as a Jew, and the Jew who breaks the law will be regarded as "uncircumcision" (vv. 26-27, AT). In short, God is not bound by the dilemma of either. That, among other things, is what the otherness of God is all about.

The Integrity of God's Rectitude (3:1-18): Paul now has the imagined Jewish interlocutor raise issues that the apostle must address. (In 2:17-24 Paul portrayed the interlocutor but did not have him speak; now he does.) Since the interlocutor, in accord with the diatribe style, is the speaker's rhetorical device, the whole passage is Paul's creation (even if it might reflect his previous discussions in various synagogues). The passage has two parts (vv. 1-8 and 9-18), each beginning with the interlocutor's leading questions. The *first* (v. 1) clearly reflects 2:17-29 by asking about the Jews' advantage and the value of circumcision; the *second* (v. 9a) restates the issue in a way that prompts Paul to formulate the conclusion of his analysis of the dilemma of both Gentiles and Jews (v. 9b), which he then supports in verses 10-18 with seven biblical quotations. (In verses 19-20 Paul states the conclusion toward which his whole argument has pointed since 1:18, and so sets the stage for the next phase of the discourse, 3:21–5:11.)

While many commentators have recognized the diatribal character of verses 1-9, Stowers has exploited this feature of the text most fully (Stowers 1994, 159-75). Noting that both Paul's style and vocabulary resemble those of Epictetus's diatribe, he infers that also Paul so designed the exchanges that the interlocutor admits Paul's basic points, and so moves the argument forward. According to Stowers, Paul constructed the dialogue as follows:

Interlocutor	v. 1
Paul	vv. 2-3
Interlocutor	v. 4
Paul	v. 5
Interlocutor	v. 6
Paul	vv. 7-8
Interlocutor	v. 9a
Paul	v. 9b

On this basis, the "we" in verse *9b* implies that Paul has succeeded in persuading the interlocutor to agree with him—understandably, since the apostle formulates both sides of the exchange. Following the argument does not, however, require knowing exactly who says what.

Responding to what Paul had said in 2:17-29, the interlocutor's double question (v. 1) raises the key issue: What is the advantage of being a Jew anyway? Paul's answer is unexpected. (In v. 2, "in the first place" is not followed by "the second.") Since he has been speaking of the law (ten times in 2:1-29), one expects him to say that the Jews' advantage is that they have the law. Instead, he says they "were entrusted [by God] with the oracles of God" *(ta logia tou theou),* an expression that in nonbiblical Greek referred to divine oracles whose receipt often entailed accepting an appropriate duty (so Doeve 1953, 116). The LXX consistently used *logia* for God's utterances of commands and promises (so Manson 1960, 87-96); indeed, Ps 119 (LXX 118) repeatedly speaks of God's beneficent actions according to his *logia* (e.g., vv. 41, 58, 76, 116, 123; NRSV renders the Hebrew behind *logia* as "promise"). Doeve's and Manson's data suggest that in Rom 3:2 Paul had in view God's spoken promises (so also Williams 1980, 266-67; Stowers 1994, 166-17; Moo 1996), not a general reference to scripture or to God's general self-disclosure. But which promises? The "entrusted" gives the clue, for Paul consistently uses this verb to refer to his being given the vocation of preaching the gospel (1 Cor 9:17; Gal 2:7; 1 Thess 2:4). Accordingly, Paul probably alludes to God's entrusting the Jews with the promise to Abraham that envisages the Gentiles being blessed though him and his descendants (Gen 12:1-3; 22:15-18); for Paul, such an entrustment entails the Jews' responsibility to live accordingly. Thus Paul's response formulates precisely the point of being a Jew in a Gentile world: being a steward of God's promise. Elements of that responsibility are visible in 2:17-20, where Paul accused the interlocutor of distorting his vocation into a tacit claim to superiority.

The disparity between the Jew's behavior and his privileged vocation (2:17-29) now becomes the unstated basis on which Paul develops his vindication of God's integrity by asking three questions, each beginning with "if." Because Paul is arguing, each "if" states the logical, valid premise of the question that follows:

v. 3 if some were unfaithful *(ēpistēsan)*
v. 5 if our unrighteousness *(adikia)* demonstrates *(synistēsin)* God's righteousness
v. 7 if in my falsehood the truth of God abounds for his glory. (AT)

Each question that follows expresses the wrong conclusion, which the interlocutor rejects vehemently with *mē genoito!* ("By no means!"; often used by Epictetus and Paul [e.g., 6:2, 15; 7:7]; see Malherbe 1989, 25-33). If Stowers is right, Paul deliberately formulates the wrong inference in such a way that the interlocutor cannot avoid rejecting it, thereby making Paul's point for him—a way of persuading the hearers, who may have the same questions.

Unfortunately, NRSV, NIV, and REB translate Paul's first question (v. 3) as if it could be answered either Yes or No. But the question's initial *mē* signals that a negative reply is expected: "Their faithlessness *[apistia]* will not nullify God's faithfulness *[pistis]*, will it?" The interlocutor's vehement "By no means!" has the effect of a vigorous affirmation: "If some were unfaithful, their faithlessness does *not* annul God's faithfulness"—an axiom undergirding the whole theological argument in Romans. (Their *apistia* is not their "unbelief" [NASB], or "lack of faith" [NIV]; the issue is not their "faith" but their infidelity with respect to God's *logia*.) Nor is Paul's faithless "some" a "delicate way" of saying that "not all Jews" have responded to the gospel (so Dunn 1988, 1:139), for that is not on the table here either. Rather, God's faithfulness persists despite some (not all!) Jews' faithlessness, just as the truth of God persists despite the Gentiles' exchanging it for a lie (1:25).

Paul has the interlocutor do more than reject the wrong inference. In keeping with the motif of the Judgment (2:16, 27), now visualized as a courtroom, the interlocutor continues: "Let the verdict be that God is true but every person a liar" (v. 4, AT). This declaration universalizes the contrast between God and humans ("everyone is a liar" is a line from Ps 116:11 [LXX 115:2]). God is not "true" in the sense of conforming to an external norm; rather, God is true to God's own self (i.e., God has integrity).

In the court of the Judgment, God's integrity/truthfulness will be confirmed—precisely in light of every human's lack of integrity/truthfulness. The otherness of God could hardly be expressed more dramatically.

The biblical quotation that follows (the latter half of Ps 51:4 [LXX 50:6]) supports this declaration. The psalm's superscription claims it is David's penitential response when the prophet Nathan exposed the king's sin in making Bathsheba pregnant while her husband is away at war and then having him killed (2 Sam 11:1–12:10). The quoted lines express David's acknowledgment to God that his sin warrants God's verdict. The NRSV renders the interlocutor's quotation this way:

> . . . so that you may be justified [vindicated] in your words *(logois)*
> and   [may] prevail   in your judging

If Stowers was right in regarding verse 4 as the words of the interlocutor (accused in 2:23 of being a transgressor of the law [as was David!], and so one of the faithless "some" of v. 3), then Paul has him acknowledge that God's being "true" includes God's negative judgment on him. That is, the interlocutor confesses his own sin as a "liar" (i.e., one whose deeds do not match his words to others).

Paul's second question (v. 5) responds to the quotation in verse 4, which expressed the vindication of God's verdict on all human falsehood (an echo of 1:18 should be heard). The introductory "if . . ." clause assumes that the vindication and triumph of God's verdict demonstrate *(synistēsin,* show, confirm) God's righteousness (that God is in the right) because the accused has lost the case; indeed, given the courtroom imagery, it was precisely the wrongdoer's conviction that showed that God was in the right. That being the case, Paul now asks the wrong question (again beginning with *mē):* "God who inflicts the wrath [on us Jews] isn't unjust *[adikos],* is he?" The question is poignant, for the wrath-inflicter is the God who established a special relation to "us Jews" by the covenant and entrusted "us" with God's own oracles, thereby making "us" stewards of God's will and promise. And since God remains faithful despite the faithlessness of "some," and since "our" wrongdoing *(adikia)* shows that God is right, we can't really say that the wrath-inflicting God is unfair, can we? "No way!" replies the interlocutor. Consequently, the God who inflicts the wrath on "us" is indeed fair, just, righteous. The penitent David was right: God does prevail in judging.

When Paul adds the parenthetical comment, "I speak in a human way," he does more than recognize his limited human standpoint; he also acknowledges that his question, raised on behalf of the privileged yet faithless Jews, expresses a very human desire to question God's fairness. When Job too questioned God's fairness, he was protesting on the basis of his own innocence; Paul's question, on the other hand, arises from the premise of "our *adikia*," our unrighteousness (NRSV: "injustice").

In verse 6 the interlocutor supports his "By no means!" by asking a question that exposes the consequences if Paul's question were not rejected as wrong (i.e., if God *were* unfair). (The question assumes that God will judge the world, and that the judgment will be impartial because God is "true," v. 4.) He notes that unless one rejects the notion that God is unfair (toward "us Jews"), God will not *judge* the world—that is, God would merely react to it, whether arbitrarily or impulsively. Were that the case, God's judgment would be amoral. Paul's interlocutor assumes that because God is impartial, God's treatment of Israel is consistent with God's treatment of the whole accountable world (3:19).

In verse 7, Paul's third question presses the issue of God's fairness. This time the premise picks up the key terms of verse 4 (God's truthfulness *[alētheia]* alludes to "Let God be true" *[alēthēs]*, and "by my falsehood" *[pseusmati]* alludes to "everyone a liar" *[pseustēs]*). Now the issue escalates from God's judgment being amoral to being immoral: If my falsehood benefits God by enhancing God's glory, "why am I still being condemned?" Shouldn't God perhaps even reward me for being useful? (The move from "their faithlessness" [v. 3] to "our wrongness" [*adikia*, v. 5] to "my falsehood" [v. 7] is not autobiographical but rhetorical.)

The rhetorical "I" of verse 7 prompts Paul to move to an autobiographical "I" (built into "slander us" *[blasphēmoumetha]*). NRSV, NIV, and REB helpfully disentangle Paul's cumbersome sentence by separating his self-reference from the question, "Why not say . . . 'Let us do evil so that good may come'?" Since the question is triggered by verse 7, Paul asks why one should not take advantage of the way human wrong enhances God, and deliberately do evil so that good may come—to God. That is, instead of *being used* by God for God's self-glorification, why not take the initiative and deliberately *use* the effect of God's judgment, and so put God in the wrongdoer's debt? Into this wrong inference Paul inserts a parenthesis in which he discloses that some people are saying that Paul actually teaches this absurdity. That is, they have assumed that Paul's teaching leads to abandoning moral seriousness. But for Paul, their taunting slogan expresses the arrogant sin of manipulating God. Paul does not dignify such thinking by answering it; instead he reaffirms God's impartiality in judgment: "*Their* condemnation is deserved." In 6:1 Paul will return to this distortion of his thought.

The second part of the passage begins at verse 9, where the interlocutor, ignoring Paul's comment in verse 8, returns to the issue raised in verse 4, by asking a question consisting of a single word, *proechometha*—perhaps the most problematic term in the whole passage (the problems are discussed by Moo [1996]). The meaning of this vexing verb is inseparable from Paul's emphatic negation that follows: *ou pantōs*, which can mean either "not at all" or "not completely." If one thinks that *proechometha* (middle or passive voice) here has an active meaning (as do most commentators, as well as NRSV, NIV, NASB, and NJB—though no such use of the word has been found elsewhere), then the interlocutor asks, "Are we [Jews] any better off [than Gentiles]?" If one thinks Paul's reply means "No, not at all" (as in NRSV, NIV, REB), then Paul now contradicts his reply in verse 2: "Much, in every way." If Paul's *ou pantōs* means "Not completely" (so Byrne 1996, *ad loc.*), he would be modifying verse 2 without explaining what a partial advantage might be. It is therefore better (with NRSV alternative and Fitzmyer 1993) to rely on the natural meaning of *proechometha* as a middle and passive verb and render it, "Are we surpassed [by Gentiles]?" In other words, "Are they better off than we?" Then Paul's "Not at all" does not conflict with verse 2 and instead reaffirms the impartiality of God in judging Jew and Gentile. In short, just as Paul used the interlocutor's opening question in 3:1 to counter the inference that he had undermined the significance of being a Jew at all, so in verse 9 he used the interlocutor's question to deny that what he had said in verse 5 about God's wrath on "us Jews" actually puts them in a worse situation at the Judgment than the Gentiles.

Paul follows his brusque "Not at all!" by explaining the reason for it: "For we have already charged [*proētiasametha*, REB: "already drawn up the indictment"] that all, both Jews and Greeks, are under the power of sin"(lit., "under sin," NRSV and REB insert "the power of"). Paul then claims that this explanation is supported by scripture (vv. 8-10).

Some recent interpreters (e.g., Sanders 1983, 125 and Donaldson 1997, 139) have contested Paul's claim that in 1:18–2:29 he has "already charged that all . . . are under sin," claiming that his case is unconvincing, internally inconsistent, and exaggerated. Indeed, the step between the faithlessness of *some* Jews (3:3) and the assertion that *all* of them are "under sin" is rather long; likewise, saying all Gentiles "are under" sin seems at odds with the claim that they can do what the law requires (2:14, 27). Such verdicts may be premature in light of the function of verse 9. This verse does not summarize what Paul had said in 1:18–2:9; rather, it *interprets* what he had said by disclosing its import: The plight of the Gentiles and Jews is the same because what will count on Judgment Day is deeds. That is, Gentiles will *not* fare better then. (By saying that both Jews and Gentiles are "under sin," Paul looks ahead to what he will say in 5:12-21 about Adam and to what 11:32 will conclude: "God has imprisoned all in disobedience so that he may be merciful to all.") By saying that the assertion in verse 9 agrees with a list of scripture lines beginning with "There is no one who is righteous, not even one" and ending with "There is no fear of God before their eyes" (forming an *inclusio*), Paul implies that his assertion in verse 9 expresses also God's judgment (so also Barrett 1994, 81).

It is quite unlikely that Paul composed this chain of quotations *ad hoc*; rather, it probably was created independently, probably not even by Paul (for a full discussion, see Keck 1978, 141-57). Whatever its original purpose, Paul finds its relentless negative characterization of all humanity useful, for there is not even a hint of exceptions or extenuating circumstances. The basic thought is not developed but emphasized by repetition: the opening denial ("There is no one . . . ," v. 10) is repeated five times in verses 11-12. Next, the unrighteous are characterized by using the imagery of speech organs four times (vv. 13-14); this leads to three explicit accusations using the imagery of walking (vv. 15-17) before the concluding line in verse 18 announces that "there is no fear of God before their eyes."

All the quotations are from the LXX, but none is from the Pentateuch. Oddly, "as it is written" (v. 10) is followed immediately not by an actual quotation but by a paraphrase of Eccl 7:20: "There is not a righteous person on earth who does good and does not sin" (AT), which is simplified: "there is no one who is righteous, not even one." Verses 11-12 are derived from Ps 14 (LXX 13):2-3, which begins by saying that God looked down from heaven to see if there are any who have understanding or who seek after God. The compiler changed verse 2 to express, apparently, what God in fact saw: "There is no one who has understanding; / there is no one who seeks God." The compiler left Ps 14:3 unchanged. As a result, verses 10-12 are rhetorically effective:

> There is no one who is righteous, not even one . . .
> There is no one who seeks after God.
> All have turned aside,
> together they have become worthless;
> there is no one who shows kindness,
> There is not even one. (AT)

The chiastic structure (reverse sequence) of verses 13-14 is evident when they are rendered more literally:

> An open grave is their *throat*
> With their *tongues* they deceive.
> The venom of vipers is under their *tongues*
> Whose *mouth* is full of cursing and bitterness. (AT)

The first two lines of verse 13 quote Ps 5:10 unchanged; the third line quotes Ps 140:3 (LXX 139:4), also unchanged. Verse 14, however, not only abbreviates a line from Ps 10:7 (LXX 9:28) but also changes the word order so that "mouth" comes at the beginning in order to create the chiasm. Such careful attention to detail is the mark of bookishness.

Verses 15-17 shorten LXX Isa 59:7. Isaiah 59, before celebrating God's righteous wrath by which God will repay his enemies "according to their deeds" (vv. 10-19), indicts Israel's wickedness for delaying God's salvation. LXX Isa 59:7-8 says,

> And their feet run toward evil,
> they are swift to shed blood.
> And their reasonings are the reasonings of fools.
> Ruin and misery are in their paths,
> and the path of peace they do not know,
> and judgment is not in their paths.

This is condensed in order to accent violence:

> Swift are their feet to shed blood
> Ruin and misery are in their paths
> And the path of peace they do not know. (AT)

The concluding line (v. 18) is taken unchanged from Ps 36:1 (LXX 35:2). The psalm begins with an extended description of the wicked (vv. 1-4), then celebrates God's mercy, truth, righteousness, and judgments (vv. 5-9). The compiler used only the line in verse 1 that served his purpose: "There is no fear of God before their eyes." By ending on this note, he implied that this is the ground of evils in the whole list. For Paul, the lack of fear (awesome respect) restates the refusal to honor God as God in 1:21.

Whatever motives led to the creation of this compilation, what matters is its significance for Paul. Its prominent location—between verse 9 and verses 19-20 (the concluding statement that is the counterpart of 1:18)—shows that he regarded it as an appropriate, authoritative body of evidence for his whole argument to this point. In fact, since the compilation begins, "There is

no one who is righteous," he could use it to support his own "all
. . . are under sin"; likewise, he could regard "under sin" as an apt
way of accounting for this roster of sins as a whole. This compilation of sins functions as the biblical counterpart of the Greco-
Roman vice list in 1:29-31. Although these compilations surely
had separate origins, many of the offenses or clusters of offenses
in verses 10-18 have their counterparts in the vice list.

3:10   There is no one who is righteous *(dikaios)*
1:29   filled with all unrighteousness *(adikia)*

3:11   There is no one who understands *(ho syniōn)*
1:31   They are foolish *(asynetous)*

3:12   There is no one who shows kindness
1:31   They are heartless, merciless

3:13   The venom of vipers is under their lips
1:30   They are slanderers, gossips

3:15   Their feet are swift to shed blood
1:29   They are full of murder

3:17   The path of peace they have not known
1:29   They are full of strife

3:18   There is no fear of God before their eyes
1:32   They know . . . that those who do these things deserve to
       die, and yet they not only do them but applaud those who
       practice them (Paul's addition to the vice list, AT)

◊ ◊ ◊ ◊

Beneath Paul's question, "Their faithlessness will not nullify the
faithfulness of God, will it?" lies an understanding of God whose
pertinence exceeds by far the circumstances in which it was asked,
namely, God really is "other." So profoundly "other" that, instead
of having to react to human deeds, God can initiate creative action
because God is free to be God in God's own way. If Paul was not
right, would Easter have occurred?

The Human Dilemma: Being Accountable (3:19-20): Janus-like, this important paragraph looks backward and forward: backward by stating the conclusion of the argument begun at 1:18, forward by stating the dilemma in a way that anticipates the discussion of salvation that begins at 3:21. A key factor in the dilemma is the law, mentioned four times in these verses.

By beginning with "now we know" (REB defers the phrase), the paragraph implies that what follows is not contested (by the interlocutor? the reader?) and so is the shared point of departure. What is known is that "whatever the law says, it speaks to those in the law" (AT; *en tō nomō,* the phrase used in 2:12 to identify the domain or sphere of jurisdiction within which Jews sin, whereas Gentiles sin *anomōs,* without the law). This is probably Paul's way of referring to the "world" of the Jews: They live within the law's jurisdiction, where they are addressed by the law (it "speaks," i.e., articulates God's will). Since the statement follows the biblical quotations in verses 10-18, none of which is from the Pentateuch, "the law" here refers to scripture as a whole (so also Cranfield 1979, 1:195). As a result, every mouth is silenced; that is, no Jew has an excuse or basis on which to protest innocence.

Noteworthy is the second result of the law addressing those within its sphere: the whole world is "accountable to God," liable to God's judgment. But if being "in the law" distinguishes Jews from Gentiles, how does what the law says to Jews within its domain result in the accountability of those "outside" its domain? Paul offers no explanation, perhaps because the accountability of the Gentiles has been evident ever since 1:18 (and especially since 3:6 acknowledged that God judges the world). Moreover, in verses 10-18 he has just quoted scripture (the Jews' ambience), namely, "There is no one who is righteous," implying that the whole world is accountable because scripture says so, even if it says it to those "in the law."

What makes this universal accountability a real dilemma, especially in light of God's impartiality in judgment, is stated in verse 20, which translated more literally says, "on the basis of works of the law [*ex ergōn nomou*] all flesh will not be rectified/justified before him"; more precisely, "it is not the case that all flesh will be justified before him on the basis of works of the law." In God's court, no one's "deeds prescribed by the law" (NRSV) will do what needs to be done. Why not? "Because through the law comes knowledge of sin" (AT). Taken by itself, verse 20 looks like a flat contradiction of 2:13, according to which it is not the hearers of the law (those to whom the law "speaks") but the "doers of the law who will be justified." Actually, neither statement should be extracted from its context and simply juxtaposed, as if Paul had written nothing relevant in between; rather, they should be juxtaposed *in situ*, so that their functions in the argument can be given their due.

The statement in 2:13 is the logically necessary consequence of Paul's assertions that God's retribution/reward will be based on deeds because God is impartial (2:6-11). Once the law is brought into the discussion (as it must, given the repeated "the Jew first and also the Greek" in 2:9-10), having or hearing the law must be distinguished from doing it (the deeds on which God's reward will be based); otherwise there would be no basis for saying "also the Greek," and God would reward Jews simply for being Jews with the law. But then, God would be partial, not impartial. Moreover, it is precisely the emphasis on deeds that allows Paul to acknowledge that Gentiles do "what the law requires" without actually having the written law. In other words, without the assertion that it is "the doers of the law who will be justified" (declared to be right), the whole argument collapses.

Whereas 2:13 says *who* will be declared righteous/justified on Judgment Day, 3:20 states the *basis* on which God's verdict of acquittal/being in the right will be pronounced for everyone—better, the basis on which it will *not* be pronounced for anyone: the deeds "prescribed by the law." Why are they not the basis? Because both Jews and Greeks "are under the power of sin" (3:9); consequently, "through the law comes knowledge of sin" (v. 20, AT). Moreover, according to 2:14-16, Gentiles will be declared right on the basis of doing what is required, not by the written law, which they do not have "by nature," but by doing what is required by the law written in their hearts—if their conscience does not accuse them. In other words, the role of conscience implies that also through this inner law comes "knowledge of sin"—not information about what is and is not sin, but knowledge of sin itself as a power under which they too live. Even when they "do the works of the law written in their hearts," their justification does not occur on the basis of deeds prescribed by the written law. In short, the alleged contradiction between 3:19-20 and 2:13-16 dissolves once we see that the two passages are talking about different things.

Of recent translations, only NRSV recognizes that Paul, in clinching his argument here, cites scripture, for it alone puts quotation marks around "no human being will be justified in his sight." This is Paul's appropriation of Ps 143 (LXX 142):2, which begins by pleading, "And do not enter into judgment with your servant, because no living person will be *dikaiothēsontai* [acquitted, pronounced right, justified] in your sight" (AT). By replacing "your sight" with "his sight" Paul transforms the person's plea into a general pronouncement, and by adding "by deeds prescribed by the law" he exposes what makes the dilemma so hopeless without the gospel.

◊ ◊ ◊ ◊

Unexpected is Paul's assertion that "through the law comes knowledge of sin" (AT; not "All the Law does is to point out our sin," CEV). Does not scripture also bring knowledge of the good? Doubtless, Paul would agree, though that is not a point he must make here. Actually, the knowledge of sin that Paul has in view is the dark side of knowing the good in scripture. It is not conceptual (theological) knowledge of good and evil that is on stage here, but the somber self-knowledge that results from hearing the good in the law. This is not knowledge of sin as a possible outcome of a course of action, but of sin as an already occurred fact, and of sin as the consequent destroying factor in one's existence. In that situation, knowing the law inevitably brings knowledge of sin— something the arrogant Jew, who in 2:17-29 instructs others, has overlooked in himself.

The Impartiality of God's Rectifying Rectitude (3:21–5:11)

Having formulated in 3:19-20 the dilemma in which both Gentiles and Jews are caught, Paul now turns to its solution, the

Good News of God's righteousness/rectitude manifested in the event of Jesus Christ. In 1:16-17 he had asserted that the gospel message *is* God's salvific power because in it God's rectitude is being disclosed. Now in 3:21-31, the messenger explains and defends the message, then elaborates and confirms it by discussing Abraham (4:1-25). The whole discussion is rounded out in 5:1-11, which also points ahead to the next section, 5:12–8:39 (many see it beginning at 5:1).

God's Rectifying Rectitude Apart from the Law (3:21-31): In stating more fully the gospel of God, Paul's argument now combines for the first time the theme of God's righteousness/rectitude *(dikaiosynē)* and Christ's death. The result in verses 21-26 is a syntactically complex paragraph whose theological content is one of the densest in the whole letter. Then Paul uses the interlocutor's questions (3:27–4:2) to lead into a discussion of Abraham in order to show that the gospel indeed had been promised beforehand in scripture (1:2), where it bears witness to the rectitude of God now manifest.

◊ ◊ ◊ ◊

At this point, it is useful to identify some of the matters that require attention in the course of the exegesis, which demands attention to every detail: (a) the meaning of key words: God's *dikaiosynē* and related terms (used seven times); *pistis* (faith/faithfulness) and related words (used four times), especially the *pistis* of Jesus (two times); and *hilastērion* (NRSV: "sacrifice of atonement"); (b) the possibility that Paul appropriates an identifiable piece of early Christian tradition; and (c) the most likely explanation of the awkward syntax. (For a perceptive discussion of these problems, see Campbell 1992, to whose analysis of the passage's rhetorical features this interpretation is indebted.)

When looked at as a whole, the passage has three significant features. *First*, it is framed by an emphasis on the present: It begins, "But now . . ." and in verse 26 ends with "at the present" (lit., "in the now time," *en tō nun kairō*). *Second*, it contains three repetitions: (a) "The righteousness of God" in verse 21 is repeated in verse 22 in order to continue the thought after the intervening reference to scripture. (b) Three phrases begin with the same word "through" (*dia* + genitive noun), all pertaining to Christ (vv. 22, 24, 25). Ancient rhetoricians called this phenomenon *epanaphora*. (c) "For the demonstration of his righteousness"(AT) in verse 25 is repeated in verse 26, and each time is followed by a phrase that begins with "in" ("in his divine forbearance" and "in the present time")—rhetorically, an isocolon because both lines are of equal length. *Third*, in the middle of verse 22 Paul inserts an explanatory parenthesis beginning with "For there is no distinction" and ending with "his grace" in verse 24 (so Campbell 1992, 87-92 and Talbert 2003, 109). When the parenthesis is removed and the elaborating phrases omitted from what remains, the basic structure of verses 21-26 emerges quite clearly:

> God's rectitude is manifested apart from the law
>> God's *dikaiosynē*
>>> through the *pistis* of Jesus Christ
>>> through the redemption which is in Christ Jesus
>>> through the *pistis* [evidenced] in his blood
>> for the demonstration of his *dikaiosynē*
>>> in God's forbearance
>> for the demonstration of his *dikaiosynē*
>>> in the present time

This analysis has three advantages: (a) identifying the parenthesis alleviates the syntactical problem; (b) one can acknowledge that Paul is using traditional language without trying to identify a fixed tradition's beginning and end or Paul's alleged additions to it; and (c) the christological center of the passage (the "through" phrases) and its relation to the christological focus of "the gospel of God" in 1:2-4 is clearer. The whole paragraph grounds the rectifying character of God's rectitude in the event of Jesus Christ, viewed from a particular standpoint. In light of the statement in verse 20, that no one will be *dikaiothēsetai* (pronounced righteous, justified, vindicated) in the Judgment "on the basis of the works of the law," the final words of verse 26 ("on the basis of Jesus' faithfulness") deliberately contrast the ground on which rectification does occur now with the ground on which it does not occur.

It is not only verse 26 that connects this paragraph to verse 20, but also verses 21-26 as a whole, though not as explicitly as one would like. As noted, in verse 20 the words "no human being will be justified in his sight" are taken from Ps 143:2, which states the reason the poet asks God not to judge him: He will lose the case. In Ps. 143:1 the poet implores God to respond to his plight "in your righteousness." So if Paul had verse 1 in mind when he appropriated verse 2 (so Hays 1980), then the poet's plea is in effect answered in verses 21-26. To see this more clearly, one must discern the underlying logic that links verse 20 and verses 21-26. If God responds not in judging impartially but rather "in his righteousness," then God's rectitude will not condemn the person pleading for God's righteous action but instead will pronounce him or her to be righteous; this pronouncement *makes* the relation right (it rectifies). But does that not violate God's impartiality, God's own integrity, God's own rectitude? Not if God's rectitude is made manifest "apart from the law." For Paul, that manifestation occurred in the event called "Jesus Christ."

In 1:17 Paul had said that God's righteousness/rectitude "is being revealed" (*present* passive) because he was speaking of the currently preached gospel, but now in 3:21 he used the *perfect* passive to say that God's rectitude "is manifested" (*pephanerōtai*) because this tense expresses the ongoing import of a completed event in the past, here the Christ-event. Moreover, because the verb *phaneroun* means making perceptible, Paul used it to underscore the claim that in the Christ-event God's rectitude became, and consequently now is, evident.

The foregoing observations are additional reasons for taking *dia pisteōs Iēsou Christou* to mean "through the faithfulness of Jesus Christ" (v. 22) not as "through faith *in* Jesus Christ" (so NIV, and still defended by some, e.g., Cranfield 1975, Fitzmyer 1992, Moo 1996; for a recent defense, see Dunn 1997, 61-81; on the other hand, Hays [2002] continues to champion "through the faithfulness of Jesus Christ"). It is highly unlikely, however, that the *pistis* of Jesus refers to his "faith" (NRSV alternative); it refers rather to his faithfulness, his fidelity, his obedience to God (which was, of course, not unrelated to his "faith"). In any case, were Paul to say that God's rectitude is manifested "through faith in Jesus Christ," he would claim that it is through *our* believing that God's rectitude is made manifest; but this translation virtually substitutes the requirement to "have faith" for the requirements of the law. In addition, the final phrase of verse 26 *(ton ek pisteōs Iēsou)* simply cannot be translated as "those who have faith *in* Jesus"* (NIV) since the almost identical phrase in 4:16 *(ek pisteōs Abraam)* does not mean "faith in Abraham" but "the faith/faithfulness of Abraham."

Because God's rectitude is manifested "apart from the law," the rectitude itself is "apart from the law," for the means of manifestation are consistent with what is manifested. That being the case, what occurred in Jesus' faithfulness too is "apart from the law," though not contrary to it. Such a rectitude, by definition, does not operate according to the rationale of the law (command, obedience, reward), and so is neither accountable *to* the law nor to be assessed *by* the law, for such rectitude functions according to its own inner logic, which is distinct from that of the law. This logic is consistent with God's otherness, God's freedom to act otherwise than within the framework of the law. The boldness of Paul's thought is nowhere more evident than at just this point, where he dares to assert that the law and the prophets themselves point to this apart-from-the-law rectitude of God the Other who acts otherwise. Consequently, instead of fitting God's rectitude that is manifested through Jesus' faithfulness *into* the framework of the law's rationale, the law (and the prophets) are to be read in such a way that they signal the rectitude that is *apart* from the law. In other words, here Christology generates a particular hermeneutic. What is implicit here becomes explicit in chapters 9–11.

In verse 22 Paul adds that God's rectitude is manifested "for *all* who *believe*," and so picks up the emphasis on *pistis/pisteuein* in 1:16-17, on the one hand, and the "all" in 3:9 and 3:19-20 (where translations obscure its threefold repetition). This "all" prompted Paul to insert the parenthesis that begins, "For there is no distinction" (between Gentiles and Jews) and ends in verse 24 with "rectified freely by his grace" (AT). The parenthesis is the only place in the whole paragraph where the emphasis is on the import of God's rectitude for Gentiles and Jews. The bulk of the parenthesis is devoted to the significance of Jesus' death for the rectifying rectitude of God; that is, its primary content is theological and christological, not soteriological.

The content of the parenthesis merits close attention. For one thing, its initial "for" (v. 22*b*) indicates that what follows is the basis of the claim that God's rectitude is manifested for *all* who believe. (Evangelical Protestants tend to emphasize "believe," but Paul, concerned with the issue of Gentiles and Jews, probably accented the "all.") What he means by "no distinction" (anticipated in 3:9 and repeated in 10:12) is expressed in the two clauses that follow, the first stating the shared dilemma, the second the shared answer to it:

> since all have sinned and fall short of the glory of God
> they are now justified [rectified] by his grace as a gift.

In the first line "and" really means "and consequently," as the shift from the past tense ("have sinned") to the present tense ("fall short") confirms. Less clear is whether "fall short" adequately renders *hysterountai*, because it can be either a middle or a passive verb; "fall short" (NRSV, NIV) assumes it is middle, and implies that they do not reach their goal (so Moo 1996). However, REB takes it as a passive: "they are deprived [by God] of the divine glory" (so also Scroggs 1966, 73 n. 42). The former has Paul say that sin precluded attaining human destiny, sharing God's glory (= excellence evident in splendor); the latter has him say that the loss of the original status is God's punishment. Neither construal—failure to attain or deprivation—points as clearly to Adam, whose primordial glory is often mentioned in Jewish texts (e.g., *Apocalypse of Moses* 20:23 [quoted in Boring et al. 1995, 352]; 1QH[a] 17:15), as a number of commentaries confidently claim (e.g., Dunn 1998 and Moo 1996 but not Fitzmyer 1993), for Paul wrote of "the glory of God," not the "glory of Adam." In any case, the first line asserts that the present human condition is the result of human sinning; humanity is not the victim but the responsible agent of its undoing. (Lacking God's glory is a *condition*, not a dilemma like facing the judge.) Over against the assertion of human responsibility in the first line stands the second, asserting that rectification occurs through the free gift of God. The rationale of grace (undeserved favor) will emerge more clearly in the course of the letter. To be noted here, however, is that the parenthesis states the gospel in a nutshell.

Just as "all who believe" prompted Paul to begin the parenthesis with "for there is no distinction," so "by his grace" at the end suggested that he resume his complex sentence by explaining that God's grace occurs "through the redemption that is in Christ Jesus." This is the second of three phrases that interpret God's rectitude christologically. Whereas in the first (v. 22), God's rectitude is manifested through Jesus' faithfulness, in the second it is manifested through what that faithfulness achieved—redemption *(apolytrōsis)*. The noun is rare in Paul's letters, appearing elsewhere only in 8:23 ("the redemption of our bodies" from corruptibility) and in 1 Cor 1:30 (Christ was made "for us wisdom . . . and righteousness and sanctification and redemption"; see also Eph 1:7; 4:30; Col 1:14). Paul uses the verb "redeem" only in Gal 3:13 and 4:5, where it refers to liberation from the law. Never does Paul, or anyone else in the New Testament, actually call Christ the "Redeemer," the word used repeatedly by the book of Isaiah for God (as in Isa 41:14; 43:14; 59:20); "Deliverer" in 11:26 renders a different word. (Among those who think Paul is quoting a tradition, some hold that the quotation begins here; others that it begins at v. 25.) Since *apolytrōsis* is related to *lytron* (ransom, used in Mark 10:45: The Son of Man came to give his life "as a ransom"), some have argued that Paul too understands Jesus' death as a ransom—especially since elsewhere he referred to Christians as belonging to Christ because they have been "bought with a price" (1 Cor 6:20; 7:23). "Redemption" and "redeem" are in fact metaphors drawn from various forms of buying the freedom of slaves and captives. This language expresses the radical, positive import of God's action in Christ; moreover, because it implies that the freed have been enslaved, it is consistent with their being "under sin" in verse 9. Nonetheless, the point here is not the price but the result.

In the parenthesis of verses 22b-24a Paul insists that God's rectitude is manifested through the redemption/emancipation from sin that occurs in Christ. The theological implications of this astounding assertion are far more important than the rationale implied by the metaphor itself. To be noticed, therefore, is that the text does not say that God's rectitude is manifested in Jesus because his own moral excellence mirrors it, however true that may be; nor does it say that Jesus' own "faith" (his "spirituality") disclosed it. Rather, the text claims that it is through the emancipation of those "under sin" that God's own rectitude, God's self-consistency, God's integrity, is manifested, and that this emancipation is effected by means of a particular human figure (REB: "through his act of liberation in the person of Christ Jesus"). What, then, is the basis for saying that through *Christ* there is redemption that manifests *God's* own rectitude?

Paul's answer is found in the clause that begins verse 25: "whom God put forward *[proetheto]* as *hilastērion.*" What is that? Is it "a sacrifice of atonement" (NRSV, NIV), a "means of expiating sin by his death" (REB), "a propitiation" (AV), "a sacrifice for reconciliation" (NJB), "the means of expiating sin by his sacrificial death" (NEB), or simply "a sacrifice" (CEV)? In the New Testament, the word is used only here and Heb 9:5; there too the translations differ: "mercy seat" (AV and NRSV), "atonement cover" (NIV), "the throne of mercy" (NJB), "the place of expiation"(NEB) or "of mercy" (CEV).

In the LXX the word translates the Hebrew *kappōret*, the lid on the chest, the ark of the covenant, in the sacred tent first used by Israel in the wilderness. On the Day of Atonement (Yom Kippur) the priest would sprinkle the blood of a sacrificed bull, then of a goat, on the ark and its lid as part of the annual ritual for dealing with Israel's sins (Lev 16). Because Heb 9:5 uses the article *(ho hilastērion)*, there the word clearly refers to the lid of the ark; Rom 3:25, without the article, suggests that Paul uses the word to refer not to the object itself but to what occurred in the ritual at the ark and afterwards, sending the sin-laden "scapegoat" into the wilderness. (Talbert [2003, 110-15], after a useful survey of possible meanings [also of the related verb *hilaskesthai*], proposes that for Paul the word meant "a new locus of divine revelation.") In the centuries after Paul, Christian theology, especially in the West, emphasized ever more strongly the death of Christ as a sacrifice made for the atonement of sins, and so interpreters sought to determine exactly what Paul's *hilastērion* meant and how it "works." Is Christ's death a propitiation (an act or gift that mollifies God's wrath) or an expiation (something that removes the cause of the wrath from people)? Actually, in terms of neither ritual nor logic can the two meanings be separated neatly.

In any case, Paul uses *hilastērion* as a metaphor that interprets another metaphor, the "redemption" effected in the death of a *person*, not an animal. Such use of *hilastērion* is found also in 4 Maccabees (perhaps written in Paul's lifetime or a century later), which celebrates the voluntary martyrdom of seven brothers and their mother during the persecutions that provoked the Maccabean Revolt in 168 BCE. The author explains the significance of their exemplary deaths as the reason "our enemies did not prevail . . . and our land [was] purified, since they became, as it were, a ransom *[hōsper antipsychon]* for the sin of our nation. Through the blood of these righteous ones, and through the *hilastērion* of their death the divine Providence rescued Israel" (17:22; Charlesworth 1985 2:563; see also 4 Macc 6:28-29). Here, a thoroughly Hellenized Jew uses biblical imagery to express theologically the beneficial results of voluntary human death for a noble cause—a theme well known in the Greco-Roman world (see Williams 1975).

What is distinctive in Paul's clause, however, is the verb *proetheto* used to express God's act; it too has been translated in various ways (NRSV: "put forward," NIV: "presented," NEB: "designed," NJB: "appointed"). In the middle voice it can mean "to set forth publicly" (as well as "intend," as in Rom 1:13). Thus Paul claims that Christ's death as *hilastērion* was God's deliberate act. That is why God's own rectitude is manifested in Christ's death. In 5:8 Paul will make the same point again: "*God demonstrates his own love for us, in that while we were still sinners, Christ died for us*" (AT; see comment).

In verse 25, the word *hilastērion* is followed by the third phrase designed to illumine how God's rectitude is manifested "through" something. This time it is *dia tēs pisteōs en tō autou haimati*, "through the faithfulness [expressed] in his blood." The AV and NIV retain Paul's word order without punctuation: "through faith in his blood." Other versions, recognizing the un-Pauline character of the phrase in this English rendering, translate Paul's words as "by his blood, effective through faith" (NRSV, NEB, REB). Those who think Paul is quoting a tradition often claim that he inserted the reference to faith. All these ways of coping with the difficulties *assume* that what Paul has in mind is the believer's *pistis* (faith). But since verse 22 refers to Christ's faithfulness, it is altogether likely that verse 25 does so as well (indeed, many good manuscripts simply read "through his faithfulness"). In short, Paul says that Christ's faithfulness was made explicit in (by means of) his sacrificial blood (also in 5:9 Paul speaks of being rectified "in his blood"). The blood itself is not the point; the "blood" signifies that Jesus was slain, sacrificed (in keeping with the *hilastērion* imagery).

Having used the three Christ-centered "through . . ." phrases to explain the *means* by which God's rectitude is manifested (through the faithfulness of Jesus, through the redemption which is in Christ, through the faithfulness expressed in his blood), in verse 25b Paul continues his complex sentence by focusing on the *purpose* of the threefold means. Here too, Paul's formulations are so terse that their precise meaning still eludes a broad consensus among exegetes; the diverging views expose significant rifts in the understanding of Romans in particular and of Paul generally. To penetrate the meaning, one must attend not only to the rarely used words but above all to the prepositions that signal their function. Paul's Greek is not as clear as translations try to make it. As noted, repetitions are a feature of the passage:

> . . . for a demonstration of his rectitude
> on account of the passing over of previously committed sins
> in the forbearance of God,

for the demonstration of his rectitude
    in the now time
so that he is [or, might be] righteous
    indeed by rectifying the one who lives out of the faithfulness of
    Jesus. (AT)

Basic for the meaning of these lines is the repetition of "demonstration" and the shift from the past ("previously committed sins") to the present ("the now time"). The careful composition is blurred by NRSV because it uses two different verbs ("show," v. 25; and "prove," v. 26) to translate the same Greek noun *endeixis* (demonstration), which refers back to verse 21 where Paul said that God's rectitude is manifested apart from the law. The purpose of this "demonstration" (not "proof") is expressed in the last two lines.

Vexing problems lurk in the clause that states the reason the "sacrificial death" *(hilastērion)* serves as a "demonstration" of God's rectitude: "on account of the passing over *[dia tēn paresin]* of previously committed sins in the forbearance *[anochē]* of God." Since *paresis* occurs neither in the LXX nor elsewhere in the New Testament, its meaning here depends on God's *anochē*, holding back. When used of a person or God, *anochē* means self-restraint, deliberately not acting as expected (as the verb in Wis 2:14 and LXX Isa 42:14; 63:15; 64:12 indicates). In using *anochē* here, Paul alludes to his questioning accusation of the Gentile judge in 2:4-5: "Do you despise the riches of his kindness and forbearance *[anochē]* and patience? But by your . . . impenitent heart you are storing up wrath for yourself on the day of wrath." In other words, "the passing over of previously committed sins" was an expression of God's holding back the deserved punishment, a self-restraint that was both merciful and ominous. Paul apparently implies that God exercised this self-restraint by "handing over" the Gentiles to the consequences of their idolatry (1:18-32) rather than destroying them promptly. Therefore "the passing over" does not refer to God's forgiveness (as is claimed by some), nor does it imply that God "overlooked" previous sins (as in REB); rather, God declined to punish them completely before "the day of wrath" had arrived.

What, then, does Paul mean by saying that God's not acting punitively as an expression of self-restraint is the reason ("on account of") Christ as *hilastērion* demonstrates God's rectitude? Does not God's refusal to punish demonstrate instead God's lack of rectitude, God's unfairness? It would *if* God's rectitude operated according to the law (recall v. 20 and 3:3). In providing the *hilastērion*, the rectitude of God *is* the rectitude manifested apart from the law, the rectitude manifested through Jesus' faithfulness. In other words, because God's not meting out deserved punishment for previous sins is of a piece with God's providing the *hilastērion* (though separated in time), God's passing over of earlier sins does show that God's rectitude is manifested apart from the law. Therefore, what God's act in Christ achieved—free (undeserved) rectification through redemption (v. 24)—does not introduce a historically *new* rectitude but reveals a wholly *different* one from that of the law. A historically new rectitude would imply that God is inconsistent, acting one way in the past but another way now. But God is consistent because the other rectitude (apart from the law) confirms "the passing over" of previous sins. Consistency across time is what matters here.

But whose sins were passed over in God's forbearance? According to Dunn (1988) and Byrne (1996), they were Israel's sins; but Williams (1975, 32) and Stowers (1994, 204), relying on what Paul said in 2:4-5, plausibly argue that they were the Gentiles' sins. Actually, a choice is not necessary, given the parenthetical observation that "there is no distinction, since all have sinned" (vv. 22-23). Consequently, rather than inferring that Paul implies that Jewish atonement rituals are inadequate (as some think and Heb 7:11, 18-19; 8:6-13 assert), one should infer that he regarded them as pointing ahead, as foreshadowing the *hilastērion* in Christ. Paul explicitly said in verse 21 that the law and the prophets bear witness to God's rectitude apart from the law, and in 1:2 spoke of the gospel precisely as promised in scripture. Paul reads scripture through the lens of Christ; he does not criticize it in the name of Christ.

Paul concludes this tightly packed paragraph by stating the purpose (or result) of the dual demonstrations of God's rectitude: "so that he might be righteous [dikaios] and rectify [dikaiounta] the one who lives out of [or on the basis of] the faithfulness of Jesus." This is the only time Paul says that God is righteous. He does so in order to emphasize that the rectitude that is manifested apart from the law in no way compromises God's own rectitude—God's integrity, God's trueness to God's nature and character—but expresses it definitively, and that it does so precisely by rectifying the person who lives on the basis of Jesus' faithfulness, actualized in his blood-death. In short, God is never more true to God's Godhood as the radically Other than when God rectifies the person who lives by Jesus' faithfulness. When God's rectitude rectifies, God "comes through" as the reality called "God" really is. God's rightness does not merely identify and reward/punish whoever is right or wrong, but also makes right whoever is not right. In 4:5 Paul will put it sharply when he refers to God as the One who "rectifies the *un*godly." Delineating what this understanding of God's rectitude means will energize the apostle's theological capacities in the rest of the letter, beginning with 3:27.

Before proceeding to that verse, however, it is important to note that what Paul means by living out of Jesus' faithfulness is not identical with the disciple's resolve to take up one's own cross, as in Mark 8:34, though they are not incompatible. Paul emphasizes that Jesus' faithfulness (which indeed took him to the cross) was *God's act*, God's own free movement into the human condition "apart from the law," a sheer gift that God "put forward." Even if it is the case that what Paul *asserts* in a theological statement Mark builds into a narrative *account*, it is nonetheless the case that Paul does not ask people to follow Jesus' way to Golgotha, but rather to *appropriate* Jesus' death by participating in it through baptism, as chapter 6 will show. It is not accidental that the word "disciple" does not appear in Paul's letters. That the appropriation does shape the believer's life, as does discipleship, is also clear, but for Paul this shaping does not depend on one's resolve to be a disciple, or on the *follower's* faithfulness, but on the power of the gospel.

In 3:27 Paul returns to the diatribe mode in order to formulate sharply the implications of 3:21-26 and to segue to a discussion of

Abraham in chapter 4. Because some of the exchanges with the interlocutor are terse, the argument moves rapidly. Understanding it is easier if one "slows it down" in order to examine it carefully. In accord with Stowers (1994, 233-34) the dialogue in 3:27–4:1 occurs as follows:

Interlocutor: Where, then, is boasting?
Paul: It has been excluded.
Interlocutor: Through what sort of law? of works?
Paul: No, but through the law of faith. For we reason that a person is rectified by faith apart from the works of the law. Or is God the God of Jews only? Is he not God of Gentiles too?
Interlocutor: Yes, also of Gentiles.
Paul: If [or since] God indeed is one, who will rectify the circumcision on the basis of faith [ek pisteōs], he will rectify also the foreskin dia tēs pisteōs [through the faith].
Interlocutor: So then, do we destroy the law through the faith [dia tēs pisteōs]?
Paul: By no means! Rather, we maintain the law.
Interlocutor: What, then, shall we say? Have we found Abraham to be our forefather according to the flesh? For if Abraham was rectified on the basis of works [ex ergōn], he does have a boast.
Paul: But not toward God! For what does the scripture say . . . ?

At issue is the impact that God's rectifying apart from the law has on Jewish identity and self-understanding in relation to Gentile salvation. Consequently, Paul has the interlocutor respond to verses 21-26 by asking, "Where, then, is boasting?" (v. 27), and later ask about Abraham in relation to boasting. By bringing up "boasting" the interlocutor is not simply requesting information; he is defending his sense of identity. His question implies that he has accepted Paul's characterization of him in 2:17-23: He calls himself a Jew; he relies on the law and *boasts* in God; having the truth in the law, he teaches Gentiles; he *boasts* in the law. The threat to Jewish self-understanding as a privileged people is implied by NJB: "So what becomes of our boasts?" REB's universalizing paraphrase, "What room then is left for human pride?" changes the point.

Paul's reply is terse: "It has been excluded." The passive implies that it was God who excluded it—namely, in God's action in Christ as set out in verses 21-26. The interlocutor then asks Paul to clarify the rationale that warrants the exclusion: "Through what sort of law did God exclude boasting? Was it through the law of works?" Paul first rejects this idea, and then identifies the sort of law through which boasting *was* excluded: "the law of faith" *(dia nomou pisteōs)*. Now, *we* want to ask, "What sort of law is *that?"*

Some interpreters (e.g., Fitzmyer [1993], Moo [1996]) think that here *nomos* means "principle" (so also REB, NIV, NJB). At first glance, such an interpretation makes sense. But is it Paul's sense? Several considerations, taken together, indicate that here too *nomos* means "law." For one thing, "by the principle of works" requires that also the contrasting phrase *dia nomou pisteōs* be translated "by the principle of faith"—hardly Paul's view of faith. (REB avoids the problem by paraphrasing: "And on what principle? The keeping of the law would not exclude it, but faith does"; likewise NJB has: "On what principle—that only actions count? No; that faith is what counts.") Moreover, not only do both instances of *nomos* in verse 31 clearly refer to the law, but so do the four previous uses of the word in verses 19-21. It is therefore improbable that in the midst of a discussion of the law Paul would suddenly have the interlocutor use the word in a different sense and then return to its customary sense in verse 31.

Manifestly, "the law of works" is a deliberate rephrasing of "the works of the law" on the basis of which "all flesh will not be rectified" (v. 20). So if "the works of the law" are deeds prescribed by the law, "the law of works" is the law that prescribes the deeds. The phrase "the law of faith" (used only here) looks like a deliberate oxymoron created *ad hoc* to express a totally different mode of existence in light of verses 21-26 (so also Moo 1996, 249), not a different way of viewing the same law (as Rhyne 1981, 90, Dunn 1988, 1:185, and others hold). In effect, Paul claims that the law that prescribes the deeds is not the means by which boasting is excluded because that law cannot exclude boasting in Jewish identity and privilege, which is based on that same law. But boasting can be, and has been, excluded because in the Christ-event God's rectifying rectitude is manifested apart from the law altogether. And that event has its own rationale, one that is capable of excluding boasting in the law.

Accordingly, in verse 28 Paul explains what he means by "the law of faith"—a person is "rectified by faith apart from the works of the law." (He had said virtually the same in Gal 2:16.) Rectification apart from the works of the law is the consequence of God's own rectitude having been manifested apart from the law. Paul's argument is not that faith excludes boasting (though it does) but that God's action in Christ has already done it; it is not the believer who excludes boasting (say, by deciding to give it up), but the rationale of God's act in Christ.

Not to be overlooked is that Paul speaks of the rectification of "a man" (*anthrōpos*, used generically). The generic, inclusive sense of "man" smoothes the way for his question, "Or is God the God of Jews only? Not also of Gentiles?" The interlocutor agrees, "Yes, also of Gentiles" (v. 29). Because this agreement expresses common Jewish thought, it is the basis *from which* Paul now proceeds. Were God not God of both Jews and Gentiles, one might infer that rectification apart from the works of the law is a concession to Gentiles who did not have the law "by nature" in the first place (2:14), while God treats Jews differently. Not so, as Paul goes on to argue: Since God is one (alluding to the Shema, Deut 6:4—the foundational conviction of Jews), he will rectify circumcision and foreskin on the same basis. The one God provides the one solution to the one human dilemma. It is this conviction that makes Paul's theology in Romans a theology of mission.

Paul's formulation, however, raises questions, partly because he uses different prepositions (*ek*, "out of" or "on the basis of," and *dia*, which combined with a genitive noun means "through, by means of"), and partly because he puts the definite article before *pistis* ("the faith/faithfulness") only in the last clause. Does he mean that Jews will be rectified on the basis of *(ek)* faithfulness (to the law), while Gentiles will be rectified through/by means of *(dia)* the faithfulness (viz., the faithfulness of Jesus, v. 26)? Or are these differences only stylistic variations? Most interpreters think the latter is the case (i.e., here the prepositions are used interchangeably) and render both uses of *pistis* as (the believer's) "faith" rather than "faithfulness," and take "through the faith" to mean something like "by the same faith" (so NRSV and Moo [1996]; but Stowers [1994, 237-41] argues that *dia tēs pisteōs* means "through the faithfulness of Jesus"). This passage, understandably, has been important in recent debates over whether Jews are saved apart from faith in Jesus Christ—a complex issue that exceeds the scope of this commentary—though the topic will reappear at 11:26.

In verse 31, the interlocutor uses Paul's last phrase (in v. 30) to put his objection as a question, "Do we then destroy the law 'through the *pisteōs*?'"(through "faith" or "the faithfulness [of Jesus]"). What the interlocutor finds objectionable is not the way Gentiles are rectified but the idea that Jews are rectified in exactly the same way, for this appears to threaten the pivotal significance of the law for Jewish existence.

Paul's response is unequivocal: "By no means! Rather, we maintain the law." Understandably, this forthright claim has generated many attempts to determine its exact meaning (conveniently summarized by Moo [1996]; unconvincing, however, is his claim that Paul means that "the Christian faith . . . provides [and for the first time!] the complete fulfillment of God's demand in his law"). The interlocutor does not ask, "What, then, is the place of the law in Christian thought and life?" His question responds to what Paul had asserted in verse 30—that God rectifies Jew and Gentile on the same basis. By asking whether Paul's assertion destroys the law, the interlocutor puts negatively (and more pointedly) what he had asked in 3:1: "What is the advantage of the Jew, or the value of circumcision?" In light of God's rectifying any and every person apart from the law, the question goes to the root of Jewish identity. And at the root, there is Abraham.

◊ ◊ ◊ ◊

The rationale of what Paul says in 3:21-26 about Christ's death is the opposite of the rationale operative in sacrifice, animal or human, where the offering is given to the deity in order to win (or sustain) favor or to avert anger. When a child is sacrificed in times of crisis, the community offers its very future in order to secure its future. But according to Paul, it is God who makes the offering in order to emancipate (redeem) humans from their enslavement to their illusions about God and the consequences of that bondage. Such a view of Jesus' death could have been conceivable only for those who have been emancipated by it. Paul had already said so in 1 Cor 1:21-25.

Abraham, the Prototype (4:1-25): The interlocutor does not pursue directly Paul's unqualified assertion, "we maintain the law" (3:31, AT); instead, he asks about Abraham as a way of questioning what Paul had said about the impact of "faith" on the law. This question rests on the common Jewish assumption that Abraham (epitomizing Israel's election) and the law are inseparable. So Paul's task is to interpret Abraham in a way that separates him from the law, without at the same time dissolving the claim that emphasizing faith actually maintains the law. Remarkably, what Paul says about the law seems not to "maintain" it because everything he says about it is negative. Nevertheless, Paul presents Abraham as convincing evidence that the patriarch too was rectified "apart from the works of the law," and so is the prototype of all those who trust in the God who raised Jesus from the dead. In treating Abraham this way, Paul is convinced that he *is* maintaining the law in its proper role—bearing witness to God's rectitude apart from the law. Paul ignores most of what Genesis reports about Abraham, and instead emphasizes one verse (Gen 15:6): "Abraham believed God, and it was reckoned to him as righteousness." For Paul, the key word in this quotation is "reckoned" (repeated nine times).

His argument moves in five steps: (a) In verses 1-8 he insists that Abraham's *faith* is reckoned as righteousness/rectitude. (b) In verses 9-12 he shows how "reckoned" implies that Abraham is the "father" of Gentiles as well as Jews, then (c) argues in verses 13-17 that God's promise to Abraham was not based on the law.

(d) In verses 18-22 he explores Abraham's faith. (e) Not until verses 23-25 does Paul explicitly link Abraham's reckoned rectitude to Christian believers. Paul had used Gen 15:6 in Gal 3, but there he did not emphasize "reckoned" because he had a different task. It is important, therefore, not to conflate the Abraham of Galatians and the Abraham of Romans.

◊ ◊ ◊ ◊

Abraham's Rectitude, Earned or Unearned? (4:1-8): Various forms of Jewish thought had long revered Abraham both as the beginning of God's chosen people and as the idealized paragon of Israelite/Jewish life. Already in Gen 26:5 God promises prosperity to Isaac "because Abraham obeyed my voice and kept my charge, my commandments, my statutes, and my laws" (though living long before Moses). This reverence produced legendary embellishments of the Abraham stories in Gen 12–25, and generated wholly new legends, evidenced especially in *Jub.* 11:14–23:10 (the whole corpus of traditions is summarized in Sandmel 1956, 30-95). *Jubilees* ends its account of Abraham with a laudatory statement: Abraham "was perfect in all his actions with the LORD and was pleasing through righteousness all the days of his life" (*Jub.* 23:10; see also 18:16). *Jubilees* notes that God tested Abraham ten times, and observes, "And in everything in which he tested him, he was found faithful" (17:18).

Running through the varied portrayals of Abraham is the theme that God rewarded him for his faithfulness and obedience. Thus Sir 44:19-21 says that "no one has been found like him in glory. . . . He kept the law of the Most High . . . and when he was tested he proved faithful. *Therefore* the Lord assured him . . . that the nations would be blessed through his offspring." The *Damascus Document*, apparently alluding to Isa 4:8 where God calls Abraham "my friend," says that "Abraham . . . was accounted a friend of God *because* he kept the commandments of God and did not choose his own will" (CD 3:10; cited from Vermes 1991, 98). Philo goes farther: "God marveling at Abraham's faith in Him *repaid him [antididōsin autō]* with faithfulness by confirming . . . the gifts which He had promised" (*Abr.* 273). Paul, however, must interpret Abraham differently if he is to adduce Abraham as evidence that "a person is justified apart from the works of the law." And that, in fact, is precisely what he undertakes in Rom 4.

Read as a diatribe, Paul begins by having his interlocutor raise the question of Abraham's ethnic significance: "What, then, shall we say? Have we found Abraham to be our forefather according to the flesh?"(so Hays 1985, 81)—that is, is Abraham our forefather by lineage? The interlocutor then reveals his real objection to Paul's claim that "boasting" is excluded (3:27): "For if Abraham was justified by works, he *has* something to boast about." Paul's curt reply, "But not toward God!" is then developed in the rest of the chapter. According to the traditional reading reflected in all translations, verse 1 is Paul's own open-ended question, focused on what Abraham "found" (NRSV: "gained"): "What, then, are we to say was gained by Abraham . . . ?" (REB ignores the troublesome "found" and simply has, "What, then, are we to say about Abraham, our ancestor by natural descent?") In any case, the phrase "but not toward God" implies that if Abraham had been "justified by works," he *would* have "something to boast about," both before God and in comparison with others. He could say what *Jub.* 21:2-3 has him say:

> Behold, I am one hundred and seventy-five years old, and throughout all the days of my life I have been remembering the Lord and sought with all my heart to do his will and walk uprightly in all his ways. I hated idols, and those who serve them I have rejected. And I have offered my heart and spirit so that I might be careful to do the will of the one who created me. [For comparable claims to obedience in second temple Judaism, see Gathercole 2002, chap. 5.]

Indeed, Paul himself could speak this way when looking back at his pre-Christian life (see Phil 3:4-6); his ironic boasting of his "weakness" in 2 Cor 11:21–12:10 expresses his current Christian attitude.

As Paul sees it, Abraham had nothing to boast about before God because he was *not* "justified by works"; as verses 3-8 are to demonstrate from scripture (Gen 15:6), Abraham's rectitude was a *reckoned rectitude* because scripture says he "believed God, and it was reckoned to him as righteousness." Here, to be "justified [dikaiousthai] by faith apart from the works of the law" (3:28, AT) is interpreted as having one's believing "reckoned as righteousness" (dikaiosynē, rectitude, rightness, requisite justice).

Even so, Paul apparently senses that, strictly speaking, Gen 15:6 does not preclude the idea that Abraham's justification was based on "works," on what he did, for one *could* read the text as implying that Abraham's faith was an accomplishment so remarkable that God recognized that it deserved to be reckoned as righteousness (as in Philo, who called faith "the most perfect of virtues," *Her.* 91). In other words, there is an ambiguity in the sequence: "Abraham believed . . . *and* it was reckoned." It is just this ambiguity that Paul removes—first in verses 4-5, then in verses 6-8— by explaining that "reckon" *(logizesthai)* and "works" *(erga)* in verse 2 are mutually exclusive.

In keeping with the use of *logizesthai* (reckon, count) in commerce, in verses 4-5 Paul points out that the worker's pay is not counted or reckoned as a favor (lit., "according to grace") but as "something due"—as an obligatory compensation for work done. The worker's pay is not a gift, for it has been earned. Paul applies this commonsense observation to Abraham by using the vocabulary of Gen 15:6 to contrast the worker in verse 4 with the nonworker in verse 5: "But to the nonworker [Abraham] who trusts the one who justifies [makes right] the ungodly, *his trust [pistis]* is reckoned as righteousness" (AT). This astounding statement is offensive because it implies that Abraham is ungodly! (By calling him "ungodly" *[asebēs]* Paul clearly alludes to 1:18, which states that God's wrath is against all human *asebeia*, ungodliness.) But God is so gracious that Abraham's undeserved rectification (being declared right) is a sheer gift. Contrary to a common reading of 4:3, Paul does *not* say that Abraham's faith *made* him righteous (then he would have had something to boast about), but says that God "reckons" (considers, counts) as rightness Abraham's trusting in God as the rectifier of the ungodly. Paul sees that only the *un*godly trust such a God; the godly trust the God who counts their godliness as righteousness.

Not to be missed is the radical otherness of God that is built into Paul's characterization of God as "the one who justifies/rectifies the ungodly," for this action challenges the commonsense view of fundamental justice. Indeed, according to Exod 23:6-8 LXX, God forbids acquitting the ungodly (*ou dikaiōseis ton asebē*; in the Hebrew text, God says, "I will not acquit the guilty"). Because God's justifying /rectifying action is not a matter of distributive justice, in which everyone gets exactly what is due, Paul insists that justification/rectification is "apart from works" altogether and instead is a matter of grace, a sheer gift given to the undeserving believer. The rectification of the ungodly calls into question God's own rectitude whenever that is understood in terms of distributive justice, which is based on law. Paul also insisted that in the Christ-event God's rectitude is manifested "apart from the law" (3:21), because the justification of the ungodly results from the manifestation of God's righteousness apart from the law.

Paul had claimed that God's rectitude apart from the law is attested by the law and the prophets (3:21); now, in verses 6-8, he notes that David had foreseen it in Ps 32 (LXX 31):1-2, even though the psalm does not use the word "righteousness." That does not deter Paul, however. Like the rabbinic practice of letting one passage interpret another when the same word appears in both, Paul cites this psalm because, like Gen 15:6, it too uses the word "reckon" (v. 8). Before Paul quotes it, he explains its relevance: David blesses those "to whom God reckons righteousness apart from works." The psalm, however, speaks of forgiveness, which is not part of Paul's soteriological vocabulary. (When Paul writes of forgiveness elsewhere, he refers to Christian forgiveness [2 Cor 2:7, 10; 12:13]; only here does he use the word to refer to God's saving act.) Since forgiveness is the cancellation of a debt, the nullification of a person's unfulfilled obligation, David can say that forgiveness occurs when "the Lord will not reckon sin," when God does not count it, does not allow it to determine one's relation to God. By definition, forgiveness occurs "apart from works"; otherwise it would be earned, like a wage. The forgiven person, like the justified Abraham, has nothing to boast about. Important as it is to recognize that in adducing David to support the interpretation of Gen 15:6 Paul follows rabbinic practice, it is even more important to understand the unstated theological

rationale by which Paul juxtaposes two quite different terms—
"reckon" and "justify"—so that verses 4-5 and verses 6-8 are
truly complementary, and the paragraph is coherent. And that
entails looking more closely at "reckon."

The verb *logizesthai*, used primarily in mathematics (to calcu-
late) and in commerce (to credit), was also used to refer to cognitive activity (to count, consider, regard), the result of which is
logismos (calculation, thought, conclusion). When Paul writes,
"Let a person think of us/consider us *[hēmas logizesthō]* as servants of Christ" (1 Cor 4:1, AT), he means that "servant" is the
appropriate way to regard him. Here the reckoning is appropriate
because it accords with reality, with Paul's self-understanding. But
when Luke 22:37 says that Jesus was *meta anomōn elogisthē*
("he was counted among the lawless," quoting Isa 53:12), this
"counting" is regarded as improper (though ultimately appropriate on theological grounds). In other words, the word "reckon"
alone does not determine whether the regarding or crediting someone with something is proper or improper. This ambiguity became
significant centuries later when Christian theology sought to
understand more precisely what Paul had said about justification.

According to the logic of the quoted line from Gen 15:6, one
entity (viz., faith) was regarded/reckoned as a different entity (viz.,
righteousness). Was this reckoning an improper one—a reckoning
that is simply arbitrary? Were that the case, it would undermine
God's own righteousness. Or was it appropriate—that is, is there
a substantive basis for such a reckoning? If so, God's own righteousness would not be impaired. Had Paul agreed with the widespread Jewish view of Abraham as the paragon of virtue, he
would have understood Gen 15:6 to say that God acknowledged
and rewarded the faith/faithfulness of the law-observant Abraham
by reckoning it as righteousness. From *that* viewpoint, God's reckoning would have been appropriate. But because Paul regards
Abraham as "ungodly," his trusting/believing was reckoned as his
righteousness *despite* the fact that he was not actually righteous.
From the common point of view, that would be an improper act,
contrary to fact; and that would call the prevailing view of God's
own rectitude into question. Does God, then, treat him *as if* he

were righteous, knowing that he was not righteous? To avoid that inference, some theology has argued that in response to faith, God credits or "imputes" *Christ's* own righteousness to the sinner, thereby providing the appropriate ground for God's "reckoning." But while this preserves the integrity of God's rectitude, it treats Christ's rectitude as a transferable good, like money in a bank account. Nor is it evident that this interpretation is faithful to what Paul says. A more careful look at our passage is called for.

By adducing Gen 15:6 as evidence of Abraham's justification/rectification without works, Paul implies that this rectification occurred when God reckoned Abraham's faith as righteousness. Since *dikaiosynē* means that the relation to a norm is right, what occurs in justification/rectification is making right the relation to the norm, namely, God. Justification/rectification does not make one good. It corrects the relationship so good can follow. By making the relation to God right, justification/rectification frees for the future. When Ps 32 speaks of forgiveness, it too has in view liberation from the past and for the future. Consequently, Paul sees that what occurs in forgiveness restores and rectifies the relation to God. And that relation is made right when the ungodly entrust themselves to God the rectifier. When God reckons/considers/regards the ungodly's self-entrustment (or faith) as righteousness, God's reckoning occurs "apart from works," that is, "apart from the law" (3:21). Only on *this* basis is God's reckoning the sheer trust of the ungodly *as* rectitude appropriate, for trust *is* the right relation to God.

It is worth repeating that Paul does not say that Abraham (or anyone else) was "justified by [his] faith," but rather by God's grace (3:24); nor does he imply that by faith Abraham was made a righteous (good) person, or that God treated Abraham as if he were righteous (though he was actually ungodly), or that God imputed Christ's righteousness to Abraham so that he could treat him appropriately as a righteous person. Such construals wrongly assume that righteousness/rightness/rectitude is a moral quality, just as they overlook that for Paul the faith that God regards as a right relation is the ungodly person's utter reliance on *God's* making the relationship right. In short, for Paul, neither affirming right ideas about God nor believing in God generally is enough for a right relation to God, for that can conceal an illusory self-understanding that one is godly; what *is* enough for a right relation to God is entrusting oneself to God. What Paul assumes here he will declare later: "It is God who justifies" (8:31).

Abraham as Our "Father" (4:9-12): In Abraham's rectification apart from "works," Paul sees the rationale that supports his assertion that God rectifies Jews and Gentiles alike "apart from works of the law" and on the basis of faith instead (3:28-29). (What Paul sees invalidates the claim that Paul's theology is focused not on how one finds acceptance by God but on the relation of Jew and Greek; actually, the former is the theological ground on which Paul deals with the latter. This false alternative, popular as part of the recent determination to free Paul from his "Lutheran" captivity, has wrought much mischief in the interpretation of Paul.) To use the psalm for his argument, Paul asks an unexpected question: Does the blessedness of which David sang apply to Gentiles as well as to Jews? (v. 9). Then he restates Gen 15:6 in order to ask another question, *"How* was Abraham's faith reckoned as righteousness?" (v. 10, AT). This "How?" refers not to the mechanism of the reckoning (How did it happen?) but to its "when": Was Abraham circumcised at the time he was "justified," or afterward? The sequence is important; if Abraham was already circumcised when he was "justified," his justification could be seen as God's reward for the patriarch's obedience (analogous to the worker's wage). But Paul points out (v. 10) that he was justified *before* he was circumcised. (Paul assumes that readers know that Abraham's circumcision is reported in Gen 17, well after Gen 15:6.) So, then, Abraham's justification was not God's response to his circumcision. But what then is the significance of that circumcision? It was a subsequent confirmation ("seal") of the faith-righteousness that was reckoned to him while he was an uncircumcised Gentile. (Even if Paul's opponents in Galatia had used the sequence "believe-circumcise" to argue that Gentiles must be circumcised after they believed the gospel, there is no evidence that Paul had to deal with that issue in Rome.) The theological significance of the sequence pertains not only to Abraham, however, for it determines the sense in which he is "father": He is the prototype for *all* subsequent believers—for Gentiles because righteousness is reckoned to them as it was to Abraham in his Gentile state, as well for those Jews who, in addition to being circumcised, also recapitulate father Abraham's faith, namely, Christian Jews (vv. 11-12).

Two things must be noted in verses 9-12. One, by rendering *patēr* as "ancestor" instead of "father," NRSV obscures the argument, for Abraham is the Christian Gentiles' prototype, not their ancestor; neither his circumcision nor their faith makes Abraham their ancestor. "Father," on the other hand, means more than paternity; it implies that as the starting point of the people of God, Abraham was definitive for what follows. Two, even though male Jews had been circumcised before they believed the gospel, Abraham becomes also their prototype when they subsequently accept the gospel and so repeat the faith of Abraham. But NRSV, by rendering Paul's Greek as "follow the example," replaces the Abrahamic prototype (or paradigm) with a mere commendable precedent. But for Paul, Abraham's justification/rectification is *not* exemplary; it is defining. Paul never advises his Christian readers to imitate Abraham's believing because for Paul the "structure" or "logic" of Abraham's believing is by definition the structure of Christian believing. That's what makes him the "father," the defining starting point. In short, Christian faith is by definition "Abrahamic." Paul has not found Abraham to be "our forefather according to the flesh" (our lineal ancestor), as in the traditional translation of verse 1, but our prototypical "father" according to grace, be one Jew or Gentile.

Promise and Law (4:13-17): In verse 13 Paul specifies the promise (Abraham will "inherit the world") as well as the basis on which it was made. Although the promise passages regularly refer to the land (Gen 12:2; 13:6; 15:5; 17:4-6, 16-20; 22:18), none of them promise the *world*—though Sir 44:21 comes close: God will give Abraham's offspring "an inheritance from sea to sea, and from the Euphrates [lit., "the river"] to the ends of the earth." Perhaps Paul spoke of "the world" (*kosmos*, not *gē*, earth) to signal that all Gentiles are included in God's promise. More important for his argument is his assertion that the promise was not mediated by the law *(dia nomou)* but through *(dia)* "the righteousness of faith"—a phrase that abbreviates the point of the previous discussion. Pointedly, though, Paul says the promise was made *also* to Abraham's "seed" (NRSV: "descendants"), thereby preparing the way for the redefinition of the "seed" in verses 16-17. In verse 14 Paul explains why Abraham and his seed are not inheritors of the world on the basis of the law *(ek nomou)*; were that the case, then both faith and the promise would be destroyed—precisely as faith and promise. Verse 15 states the reason for that result: "for the law brings about *[katergazetai]* wrath" [AT; REB goes beyond the text: "law can bring only retribution"). Attached to this explanation is a statement that looks like a maxim: "where there is no law, neither is there violation," adduced here to explain why the law produces God's wrath. The explanation, however, seems incomplete until it is fleshed out: (a) Law and transgression *(parabasis)* go together: no law, no transgression; (b) but ever since Moses there is the law, (c) consequently now there is transgression and its consequence, God's wrath. (d) Therefore the earlier promise to Abraham's seed does not come through the law but through the righteousness of faith.

According to verses 16-17, two purposes (or results) explain why the promise to Abraham and his "seed" is made on the basis of faith *(ek pisteōs)*. (a) "So that it might be according to grace." Since in verse 4 this phrase refers to the basis of God's "reckoning," neither the reckoning of Abraham's faith nor the promise of inheriting is a reward; both are acts of God's grace. (b) "So that it might be *bebaion* [firm, reliable, valid; NRSV's "guaranteed" is excessive] for all the seed"—that is, "all the seed" can count on it.

But why does the reliability of the promise depend on its being made on the basis of faith *(ek pisteōs)* and not "through the law"? The answer lies not in the nature of the promise but in the identity of "all the seed," which for Paul is not simply (physical) "descendants." Apart from verse 17, "all the seed" in verse 16 is ambiguous: the promise is "not only to the adherents of the law but also to those who share the faith of Abraham (for he is the father of us all . . .)." By itself "father of us all" could refer to all

Jews, some of whom have become Christian Jews, but verse 17 cites a line from Gen 17:5, "I have made you the father of many *ethnōn*," a word meaning both "nations" and "Gentiles." In other words, by citing Gen 17:5, Paul expands Abraham's role as "the father of us all" to include Christian Gentiles. This expansion, however, now makes it unclear whether the "adherents of the law" refers to Christian Jews (so, e.g., Moo 1996) or to all observant Jews. In light of 9:4-5 and chapter 11 (especially 11:25-32), however, the latter is the more likely. If so, Abraham is the common forefather of all Jews by lineal descent, and of all Christian Gentiles by Abrahamic faith.

Aged Sarah and Abraham being *childless*, Abraham could only *believe* the promise, and that entailed trusting a God capable of keeping such a promise—namely, "the God who gives life to the dead and calls into existence the things that do not exist" (v. 17*b*). Perhaps this characterization of God as the vivifier of the dead alludes to a line from the ancient Jewish prayer, The Eighteen Benedictions, "You, O Lord, are mighty forever, for you make the dead alive."

In any case, this characterization of God is the closest the New Testament comes to stating the doctrine of *creatio ex nihilo*. The idea was being taught also by Hellenized Judaism, which rejected the Platonic idea of a Demiurge creator who shapes already-existing matter into the cosmos, for such a view implies that the existence of matter itself is not contingent on the creator. Philo is explicit: God "called the non-existent into existence" (*Spec. Leg.* 4.187; in *Mos.* 2.100 he refers to God as the one who "brought into being what is not"; see also 2 Macc 7:28 and 2 *Bar.* 21:4; 48:8). By characterizing God this way, Paul connects creation, resurrection, and Sarah's conceiving Isaac—each being a completely fresh start because none has an antecedent cause that explains it historically. Each is as discontinuous from what preceded it as the coming of the New Age (see introduction, p. 34); at the same time, each expresses God's freedom to act. Nowhere is the radical otherness of God expressed more trenchantly.

Abraham's Faith (4:18-22): In sketching briefly what Abraham's faith entailed, Paul shows that his trusting God is not an example to be imitated, not an achievement to be admired or venerated. Rather, as portrayed here, that faith instantiates in the patriarch's circumstance the essential features of faith/trust itself. The function of the portrayal is to make the paradigmatic character of Abraham's faith concrete. Verse 18 does not speak of a general, naive faith in God, but of the patriarch's struggle to believe, using the strange expression "hope against hope" (AT; REB paraphrases: "When hope seemed hopeless"). That is, given his and Sarah's age, there was no apparent reason to hope that the promise would be kept; nonetheless, he believed, and so became "the father of many *ethnōn*" (as Gen 17:5 said). Paul supports this by citing words from Gen 15:5: "So [numerous] shall your seed be," namely, as numerous as the stars.

What Paul means by "hope against hope" emerges in the rest of the complex sentence (vv. 19-21) according to which Abraham "did not weaken with respect to faith *[tē pistei]* . . . but was made strong with respect to faith" *(enedynamōthē tē pistei)*. The repetition of *tē pistei* is deliberate; both are probably datives of respect, as in the translation above. Accordingly, "he did not weaken in faith" (NRSV) is better than REB's "his faith did not weaken," for the sentence concerns Abraham, not what happened to his faith. In verse 19 Paul says Abraham did *not weaken* (*mē asthenēsas*, active participle), but in verse 20 Paul deliberately uses the passive verb, *enedynamōthē* —"was made strong," namely by *God*. Some translations replace God's strengthening action with Abraham's (NRSV and NASB: "he grew strong in faith"; REB oversimplifies: "strong in faith"; NJB: "drew strength from faith"). In other words, Paul avoids implying what these translations make him say—that Abraham believed more strongly, as if he were the source of strengthened faith.

Modern translations are not the first to change Paul's thought here, for many manuscripts (including those used by the AV) insert a negative in verse 19, thereby making Paul say, "he did *not* consider his own body as good as dead." But without the negative (surely the preferred reading), Paul says that Abraham *did* consider the effect of his and Sarah's age on the likelihood that they would become parents, and nonetheless was convinced that the Promiser is able to keep the promise. According to the variant reading, Paul thinks Abraham's faith ignored the empirical evidence; according to the preferred reading, his faith was a resolute "nevertheless" in the face of the evidence because the One who made the promise is able also to keep it, for God is the one "who gives life to the dead"—including the "deadness" of the aged bodies of Abraham and Sarah.

Paul claims that "no distrust [apistia] made him waver concerning the promise of God" (v. 20; AV: "he staggered not . . . through unbelief"). Yet according to Gen 17:15-17, when God repeated the promise of a son, "Abraham fell on his face and laughed, and said to himself, 'Can a child be born to a man who is a hundred years old? Can Sarah, who is ninety years old, bear a child?'" Either Paul ignores this report, or he does not regard Abraham's laughter as "distrust," because this laughter actually underscores the radical otherness of God's promised action.

Paul also says that Abraham was made strong in faith "as he gave glory to God" (v. 20), though nowhere does Genesis say this. By making the comment he clearly contrasts Abraham—still an uncircumcised Gentile—with the Gentiles in 1:21, who knew God but "did not honor him as God or give thanks to him." To give God glory is indeed to honor God as God and to be grateful—that is, to acknowledge one's utter contingency on the One who can keep the promise. Having pointed that out, as well as having said that God strengthened Abraham in believing, Paul can add, "therefore his faith was reckoned to him as righteousness" without suggesting that Abraham earned this reckoning. God's response is not to be confused with reward.

Abraham's Faith and Christian Faith (4:23-25): In concluding the whole discussion of Abraham on this note, Paul has left behind the interlocutor's question (4:1), and now explicitly links the patriarch to the readers by claiming that what scripture says about Abraham has a purpose greater than simply providing information. It was written "also for our sake"—Paul's and the readers'—because what was true of Abraham is true also of them: To them, too, faith will be reckoned as righteousness. The futurity of this reckoning is somewhat surprising since 5:1 begins,

"Now that we have been justified" (REB). Though the "reckoning" in view here may be simply a logical future, it probably refers to the future Judgment when present justification will be completed and confirmed.

In any case, Abraham is pivotal for Paul's argument because what was written about him was written also for our sake—all who are Abraham's "seed." Otherwise Paul shows no interest in Abraham as a historical figure; nor, despite the "hope against hope" theme, does he show any interest in the story of the binding/near sacrifice of Isaac (Gen 22), even though Genesis regards that as God's test of Abraham's faith and obedience. Indeed, Genesis says God will reward him for it: "*Because* you have . . . not withheld your son . . . I will indeed bless you, and I will make your offspring as numerous as the stars," etc. (Gen 22:16-17). So, too, Abraham's abandonment of polytheism for devotion to the one true God, so important for Philo, is ignored here—even in a discourse that begins with an indictment of idolatry! Paul's characterization of Abraham is actually inferred from the apostle's understanding of Christian faith and righteousness, and their significance for the Gentile mission. (Paul also says almost nothing about Abraham's significance for the mission to Jews.) It is at least doubtful whether it is appropriate to speak of Abraham's role in "salvation history," as is often the case, for while Abraham does appear at the beginning of God's people, there is no evidence that Paul saw him as inaugurating a history, a continuing story. Rather, as the originating paradigm, Abraham is the recorded promise. To confuse or conflate promise with history, as is often done, is to misconstrue Paul's thought at a key point.

Although the faith of Christians, be they Jews or Gentiles, too will be reckoned as rightness with God—because the *character* of "faith" is the same—Paul is quite aware that the Christ-event makes the *content* of that faith different from that of Abraham. Consequently, not until the very end of the whole chapter does Paul mention Christ (vv. 24-25). But even here, the accent is on *God's* action in the Christ-event. In this context, Christians believe in God who, as in verse 5 and verse 17, is characterized by what God *does*: here, "raised Jesus our Lord from the dead." With this formulation Paul links Christian believing with that of Abraham who trusted the God "who gives life to the dead" (v. 17), thereby indicating that when Christians believe the gospel they believe in the God whom Abraham trusted. Though Paul's argument would have been complete had he stopped at the end of verse 24, he added verse 25, whose passive verbs ("was handed over" and "was raised") again emphasize God's action.

Verse 25 is often regarded as a piece of Christian tradition that Paul cites; its parallel structure is obvious:

handed over [NRSV adds "to death"] for our trespasses
paredothē   *dia ta paraptōmata hēmōn*

raised   for our justification
ēgerthē   *dia tēn dikaiōsin hēmōn*

If Paul is indeed quoting a fixed tradition, the historical implications would be significant: he inherited the view of Christian salvation as justification/rectification, which he then developed in his own way. Exploring the consequences of that possibility, however, belongs to the history of early Christian theology, not to the exegesis of the text before us. In any case, the first line is similar to the tradition quoted in 1 Cor 15:3, though the vocabulary differs. That Jesus was "handed over" is said also in the Lord's Supper tradition quoted in 1 Cor 11:23 ("in the night in which he was *paredothē*" [AT], which probably means "handed over" rather than "was betrayed"). All three formulations reflect the appropriation of Isa 53:12—"because of their sins he [the Servant] was handed over [*paredothē*]" (AT). Further, this line agrees with 3:25—God put Christ forward as "a sacrifice of atonement" (the *hilastērion*; see above).

The second line connects Jesus' resurrection with "our justification" (*dikaiōsis* refers to the action itself). It would be a mistake, however, to compartmentalize the Christ-event so that his death effected atonement and his resurrection our justification, for the whole clause has been formulated with rhetorical balance in mind. Moreover, by ending the sentence this way, Paul has set the stage for 5:1, which follows immediately with, "Therefore, having been justified . . ." (AT).

The Epistle of James too quotes Gen 15:6, but draws a quite different conclusion from that of Paul (see Jas 2:14-26, esp. vv. 23-24): "You see that a person is justified by works and not by faith alone." True, this epistle adduces Abraham to argue that "faith by itself, if it has no works, is dead" (2:17), in order to attack those Christians who ignore the plight of the poor. So it is often said that James does not oppose Paul himself but a gross distortion of Paul, since Paul is no less insistent on charitable deeds than James (see, e.g., Rom 12:13, 20; 1 Cor 11:21-22; Gal 6:10; Phil 2:4; 1 Thess 5:15).

◊ ◊ ◊ ◊

Paul did not believe in faith. He believed in God and emphasized faith—not because faith is powerful but because God is. When Paul wrote that Abraham, despite his and Sarah's age, "grew strong in faith," he did not suggest that faith enabled the aged pair to recover their fecundity. The possibility of such psychosomatic effects of faith was beyond his horizon. Indeed, he shows no interest whatever in explaining "how faith works," because, from his perspective, it is not faith that is "the power of God for salvation" but the *gospel*. Had Paul been interested in the power of faith, in the potency of our trusting, he might have organized "faith clinics" in which he taught people how to "believe harder" so that their faith would be more powerful. Then, of course, he would have said that God justifies the godly.

Beyond Rectification: Rescued and Reconciled (5:1-11): That chapter 5 marks a major turn is signaled by the concluding lines of chapter 4, for from this point on—even in chapters 9–11—the focus is on the readers. That chapters 5–8 constitute a distinct section is also obvious from the peroration with which they conclude (8:31-39). Less obvious, however, is whether 5:1-11 ends the section that began at 1:18 or begins the next one. A firm decision, however, is unnecessary, since verses 1-11 are a hinge between what Paul has already said and what he is about to say. Rhetorically, it fits what the *Rhetorica ad Herennium* (attributed to Cicero) calls a *transitio*: "a figure which briefly recalls what has been said, and likewise briefly sets forth what is to follow next" (4:26, 35). Theologically, it presents Christian existence between two events, between what God has already done and what God has yet to do, between "the already" and "the not yet." This dual horizon shapes chapters 5–8 as a whole, and provides warrants for Christian life in the present. The passage looks beyond rectification toward the completion of God's saving activity through Jesus Christ. Every sentence in it leads the hearers' thought to the future, expressed in various terms, when "we will be saved" (v. 9, repeated in v. 10).

Paul, knowing that the letter would be heard before it would be studied, here ceased arguing closely from scripture (as in chap. 4), eschewed writing a dense paragraph (like 3:21-26), and abandoned the diatribe (as in 2:17–3:31); instead he composed a passage whose pervasive use of "we," "our," and "us" draws the hearers (and today's readers!) into its celebratory, confessional posture (begun at 4:23). He will resume careful argument at 5:12-21, but this transitional passage allows the hearers to catch their breath while at the same time inviting them to think afresh about the effects of God's act in Christ on their present and future existence.

While he does not argue, he does reason, relying on well-known rhetorical constructions and devices to make his assertions effective in moving the hearers to share his own confidence in God (Keck 1993, 80-89). For example, the repetition of "we boast" that appears at the beginning (v. 2) and end of the passage (v. 11) creates an *inclusio*, as does the repetition of "through Jesus Christ our Lord" in verse 1 and verse 11. In our passage Paul also relies on three constructions to lead the readers' thought forward to the main point: (a) "not only . . . but . . ." (vv. 3, 11); (b) "if X, how much more Y" (vv. 9-10); and (c) *gradatio*, the ancient rhetoricians' term for a figure in which the last word of one phrase is also the first word in the next:

> our justification (4:25).
> justified . . . we boast
> we boast in suffering
> suffering produces endurance
> endurance produces character
> character produces hope
> hope does not disappoint. . . .

Paul skillfully repeats certain key terms that link the passage to chapters 1–4; he also introduces motifs that reappear in chapter 8. Moo (1996, 293) provides a list of the latter, but the list of the former is even longer:

v. 1	justified	3:20, 26, 28, 30
	by *(ek)* faith	3:30; 4:16 (3:26; 4:16)
v. 2	grace	4:16
	boast	3:27; 4:2
	hope	4:18
	glory of God	3:23
v. 9	blood	3:25
	wrath	1:18; 3:5; 4:15
	now	3:21, 26
v. 10	God's Son	1:3-4

◊ ◊ ◊ ◊

The long topic sentence (vv. 1-2) contains an important text problem: Did Paul write "let us have *[echōmen]* peace with God," as most manuscripts say, or "we have *[echomen]* peace"? Since the former exhorts, the latter is preferred, partly because there is no exhortation in the rest of the passage. (Fee [1994, 495-96 n. 66], however, makes a strong case for "let us have" and "let us boast," vv. 3, 11.) Thus Paul begins by pointing out that, "having been justified on the basis of faith" *(ek pisteōs)*, there is no hostility, no animosity with God (reformulated in vv. 10-11 as "enemies" who have been reconciled to God). In keeping with the celebratory character of the whole passage, Paul does not dwell on the animosity but on its resolution—peace, the result of being rectified on the basis of faith. Paul is not talking about "peace of mind" but about the definitive consequences of God's act. By adding "through our Lord Jesus Christ," Paul says that Christ is the means by which God's action occurred. In fact, this passage repeatedly speaks of Christ as the means, using *dia* + genitive noun (= through).

v. 2	through whom *(di' autou)* we have access
v. 9	through whom *(di' autou)* we will be saved
v. 10	through *(dia)* the death of his Son we were reconciled
v. 11	through *(dia)* whom we have received reconciliation

These usages agree with 3:22 (God's righteousness is manifested "through *[dia]* the faithfulness of Jesus Christ"). All these statements clearly assert that the benefits mentioned are contingent on the Christ-event, and so would not have occurred apart from Christ. In verse 2 Paul uses a wordplay *(paronomasia)* to express that benefit: "we have obtained access *[eschēkamen]* to this grace in which we stand *[hestēkamen]*." Here "grace" *(charis)* is imaged as a status or a space, a domain in which the believer now "stands," having arrived there through Christ. To "stand" in grace is to have one's ongoing existence firmly and unwaveringly determined by God's undeserved favor, well expressed in "Amazing Grace."

The opening sentence concludes by naming another benefit, this one combining the present ("and we boast") with the future— "our hope of sharing the glory of God" (REB: "hope of the divine glory that is to be ours"). The glory that is hoped for will replace the lack of glory because of sin (3:23). Paul had spoken negatively of "boasting" in 2:17; 3:27; 4:2 where it referred to Jewish "confidence that God would vindicate Israel on the basis of both election and obedience" (Gathercole 2002, 226). Here, and in verse 11, he regards it positively because it expresses confidence in future salvation that results from being rectified. Paul evinces no regret that this "glory" is "not yet," for like Abraham, he is "fully convinced that God was able to do what he had promised" (4:21)—here, the completion of presently "standing" in the domain of grace. In chapter 8 Paul will return to this theme of the glorification of the believer (8:17, 18, 21, 30).

When Paul continues (vv. 3-4) with "and not only that," one expects him to write of something that even exceeds this future glory. Instead, he abruptly speaks of the painful present ("sufferings") between "the already" and "the not yet." In this context, sufferings are the opposite of glory; they are the hallmarks of the yet-unredeemed world, a brutal reminder of the "not yet." And what is the appropriate Christian attitude toward sufferings (the plural suggests both variety and frequency)? "We also *boast* in our sufferings."

Every item in this clause requires comment. (a) "Sufferings" renders the plural of *thlipsis,* which Paul used at 2:9 to speak of

God's painful punishment (NRSV: "anguish"; REB: "affliction"), which is hardly the meaning here. *Thlipsis* was used for a range of sufferings, from internal "distress" (as in 2 Cor 2:4) to external persecution (John 16:33); it appears in Paul's hardship lists (2 Cor 4:8-9; 6:4-10) and was used also to refer to the tribulations expected at the End Time (Dan 12:1; Matt 24:29; Rev 7:14; and Matt 24:21 speak of "the great tribulation"). Here, however, the word probably refers to what Paul will call "the sufferings of this present time" (8:18), such as those listed in 8:35 (hardship, distress, persecution, famine, nakedness, peril, sword). The man who wrote this way about suffering had himself endured much of it, as he points out in 2 Cor 11:24-29. (b) The expression "boast in" can refer to the *circumstances* in which boasting occurs, or to the *content* of the boasting. If Paul means the former, sufferings are the context in which Christians boast about the hope in verse 2; if he means the latter, then Christians boast about their sufferings. Since boasting "in" refers to the content also in 1 Cor 1:31; 3:21; Gal 6:13; Phil 3:3, the latter is preferable here as well. (c) Since *kauchōmetha* in verse 2 means "we boast," the same verb probably has the same meaning in verse 3 (though grammatically it might also mean "let us boast"). In a word, Paul says, "we boast about [our] sufferings!" (AT). But why? Not because suffering is enjoyable, for Paul is no masochist. Rather, the reason for this stance lies in what "we know"—namely, what that suffering produces *(katergazetai)* or achieves, as Paul now spells out in the *gradatio* that ends in verse 5.

Paul ignores the negative things that suffering often produces (e.g., anger, bitterness, depression), and instead writes only of its positive consequences for the sufferer, thereby ignoring also its possible effects on others—especially those who are close to the sufferer. He is not, of course, outlining an essay on suffering. Rather, by highlighting the positive moral consequences of suffering, he leads the hearer/reader back to the theme of hope, his real interest here. This interest in hope—the hope of God's glory—distinguishes Paul's treatment from two other ancient perspectives on suffering, one found in scripture and in early Jewish writings, the other in Greco-Roman moralists. To oversimplify, the former often viewed suffering as God's harsh discipline designed to correct waywardness, as in *Pss. Sol.* 16:11, "If I sin, discipline me that I may return" (see also Prov 3:11-12; Jdt 8:27; Sir 18:13). The latter emphasized the role of suffering in developing character and the virtuous life (see Talbert 2003, 134-35).

The sequence (suffering, endurance, character, hope) does not imply stages through which one passes (though that is not excluded); it refers to the development of virtues—clearer in Paul's Greek than in translations, especially because of what endurance produces: *dokimē*, tested genuineness. Neither "character" (NIV, NRSV) nor "approval" (REB) is as adequate a translation as "proven character" (NASB) or "tested character" (NJB). Unexpected is the claim that "tested character" produces hope. Since Paul is asserting rather than arguing, what he means by this claim can only be inferred. Perhaps the statement means that by being tested one hopes more intently for the glory of God, which will replace the present arduous existence.

In any case, in verse 5 the passage nears its goal when it explains why the hope does not *kataischynei* (to disgrace, shame; NRSV: "disappoint"; REB paraphrases: "such hope is no fantasy"). What is hoped for is real, and its reality will be evident; otherwise its illusory character would disgrace those who hope. How does Paul know this? "Because God's love has been poured out [*ekkechytai*, perfect tense: it has been and so now is poured out] into our hearts through the Holy Spirit that has been given to us." Although Titus 3:6 can speak of the Spirit being poured out—perhaps influenced by Joel 2:28-32, quoted in Acts 2:17 and applied to the Pentecost event in Acts 2:33—here Paul says that God's *love,* not the Spirit, is poured into the core of the self, the heart. Here the Spirit is the means by which God's love reaches the human heart where it is experienced (emphasized by Fee 1994, 496-97). Thus Paul avers that the experience of God's love generates the assurance that the hoped-for glory is real, since God's love does not deceive. Paul does not say when the Holy Spirit was "given"; many assume Paul thinks of baptism, but the occasion is unimportant for Paul's point.

The step-by-step development of thought reaches its high point in verse 8, which picks up the reference to God's love in verse 5 and reformulates it as an astounding assertion: "God proves [*synistēsin*, here demonstrate, confirm as in 3:5] *his own* love for us in that while we were still sinners *Christ* died on our behalf [*hyper hēmōn*]" (AT). While the statements about Christ in 1:3-4 and 4:25 may well be quotations of early Christian traditions, verse 8 is surely Paul's own formulation. *This is Paul's Christology in a nutshell.* This coalescence of God's love and Christ's death on our behalf is the way God demonstrates convincingly (present tense!) *God's own* love for us. However true it may be that by accepting the cross Christ showed his love for God (and his love for us, as Gal 2:20 says), that is *not* what Paul says here (see Furnish 1993, 113-21). Rather, he asserts that while we were still wholly undeserving, enemies in fact (v. 10), Christ died on our behalf, for our sakes. By using the present tense, Paul says that God demonstrates that love now, in the heart—the core of the self and the seat of the will. God's love, expressed in Christ's death, can be argued convincingly in the mind, but it is experienced convincingly in the heart.

The more clearly one grasps the structure and flow of thought in verses 1-11, the more odd verses 6-7 appear. Until now, they have been bracketed out of the discussion because they may well have been added to what Paul had written (so Keck 1979, 137-48). A number of considerations point to this conclusion. (a) The Greek text of verse 6 is unstable, and there is little agreement on which of its seven forms is to be preferred. (b) Verses 6-7 interrupt the clear connection, formal and conceptual alike, between verse 5 and verse 8. (c) Verse 6 regards the human condition as weakness, whereas the rest of the passage sees it as hostility toward God (implied in "we have peace" in verse 1 and explicit in verse 10: "enemies"). Moreover, elsewhere Paul uses "weak" to speak paradoxically of Christian existence (2 Cor 10–12), but nowhere else does he regard the human dilemma as being "weak" (with respect to what; in 8:3 he says that the law was "weakened," not persons). Further, the antidote for weakness is strength, not reconciliation or peace. (d) Verse 7 is a comment designed to help the reader appreciate the magnitude of Christ's death for sinners by comparing it with an unrequired self-sacrifice for a righteous person, perhaps even for a good one (possibly an allusion to one's benefactor; so Cranfield 1975, 1:264-65; Winter 1994, 35). But elsewhere Paul never enhances the significance of Christ's death by such a comparison. For him, Christ's death is *the* eschatological event through which the New Age breaks into the present, comparable to creation, not a specially impressive instance of self-giving.

The copyist who later inserted verse 7—perhaps from a comment in the margin of the text being used—into the text, probably created verse 6 as a transition. And while he appropriated Paul's "ungodly" from 4:5, he also replaced the *confessional* character of Paul's reference to Christ's death ("on our behalf"; see 1 Thess 5:10; Gal 1:4; 2:20; 3:13; 2 Cor 5:21; Rom 8:32) with a phrase that *views* that death from the standpoint of an observer. As a result, in verses 6-7 the tone has changed from the immediacy in Paul's surrounding statements to that of reflection on what Paul had written. The verses belong to the history of the interpretation of Paul.

In verses 9-11 the emphasis shifts to the future. Using the "how much more" construction (from the lesser to the greater), Paul reasons from the present ("now") to the future when "we will be saved." "By his blood" connects verse 9 with verse 8 by metonymy (the substitution of a different word to say the same thing, here "Christ died"), and deliberately recalls the same phrase in 3:25. Paul uses these syntactical and rhetorical devices to say, in effect, that we who have now been rectified by Christ's death will be saved from the impending wrath of God by the same Christ. The passage turns the didactic statement about the significance of Christ's death in 3:21-26 into a celebrative confession. Here rectification is linked to Christ's death, whereas the tradition used in 4:25 linked it to his resurrection. For Paul, this difference is inconsequential, since he views the death and resurrection of Jesus as one event; he can therefore refer to whichever moment is pertinent to the immediate discussion: Christ's dying in verse 8 suggests rectification through his death in verse 9.

In 1 Thess 1:10 Paul wrote of God's Son whom God "raised from the dead—Jesus, who rescues us from the wrath that is coming." Now, in Rom 5:9 he appropriates that motif in order to say that future salvation from the wrath of God confirms the rectification that has already occurred. Here *dikaiōthentes* ("having been justified/rectified") retains its juridical aspect of acquittal: To be "declared in the right" in the present is to anticipate the eschatological verdict of the Judge. Consequently, Paul can assert, without any qualifying phrase, "We will be saved from the wrath" when it arrives; the Judge has already declared us to be "in the right." As Paul understands it, "justification by faith" anticipates the future, and by that very means rectifies the present relation to God.

Noteworthy is the apostle's freedom to formulate his basic ideas in quite different idioms, seen in the ease with which he moves from rectification/justification, which prevailed in chapters 1–4, to reconciliation. Whereas the former was the appropriate idiom for the resolution of the human dilemma understood as culpability for a wrong relation to the impartial God (3:19), reconciliation is the proper antidote for being "enemies" (v. 10). For Paul it is we who are reconciled to God (see 2 Cor 5:18-20), not God to us. It is we, not God, who need to be changed, for sin estranges one from God, and disobedience makes one God's rebellious enemy, subject to God's wrath. God's wrath is the logical expression of God's holiness, that unity of ontic and moral otherness that makes God God.

One should not, then, either overlook or evade the taut paradox that marks Paul's understanding of God in this passage. Here the otherness of God that manifests itself as wrath is the same otherness that demonstrates itself as love. Further, because Christ's death and resurrection is the self-investment of God the Other for the sake of the enemies, God the Other is God the Reconciler.

◊ ◊ ◊ ◊

This paragraph clearly shows that Paul's theology in Romans is theocentric but christomorphic—focused on God as understood in light of Christ. Christ is the means through which we have peace with God, access to grace, justification, reconciliation, salvation from wrath—all of which are God's doing by means of Christ. So it is not surprising that in response we "boast in God through our Lord Jesus Christ." Further, also God's rectifying rectitude is manifested "through the faithfulness of Jesus Christ" (3:22, AT), and justification occurs "through the redemption that is in Christ Jesus," the *hilastērion* ("sacrifice of atonement") that God provided (3:24-25) and whom God "handed over [to death] for our trespasses and was raised for our justification" (4:25). Through Christ's death, God "demonstrates his own love for us." The letter's opening lines pointed in this direction by speaking of "the gospel of God" (1:1) before referring to "the gospel of his Son" (1:9). Throughout Romans, the idioms vary but the theme is consistent: It is through Christ that God acts redemptively. Paul takes such "through" language seriously. For him, Christ is not a symbol of the power of self-giving (a Christ-figure) but *the* God-involving event—indeed, the redefining eschatological event. That is what makes the gospel of God simultaneously the gospel of the Son.

Liberation from Bondage (5:12–8:39)

While all interpreters of Romans recognize that the character and content of chapters 5–8 differ from those of chapters 1–4, they rarely ponder seriously enough *why* they do—to be more precise, whether and to what degree the theological content of 1:1–5:11 *requires* Paul to take up the topics of this second major section. Would it not have made more sense to follow the discussion of Abraham and his "seed" in chapter 4 with the discussion of Israel in chapters 9–11, instead of delaying it in order to treat the topics of 5:12–8:39? This commentary proposes, instead, that there are two basic *theological* reasons why 5:12–8:39 stands where it does, both required by what Paul did *not* say in chapters 1–4, the one centered in anthropology (the view of the human condition), the other in the correlate of anthropology—Christology/soteriology.

In chapters 1–4 the discussion of the Gentiles without the law, and of the Jews with it, makes several assertions about the *human* dilemma before the impartial God: " 'No human being will be justified in his sight' by deeds prescribed by the law, for through the law comes the knowledge of sin" (3:20), and "all have sinned and fall short of the glory of God" (3:23). But Paul has not explained why knowledge of sin precludes justification by doing what the law requires; nor did his extended discussion of the Gentiles' refusal to honor God as God (in 1:18-23) explain why they did so; the passage simply describes *what* they did and the consequences. Without further explanation, Paul's discussion of the human plight is essentially a stream of assertions; it is not yet an argument that accounts for it. Paul, seasoned preacher and theologian, apparently realizes that he must account for the human plight more fully by going to the root of the dilemma if his claims about the gospel are to be persuasive, particularly to those in Rome whose support he desires for the mission to Spain.

The second thing not yet said—the christological/soteriological correlate of anthropology—is the obverse of the first. Here too, chapters 1–4 have made bold claims about Christ, albeit often in passing. In one way or another, Paul has asserted *that* the Christ-event, over two decades ago, is the God-given answer to the human dilemma. But he has not yet explained *how* it is the answer. Indeed, in the transitional passage (5:1-11) he asserted that "through Christ" there is peace with God, access to grace, justification in Christ's blood, salvation from God's wrath, reconciliation with God, salvation by his (resurrection) life, and boasting about God—an impressive list of benefits—without explaining how these benefits actually flow from that one event to all who believe the gospel. Paul realizes, one may infer, that if he does locate the root of the human plight, he must also show how the Christ-event deals decisively with it. Otherwise the problem will be beyond the reach of the solution.

Though Paul does not comment on the moves he makes (as he does in 2 Cor 11:1, 16-18), we may surmise that it is these theological necessities that generated 5:12–8:39. In one way or another, this section accounts for the human dilemma by probing it more deeply; it also explains how the Christ-event overcomes it (Keck 1995, 23-29). When Paul goes deeper into the human plight, he needs a different vocabulary. In chapters 1–4, being wrong and being wrongly related to the impartial judge is the human *dilemma;*

now, however, the plight is a *condition* in which the self is trapped, the tyranny of sin and death. Unless these malign tyrannies are broken and replaced by beneficent sovereignty—a different condition—there is no real salvation. Before concluding chapter 8, Paul not only has gone deeper but wider as well, for he has seen that the human condition is inseparable from the condition of the whole creation. Accordingly, Christ's import is creationwide as well. Were that not the case, he would not be the true eschatological event, but only a very important figure in the history of religious thought.

Once one sees the way chapters 6–8 continue and deepen chapters 1–4, one can give full weight to the different vocabularies without becoming embroiled in the 150-year-old argument about whether the juridical language in chapters 1–4 or the participatory language in chapters 6–8 is the more important. Much of that argument was specious because it missed the underlying coherence of Paul's way of thinking. Moreover, the view proposed here allows the function of chapter 7 to emerge more clearly: it no longer interrupts the flow of thought but actually supports it by rejecting the law as an adequate alternative solution to the human condition, as well as by exposing the deepest dimension of the human condition for which chapter 8 provides the solution. That is, chapter 7 supports the previous argument by rejecting its opposite (arguing *e contrario*) and by preparing the ground for chapter 8.

Partly because the discussions in chapters 6–8 are concise and closely reasoned, and partly because Paul keeps many balls in the air, but largely because he did not think or write in terms of "topics" as we understand them, this section resists a detailed outline based on nouns. Nonetheless, the general structure is reasonably clear:

5:12-21	The Human Dilemma as Condition
6:1–7:6	Liberation from Sin, Death, and the Law by Solidarity with Christ
7:7-25	The Role of the Law in the Reign of Sin
8:1-30	Liberation from Flesh by the Resident Spirit
8:31-39	Conclusion: God's Love Celebrated

Also clear is that the conclusion celebrates the solution to the problem outlined in 5:12-21, thus forming a theological *inclusio*.

The Human Dilemma as Condition (5:12-21)

This famous discussion of Adam and Christ is a theological tour de force. Its function is to prepare the way for chapters 6–8 by describing the human dilemma as a *condition* for which God has provided an appropriate solution. Accordingly, the celebratory, confessional character of verses 1-11 (evident in the frequent use of "we") is replaced here by the observer's "they" or "those who." In portraying the human condition and its resolution, Paul reaches for the language of *participation*, for which he prepares the way by comparing two figures, Adam and Christ, because now redemption entails exchanging one's participation in one condition (Adam) for participation in another (Christ). The passage is unusually dense because in fleshing out this logic in a preliminary way, Paul finds that in addition to Adam and Christ there are also nonhuman actors on stage (sin, death, law, grace) who do things that humans do (enter, spread, abound, receive, multiply, reign [NRSV: "exercise dominion"]). These nonhuman actors are also realities that wield power. Thereby Paul situates the self on a stage where many things *happen*. The passage does not define the actors on the stage; their identities are disclosed by what they *do*. Indeed, just as the human condition is the result of what *happened* in Adam, so liberation from that condition is the result of what Christ *did*.

Further, the passage is also complex because Paul relies on four kinds of argument. (a) He asserts and provides warrants for what he has just said ("for . . ."); (b) he compares (as A, so also X) and contrasts (not as A, so also X); (c) he argues from the lesser to the greater (if this is the case, how much more is . . .); and (d) he states purpose or result. In verses 20-21 he combines several modes of argument in the same sentence, not unlike the way a classical symphony's last movement combines themes developed earlier.

It is easier to understand the passage, however, if one identifies some assumptions that underlie Paul's reasoning. (a) He assumes a particular reading of Gen 2–3, namely, that Adam, like Christ, was a historical person, not a symbol. (b) He also assumes that Christ was not only historical but the eschatological person—that is, he stands at the beginning of the New Age, as Adam did at the beginning of the Old Age. (c) He assumes that what each figure did affects those involved with him; that is why the two can be compared and contrasted. (d) He assumes that the nature of the effect accords with the nature of the deed. As assumptions, none of these things are argued *for*; rather, they are ideas that Paul argues *from*.

In this passage, Paul shows little interest in Adam and Christ themselves. What interests him is the effect of each one's deed: In the effects of Adam, Paul detects the human condition, and in the effects of Christ, he sees its resolution. Even though the passage speaks of Adam before it speaks of Christ, it is "Christ and his benefits" that has determined what Paul says about Adam. Paul's *thought* moves "from solution to plight" (as E. P. Sanders put it), even though he *argues* from plight to solution. (We will return to this feature of Paul's argument in connection with v. 14.) In other words, verses 12-21 are the result of Paul's seeing that Christ's death and resurrection broke the power of sin and death, the hallmarks of the human condition. Here Adam is important because his deed accounts for their malign power. That is the only reason Adam appears explicitly in Romans at all. (As noted, whether he appears implicitly in 1:18–2:16 remains disputed.)

Given the unusual expressions, multiple forms of reasoning, and long complex sentences, it is easier to understand the passage when its overall structure is *seen*. Though proposed structures vary, the analysis printed below relies on formal considerations—that is, signals in the text itself—and yields a chiastic structure.

> v. 12   opening statement of the human condition
>   vv. 13-14   the law factor
>   vv. 15-16   two contrasts (not like) + warrants (for . . .)
>   v. 17   warranting conclusion (emphasizing "reign")
>   vv. 18-19   two comparisons (as . . . so . . .)
>   v. 20   the law factor
> v. 21   conclusion (emphasizing "reign")

The opening statement (v. 12) begins with "Therefore," implying that what follows is the conclusion to be drawn from what has just been said. Since the content of verses 12-21 does not follow from verses 1-11, "therefore" may simply indicate a transition. More significant is the fact that the dash at the end of verse 12 (NRSV, NIV) signals that the opening sentence is broken off here, so that the comparison that begins with "just as" is not completed. Verse 13 moves in a different direction (a phenomenon called *anakolouthon*, something that does not follow). Even so, what Paul asserts in verse 12 is clear enough to set the stage for the rest of the passage by speaking of sin not as something that one does, but as a reality that itself "does": It entered the world, where, as verse 21 will say, it exercised kingly rule (*ebasileusen*; a *basileus* is a king). This view of sin as a controlling power accords with 3:9: "all . . . are under the power of sin."

While Gen 3 does not actually say that Adam and Eve had once been immortal but *became* mortal because of their disobedience, Gen 3:19 and 22-24 imply that death was part of their punishment, and some early Jewish writers drew this conclusion. For example, Sir 25:24 says, "From a woman sin had its beginning, and because of her we all die." And *4 Ezra* 3:7 says, "And you laid on him one commandment of yours, but he transgressed it, and immediately you appointed death for him and for his descendants." That author's apostrophe is well known: "O Adam, what have you done? For though it was you who sinned, the fall was not yours alone, but ours also who are your descendants. For what good is it, if an eternal age has been promised to us, but we have done deeds that bring death?" (8:48-49).

Paul too thinks that Adam's "fall" was repeated by everyone afterward, though like *4 Ezra* he does not explain clearly just how this repetition came about. Having said that through Adam sin entered the world, and through sin also death (v. 12), he continues, "and in this way [*kai houtōs*] death came to all men, because all sinned" (NIV). By translating *kai houtōs* as "and so," NRSV wrongly suggests that "death came to all" as a *result* of Adam. But *kai houtōs* means "in this way." In other words, this is *how* death came to everyone—through sin. This clearly implies that everyone sinned, thereby repeating what occurred in Adam's case. Had Paul stopped here, he would have said what *4 Ezra* said. But Paul added the troublesome phrase "*eph hō* all sinned," which NRSV and NIV render as "*because* all sinned." Unfortunately, *eph hō* probably does not mean "because." Nor does it mean what the Vulgate says: *in quo* (in whom)—that is, "in whom [Adam] all sinned." This view, adopted by Augustine, became so firmly entrenched in the West that the Puritan primer (used to teach the alphabet) taught children that A is for Adam "in whose fall we sinnéd all." The exhaustive investigation by Fitzmyer (1993, 321-39; summarized in his commentary, 413-17) led him to conclude that the words express consequence, not cause ("because"): "Death spread to all human beings, with the result that all have sinned" (so also Talbert 2003).

But this translation, exact as it may be, suggests that the ubiquity of death resulted in the universality of sin—the opposite of what Paul had just said: Death *follows* sin. This conundrum can be avoided by recognizing the elliptical character of verse 12: "with the result that all have sinned" is the logical inference *from* the ubiquity of death. The phrase does not trace sin to death. Such a view would also be incompatible with 1:18-32, where sin is not the result of being mortal but of refusing to honor God as God. Moreover, if sin comes from death, then people *do* have an excuse and the whole world would not be accountable to God (2:1; 3:19-20), for they could blame their sin on their mortality, on a flaw in creation. Valid as it may be that having to die can produce angst, which generates all sorts of destructive behavior, there is no evidence that Paul thought in these terms (though Heb 2:14-15 came close).

Paul emphasizes *how* death spread to all because he is interpreting Gen 2–3; viewed theologically, he emphasizes the repetition of Adam's sin because thereby he continues to hold humans accountable. He anticipated what the *Apocalypse of Baruch* said a few decades later: "For although Adam sinned first and has brought death upon all who were in his own time, yet each . . . who has been born from him has prepared for himself the coming torment. . . . Adam is, therefore, not the cause, except only for himself, but each of us has become our own Adam" (*2 Bar.* 54:15, 19). Like *4 Ezra, Pseudo-Philo* (1st c. CE) reports that God said,

"That man [the first formed, the protoplast] transgressed my ways and was persuaded by his wife, and she was deceived by the serpent. And then death was ordained for the generations of men." Lest Adam forget what he had done, the author adds, "The Lord continued to show him the ways of paradise, and said to him, 'These are the ways that men have lost by not walking in them, because they have sinned against me'" (13:3-8). These texts trace the dilemma to Adam, yet refuse to regard all humans as innocent victims of his deed. So too, in Rom 5:12, the accent of the last clause is on individual guilt and responsibility (so also Wedderburn 1973, 351). Paul does not mention Satan, as does Wis 2:24: "God made us for incorruption . . . but through the devil's envy death entered the world, and those who belong to his company experience it." Nor does he minimize the import of Adam's sin, as does Wis 10:1-2: "Wisdom protected the first-formed father of the world, when he alone had been created; she delivered him from his transgression and gave him strength to rule all things."

It is important to note also some other things that Paul does not say. Not a word is said about the origin of sin, nor about either the serpent or Satan, nor about any other detail in the Genesis story. Nor does Paul blame Eve, as does Sir 25:24 quoted above (probably because it would have seemed odd to say that a woman was a "type" of Christ, v. 14). Nor does Paul explain why God allowed sin to enter the world. What matters for him is *that* sin and death are intruders. They are not part of creation as God made it; as powers they are usurpers, squatters who entered the estate and now rule its inhabitants. For Christian theology, this view of sin and death is crucial: They are not traced to a flaw in creation or to some fault in the Creator. Their tyrannical presence makes sinning and dying unavoidable, but not "natural." Paul regards them both as profoundly "unnatural"; for him, the present human condition contradicts the original condition. He draws on the ancient Near East view that death is an enemy, indeed for him the ultimate enemy, as he said in 1 Cor 15:26. (For a perceptive overview, see Black 1984, 413-33.)

In imaging death as a power that tyrannizes and mars human existence, Paul did not abandon the literal meaning of the word "death," the inevitable termination of physical life; nor did he simply regard it as an immutable fate or as a morally neutral "fact of life." Rather, he not only saw it as a moral/theological issue by linking it with sin, but he also denied that it is invincible, for he viewed it through the prism of an event that broke its power— Jesus' resurrection by the radically Other, God. For Paul, the literal and the metaphorical meanings of "death" are distinguishable but not neatly separable.

No one knows why Paul did not finish the sentence in verse 12, and instead began talking about the law, but the content of verses 13-14, beginning with the word "For" (omitted by NRSV!) points to a plausible explanation: Verses 13-14 are needed because Paul's assertions in verse 12 create a logical problem. Since there is no transgression if there is no law to transgress (4:15), how can all have sinned, and have been accountable for it, before the time of Moses? (Paul simply ignores the so-called Noachic law in Gen 9:4-6.) Paul explains that "sin was indeed in the world before the law," though it was not "reckoned"—that is, not entered into the books (alluding to the image of the heavenly books in which human deeds are registered until the Day of Judgment; see *Jub.* 20:17-23; *2 En.* 104:7; *2 Bar.* 14:1; Rev 20:12). Thereby Paul acknowledges the presence of sin as a power that results in death, even though individual sins (transgressions) are not yet recorded. In the absence of the law, their sins "were not like the transgression of Adam," because (we may assume) he transgressed God's prohibition against eating from "the tree of the knowledge of good and evil," lest he die (Gen 2:15-17). Even though sins were not recorded between the time of Adam and Moses, death "exercised dominion" (*ebasileusen*, ruled as king) nonetheless. After Adam, the inevitability of death was the mark of the human *condition*. Existence itself is now marred. Not even obedience to the law, once it arrived, could undo this condition; indeed, the law made matters worse, for not only were sins now recorded as transgressions, but now "trespass multiplied" (v. 20); moreover, according to 3:20, the law brings knowledge of sin.

Since the human condition is not the result of gradual deterioration but of an event at the outset of the human story, transforming that condition requires undoing what had occurred at the beginning; otherwise the consequences would be addressed without dealing with the cause. What is needed is a figure who undoes what Adam did. In such a perspective, Adam is viewed as "a *type* of the one who was to come," namely, Christ. Basically, a "type" is a prefiguration that one detects (retrospectively!) in a pattern of similarities and contrasts between two entities, whether persons, events, or things. By definition, a "type" is recognizable only in light of its subsequent counterpart, which therefore is always the more important (otherwise the counterpart would not be an effective alternative). Understandably, then, whether Paul identifies differences or similarities between Adam and Christ, he invariably finds what occurs through Christ *reverses and surpasses* what occurred through Adam. Whereas much Christian theology in the West, especially after Augustine, has concentrated on verses 12-14 as the basis for the doctrine of "original sin," Paul was more interested in verses 15-21.

The discussion of Adam and Christ (vv. 15-19) lies at the heart of the chiastically constructed passage (vv. 12-21), as noted. Paul first points out two *differences* between them (vv. 15-16) by relying on a formulaic sentence structure not repeatable in felicitous English: "*Not* like A is X." The center of the chiasm, and therefore the most important, is verse 17. In verses 18-19 Paul points out *similarities*, also relying on a formula: this time "*As* A . . . so also X." Running through verses 15-19 is the repeated "through one man"; indeed, it frames the whole discussion (vv. 12, 21). In addition, the various modes of reasoning (noted on p. 145) give the whole passage a remarkable architectonic character in which an amazing variety of ideas are coordinated.

That Paul is more interested in what Adam and Christ *did* than in the figures themselves is signaled by the opening salvo in verse 15: "Not like the trespass is also the *charisma*" (AT; *charisma is* a concretion of grace [*charis*], a "begracement," obscured by NRSV's "free gift"; REB paraphrases exuberantly: "God's act of grace is all out of proportion to Adam's wrongdoing"). *Charisma* (not used in LXX) is a distinctly Pauline word (14 of 19 uses in the NT; in Romans, used also at 1:11; 6:23; 11:29; 12:6), but nowhere in Romans is it linked with unusual activity like *glossolalia* ("tongue-speaking"), as in 1 Cor 12:4-11 (see Nardoni 1993, 68-80). "Trespass" *(paraptōma)* is the equivalent of "transgression" *(parabasis)* in verse 14; ancient rhetoricians would have recognized this change of words for the same thing as a *metalepsis.*

The unexpected contrast between "the trespass" and "the begracement" is deliberate. At first glance, it might appear that Paul is contrasting incommensurate entities (like apples and lamb chops); a second look, however, reveals that this disparity is precisely the point: The baleful import of "the trespass" is of a quite different order than the beneficent result of Christ's deed. (Although Paul does not say so, this disjunction is of a piece with the disclosure of God's rectitude apart from the law.) *Why* there is such utter disparity between "the trespass" and "the begracement" is explained in the warrant that follows, which is complex because it combines reasoning from the lesser to the greater and the contrast between "the one and the many." "If it is the case that by the trespass of the one man many died, how much more is it the case that the grace of God and the free gift in the grace of the one man Jesus Christ have abounded for the many" (AT; in this context "the many" is a *metalepsis* for "all" in v. 12; it does not refer to a lesser number or to a restricted group). Built into this rather overloaded sentence is an unstated contrast: Death happened *to* the "many" as a consequence of their own trespasses (v. 12), but what occurred *for* the many was *not* a consequence of what they did but solely the result of God's grace actualized in Christ's grace (not his gracious demeanor but the man himself as the grace-event). Over against the deserved consequence of Adam stands the undeserved consequence of God's gift. "The trespass" is indeed not like "the begracement."

The second contrast (v. 16) restates the same point: "And not like the sin of the one man is the free gift" (AT, *dōrēma*, picking up "gift" *[dōrea]* in verse 15, and alluding to *dōrean* in 3:24). The warrant for this difference is formulated in juridical language and is expressed elliptically; the reader must supply the missing words (including the verbs): "The verdict [*krima*, judgment] that followed from the one [trespass] led to condemnation *[katakrima]* [of many] but the *charisma* [i.e., the Christ-event] which followed many trespasses leads to *dikaiōma*" (NRSV and NIV: "justification"; here REB is better: "verdict of acquittal").

The central statement (v. 17) is longer and more complex because it picks up important terms in verses 15-16 and correlates them with the key word "reign" (*basileuein*, used in v. 14 and twice in v. 21). Like verse 15, this statement reasons from the lesser ("if it is the case that by the trespass of the one man death reigned through the one man") to the greater: "how much more is it the case that those who receive the abundance of grace and of the gift of rectitude *[dikaiosynē]* will reign in life through the one man Jesus Christ" (AT). As a result of Adam's trespass, death reigned; through Christ, the recipients of rectification will reign in life. That is, being ruled by death is replaced by ruling in life (= over death).

As observed already, verses 18-19 point out two similarities between the effects of Adam and of Christ, syntactically expressed as "as A . . . so also X." The initial "for" in verse 19 implies that the second similarity functions as the warrant for the first in verse 18. There are two kinds of similarities here: The one continues the "through one man" motif, the other emphasizes the congruence of the deed and its effects. Moreover, since verses 12-21 have a chiastic structure with verse 17 at the center, verse 18 picks up the juridical language of verse 16; but while verse 19 formally corresponds with verse 15, the language of verse 19 moves in a quite different direction because good style required some variation.

The NIV renders verse 18 this way: "Consequently, just as the result of one trespass was condemnation for all men, so also the result of one act of righteousness *[di' henos dikaiōmatos*, repeating *dikaiōma* in v. 16] was justification that brings life *[dikaiōsin zōēs]* for all men." Paul relies on the principle that like produces like: The one righteous act results in rectifying action for all. For some reason, Paul's *eis dikaiōsin zōēs* (lit., "for rectifying of life") gets translated either as "justification that *brings* life" (NIV), or "justification *and* life" (NRSV, NJB); only NASB's "justification *of* life" recognizes that Paul is not talking about two benefits but one: the rectification of life.

The asserted similarity stated in verse 18 is supported by the similarity in verse 19, formulated in terms of disobedience and obedience, each of which produces the appropriate result. "Just as through the disobedience of the one man the many were made [*katestathēsan,* put in a particular status] sinners, so too through the obedience of the one man the many will be made [*katastathēsontai*] righteous" (AT). (As in 4:9-10, it is not clear whether the future tense is a logical future or an actual future, referring to the Great Assize.) Because like produces like, this statement is particularly important for two reasons: (a) It expresses concisely the correlation of Christology and soteriology, and (b) the right act of Christ in verse 18 is now specified as his obedience. Which is to say that through Christ's one right act of obedience, the many (everyone) will be made right. This act of obedience is the "faithfulness of Jesus Christ" (3:22, 26), actualized "in his blood" (3:25, AT), through which believers have now been rectified so that they will be "saved . . . from the wrath" (5:9).

Especially significant is what verse 20 says about the law of Moses: like sin and death, it too was not part of the creation but entered it. Moreover, like sin and death, it is an actor to be reckoned with, not an inert entity to be simply understood or followed. Indeed, "entered," like NRSV's "came in," may be too pale a translation of *pareisēlthen,* which REB renders better as "intruded." (In Gal 2:4 Paul used this verb to say that his opponents "slipped in" at the Jerusalem council.) By writing verse 20 at all, Paul precluded the inference that one is made righteous through obeying the law. Exactly what he means to convey instead, however, is not free of ambiguity, for *hina pleonasē to paraptōma* can express either purpose ("the law entered in order to increase the trespass"; REB: "to multiply lawbreaking"; similarly NIV), *or* result (as in NRSV: "with the result that the trespass multiplied"). Some interpreters (e.g., Cranfield 1975, Moo 1996, Talbert 2003) claim the former is Paul's meaning, others (e.g., Achtemeier 1985, 98) the latter. (The same ambiguity is found in Gal 3:19: The law "was added *charin* trespasses," which

NRSV and NIV render as "because of" [i.e., transgressions made the law necessary], but REB has, "It was added to make wrongdoing a legal offense.") Since Paul had already said that "through the law comes the knowledge of sin" (3:20) and that "the law brings wrath" (4:15), it is likely that also here he refers to the *result* of the law's arrival; it made matters worse. But he goes on to say that "where sin increased [here "sin" is a synonym for "trespass"], grace abounded all the more," or as Achtemeier (98) puts it, "Grace simply out-increases sin." God's grace is more than equal to any sin.

The sentence begun in verse 20 continues in verse 21, which begins with *hina* signaling purpose or result. Consequently, the thought of the last clause in verse 20 ("where sin increased, grace abounded all the more") is completed in verse 21. In other words, the increase of grace has a purpose (or result): "that grace might reign." Everything else in this complex sentence is designed to enhance this goal. The enhancement begins by calling attention to the similarity between the reign of sin and the reign of grace. When Paul says that sin reigned "in death," he probably understands the phrase to mean "by means of death" because grace is to reign "through righteousness leading to eternal life." The passage began by asserting that death entered the world through sin (v. 12); now it ends with sin reigning by means of death—that is, sin's tyranny is expressed in death. Although death reigned from Adam to Moses (v. 14), the arrival of the law increased the trespass (v. 20), so that now sin reigns through what it produces, death. Sin and death are inseparably linked, but the ultimate devastator is sin—not as a wrong deed but as a malign power that controls.

But since grace abounds all the more as sin increases, grace has the last word, for it too reigns, but through righteousness (not "justification" as NRSV has it) that leads to eternal life. This righteousness is the free gift (v. 17); it is also the "rectification of life" that results from Christ's act of righteousness in his obedience (vv. 18-19). All this occurred "through Jesus Christ our Lord." It would not have occurred otherwise. Chapter 6 will explain how it occurred.

◊ ◊ ◊ ◊

Paul had written about Christ and Adam before, in a quite different context—namely, 1 Cor 15, where he explained why those Corinthians who say "there is no resurrection of the dead" are wrong. Apparently, they failed to see that Jesus' resurrection *from* the dead (which they had accepted as part of the gospel they believed [1 Cor 15:11]) is inseparable from the general resurrection *of* the dead. Paul's response included two references to Adam and Christ. (a) In 15:21-22 his reasoning anticipates that of Rom 5:15-21: "Since death came through a man, resurrection of the dead also comes through a man. For as all die in the Adam, so too all will be made alive in the Christ," at the parousia (AT). (b) A few verses later, in explaining how the dead will be raised (15:42-49), Paul distinguished the physical body *(sōma psychikon)* that is "sown" (buried) from the spiritual body *(sōma pneumatikon)* that will be raised. Next he said, "the first man Adam became a living being" *(psychēn zōsan,* quoting LXX Gen 2:7), but "the last Adam became a life-giving spirit," presumably as a result of his resurrection. Paul added that the first man was "from earth, of dust" but the second man is "from heaven," noting that "as was the man of dust, so are those who are of the dust [everyone]; and as is the man of heaven, so are those who are of heaven [the resurrected]. Just as we have borne the image of the man of dust, we will also bear the image of the man of heaven." Also in this passage, the reasoning is like that of Rom 5:15-21, even though in speaking of Christ as the last Adam, Paul had in view the resurrected Christ rather than the obedient earthy one of Rom 5:19. In both letters, the benefits enjoyed by the believers are substantively derived from what Christ does: In Rom 5:19, Christ's rectitude in obedience yields rectification, just as in 1 Cor 15:45 Christ's being a life-giving Spirit enables him to vivify the dead.

Liberation from Sin, Death, and the Law (6:1–7:6)

The discussion of Adam and Christ in 5:12-21 set the stage for chapters 6–8 by tracing the human dilemma to a condition, a state, marked by the reign of sin and its consequence, death. Because this condition was brought on by Adam at the outset of human existence, it is universal, qualifying all humans afterward.

By saying that sin and death reign, Paul signaled that they are experienced as powers operating in a field of force from which one cannot emigrate by deciding to leave, by an act of will. The subsequent arrival of the law does not change the condition but instead exacerbates it into the dilemma of being accountable, for the law brings knowledge of sin (3:20) and increased trespass (5:20), now recorded in the heavenly ledger until Judgment Day (5:13). Emancipation from the condition comes in the same way that the enslavement to sin and death occurred—through the act of one man, Christ, in whose domain, marked by the reign of grace, there is rectitude and life instead of sin and death.

In 6:1–7:6 Paul discusses how one is freed from the domain of sin and death and transferred to the domain where grace reigns in life, namely, "through Jesus Christ our Lord" (5:21)—specifically, through solidarity with *his death* there is life—not in the sense of life *after* death, but rather indestructible life through a "dying" that occurs while one is still alive. The discussion moves in three steps: (1) 6:1-14 explains how Christ's death and resurrection free one from sin and death and effect new life; (2) 6:15-23 explains how those emancipated from slavery to sin and death are now "enslaved" to righteousness; and (3) 7:1-6 explains how, being freed from the law through Christ, one is "enslaved" to the new life of the Spirit; these verses end in a way that sets up what follows: the dilemma created by the law (7:7-25), and life empowered by the Spirit (8:1-30). The shocking use of slavery to characterize freedom reflects Paul's conviction that there is no such thing as a truly autonomous self, that one is always beholden to some structure of power, that the self is a heeding self. According to this whole section, having to obey is itself not the problem; the real problem is what or whom one obeys, for therein lies the difference between two destinies—the wrath of God or eternal life.

◊ ◊ ◊ ◊

Freed from Sin and Death (6:1-14): The opening question, "What then are we to say?" introduces a wrong inference, not from verse 21 but from verse 20: "Where sin increased, grace abounded all the more." (It does not really matter whether the question comes from an interlocutor or whether Paul himself raised it as a springboard for what he wants to say because the interlocutor is Paul's creation.) After brusquely rejecting the inference that we "should continue in sin in order that grace may abound," Paul asks two questions that signal the theme of the paragraph: "How can we who died to sin go on living in it?" (v. 2) and "Do you not know that all of us who have been baptized into Christ Jesus were baptized into his death?" (v. 3). The juxtaposition of these questions implies that for Paul death "to sin" is the consequence of being baptized "*into* Christ's death" (the prepositions are important!). To explain this consequence, Paul discusses the questions in reverse order: verses 4-5 interpret baptism "into" Christ's death, and verses 6-11 explain dying "to" sin. Verses 12-14 translate the theology of verses 2-11 into imperatives for those who "died to sin" by being "baptized into" Christ's death. Understanding this passage—and the whole section, in fact—requires being alert to the imaginative, multilayered meanings of key terms, as well as the assumptions on which the usage rests.

According to verse 2, dying "*to* sin" precludes living "*in* it." To live "in sin" is more than having a particular lifestyle; it is living in the domain where sin reigns, and from which there is no escape except by death (see v. 7). While dying does terminate life in sin's domain, the death "to sin" that Paul has in view is not sheer physical death, but a ritualized dying that has occurred before one expires. By this dying "to sin," sin's power is terminated. Sin itself has not died; it is the Christian who has died to it, has become "dead" to its power. This is why continuing to live "in" its domain contradicts what has happened. Paul is not saying that Christians no longer commit sins; such a view would make the exhortation in verse 12 pointless. Rather, because the reign of sin has been terminated, one need not sin; therefore, to sin deliberately is preposterous.

In verse 3, Paul introduces his point with the question, "Do you not know?" He expects a positive answer, "Yes, of course we know." That is, he counts on what they already know and accept to be the basis *from* which he can reason. But what do they know? He assumes they know that being baptized means being "baptized into Christ Jesus." For the history of the Christian theology of baptism it is significant that Paul assumes that his understanding of baptism "into Christ" is shared by the readers to whom he had not taught it. They probably did not know—though we do—that also in Gal 3:27 he had written of being "baptized into Christ," and that he took "into" quite seriously, as "clothed yourselves with Christ" indicates; indeed, the whole argument in Gal 3:23-29 turns on being "in Christ" as a result of being baptized "into" him. Also in 1 Cor 10:2, he had used the same idea: The Israelites were "baptized into Moses." But what are we to make of such language?

For Paul, being baptized "into" someone makes one a participant in that person's significance by entering into it, by sharing it, and so accepting that person's significance as authoritative for one's life. In this light, one can understand why, in 1 Cor 1:13, Paul taunts the faction-ridden Corinthian church by asking, "Were you baptized in the name of *Paul?*" (the name represents the person here). For Paul, baptism "into Christ" makes one a participant in an *event*, not an ideal or a myth. Basic for this understanding is the conviction, widely held at the time, that a religious ritual *does* what it symbolizes. No one then would have understood the statement, "It's only a symbol." Paul's understanding of baptism is marked by this "realism." Without this realistic view of what occurs in the baptismal rite, it is hard to see how he could have written 6:3-11. In his missionary situation, he assumes, of course, that it is new believers who are baptized. Here he reinterpreted baptism "into Christ" (Gal 3:23-29) as baptism into *Christ's death* (so also Betz 1995, 107). In the history of Christian theology of baptism, this reinterpretation was new (even if Paul did not announce it as such). And it was essential for the argument.

In verse 4, Paul begins to draw the inferences ("Therefore") from his assertion that all the baptized were baptized into Christ's death. The wording of the inference deserves careful scrutiny. From being "baptized into his death" Paul infers that by baptism we "have been *buried with him*" (*synetaphēmen*, lit., co-buried). This is the first of several verbs with the prefix *syn-* (= co-) used in this passage: "co-planted" (v. 5; NRSV and NIV: "united with him," REB: "identified with him"); "co-crucified" (v. 6); "co-live" (v. 8)—all of which express solidarity with Christ. The act of baptism unites the baptized with Christ, establishes solidarity with his death. Paul does not say that baptism inaugurates solidarity with Jesus' mission or celebrates one's new discipleship, for however true that may be, that is not the point here, where Paul, explaining how one "dies to sin," emphasizes discontinuity between one's past and present life. In this context, the "newness of life" that Paul has in view requires death to sin, a death that occurs by ritualized burial with Christ, accomplished in baptism. Paul probably assumes baptism by immersion (*baptō* means "dip"), a ritualized "burial." Accordingly, Paul sees an analogy between Christ's being raised from the realm of the dead and the immersed being raised from the water. What actually matters here, of course, is not the analogy itself but what being baptized signifies for the one baptized—a radically transformed life.

When Paul says that it was through the Father's glory that Christ was raised, he probably means that it occurred through God's power. This act was no mere resuscitation, a restoration to status quo ante; rather, because the *means* coheres with the *result,* resurrection was a wholly new mode of existence, one that accords with God's glory (excellence manifest as splendor). If by being raised from the dead Christ had merely resumed the life he had before he died, that restoration—no matter how remarkable—would be irrelevant for the human condition, for a resumed life would be a life restored to the dominion of death. But for Paul, "Christ, being raised from the dead, will never die again; death no longer has dominion over him" (v. 9). Even so, Christ's liberation from death would still be irrelevant if it pertains to him alone. According to the logic of our passage, not even believing that Jesus' resurrection transformed *his* existence into a deathless one suffices, for one might well regard his transformation as an exception—understandable since he was the Son of God. That seems to have been the reasoning of those Corinthians who had accepted Paul's message about Christ's death and resurrection (1 Cor 15:1-11), yet said "there is no resurrection of the dead" (v. 12)—that is, for everyone else. To correct that view, Paul insisted that the resurrection of Christ is inseparable from the resurrection of all (1 Cor 15:20-23); indeed, "if *the dead* are not raised, then *Christ* has not been raised" (15:16) either. In other words, Paul's reinterpretation of Gal 3:23-29 in our passage has been deeply influenced by 1 Cor 15. Christ's liberation from death liberates those who participate in him.

The logic of solidarity with Christ underlies what verse 4 says about the purpose/result of baptismal solidarity with Christ in death: "so that . . . we *too* might walk in newness of life" (NIV: "live a new life") in the present. This is Paul's way of reminding the readers that continuing *in* sin is incompatible with dying *to* it (vv. 1-2), and of setting the stage for the exhortations that begin at verse 11. Paul does *not* say that as Christ was raised, we too have been raised, or that we have been raised *with* him. For Paul, *baptism does not end mortality; it begins a new morality,* one that must be actualized. Even Colossians and Ephesians, which speak of having "been raised *with* Christ" (Col 3:1; Eph 2:6) contain exhortations; they too have a "not yet" dimension. In Rom 6:4, the new life embodies both "the already" and "the not yet" of Christian existence. Because its moral import is anticipatory, it leans toward the future for its fulfillment, formulated in verse 5: "For if we have been united with him in a death like his, we *will* certainly be united with him in a resurrection like his." At that point, and not before, the liberation from sin and death will be complete. But it will be! Being united with Christ in baptism guarantees it, for thereby one is united with the *whole* Christ-event. (Christ's death and resurrection are distinguishable moments in *one* indivisible event; otherwise Paul could not reason as he does here.)

The *way* Paul formulates what occurs in baptism (v. 5) should not be overlooked. Three details are important. (a) The expression "united with him" renders "we have become *symphytoi*" (lit., grown together; a *phytos* is a plant), a vivid image of inseparable unity. One is united with Christ by the rite of baptism, not by an act of will or by some form of psychological identification (neither of which is indissoluble!). (b) Inseparable unity is required for the rationale built into the shift from past tense ("we have been united") to the future: "we will be united"; that is, only if the unity is unbreakable can Paul reason *from* what has already occurred in baptism *to* what will yet occur. (c) The unification with Christ in baptism occurs "by the likeness *[homoiōmati]* of his death" (AT). The rite does not *repeat* Christ's death/burial/resurrection; rather, because the burial in water that occurs in the rite is "like" Christ's burial/death, the rite does what it symbolizes—establishes the whole *person's* solidarity with Christ, not just the person's will or disposition.

In verses 6-11 Paul explains why what occurred in baptism precludes continuing to live as before (in sin's domain): "Our old self [lit., man, *anthrōpos*, understood generically] has been co-crucified [with Christ]"; this solidarity has a double purpose/ result: "so that the body of sin might be destroyed, so that we might no longer be enslaved to sin" (AT; REB: "our old humanity has been crucified with Christ, for the destruction of the sinful self, so that we may no longer be slaves to sin"). The "old *anthrōpos*" is our Adamic self. Since one does not speak of the "old" without implying the "new," Paul's phrase expresses the standpoint of those who are in the new creation, who are no longer defined by Adam but by Christ. The "old man" is not a part of the self, but the whole self ruled by sin. *That* self was co-crucified with Christ (an expression Paul had used in Gal 2:19); this is the only explicit reference to the cross in Romans. "Co-crucified" makes the salvific solidarity with Christ's death concrete and vivid, and the use of the passive suggests that this "co-crucifixion" was not the result of Paul's will but of God's action.

The first immediate purpose/result of baptismal solidarity is "that the body of sin might be destroyed," followed by the ongoing consequence: "that we might no longer be enslaved to sin." But what is the body *(sōma)* of sin? Not simply "the sinful body," as if the physical body as such were sinful. Rather, here as elsewhere, "body" refers to the concrete, phenomenal self, the whole actual person, just as in 12:1 "present your bodies" means "present yourselves." (In our common words like "somebody" or "anybody" this sense of "body" is retained.) The "body of sin," then, is Paul's shorthand for the person defined by sin, controlled by it, as the discussion of Adam outlined in 5:12-21. Indeed, "the body of sin" characterizes "the old *anthrōpos*." By being co-crucified with Christ this sinful self is "destroyed" (*katargēthē*; NIV: "done away with"); indeed, this negative consequence is essential, for on this destruction depends the positive result: no longer "enslaved to sin." The anthropology of verse 6 is noteworthy, for without lapsing into a dualism of sinful body and innocent spirit/soul, developed later by various Gnostics, Paul nonetheless distinguishes an enslaved self from an emancipated self. At the same time, the enslaved self is not an innocent victim, for in the wake of Adam, "all have sinned" (5:12); thereby the enslaved self is a culpable self enslaved also by its own actions. In verse 19, Paul will make this complicity explicit.

Verse 7 explains why dying with Christ in baptism is so important: "Whoever has died is *dedikaiōtai* from sin." By using the perfect tense here Paul implies the continuing results of completed action in the past; by using the passive voice, he implies that the subject of the verb is God. But what was the action? Because it must be similar to verse 18 where the phrase "freed from sin" occurs, NRSV, NIV, and NASB translate verse 7 as "freed from sin." The unexpected use of *dikaioō* (to vindicate, acquit, declare, or make right) has generated considerable discussion (see Fitzmyer 1993), as well as various translations: REB: "death cancels the claims of sin"; Fitzmyer: "is acquitted of sin"; NJB: "no longer has to answer for sin"; CEV paraphrases: "sin doesn't have power over dead people." Whatever the exact nuance, the point is clear enough: Dying with Christ terminates the reign of sin over the baptized.

In verse 8 Paul restates the point with reference to the future, "We will also live with him" (another co-verb: *syzēsomen*); 2 Tim 2:11 virtually repeats our verse: "If we have died with him, we will also live with him." (Second Timothy 2:11-13 quotes a well-known "saying" that has developed Paul's statement in Rom 6:8.) Although one is no longer "enslaved to sin" (the "already"), the future life with Christ (the eternal life mentioned in 5:21) remains a matter of hope (5:2) and of faith: "we *believe* that we will also live with him." But what is hoped for and believed is warranted by an event: Christ's resurrection, which by definition implies that "he will never die again" (v. 9). And that means, Paul continues, that "death no longer lords it over him" (AT of *autou ouketi kyrieuei*). Because "death no longer has dominion" (NRSV) over the resurrected Jesus, solidarity with him is the means by which humans too will be freed from death's dominion. And since Jesus is the first to be freed totally from death, he stands at the head of a whole new creation; that is, he is the New Adam.

But even freedom from death falls short of the emancipation that really matters, for death is the consequence, and therefore the symptom, of sin (5:12, 17). To be liberated from the symptom is not yet to be liberated from the cause. Therefore verse 10 points out that "the death he [Christ] died, he died to sin." By using the same clause for Christ that was used of Christians in verse 2, Paul again underscores the solidarity between Christ and the baptized believer. Moreover, to express the absolute, unique, definitive significance of Christ's death to sin, Paul adds the word *ephapax*, "once for all" (time). In short, Christ's death, together with his resurrection, is the eschatological event, not merely an important event. And by definition, the eschatological event terminates the old and inaugurates the utterly new. What occurred in the Christ-event is the prototype of what occurs and will occur for those who participate in it.

Since for Paul Christ's death and resurrection are one salvific event (despite the temporal interval ["on the third day," 1 Cor 15:4]), he continues, "but the life he lives, he lives to God." That is, his resurrection life is totally oriented *to* God because it is completely dependent *on* God who raised him from the dead. (Paul does not, thereby, imply anything negative about Christ's dependence on God before his death.) The present import of Paul's exposition is stated as an imperative, well put by REB: "In the same way [*houtōs kai*, the same phrase used in 5:18, 19, 21; 6:4] you must regard yourselves as dead to sin and alive to God, in union with Christ Jesus." In verse 2 Paul assumed that we "died to sin"; now he points out that what has occurred must be actualized, first of all by one's self-understanding; one's "self-image" or self-regard is to be a christologically determined paradox: dead to sin, alive to God. How this self-understanding is to be actualized is outlined in verses 12-14.

The tension between "the already" and "the not yet" generates the need to identify the traits of each clearly enough that "the already" does not make one over-confident in the present or "the not yet" generate doubt or despair about the future. Paul addresses this need in verses 12-14. To guard against over-confidence, he begins with an unexpected negative imperative: "Do not let sin reign in your mortal body so that you obey its desires" (AT). In other words, what "the already" makes possible, "the not yet" makes necessary. Why does Paul point to the *mortal* body as the battleground of resistance to sin's reign? Having insisted that "you also must *consider* yourselves dead to sin and alive to God in Christ Jesus" (v. 11), why does he not single out the mind instead? And why does he remind the readers that the body is mortal? Because the mortality of the body is itself evidence of "the not yet"; that is, until one participates in Christ's resurrection, the body is still subject to the inevitability of death and vulnerable to the power of its desires. "Whoever has died is freed from sin" (v. 7), but not yet from (physical) death. Not even dying with Christ ritually in baptism does that; if it did, baptism itself would confer immortality. Until the impending coming of Christ (the parousia), when everyone will be transformed (the living as well as the dead, as 1 Cor 15:50-57 insists), the resistance to sin's rule occurs in the not-yet transformed body because its "desires" (*epithymiai;* NRSV: "passions") remain potent. The rule of the desires, one is expected to remember, is God's basic punishment for idolatry (1:24; NRSV: "lusts"). Paul will write again about "desires" in 7:7-8; 13:14; and especially in 7:7-25. By using "passions" instead of "desires" in verse 12, NRSV properly avoids suggesting that Paul regards body-desires *per se* as sinful. What matters for Paul is whether desires, as passions, control the self. Significantly, he clearly assumes that the baptized who "walk in newness of life" (v. 4) *can* prevent sin from reigning in their mortal bodies, though neither here nor elsewhere does he assume that they are thereby guarding their sinlessness. Nothing that Paul has said in verses 4-12 has diminished one's responsibility; rather, what he said increased it: you *must* because *now you can!*

Whereas verse 12 stated only the negative imperative that makes concrete the new self-understanding, verse 13 states both the negative and the positive, using different imagery to accent the personal responsibility implied in verse 12. The imagery of "presenting," introduced here, will be important also in verses 15-19. Likewise, using "members" (= particular parts of one's body) anticipates what he will say about one's "members" in 7:5, 22-23. In effect, verse 13 explains how the prohibition in verse 12 is to be carried out. In verses 11-13, Paul's admonitions become increasingly concrete and more focused on one's responsibility: from a general self-understanding (dead to sin, alive to God), to a prohibition against letting sin reign in the body with its desires, to the imperative, "do not present your members to sin . . . but present yourselves to God." Characterizing one's body parts as "weapons of *adikia*" (wickedness; a key word in 1:18, 29; 2:8; 3:5) makes it clear that resisting sin's effort to "exercise dominion" in (or by) the mortal body is a real battle, a nuance diminished by translating *hōpla* as "instruments" (NRSV, NIV) or as "implements" (REB). Paul was not gun-shy of military imagery. In 13:12 Paul uses the same word (NRSV: "armor") when telling the Romans not to gratify the desires of the flesh, and in 2 Cor 6:7 he wrote of "the weapons of righteousness," as he will do at the end of Rom 6:13. His imagery implies that when one obeys the desires, they become weapons in the hands of wickedness. Here, *adikia,* like sin, is not viewed as a characteristic of deeds done *by the self* but as something done *to the self.* To "present" oneself, or one's "members," is to make oneself available, to become accessible to a governing reality, well put by REB: "You must no longer put any part of it [the body] at sin's disposal." To put oneself at the disposal of God, on the other hand, is what it actually means to be "alive to God." Then one's "members" are not weapons of *adikia* but of *dikaiosynē* (righteousness), that is, instruments in the struggle to be right and do right.

In verse 12, by using the third singular imperative ("do not let sin exercise dominion") Paul no more means "do not *allow* sin" to reign than "Let your kingdom come" (Matt 6:10) asks God to allow it to arrive. In both cases, the third singular imperative "let" means "cause it to happen" (so also Col 3:15-16), as often in the Psalms (see, e.g., 7:7; 9:19; 31:17-18). Against sin's dominion, then, Paul calls for active struggle. Marcus (1988, 86-91) suggested that here Paul appropriates and adapts the ancient biblical motif of God's holy war against the enemies of God. If so, then Paul summons the readers to participate in God's overthrow of sin, made explicit in the second plural imperative in verse 13: "Do not present your members as weapons of wickedness" (NRSV, alt.).

In verse 14 Paul concludes his exhortation by explaining why this struggle will not be lost: "You are not under law but under grace." To be "under grace" is to live in the domain where grace reigns (5:21), to live in the grace "in which we stand" (5:2), to "exercise dominion in life" because one has received "the abundance of grace" (5:17). It is to live a life so different from that defined by Adam that one lives like someone "brought from death to life" (v. 23). To live "under grace" is to have one's life controlled by grace and giftedness, instead of being controlled by the law.

In this passage, as in the rest of the section, Paul's thought expresses stark contrasts, radical alternatives; it is either/or. No place is granted to mixed situations, to piecemeal or gradual transitions, or to uncertainties or hesitations. The imperatives show that the language of Rom 6 does not simply *describe* the new Christians. Rather, it summons them to be what they became in baptism. Paul did not use such language to make the readers feel guilty for not living up to it, but rather to express the consequences of the Christ-event as the breakthrough of the New Aeon into the present sin-dominated Age. From that perspective, the relation of the Old Age to the New is not like the transition from dawn to daylight, but like a disruptive earthquake. It is the discontinuity inherent in this perspective that evokes both the either/or language and the interpretation of baptism. Because the occurrence of the Christ-event ruptured the tyranny of the Old Age, one's solidarity with that event inevitably calls for discontinuity from the past and being shaped now by what is yet to come. Moreover, Christian life, begun at baptism, should—and therefore can—conform to Christ because Christian life is as much an act of God's grace as Christ himself. Were that not the case, solidarity with Christ would be a nice idea. Paul is not portraying ideals toward which one must strive. Were that the case, he would be putting the readers "under the law," even if it were a Christian law. Even less is he asking them to strive to "be like Jesus." He is thinking rigorously and penetratingly about the consequences of an event that was an act of God's love "while we were still sinners" (5:8, AT), an act that put the participants in that event "under grace." What occurred "apart from the law" (God's rectifying action, 3:21-26) produces an existence that is not "under law but under grace."

Freed from Sin, Enslaved to Rectitude (6:15-23): This paragraph begins, like verses 1-14, with a curt rejection of the wrong inference from what Paul has just written, this time in verse 14: "Sin will not lord it over you, because you are not under law but under grace" (AT). If that is true, what follows? That "we should sin" (rephrasing v. 1)? Does being "under grace" give one a license to sin, especially since "where sin increased, grace abounded all the more" (5:20)? Although the issue embedded in the false inference in verse 15 had emerged in 3:5-8 (see comment), here the matter is even more urgent because the question, "Should we sin?" comes from one who now is "not under law but under grace." Had Paul not rejected it, the door would be open to misunderstanding grace as God's unchanging benign disposition; but here, grace is a different order (see 5:15) with its own mandates and accountability. According to 5:21, also grace "reigns," and it does so "through righteousness," not indulgence. Our passage, then, explains why this is the case. (As in 6:1, here too it is unimportant whether the interlocutor or Paul raises the question.)

Paul's response in verses 16-23, however, lacks the clear reasoning that characterizes verses 1-14, and especially 5:12-21. Verses 17-19a interrupt the flow of thought, which resumes at verse 19b ("For just as . . ."); moreover, the content of verses 17-19 is less than clear. The same must be said of verse 16.

Although verse 16 begins like verse 3, it loses its clarity as it grows more cumbersome. For one thing, what appears to be an appeal to common sense is expressed oddly: "Don't you know that when you offer yourselves to someone to obey him as slaves [lit., "for obedience"], you are slaves to the one whom you obey?" (NIV). The problem lies not in the allusion to the widespread practice of volunteering to become someone's slave in order to escape destitution or even move up the social ladder, but in the banality of the question. To say that one is an obedient slave to the person to whom one offers himself as a slave in order to obey him is "not an impressive truism" (Pallis 1920, 89). The logic of what follows is no better: "either [slave] of sin . . . or of obedience," for what does it mean to be a slave of *obedience*? Nor is it clear how being a slave of obedience "leads to righteousness"; verse 18 is clearer in saying that those freed from sin "were enslaved *to* righteousness" (NRSV: "of righteousness"); clearer too is "enslaved to God" (v. 22). Compared with the clarity of Jesus' word in John 8:34, "everyone who commits sin is a slave of sin," something is amiss here, though Paul's point is the same.

Verses 17-18 present different problems. To begin with, what has "having been freed from sin you were enslaved to righteousness" (AT) got to do with becoming "obedient from the heart to the form [*typos*, pattern] of teaching to which you were *handed over [paredothē]*"? (AT; REB's "to which you were made subject" is better than "to which you were entrusted" [NRSV and NIV], and much better than NJB: "to which you were introduced"— none of which say what Paul wrote). Moreover, assuming that the "*typos* of teaching" refers to some unspecified body of instruction (pre-baptismal catechetical instruction, moral counsel, and christological teaching have been nominated), one expects the text to say that the teaching was handed over to the Christians (as in 1 Cor 15:3), not that they were "delivered up captive to Christian doctrine," as Matthew Black's commentary puts it. Unconvincing too is the view of Stowers (1994, 258) that Paul is referring to the law to which God handed over the god-fearing Gentiles. Further, there seems to be no reason why Paul would suddenly interrupt his argument with an apostrophe ("Thanks be to God . . .").

Indeed, he might not have done so, if verse 17 is a later insertion (so Furnish 1968, 193-98, following Bultmann, who called it a "stupid interpolation"; recently Gagnon [1993, 671-73] denied the interpolation hypothesis). Strange too is verse 19*a*: "I am speaking in human terms because of the weakness of your flesh" (AT; NRSV: "your natural limitations"; REB: "to use language that suits your human weakness"; CEV: "I am using these everyday examples, because in some ways you are still weak"). Also at 3:5 Paul pointed out that he speaks "in human terms," but there his comment is understandable because he is questioning God's justice or fairness from the standpoint of the human recipient of it. Here, however, neither the language he has already used in chapter 6 nor which he is about to use explains why he suddenly blames the *readers'* limitations for the way he uses language. Moreover, what sort of "weakness" is in view here? Is it cognitive—that is, is Paul prejudging their capacity to follow the argument or to see that he is using language metaphorically? If so, would he not have written of the weakness of the *mind* (or even of the *strength* of the flesh as the inhibiting factor)?

The tortured style and the awkward ideas are left behind, fortunately, at verse 19*b*, where the argument continues and the complex sentence structure repeats that of verse 4: "as . . . so also." Paul uses this comparison to contrast the readers' lives before the impact of the Christ-event with the imperatives for the present (repeating the idiom of "presenting yourselves" or "your [body] members" in v. 13). The result is a rhetorically effective parallelism:

Past

| presented | members | as slaves | to | impurity & iniquity |
| leading to | iniquity | | | |

Present

| present | members | as slaves | to | righteousness |
| leading to | sanctification | | | |

"Impurity" *(akatharsia)* is not ritual "uncleanness" but the moral pollutedness delineated in 1:24-32, where the desires of the heart that lead to "impurity" head the list. REB's rendering is dramatic:

"to the service of impurity and lawlessness, making for moral anarchy." Verse 19 reveals that Paul has Christian Gentiles in view. Still, the focus on Gentiles does not exclude Jews, for they too participate in Adam and his consequences, especially since they too are subject to death (see also 3:9, 22-23).

Whereas the English word "sanctification" can refer to either the process or the result (as does "radiation"), Greek vocabulary allowed one to indicate one or the other. To express result, Paul probably would have used *hagiōsynē* as in 2 Cor 7:1 and 1 Thess 3:13. Here, however, he uses *hagiasmos,* the process of making holy, that is, hallowing. Although the word is not common in Paul's letters, he did tell the Thessalonians that sanctification was God's will, and then he spelled out what that should mean for the sexual side of marriage. In 1 Cor 6:11, part of a section dealing with sexual morality, sanctification marked the transition from an immoral life: "you were washed, you were sanctified, you were justified." In light of the biblical mandate to Israel, "You shall be holy, for I the LORD your God am holy" (Lev 19:1), the significance of Paul's emphasis on sanctification emerges clearly. The sanctification of the Gentiles, to be actualized in their new morality, is a sign of their inclusion in the people of God. It is not surprising, then, that Paul frequently addresses the (predominantly Gentile) readers of his letters as "saints" (holy ones; see Rom 1:7; 1 Cor 1:2; 2 Cor 1:1; Phil 1:1; see also the concluding greetings in Rom 16:15; 2 Cor 13:12; Phil 4:21-22). In our verse, Paul says in effect, obligate yourselves to righteousness because the end result is the hallowing of life.

To undergird the imperative in verse 19, verses 20-22 elaborate the contrast between the readers' past and present ("When you were . . . But now . . .").

	Condition	Current Outcome ("fruit")	Final Result (telos)
Past:	slaves of sin free regarding righteousness	shameful things	death
Present:	freed from sin enslaved to God	sanctification	eternal life

Rhetorical considerations account for the striking formulation of verse 20: "When you were slaves of sin, you were free in regard to righteousness"—for Paul, a spurious freedom. The mandate now, however, is to "present your members as slaves to righteousness" (v. 19) because "having been freed from sin, you were enslaved to righteousness" (v. 18, AT). In using the language of slavery and emancipation this way, Paul expresses the conviction that "freedom from" always entails an obligatory "freedom for." He never envisages total absence of obligation, for precisely those who are not "under law" are "under grace." As Paul sees it, one is always "under" some structure of obligation, beholden to some power and authority.

The "things of which you now are ashamed" are the "shameful lusts" (NIV for *pathē atimias* in 1:26) and the "things that should not be done" in 1:28. Even though Paul had not yet been to Rome, he knows enough of the Gentile world to remind the new Christians in Rome of their changed morals.

Verse 23 concludes the discussion by reformulating 5:15 ("the *charisma* [NRSV: "free gift"] is not like the trespass"): God's *charisma* (begracement) is eternal life, but death is the earned wage. Whether sin's wage, death, is total annihilation is as unclear as when the wage will be paid—though one may surmise that payday will be the day of wrath. Probably "death" refers to both the termination of physical life and a moral or "spiritual" deadness. Paul has referred to eternal life several times (2:7; 5:21; 6:22), and this is the last time he mentions it explicitly in Romans. The life that is eternal *(aiōnios)* is the life of the New Aeon; the emphasis is on its qualitative otherness, not on its endless duration, which, of course, is inherent in its otherness. For Paul, this "aeonic" life does not commence when present life expires; it begins during our mortality—a mark of the "already–not yet."

◊ ◊ ◊ ◊

To understand better the significance of chapter 6 as a whole, it is useful to recall that from time to time ethicists argue whether it is possible to derive an imperative from an indicative—whether what *is* implies what *ought to be*. In verses 15-23 it is evident that

Paul insists that the indicative does indeed imply an imperative. Why? Because for him, the believer's indicative—what actually is—results from an event that inaugurated a change that is not yet completed. In fact, the actuality of that event—the death and resurrection of Christ to which the baptized is now bonded—itself requires completion at the parousia (as Paul pointed out in 1 Cor 15:24-28). Precisely *this* indicative has an imperative built into it for those participating in it by baptism. Otherwise, the Christ-event would not really signal the irruption of the New Age, and then the new self-understanding would be a romantic sentiment, not a necessary mandate.

Freed from the Law (7:1-6): Although Paul has asserted that Christians are "not *under the law* but under grace" (6:14-15, AT), he has not yet explained how this transition came about. Providing this explanation is one task of this unit. Another task is to state the positive consequences of being freed from the law, just as his earlier references to emancipation from death and sin were followed by statements of the positive results. The third task is to set up the discussion that follows in the rest of chapter 7.

This is not the first time that Paul wrote about freedom from the law, for his letter to the Galatians says that "God sent his Son, born of a woman, born under the law, in order to redeem those who were under the law"; it also states the purpose/result: "that we might receive adoption as children" (Gal 4:4-5). This statement is part of a complex argument that Christian Gentiles need not, and must not, be circumcised in order to be bona fide children of God, as some traveling Christian Jewish "teachers" were insisting. But there is no evidence that our letter addresses similar issues—though perhaps Paul hoped this letter would prevent in Rome what had happened in Galatia. Be that as it may, the discussion of freedom from the law here lacks the polemical tone of Galatians.

Still, up to now, apart from the witness of the law and the prophets (3:21) and the assertion that his emphasis on faith actually upholds the law (4:31), Paul has said nothing positive about the law. Rather, it brings God's wrath (4:15), increases the trespass (5:20), and has power over people (6:14-15) whom it addresses in its domain (3:19), where it brings knowledge of sin (3:20). It neither conveyed the promise to Abraham nor actualized it to his seed (4:11-14). Understandably, God's rectifying rectitude is manifested wholly apart from the law (3:21). Also in 7:1-6 Paul writes negatively about the law: It is a power that binds (v. 6) and from which one is released only by dying to it (v. 4), just as one must die to sin and death (chap. 6). In short, the law does not provide the solution to the human dilemma because by entering it (5:20) the law has become part of the dilemma. Yet Paul will deny that the law itself is sinful (7:7) and insist instead that it is holy (7:12). Remarkably, as in the case of sin and death, he speaks of the law only in terms of its effects on the self. He is not concerned to explain what it *is*, but only what it *does* (and does not do) with respect to the human condition. It is a mistake, therefore, to talk of Paul's "doctrine of the law"; what we find is his focused argument about the law. While the latter draws on the former, the two are not the same.

Where did this negative view of the law come from? Though no one knows how Paul came to think what he thought, some possible inferences are worth noting. This view of the law did not suddenly occur to him as he was dictating Romans, for he had already written of God redeeming "those who were under the law" (Gal 4:5), and in Gal 2:19 he spoke of his dying to the law: "For through the law I died to the law, so that I might live to God." His own dying to the law suggests rather strongly that his thought cannot be separated from his life experience, that dying to the law was not painless for him, for while he was a zealous Pharisee he had not found the law to be an enslaving power (see Gal 1:14; Phil 3:4-6). This view of the law somehow resulted from his "conversion." In speaking about dying to the law, then, Paul knew first-hand what he was talking about. Nonetheless, nowhere does Romans describe that experience.

In verse 1 Paul suddenly addresses the readers directly, calling them "brothers and sisters" (lit., brothers), which he had not done since 1:13. Thereby he both reminds them subtly that he writes as a fellow member of the (fictive) family of believers and implies that they should note carefully what follows. While Paul's use of kinship language suggests a good deal about early Christian groups (well summarized by Meeks 1983, 87), its rhetorical function is also noteworthy since the letter has a persuasive task in Rome. It is not surprising, then, that he will address the readers as siblings again in verse 4, and frequently thereafter (8:12; 10:1; 11:25; 12:1; 15:14), each time probably for the same reasons. Only here, however, does he find it necessary (or useful) to characterize them as "those who know the law." Most likely they are Christian Jews and former "God-fearers" (Gentiles attracted to Judaism)—all of whom would "know the law," namely, the law of Moses. As in 6:3, Paul asks, "Do you not know . . . ?" in order to elicit their assent to the starting point of Paul's interpretation of freedom from the law.

The readers' knowledge of the law to which Paul calls attention, however, has nothing to do with its content but only with the duration of its authority—as long as one lives—because also this paragraph will emphasize the pivotal role of death. Accordingly, he deliberately uses the verb *kyrieuei* (lit., "exercise lordship"; NJB: "can control." NRSV's "is binding" conceals the use of *kyrieuei* also in 6:9 where death is the subject, and in 6:14 where the subject is sin). Thereby Paul alerts the readers that he understands the law to be a power that, like sin and death, "lords it over" a person—a reminder that one is "under the law" (6:14-15, AT).

Verses 2-3 apply the observation about the duration of the law's activity—which is true of any law—to the *wife's* relation to the law, perhaps because in a patriarchal society she is the one who is "under the law" of marriage. In any case, he chooses an appropriate word for "married woman," *hypandros* (lit., "one under a man"), found only here in the New Testament but used by both nonbiblical and biblical writers (e.g., Prov 6:24 LXX; Sir 9:9). Moreover, she is *bound* to the husband by the law. But if her husband dies, "she is discharged *[katērgētai]* from the law concerning the husband" (so NRSV), which creates a new opportunity for *her*. (Paul does not identify the believers with both the dead husband and the widow, as Thielman [1994, 196-97] says.) To make this clear, he calls attention to the difference between her situation during the husband's lifetime and afterward: If, while he is alive, she becomes involved with another man (paraphrasing the somewhat ambiguous *genētai andri heterō;* NRSV: "lives with another"; REB: "gives herself to another"; NIV: "marries another"), she will be an adulteress; but if the man dies, she is free from the law that bound her to her husband; now she is not an adulteress if she joins another man.

Unfortunately, in verse 4 the NRSV's mistranslation of *hōste* as "In the same way" derails Paul's thought, for this word, when followed by an independent clause (as here), means "therefore, so, so then" (BDAG); it signals a conclusion drawn, not a comparison. Had Paul wanted to say "in the same way" he would have used *houtōs kai* as in 6:4, 11. By translating *hōste* as "in the same way," NRSV invites the reader to look for an exact parallel in verses 4-6 to verses 2-3; yet such a parallel cannot be found, because in verses 2-3 it is the death of the *husband* that frees the woman from the law that bound her to him, but in verse 4 it is the *wife* (the Christians) who "died to the law." Even apart from the mistranslation, many commentators fault Paul for inept reasoning here. Before agreeing that here Paul suffers from "a defect of imagination" (Dodd 1932, 103), one should look more closely.

The conclusion that verses 4-6 draw from verses 2-3 is that death frees one from the law, which verse 3 actually anticipated by saying that "if her husband dies, she is free *from that law*" (not free from the husband!). Just as being "co-crucified" in 6:6 expressed vividly the necessary death that occurred in solidarity with Christ, so now Paul accents the instrumental role of Christ's death by saying that death to the law occurred "through the body of Christ"—not a reference to the church, as Dodd (1932, 101) claimed. And just as in 6:20-22 the language of liberation is followed by a statement of both the immediate result and the final purpose, so here "you have died to the law" is followed by the immediate *result* ("so that you may belong to another [Christ]"). (Oddly, the one whose death makes remarriage possible is also the new husband!) In chapter 8 Paul will explain what belonging to Christ means. Not to be overlooked is that the one to whom the remarried widow belongs is the resurrected Christ, not "the Jesus of history." Why? Because the primary purpose of death to the law is a wholly new kind of life, one that for Paul is not to be confused with adhering to Jesus as example and teacher. For Paul, Jesus of Nazareth is not a substitute for Moses (in the same game) but an alternative to Moses in a different sport. Another purpose is to "bear fruit" *(karpophorēsōmen)*. In keeping with the imagery of the passage, the word suggests childbearing, but here it relies on the metaphorical meaning of "fruit" *(karpos)*: the moral outcome of liberation from sin. The repetition of "bear fruit" in verse 5 makes this quite clear. Complex as Paul's arguments can become, they never overlook the positive mandatory moral consequences of the liberation of the self. Paul's reasoning about the wife emerges more clearly if we put his conclusion about her as a question: Apart from divorce, under what circumstances is the married woman free to join someone else without being guilty of adultery? Answer: at the death of the husband. Thereafter she is free to belong to another man and to be "fruitful."

The concluding verses 5-6 restate the substance of verse 4 (the contrast between then and now), and also introduce topics to be discussed: the law as energizer of the passions (discussed in vv. 7-13), as well as life "in the flesh" and the role of the Spirit in the new life (both discussed in 8:1-17). Strong language is used to contrast the past (v. 5) and the present (v. 6). The past was marked by moral failure and was doomed. The "sinful passions" *(ta pathēmata tōn hamartiōn)*: (a) were energized *(enērgeito)* by the law, but not controlled by it, (b) were energized "in our [body] members," which had become "weapons of unrighteousness" (see 6:13), "slaves to impurity and to iniquity *[anomia]* leading to iniquity" (see 6:19); (c) "bore fruit" for death (i.e., they served to bring on death)—a deliberate contrast with the "remarried widow" who bears "fruit for God." *But now* (the phrase used at 3:21), this disastrous situation is replaced by being (a) "discharged from the law" (picking up the wording of v. 2), (b) being "dead to that which held us captive," and (c) serving as slaves "not to the oldness of the letter" but *in* the "newness of the Spirit" (AT—not "slaves *to* the Spirit," for the Spirit brings freedom "from the law of sin and death," 8:2). The contrast between the letter and the Spirit appeared in 2:29, where it was used to distinguish physical circumcision from the circumcision that really matters (see comment).

◊ ◊ ◊ ◊

Before proceeding, it may be useful to reflect on the significance of Paul's understanding of sin, the real culprit at work in death and in the law. While sin always involves a hostile act against God's will, deliberate or unintended, for Paul sin is more than disobedience (trespass, transgression); if it were a matter of trespass, it could be dealt with by forgiveness and the command, "Don't do that again!" coupled with "Do this instead." But Paul evidently regarded such a view as superficial, because for him sin was an insidious power that creates a destructive condition that ultimately must be reversed, and from which one must be freed in the meantime. In 6:1–7:6 the human condition, for which God's act in Christ provides the remedy, is portrayed as bondage, traced to Adam in 5:12-21.

6:6	enslaved to sin
12	sin reigns, making one obey passions
14	sin rules as lord
17	slaves of sin
18	enslaved to sin (implied by "freed")
19	one's body "members" are slaves to sin and iniquity
20	slaves of sin
22	enslaved to sin (implied by "freed")

However much Paul found his understanding substantiated in biblical and early Jewish thought, what he was struggling to comprehend was not the Jewish or Gentile plight, nor that of Rome's ruling elite, nor of any other group, be its sins venal or vicious. For him the plight was *human*. So even if the remedy had been promised in the Jews' scriptures and was provided by the Messiah of Davidic stock (1:2-4), that remedy had to address the human condition at its deepest level, or it would only enhance somewhat the various forms of "better life" already in place. But if God had resurrected Jesus, then a new reality is at hand for all who believe that God had acted in this way. And if that is the case, then Paul has to get the word out—even to Spain—that the power of sin and death has been ruptured, decisively. In the meantime, Paul must also explain why obeying the law will not produce the same result as believing the news of what God had achieved in the event called "Jesus Christ."

The Role of the Law in the Reign of Sin (7:7-25)

In this passage Paul probes to the deepest, and most disturbing, level of the human condition. As already noted, beginning with 5:12 the apostle penetrated deeper by seeing the human plight as bondage, as being "under" powers, as being ruled by realities that one cannot avoid obeying, and from whose control one must be freed if one is to be right with God and to do right by others as well. But *why* does one obey these malign powers? And why does even the law of Moses turn out to be a power "under" which one lives until liberated? Whereas the imagery used to speak of this subservience implied that the enslaving powers are external (the self is "*under*" them), now Paul explains that their power is so effective because they are also "*within*" the self. Not until this enslaving power within the self is replaced by an enabling power within the self (the Spirit) is one truly free (as chap. 8 will explain). The requisite liberation does not, and cannot, occur by resolute obedience to the law because the law has become a power from which one must be released if one is to belong to Christ (vv. 1-6). Now Paul goes on to argue that the law is part of the dilemma not despite being holy, but precisely because it is. Romans 7:7-25, then, is not a digression; it is required by what Paul has already said.

But who is the "I" that speaks here so poignantly? Interpreters' answers continue to be divided sharply. In detecting the identity of the "I" one must acknowledge but not over-emphasize the use of the past tense in verses 7-13, the present tense in verses 14-23, and the brief use of the future tense in verse 24. Using these tenses in this sequence not only gives the whole section a strong narrative character; it also is a rhetorically effective way of drawing the reader into the situation described—especially the pathos of verse 24: "Wretched man that I am! Who will rescue me from this body of death?"

Along with *ethos* and *logos*, *pathos* was an important dimension of ancient rhetoric (see Olbricht 2000, 7-22; for *pathos* in

Romans, see Keck 2000, 71-96). The influence of ancient rhetoric on this passage is especially evident in Paul's use of *prosōpopoiia* (as Stowers [1994] showed, followed by Talbert [2003]; but Thurén [2000, 118-20] is not persuaded). In *prosōpopoiia* the identity of the speaker is conveyed not by the personal name but by the speaker's self-disclosure, as Quintilian saw: "With this figure we present the inner thoughts of our adversaries as though they were talking to themselves . . . or pretend that we have before our eyes things, persons or utterances" (quoted from Stowers 1994, 20). Or, as *ad Herennium* (attributed to Cicero) puts it, this device "consists in representing an absent person as present, or in making a mute thing or one lacking form articulate, and attributing to it . . . a language . . . appropriate to its character" (4.53:66), adding that it is most useful in appealing to pity *(commiseratione)*—precisely as in verse 24.

Reading 7:7-25 in this light makes it virtually certain that the passage is not autobiographical (which is not to deny all autobiographical reference). Paul is not "sharing his story." Nor is he "taking himself as representative, first (in vv. 7-13) of mankind generally, and then (in vv. 14-25) of Christians" (Cranfield 1975, 1:34; similarly Thurén 2000, 121). Augustine's view that verses 14-25 describe *Christian* experience was repeated by Luther and Calvin, and is still championed (e.g., by Packer [1999, 73], who claims it is "surely beyond dispute"). Neither is Paul using "I" to recount the story of Israel's experience with the law (Wright 2002, *ad loc.*) or his own experience in solidarity with Israel's (Moo 1996, 431). Nor is it likely that Paul gives voice only to the dilemma of the Gentiles "who try to live by the works of the law" in order to gain self-mastery over their desires (Stowers 1994, 273). While the Greek parallels are the more prominent because Paul has *primarily* Gentiles in view (indicated by 6:21, see comment), the allusions to Genesis suggest that the "I" portrays the Adamic self (not simply Adam himself), whose plight has become clear in light of Christ. Still, no identification of the "I" has proven to be completely problem-free (for a concise summary of the major options, see Moo 1996, 424-31).

Even though the present tense first appears in verse 14, the second unit probably begins at verse 13, for here—as in 6:1, 15; 7:1—Paul first formulates an inference that is rejected immediately ("By no means!"). Thus verses 7-12 constitute the first unit, verses 13-25 the second.

◊ ◊ ◊ ◊

The Unwilling Accomplice (7:7-12): Paul, having written of living under the "reign" of sin (5:21) and "under the law" (6:14, AT), on the one hand, and of dying "to sin" (6:1, 10-11) and of dying "to the law" (7:4) on the other, is aware that one might conclude that the law itself is a form of sin. So he begins by rejecting this wrong inference with his usual "By no means!" (see comment on 3:4). Still, he would not have written this way about sin and the law if he were not convinced that somehow they *are* intimately connected. His task, now, is to show *how* they are connected even though they are not at all identical. So verses 7-12 will explain how sin reigns through the law, the very law that prohibits sin. This explanation allows him to declare that the law, far from being identical to sin, is in fact its opposite: holy (v. 12). Verses 7-12 is a carefully crafted, chiastically structured argument in which a specific commandment represents the law as such.

a the law is not sin
  b I came to know sin *through* the law (viz., the 10th commandment)
    c sin, *seizing opportunity*, through the commandment produced desires in me
      d apart from the law, sin is dead (and I am alive)
      d´ the commandment arrived, sin came alive, and I died
    c´ sin, *seizing opportunity*, through the commandment
  b´ deceived me *through* it and killed me
a´ so the law is holy, and the commandment is holy and just and good

Paul's explanation begins by pointing out, "But I would not have known sin [not simply "what sin was," as in NIV] except through the law" (AT), thereby using *prosopōpoiia* to restate 3:20: "through the law comes the knowledge of sin." The rest of verse

7 makes this observation concrete by citing the tenth commandment (Exod 20:17; Deut 5:21): "I would not have known *epithymia* if the law had not said, *ouk epithymēseis*" (usually translated as "You shall not covet," but which also means, "You shall not desire"). By ignoring the commandment's list of things not to be desired (the neighbor's possessions), Paul concentrates on desire itself; his argument does not require specifying what is desired. While he can use "desire" in a positive sense (as in Phil 1:23), here, as in most cases, the word has a negative meaning (as in 1 Thess 4:5 where he connects it with passion [NRSV: "lustful passion"]; in Rom 1:24 he states that God handed the idolaters over to their heart's desire for immoral deeds [see comment]; and in 6:12 he urged, "Do not let sin exercise dominion in your mortal bodies, to make you obey their *epithymiais* [passions]"). So too in 7:7 *epithymia* is more than ordinary wanting (as in, "I'd like to have . . ."); it is an emotionally driven wanting, an impassioned craving, a lusting for something. Since the Decalogue prohibits deeds that seem more serious (idolatry, misuse of God's name, murder, adultery, theft, false witness), why does Paul select coveting/desiring to show how "I" came to know sin through the law? Because, whereas the rest of the Decalogue prohibits *acts*, only the tenth commandment forbids an inner disposition that is prior to prohibited acts. And it is just this focus on the inner self that accords with Paul's concern to identify the locus of sin's exercise of power within the self. In short, the "I" comes to "know sin" when it understands its inevitable response to the law.

To show that also other Hellenized Jewish writers connected desire and death, commentaries sometimes cite the misnamed *Apocalypse of Moses* (the Greek version of *The Life of Adam and Eve*) and Jas 1:14-15, but miss the fact that Paul connects them in exactly the opposite way. In the former (written perhaps a generation after Paul) Eve says that the serpent "sprinkled his evil poison on the fruit which he gave me to eat which is covetousness *[epithymia]*. For covetousness is the origin *[kephalē*, lit., head, first] of every sin" (19:3). In the latter, the author points out that "one is tempted by one's own desire *[epithymias]* . . . , then desire, having conceived, it gives birth to sin, and that sin, when it is fully grown, gives birth to death." In both of these texts, sin results from desire, but in Rom 7:8 sin *produced* the desire. For Paul, the culprit is not sin-producing desire, but desire-producing sin.

What makes this productivity so heinous is sin's seizing the opportunity (mentioned twice) presented by the commandment that forbids desire, and through that very commandment effects "all desire" (REB: "all kinds of wrong desires") in the self. Consistent with the way Paul viewed sin since 5:12, here too sin is not what the self does; it is rather a power that does things to the self. In this passage, sin does not heighten desires; it *produces* them *through* the prohibiting commandment itself.

The whole passage results from the juxtaposition of, and interplay between (a) the quotation from the Decalogue (v. 7), (b) allusions to Gen 3, and (c) allusions to what Paul said in 5:12-21 about both Adam and the law. Because Paul assumes that the story of the fatal disobedience in Eden is well known, he can allude to it without actually quoting a line from it. Also, the juxtaposition of Exod 20:17 and allusions to Gen 3:1-7 accords with the rabbinic practice of correlating two quite different texts because each contains the same key word (as Paul did in 4:1-8, where the key word was "reckoned"). In this passage, the commandment's prohibition against desire alludes to Gen 3:6 (LXX 7), which suggests "desire" by saying that Eve "saw that the tree was good for food, and that it was pleasing to the eyes to see, and beautiful to contemplate." (Although the LXX does not use the term "desire," the Hebrew behind "beautiful" is *nehmād*, desirable.) Moreover, since the "I" expresses the Adamic plight as well as alluding to the Adam-event, Paul can specify what happened when "the law came in" (trespass multiplied, 5:20); here, sin produced "all desire" when the commandment arrived. So too, the assertion that "apart from the law sin lies dead" (v. 8) restates 5:13, "sin was indeed in the world before the law."

Verse 8 is formulated in a way that sets up the rhetorically balanced verse 9:

| apart from the law | sin is dead | (and I am alive) |
| the commandment arrived | sin came alive | and I died |

When verse 10 explains that "the very commandment that promised life proved to be death for me," (AT), it alludes to the implication of God's command not to eat of the tree of life lest one die (Gen 3:3)—that is, life is promised by obeying the command, as in Lev 18:5, where God promises that the person who obeys the laws "will live [find life] by them." Verse 11 restates the point more sharply: instead of "I died" (v. 10), now sin "killed [me]" through the commandment. In fact, sin used the commandment to deceive the self—probably an allusion to the serpent's lie to Eve, "You will not surely die" (Gen 3:4, AT). That is, sin deceived by inducing her to think that God would not inflict the promised punishment. In short, sin uses the law to deceive by creating the illusion that one can get away with disobedience. As Via (1990, 44) astutely observed, "The law is a power that entices me into misrepresenting itself [it?] and thus into misrepresenting the nature of my existence." It *is* this power, however, because of what it has *become:* sin's tool.

The horrendous character of what the law has become is underlined by verse 12: "The law is holy, and the commandment is holy and just and good." The real culprit is sin residing in the self before the law arrived. Understandably, verse 12 prompts interpreters to say that the passage is a defense or a vindication of the law. Valid as that judgment may be, it is only the explicit half of the story; the implicit half (in vv. 13-25) is no less important—the law's inability to prevent being used by sin. Indeed, here the law is the unwilling accomplice in sin's destructive work, the subjection of the self to death. There can be no liberation from sin by means of the law.

◊ ◊ ◊ ◊

What Paul says about the law is highly significant for Christian anthropology, the understanding of the self. In contending that the law is neither the problem nor the solution for the problem, Paul exposes two kinds of naivete—the one assumes that intuitive ("natural") goodness would flourish were it not for the law's (culturally conditioned) prescriptions and prohibitions; the other is confident that by "doing the right thing" persistently, human wickedness can be overcome eventually. From Paul's angle, the former is naive about human capacity, the latter naive about the already conditioned character of human existence that one assimilates in society. Neither one reckons seriously with the reality of that heinous power that Paul calls "sin" because each regards it as a wrong that one *does* rather than a reality that wrongs the doer and the deed alike. By no means, however, is Paul a pessimistic misanthrope. Why not? Because he views the human condition from the standpoint of what God has already done to overcome it.

The Conflicted Self (7:13-25): It is the very holiness of the law that, like the impartiality of God (2:9-11), makes the plight of the "I" so acute. Before showing why this is the case, Paul first makes sure that the law's complicity in sin's slaying the self does not imply that it was the law that brought death. As in verse 7, he formulates the wrong inference sharply in order to refute it easily: "Did what is good, then, bring death to me?" (see also 6:1; 3:4-6 and the comment there). He does not, however, state the underlying reason why it is enough to reject the inference—namely, the common conviction that like produces like (made explicit by Jesus, "A good tree cannot bear bad fruit, nor can a bad tree bear good fruit," Matt 7:18). Assuming that commonsense view, Paul simply formulates the inference in a way that exposes its self-contradiction: "Did the good bring death [the bad] to me?" After flatly rejecting this inference, Paul explains what really happened: "But in order that sin might be recognized [*phanē*, manifest] as sin, it produced death in me through what was good, so that through the commandment sin might become utterly sinful" (NIV). The totally perverse power of sin does not become evident in the grossness of the sinful act, Paul in effect argues, but in *using* the good to bring about its opposite—death. Where sin is at work, like does produce like—in spades. What Paul says here goes beyond what 5:12 said generally ("death came through sin") by explaining how it came.

Verses 14-25 explain how this comes about, thereby reaching the deepest level of the human plight. It is around these verses that the arguments continue to swirl. Probing the human condition most deeply requires Paul to focus his analytical skill on the self, for without a clear understanding of the condition of the "I" it remains unclear why obeying the holy law cannot control sin. The passage, while thoroughly concerned with anthropology, is not interested in explaining the "nature" of the human being (the relation of soul and body or of soul to spirit, being created in God's image, etc.), but solely in showing *why* "I" cannot obey the law in the first place. Thus, in light of verse 13, verses 14-25 tacitly explain why sin can use the good to produce death: The self too is an unwilling accomplice in its own condition. But if it is not the "nature" or composition of the self that accounts for its inability to obey the holy law, what does account for it?

Verse 14 gives the answer. It does so by calling attention to the radical disparity between the *state* of the self and the character of the law—a disparity based on the difference between spirit and flesh (mentioned in 7:5: "while we were living in the flesh," but not developed until chap. 8). It is the contrast between spirit and flesh that now prompts Paul to write not of the holiness of the law but of its "spiritual" *(pneumatikos)* character. Although some commentators (e.g., Barrett 1957, Cranfield 1975, and Moo 1996) say that Paul refers to the divine origin of the law, its origin is not the point but its character, because it is essential for the argument.

Whereas in 7:5 Paul spoke of living "in the flesh" (in a domain of power, a controlling field of force), here he says, "I am *sarkinos*" (fleshly; NRSV: "of the flesh"; "unspiritual" [NIV and REB] is too weak). To be "fleshly" is to be defined by flesh *(sarx)*, not in the sense, "I am a physical phenomenon," for which Paul would have used *soma* (body). Rather, "flesh" is the physical or phenomenal when it inappropriately exercises power. In this context, fleshliness manifests itself in desire; desire is the symptom of fleshliness. Physicality *per se* is not the problem; the problem emerges when physicality becomes fleshliness, when one's physicality inordinately defines the self and controls it through desire. Then one's nonphysical self—what verse 22 calls "the inner man" (NASB; REB: "my inmost self"; NIV: "my inner being")—loses control. (This is as close as Paul comes to speaking like those Greeks who regarded reason to be the "ruling part" of the self, responsible for controlling the irrational aspect of the self.) The resulting condition is bondage, as verse 14 makes clear in the explanatory phrase, "sold under sin" (NRSV: "sold into slavery under sin"). This explanation is the chief reason Paul is not talking about Christian existence.

Because "sold" is a vivid metaphor, Paul has no interest in who did the "selling," as does 1 Macc 1:15 when it uses the same verb to characterize those Jews who abandoned their religion for Gentile ways: they "sold themselves to do evil." Similar to Paul, however, is the Qumran text, "To death I belonged because of my sin, and my iniquities sold me to Sheol" (11QPsa 19:9-10, quoted by Fitzmyer 1993), because it is the enslaved *state* that matters to Paul (indicated by the participle in the perfect tense, used for the ongoing result of past action). Nor has Paul any interest in explaining exactly when this enslavement occurred—for example, when the soul entered the fleshly, material body, as some Gnostics would claim later. By interpreting "fleshly" existence as being "sold into slavery under sin," verse 14 indicates that being "fleshly" is a far more serious obstacle to obeying the spiritual law than one's finitude. At the same time, verse 14 also implies that being enslaved to sin manifests itself as fleshliness, the state in which physicality exerts inordinate and uncontrolled influence. This is the foundation on which the rest of the argument rests.

At verse 15 the "I" begins to explain how being "fleshly" manifests itself in what one *does* and *does not achieve* (*katergazomai*, used four times [vv. 15, 17, 18, 20]). The emphasis on achievement allows Paul to expose the disparity between intention or will and the actual deed (vv. 15-20), and the disparity between the inner and outer self (vv. 21-24). What emerges is not the *bondage* of the will but its ineffectiveness, its weakness, its inability to actualize itself in the deed. And since the self expresses itself in the will, this incapacity to do what is willed discloses what it means for the "I" to be fleshly, "sold under sin." In short, verses 15-25 portray the frustrations of the fleshly "I." (For an instructive discussion of how Greek philosophy did and did not discuss such issues, see Dihle 1982.)

The portrayal begins with the declaration, "I do not know what I achieve" (AT). Even if one translates *ginōskō* as "understand" (NRSV, NIV), the assertion is surprising because Paul does go on to explain what the "I" does. REB paraphrases: "I do not even acknowledge my own actions as mine," perhaps influenced by Augustine's comment that the Vulgate's *non intelligo* means *non approbo*, "I do not approve" (accepted by Barrett 1957 and Cranfield 1975). But Paul is not discussing the self's attitude toward its deeds but the deeds themselves: *why* they do not correspond to what is willed, but instead are the opposite of what is willed. That is, since like produces like, what does the hated deed imply about its doer? Paul did not need to argue the case for this disparity between intent and result, for it had been recognized often. Ovid (shortly before Paul's time) is frequently quoted: "I perceive what is better and approve of it, but I pursue what is worse" (quoted from Fitzmyer 1993); Stowers (1994, 260-64) sketches the legacy of Euripides' *Medea* (5th c. BCE) in which Medea says, "I am being overcome by evils. I know that what I am about to do is evil but passion is stronger than my reasoned reflection and this is the cause of the worst evils for humans" (see also Talbert 2003, 192-93). On the other hand, the Cynic-Stoic Epictetus (shortly after Paul) taught that since wrongdoing involves a contradiction, the wrongdoer "is not doing what he wishes"; but "as soon as anyone shows a man this, he will of his own accord abandon what he is doing" (*Discourses* 2.26.1, 4). This is exactly what Paul denies: that the contradiction between intent and deed can be eliminated by self-knowledge. For Paul, the problem is neither ignorance of the good nor lack of will to do it, but the inability to do the willed good that is known through the law. In other words, he rejects the already-ancient Greek view that knowledge of the good leads to doing the good.

In verses 16-20 he first draws out implications of the contradiction between what is willed and what is done. The first concerns the law. The argument insists that "the commandment is holy and just and good *[agathē]*" (v. 12); it also asserts that the "I" wills to do what the law commands. Consequently, from the contradiction between what is willed and the hated act that is actually done, Paul infers that the problem lies not in the law ("I agree that the law is good," *kalos* here is synonymous with *agathē*), which is external to the self; rather, the problem lies *with-*

in the self: "it is no longer I that do it, but sin that dwells within me" (v. 17). In the first clause, the "I" dissociates itself totally from the "I's" unintended act; in the second, the "I" identifies the real doer—sin, resident in the self. (So important is this diagnosis that vv. 19-20 repeat it.) This diagnosis does not imply that the self is innocent. What it does imply is that resident sin acts through the self in such a way that the sin produces a contradiction between what the self wills and the evil deed it actually does (v. 19), for which the self is accountable. Precisely this contradiction, and the plight it generates, shows that the "I" is "sold *under* sin," that is, under its control, now exposed as control exercised from within, where it *resides*. The presumed correspondence between the producer and the produced is confirmed: The real doer of the hated deed is resident sin, not the intending self.

Verse 18 gives the reason why resident sin is the real doer. Unfortunately, however, translations have Paul give the wrong reason: "nothing good dwells within me," as if he were answering the question, "How much good dwells within me?" ("nothing good" may reflect the doctrine of "total depravity"). Here is what he actually wrote: "The good does not dwell within me, that is, in my flesh" (for full discussion, see Keck 1999, 66-75). What matters for Paul's line of thought is not the *quantity* of good in the self, but *whether it resides* there. If the good is a resident, one would and *could* do the good that the law commands, for then the good law would produce the good by eliciting the inherent good. Tragically, however, what does reside in the self is sin. Moreover, it resides "in my flesh." (Locating sin's residence in the flesh explains why in 8:3 Paul will say that God "condemned sin in the flesh.") The last part of verse 18 is rendered better by REB: "for though the will to do good is there, the ability to effect it is not," for the statement is neither about the self's *ability* to will (as in NRSV) nor about its *desire* to will the good (as in NIV), but about the failure to achieve the willed—a failure made even more disastrous by the "success" in doing the hated evil instead of the willed good (v. 20).

In verses 21-24 the plight of the Adamic self is expressed most starkly. Here Paul, having said that sin resides in the self, now specifies both *where* in the self it operates—in the "members"—and *how* it does: by making the self a prisoner of war. In chapter 6 Paul had already spoken of the role of the body's "members." There, as part of his exhortations to actualize the new life, he characterized the members' role in prebaptismal life as "weapons of wickedness" (6:12) and as "slaves to uncleanness and iniquity" (6:19) in order to contrast it with their postbaptismal role as "weapons of righteousness" and as "slaves to righteousness" (6:19). Notably, in that context, the "members" are the self that one "presents," makes available to wickedness or to righteousness, implying that one is responsible for both "presentings," because one can determine their use by an act of the will. But when 7:21-23 traces the contradiction between what is willed and what is done to the conflict between the will and sin in the "members," Paul implies that one cannot determine their use by an act of will. Perhaps the portrayal here is more serious because Paul is probing, not exhorting.

In verses 21-23, the crucial clause occurs at the beginning: "So I find the law" *(ton nomon)*, which some translations regard as referring to a pattern so consistent that it can be called a "rule" (NJB), a "principle" (REB), or "a law" (NRSV). CEV has Paul say something quite different: "The Law has shown me that something in me keeps me from doing what I know is right." But Achtemeier (1997, 19) argued persuasively that what "I find" is not a law or a principle but evil "close at hand" whenever the self wills to do the good. Why? Because *ton nomon* is not the direct object of "I find" but "an adjectival accusative of reference." So he translates verse 21 as, "So when I will to do the good, with reference to the torah [that is, the good specified there], I find that evil lies close at hand to me." (Similarly Wright 2002, 570; unpersuasive, however is his claim that the evil "close at hand" alludes to God's word to Cain in Gen 4:7.)

Verses 22-23 spell out what results from *evil* being "close at hand" (not a vague "something," as in CEV) when the self wills to do the good: the self discovers that it is in conflict with itself. The "inner self" that delights in God's law is at war with a different law, located "in my members," that wins the fight by "making me

captive to the law of sin that dwells in my members." Since Paul
is partly rephrasing verses 16-17, the inner self's delight in God's
law (v. 22) restates more vividly the self's agreement that the
law is good (v. 16); both affirmations summarize what the poet
celebrates in Ps 119. But absent from that psalm is what Paul
emphasizes: the conflict between God's law that the inner self (the
esō anthrōpos) affirms and a different (heteros) law in the "members." The identity of this different law is not clear. (That it is
God's law when taken over by sin and so made into "a qualita-
tively different law" [so Meyer 2000, 1057] is not evident, for it
is doubtful whether God's law [even when controlled by sin] is
found in the members.) The reference to the "inner self" implies
that here "members" is used to express the contrasting external
self, as in REB: "In my inmost self I delight . . . but I perceive in
my outward actions a different law. . . ." Also, "the law of my
mind" does not refer to some sort of logic that governs cognitive
processes but to what the inner self affirms, namely, God's law.
Clarity here is elusive because largely for rhetorical reasons, and
in order to avoid complete repetition, Paul mentions four laws in
order to express the conflict between two of them: the law of God
(= the law of my mind) vs. the law in the members (= the law of
sin = the commanding power of sin).

Interestingly, the conflict is not described by a neutral external
observer but by the self; the "I" sees what is really going on.
Rhetorically, this detail prepares for the pained outburst in verse
24, "Wretched man that I am! Who will deliver me from this body
of death?" (or perhaps, "the body of this death"). The prisoner
cries for release from the captivity to the law of sin in the members, not for rescue *from* the body because it is mortal, for Paul
expects redemption *of* the body (8:23). By asking this question,
the self recognizes its inability to rescue itself from sin by itself,
neither by resolve nor (as pointed out by Watson 1997, 261) by
recovering the primordial right relation to the Creator that has
been suppressed by human wickedness (1:18).

Verse 25 consists of two parts, the second of which puzzles
many interpreters because after the gratitude for rescue expressed
in the first part, the restatement of the plight is unexpected. Some

(e.g., Dodd 1957, as well as the Moffatt translation) concluded that this second part got misplaced, having originally come before verse 24. Others have regarded it as a copyist's marginal comment that was added later. While most interpret the statement as part of the original text, it is hardly "an altogether appropriate conclusion" by a mature Christian who looks forward to full deliverance from the current "not yet" of salvation (so Cranfield 1975).

The rhetorically balanced conclusion emphasizes the self: "I myself" (retained by NIV but not visible in the NRSV's simple "I" or in REB's "left to myself"); this "I" is emphasized because it is divided against itself.

| I myself | with the mind | am slave | to the law of God |
| but | with the flesh | [am slave] | to the law of sin |

Here the self lives in conflict between these two simultaneous slaveries, the one positive, the other negative. Until and unless the link between sin and flesh, in which the negative bondage is grounded, is broken, obeying the law of God remains only a frustrated mental act.

◊ ◊ ◊ ◊

In verses 7-25 Paul has said so much about the dilemma of the self that it is easy to overlook what he did *not* say, which too is important. To begin with, the focus throughout is on the way sin functions as a sinister power that frustrates the self's intent to obey the holy law of God. Accordingly, he eschews all attempts to define or analyze the essence of sin, self, or law; instead, he discloses the human plight by showing sin's power to enslave, the law's lack of power to prevent being used by sin, and the incapacity of the self to actualize what it wills. Nor need he say *which* sin has this power; it is the operation of sin qua sin that must become clear.

Also absent from the whole discussion is any reference to Satan or to temptation. Had Satan been blamed, the whole analysis would have been different, for Paul would hardly have spoken of Satan as residing in the self. More important, then the plight

would have been traced to an external power that could be discussed only in mythological terms; Paul, however, treats it in
metaphorical terms. Besides, blaming Satan would have exonerat-
ed the self as an innocent victim. Had Paul discussed the role of
temptation, the self would have been *lured* to choose evil rather
than doing evil despite willing not to do it.

Paul does not trace the conflict between the power in the "members" and what the inner self intends to the conflict between the
good and evil impulses in the self, the *yeṣer-ha-ra* and the *yeṣer-ha-
tôb* (see Marcus [1986, 8-21] for similarities and differences). At
Qumran, the Community Rule calls them the two spirits, the spirit of truth and the spirit of injustice. Both spirits come from God,
who has "established" them "in equal measure until the determined end." Moreover, until the present they "struggle in the
hearts of men and they walk in both wisdom and folly" (1QS 3-
4, Vermes 1975, 73-75). By being a member of the community,
however, the evil spirit can be controlled: "No man shall walk in
the stubbornness of his heart so that he strays after his . . . evil
inclination, but he shall circumcise in the Community the foreskin
of evil inclination," presumably by strict obedience to the community's interpretation of the law. Even though Paul too talks
about a war between the law of sin in the members and the law of
the mind, he does not trace that conflict to God-given impulses
but to the power of sin; nor does he think that the evil impulse in
the "members" (if indeed he alludes to it) can be controlled by an
act of will or obedience to the law. Likewise, Paul diverges from
the assumption built into Deut 30:19, where Moses, speaking for
God, says, "I have set before you life and death, blessings and
curses. Choose life"—that is, obey the commandments. The
assumption is that you can do what you choose. That was the prevailing view also in early Jewish thought. But for Paul, the problem is neither the wrong choice nor a vacillating weak will, but the
inability to actualize the right choice. Why? Because as he saw the
self, sin-power is stronger than willpower.

Unmentioned as well is any reference to historical, social, gender, or ethnic aspects of the human dilemma. Paul concentrates the
readers' attentions on the "I," who despite the narrative quality of

verses 7-11 is somehow ahistorical, lacking any reference to God's covenant with Israel, the presupposition of the law. This "I" encounters the tenth commandment as a solitary self whose willing the good apparently is not part of a community's will or practice in which virtues are formed. Likewise, there is no reference to the social dimension to sin's operation. No allowance is made for circumstances in which one hates all the options—whether because of their character or because of their consequences—but must act nonetheless. Instead, by disregarding all contingencies, Paul's analysis moves relentlessly toward the self's discovery of its conflicts with itself, irrespective of its age, health, gender, or ethnic identity. One might well say that, as in Christ there is neither male nor female, and so forth, so in bondage to sin there is neither male nor female, Jew nor Greek, slave nor free, but only the Adamic self. Here, no qualifying considerations or extenuating circumstances are allowed to mitigate the dilemma in which the self is caught, blur what caused it, or imply a spurious solution from it. The self cannot extricate itself; it can only be rescued.

Liberation by the Resident Spirit (8:1-30)

This passage is the climax of the discussion begun at 5:12 as well as the conclusion of the letter's argument to this point. It picks up and develops themes mentioned before; it also opens windows to the widest horizon in the whole letter, the impending redemption of creation itself. Two markers in the text disclose its structure: in verses 1-17 the key word is "Spirit" (used fifteen times), whereas in verses 18-30 it is "wait," associated with "hope." Moreover, both verse 18 and verse 30 end on the same note: "glorified." Accordingly, verses 1-17 constitute the first unit, which accents the "already"; the second (vv. 18-30) emphasizes the "not yet" of redemption.

◊ ◊ ◊ ◊

The Power of the Spirit (8:1-17): In chapter 7 Paul argued that in the self sin is a resident power stronger than the will to do the good required by the good law (see 7:12, 17, 20, 23). The situation is so dire that he characterized the self as sin's slave (7:14) and as a prisoner of war needing rescue (7:24). Now the deliverance "through Jesus Christ our Lord" (7:25) is spelled out, first by explaining how it occurred through Christ (vv. 1-4), then by portraying the role of the Spirit as God's power now residing in the self. Since sin resides in the flesh, operating through the body's "members," actualizing liberation from sin entails a conflict between Spirit and flesh (vv. 5-8). The resident Spirit is also the pledge of the believer's resurrection (vv. 9-11), assuring solidarity with Christ's glorification (vv. 12-17). Paul's task is to portray the Spirit's power in a way that is simultaneously convincing and realistic; that is, the Spirit must be portrayed as powerful enough to deal effectively with the dilemma exposed in chapter 7, yet not so overstated that it becomes fanciful. This note of realism (the "not yet") is expressed in verse 17, where the assurance of sharing Christ's glory entails sharing also his suffering. The reference to suffering is the springboard to verses 18-30.

As already noted (see p. 192), some interpreters have found the transition from 7:25 to 8:1 to be so awkward that they have proposed "improving" the text by omitting the latter part of verse 25 ("So then . . ."). The difficulty, however, should not be exaggerated. In any case, the conjunction "therefore" at 8:1 is pivotal, for it announces a conclusion or inference. But from what? Not from the restatement of the dilemma in 7:25, but rather from the discussion that began with the comparison of Adam and Christ in 5:12-21. In fact, taken together, verses 1-2 allude to themes that have been prominent since 5:12. Thus the noun "condemnation" (v. 1) recalls 5:16, 18, where the same word is used (the verb appears in 8:34). In addition, the claim that there is no condemnation "for those who are in Christ Jesus" recalls 6:1-4, where Paul explained baptism "into Christ," as well as 6:23, which contrasts the wages of sin with the gift of eternal life "in Christ Jesus our Lord." So too, being freed "from the law of sin and death" (8:2, AT) explicitly refers to the enslavement to "the law of sin" in 7:25. Such allusions help the readers/hearers follow the train of thought as it now moves toward its conclusion.

Verse 1 is a verbless assertion whose warrant is stated in verse

2 (indicated by "for"), which itself is warranted by verses 3-4. These verses first state the soteriological import of God's act in Christ, then its moral purpose/result—living according to the Spirit rather than according to the flesh. Verses 5-8 explain this other mode of living.

Although the declaration, "there is now no condemnation" is phrased negatively, the content is positive, expressing the gospel in the idiom of a courtroom (as in 8:34). If there is no condemnation, the guilty are acquitted and so saved "from the wrath" of God (CEV: "You won't be punished"; see 5:9). And who are the acquitted? "Those who are in Christ Jesus" (REB: "united with Christ"). The language of participation is here linked with the forensic idiom of acquittal, being declared "in the right," a significant aspect of rectification/justification. So important is this declaration in verse 1 that "no condemnation" begins the Greek sentence: "Therefore no condemnation now for those who are in Christ Jesus . . ." (AT).

Why not? Because of the liberation from bondage that has occurred in Christ. NRSV brilliantly preserves the ambiguity of the Greek. In saying "the law of the Spirit of life in Christ Jesus has set you free," does Paul mean that "the law of the Spirit has set you free" *by means* of Christ Jesus or that "the law of the Spirit of life in Christ Jesus" did the freeing? Although "set *me* free" clearly answers the question in 7:24 ("who will rescue me?"), the more difficult reading ("set *you* [sg.] free") is preferred by most interpreters, since copyists tend to alleviate problems. The identity of this individual need not be sought, for this "you" might well be used for rhetorical effect to address each hearer/reader of the letter.

The content of verse 2, however, has become controversial because, together with verse 3, here Paul uses the word "law" three times. In verse 3, "the law" is clearly the law of Moses; in verse 2 "the law of sin and death" expands "the law of sin that dwells in my members" in 7:23. But what is "the law of the Spirit of life"? In 7:6 Paul had *contrasted* the law, "the old written code" (lit., the letter), and the new life of the Spirit. Is, then, "the law of the Spirit of life" a deliberate oxymoron, as Fitzmyer (1993) says?

Or does "law" here mean something like principle or rule (so, e.g., Talbert 2003)? Paul might have written simply, "The Spirit has freed you from the law of sin and death"; but if that is what he meant to convey, why did he complicate a clear idea with "the law of the Spirit of life in Christ Jesus"? Is he engaged in a "word play, pure and simple" (so Fee 1994, 522)?

None of the above, if Dunn (1988, 1:416-17), Meyer (1990, 62-84 and commentary 1058), Bayes (2000, 102), and Martyn (2003, 579-85) are right, for they argue that "the law of the Spirit of life" is the law of Moses, now freed from being sin's agent, as described in 7:23-25. On this reading, Paul thought that Christ liberated the law from its subservience to sin and brought it under the aegis of the Spirit so that it could then liberate persons from bondage to its previous role, sin's means of bringing death. It is difficult to be persuaded, however, that Paul would have left such a pivotal understanding unsaid. Since the troublesome phrase appears only here, it may well have been created ad hoc as a deliberate (though not exact) counterpart to "the law of sin and death"—a phrase that summarizes the plight portrayed in 7:7-25, according to which sin used the life-promising law to bring about the opposite, death. From that hopeless situation, the life-giving Spirit brought liberation. To underscore the reversal that this liberation represents, Paul referred to "the *law* of the Spirit of life" just as in 5:19 the effect of Adam's "disobedience" is reversed by Christ's "obedience." (Because vv. 3-4 explain that this liberation occurred through God's act in Christ, we can now say that the ambiguity at the beginning of v. 2 is resolved: "in Christ Jesus the law of the Spirit of life has set you free." This interpretation differs somewhat from Keck 1980, 41-58.) In verses 3-4 Paul explains what "God has done" by referring to three considerations: (a) the situation to be changed: the inability of the law; (b) God's action in Christ that changed it; and (c) the result ("so that . . .").

(a) Remarkably, the law did not weaken the power of the flesh; rather, the power of the flesh weakened the law! Paul is not criticizing the law for being innately weak or incompetent. Rather, he explains why the law could neither overcome sin, whose power has just been portrayed, nor deliver the promised life (7:10): Its capacity was vitiated by the flesh through which sin enslaved the self (7:23). As a result, the law can command and prohibit, but the self cannot do what is commanded and prohibited because the law "is unable to enable" (so Donaldson 1997, 135), or as verse 8 will say, those who live in the domain of flesh "cannot please God." Liberating the self so that it can do what it intends requires breaking sin's power. That, Paul claims, is exactly what God has done: "condemned sin in the flesh," precisely where it resides and reigns. Since God is the actor, "condemned" implies that the sentence was carried out, not merely pronounced.

(b) God's effective action occurred by means of the Christ-event, formulated in language that fits the context: "by sending his own Son in the likeness of sinful flesh, and to deal with sin" (NRSV; NIV: "by sending his own Son in the likeness of sinful man to be a sin offering"). This formulation contains three elements that invite attention. *First,* "sending [lit., having sent, *pempsas*] his own Son" paraphrases Gal 4:4, "God sent out [*exapesteilen*] his Son" (AT, viz., from heaven, not from Nazareth). This is Paul's way of referring to the incarnation of the pre-existent Son of God. (Actually, it was later Christian theologians who coined the word "incarnation" [lit., enfleshment] to name the action stated in John 1:14, the Word "became flesh." In John, Jesus often refers to his incarnation as being "sent" from God; see, e.g., John 3:17, 34; 5:36-38; 8:28-29; 12:44-45.) Because this "sending," for Paul as well as for John, assumes the Son's pre-existence, the meaning differs totally from statements about God "sending" persons like John the Baptist (see John 1:6). By inserting "his own," Paul accents God's involvement (see 5:8).

Second, "in the likeness of sinful flesh" also is Paul's adaptation for this context of what he had written in Gal 4:4—that God's Son "was born of woman, born under the law, in order to redeem those under the law" (AT)—for both passages claim that God's Son identified with the human condition in order to overcome it. In Rom 8:3, Paul inserts *in the likeness (en homoiōmati) of sinful flesh* in order to avoid saying that "God sent his own Son *in* sinful flesh," for that would have implied that the humanized Son had become another instance of the condition, so identified with it as to be indistinguishable from it. The word *homoiōma* means likeness or similarity, not sameness or identicality. (Paul had used it before in 5:14; 6:5; the Christ hymn quoted in Phil 2:5-11 used it as well [v. 7].) What Paul has in view is the pre-existent Son's solidarity with the human condition as the result of being sent by God to identify with it; Paul had made the same point in 2 Cor 5:21: "For our sake, he [God] made him [Christ] to be sin who knew no sin, so that in him we might become the righteousness of God." According to the logic of salvation based on incarnation, God's Son must become like us in order to change us, while at the same time not becoming just another one of us. This combination of similarity and difference underlies the comparison between Adam and Christ in 5:12-21. Later Christian theology would account for this combination of identification and difference by the doctrine of the two "natures" of Christ (truly divine, truly human).

Third, when Paul wrote that God sent his own Son *peri hamartias,* he probably meant either "for sin" or "as a sin offering" (NIV) rather than "to deal with sin," which NRSV and REB prefer. Since *to peri hamartias* (LXX Lev 14:19) clearly means "the sin offering," without the article *to* Paul's phrase probably means "as a sin offering," as often in the LXX (e.g., Lev 5:8; 14:31; Ps 39:6). This language of sacrifice accords with that of 3:25, where Paul refers to Christ as the one whom God "put forward as a sacrifice of atonement" *(hilastērion),* as well as with 5:9, where he says, "we have been justified by his blood." The accent here, however, is not on the atoning sacrifice of Christ's death but on how God used the Christ-event (focused on incarnation and death)— namely, to condemn sin in the flesh, precisely where it resides and operates. As a result, now it is sin that is condemned, not "those in Christ Jesus." Paul need not explain *how* this condemnation occurred, for in this context, what matters is *that* it occurred, because Paul's eye is on its purpose or result.

(c) That purpose or result is stated in verse 4, "so that the just requirement *[dikaiōma]* of the law might be fulfilled in us, who walk [= live] not according to the flesh but according to the Spirit." Pivotal here is the meaning of the *dikaiōma* of the law.

Had Paul used the plural *dikaiōma* as in 2:26, he would have said that the specific ordinances or commandments are to be fulfilled; the singular noun, however, refers to what the law rightly requires, namely, conformity to God's will and character, what the law *as such* is all about (though Ziesler [1989, 207] thinks it refers to the tenth commandment; see 7:7-10). The text does not speak of our *doing* the *dikaiōma*, but of its being "fulfilled" *(plērōthē)* in us; using the passive voice implies that God is the doer who actualizes the right requirement of the law *in* us (had Paul meant by us he probably would have written *dia hēmōn*). God fulfills the *dikaiōma in us* because the enabling Spirit resides in us (to be explained in what follows), and so enables us to live "according to the Spirit." To live "according to" something is to respond appropriately to its character. Here, too, it is clear that for Paul one always lives "according to," in accord with, a reality other than the self, because the self is never truly autonomous. In other words, as a result of God's condemning sin in the flesh, sin the resident preventer is replaced by the Spirit, the new resident enabler. Verses 5-11 will explain this new situation; verses 12-17 will point out its implications.

Understanding both units is aided by noting three considerations. *First*, Paul's understanding of the Spirit is stated in virtually interchangeable expressions. When writing of the *relation* of the Spirit to the believer, he can say:

v. 9   you are "in the Spirit" *(en pneumati)*
        the Spirit of God "dwells in you" *(oikei en hymin)*
        one "has the Spirit of Christ" *(pneuma Christou echei)*
v. 10   Christ is "in you" *(en hymin)*
v. 11   the Spirit of the Resurrecter "dwells in you" *(oikei en hymin)*
        his "indwelling Spirit in you" *(enoikountos autou pneumatos en hymin)*

When he speaks of the *effects* of the Spirit, he can say:

v. 4   "walk according to the Spirit" *(peripatousin kata pneuma)*
v. 5   "exist [NRSV: "live"] according to the Spirit" *(ontes kata pneuma)*
v. 14   "led by the Spirit of God" *(pneumati theou agontai)*

Evidently, the Spirit = the Spirit of God = the Spirit of Christ because the Spirit is both the mode and the means by which the resurrected Son exercises power in the believers who have been baptized "into Christ" (6:3). Even though Paul mentions God, Christ, and Spirit, the variety of expressions indicates that his thought is not really trinitarian (so also Fee 1994, 538), though his language here, as in 2 Cor 13:13, will lead to the later formulation of the doctrine of the Triune God.

Second, the contrasts between the Spirit and the flesh, which pervade both units, are to be understood as the tensions between two powers, *not* between two conflicting components of the self. Paul is not talking about the conflict between incompatible essences or natures *of* (or constituting) the self, but of the conflict between two powers *for* the self, for the Spirit is the power of the New Age. To read the text in terms of Greek body-spirit dualism is to misunderstand Paul completely.

Third, for Paul, the Spirit is the unmediated presence of God as power, here focused on the power that enables the believer to live in accord with God's will. Since Paul has been discussing sin's power to thwart the self's intent to obey the law, it is understandable that here the accent falls on the moral import of the Spirit's presence, and that not a word is said about the Spirit's role in generating intense experiences like tongue-speaking, which Paul dealt with in 1 Cor 10–12 (even though he was writing Romans in the vicinity of Corinth).

The explanation of the new situation created by the presence of the Spirit (vv. 5-11) has two parts: in verses 5-8, Paul describes the radical contrast between life controlled by the flesh and life under the aegis of the Spirit; in verses 9-11, he applies this contrast to the readers ("But you . . ."). Thus the former lays the groundwork for the latter.

Noticeably missing from the description in verses 5-8 is any reference to the conflict *within* the self (between the Spirit residing in the believer and the sin in the body's "members," 7:22-25) because Paul is contrasting two kinds of persons—those who exist "according to the flesh" and those who exist "according to the Spirit" (so also Fee 1994, 540). As in 6:2, 22, 24—and especially in 7:4-6—so also here the contrast is stark and absolute because the two modes of life are mutually exclusive; that is, Paul elaborates, now in terms of Spirit and flesh, the contrast between Adam and Christ that inaugurated the whole discussion. To do so, Paul characterizes both kinds of persons by first using the verb *phronein* (to set the mind) in verse 5, then the noun *phronēma* (mindset) in both verse 6 and verse 7. Setting the mind is more than cogitation; it includes also an avowed stance, a life-shaping attitude (as in Phil 2:5, "Let the same mind *[phroneite]* be in you that was in Christ Jesus"); *phronēma* is the mentality that determines what one lives by; it shapes one's existence. That, presumably, is why Paul uses the participle *ontes* (from the verb "to be") in both verse 5 (NRSV: "live") and verse 8 (NRSV: "are"). In other words, the symptom of existing according to the flesh is setting the mind on "the things of the flesh," just as the symptom of its opposite is setting the mind on "the things of the Spirit." As already noted, "flesh" *(sarx)* is not simply the phenomenal, the empirical, the physical as such, but the phenomenal functioning as inordinate power that determines the self. It is therefore as misleading to translate "according to the flesh" as "sinful *nature*" (NIV) as it is to render it as "live on the *level* of the old nature" (REB), for Paul is contrasting neither "natures" nor "levels" but sovereignties that govern one's life.

Since verse 5 begins with "for," what it says accounts for what is said in verse 4—namely, the *dikaiōma* of the law is fulfilled in those who live according to the Spirit because they set their minds on the things of the Spirit, which both accord with the spiritual law (7:14) and lead to life and peace (v. 6); the mindset of the flesh, on the other hand, leads to death or amounts to death (lit., "is death"). Why? Because, verse 7 explains, the mindset determined by flesh is "hostile" (NRSV, NIV) or marked by "enmity" (REB) to God (see 5:10). Why is this the case? Because "it does not submit to God's law" (implying that the mindset of the Spirit does submit to it). Why not? Because, by definition, "it cannot." Indeed, verse 8 continues, "those who are [*ontes*, exist] in the flesh cannot please God" (i.e., by fulfilling the *dikaiōma* of the law). To be "in the flesh" does *not* mean simply to live in the physical body, but to live in the domain of flesh, to live in the field of its power, to live "under its control" (REB). NIV introduces the word "sinful" ("the mind of sinful man," "the sinful mind," and "those controlled by the sinful nature"); the text, however, does not mention sin at all.

Verses 9-11 begin with a forthright assertion, "But *you* are not in the flesh but in the Spirit, since the Spirit of God dwells in you" (AT; because of rhetorical considerations, "in the Spirit" is coined to contrast with "in the flesh," v. 8). The accent falls on God's Spirit residing *(oikei)* in the believers, the opposite of sin's residing in the self (7:20). The Spirit that resides *in* the self puts the self *into* an environment where the self is subject to a new power. Paul supports this by stating the opposite: "Anyone who does not have the Spirit of Christ does not belong to him"; stated positively, by possessing the Spirit of Christ, one becomes the possession of Christ. Here, to be "in the Spirit" does not refer to an exceptional, ecstatic state (as in Rev 1:10, where it is the state in which the seer receives special revelation); in our passage, it refers to the normal state of the believer. That is, one is Christ's possession, but not by being mantically "possessed."

Behind the succinct verse 9 is what Paul had written in 1 Cor 6:19-20: "Or do you not know that your body is a temple of the Holy Spirit within you, which [Spirit] you have from God, and that you are not your own? For you were bought with a price [i.e., you now belong to Christ]; therefore glorify God in your body." Also in Rom 8:10-11 Paul goes on to point out the significance of the Spirit's residence for the body, first linking the Spirit with present righteousness (comparable to "glorify God in your body"), then linking it (v. 11) to future resurrection, thereby explaining the contrast with the death that results from living according to the flesh (vv. 5-6).

Verse 10 is formulated with rhetorical balance:

But if Christ is in you
the body   is dead   on account of sin *(dia hamartian)* but
the Spirit is life   on account of righteousness *(dia dikaiosynēn)*

The connection between sin and death having been stated variously since 6:1, here the accent falls on the last line, the consequence of

Christ's being "in you." ("But if" does not mean "Should it turn out that . . ."; it signals rather a mode of reasoning: If A is true [as it surely is], then B follows.) The connection between Christ "in you" and "the Spirit of life," however, is not immediately self-evident. For one thing, although *pneuma* can refer to the human spirit or to the divine Spirit (as in NRSV), it is unlikely that Paul meant to say, "your spirit is alive because of righteousness" (NIV), for that would imply that Christ's Spirit vivifies the human spirit; but verse 11 links the *pneuma* with the vivification of the mortal body.

Also problematic is the paraphrase in REB: "The Spirit is your life because you have been justified." Not only does this replace Paul's noun *dikaiosynē* with a passive verb in the past tense, but it also makes the Spirit's role dependent on action in the past, justification. (Does REB try to express the doctrine that sanctification follows justification?) Here the meaning of the preposition *dia* is crucial. *Dia* followed by a noun in the accusative case, as here, means "on account of," either as a prior cause or as the intended result ("for the sake of"). The appearance of *dia hamartian* ("on account of sin") and *dia dikaiosynēn* ("on account of righteousness/rectitude") in parallel lines (see above) does not require *dia* to have the identical meaning in both lines, as 4:25 shows. There a rather similar idea is expressed in exactly the same way: Christ was handed over on account of *(dia)* our trespasses, and raised on account of *(dia)* our rectification. In both passages, the first *dia* phrase points to the past, while the second points to the future. (Ancient rhetoricians would have called this a *traductio*, "a play on different meanings of the same word"; so Rowe 2001, 132.) So it is likely that 8:10 means that the Spirit is life (i.e., life-giving) for the sake of rectitude—that is, the Spirit's presence now makes righteousness possible, the rectitude that results from the *dikaiōma* (right requirement) of the law being fulfilled (v. 4). That the Spirit effects rectitude accords with Gal 5:22-23, which lists the moral "fruit of the Spirit."

In verse 11, the "if . . ." clause marks a mode of reasoning, exactly as in verse 10. Paul might have written simply, "the Spirit of God will give life," and so forth. He used the longer phrase, however, in order to express more clearly that the Spirit links the resurrection of Jesus and the resurrection of the believer. But here too, the same preposition *dia* is pivotal for what Paul means. Many manuscripts have *dia* + accusative ("on account of his indwelling Spirit"), while others have *dia* + genitive ("through his indwelling Spirit"). Although NRSV, NIV, REB, and NASB use the latter reading, Fee (1994, 552-53) notes that nowhere else does Paul speak of the Spirit as God's *means* of resurrection, and that the subject matter here is not agency anyway but "certainty about the future." This is on target. In short, the inner residence of the Spirit is the basis on which Paul assures the readers that they too will be resurrected, for the resident Spirit is the Spirit of the One who resurrected Jesus. Paul no more says *how* God will vivify the mortal bodies than he says how God resurrected Jesus.

Verses 12-17 continue the discussion of the Spirit by combining quite different ideas. Verse 12 introduces an exhortation based on living "according to" flesh or Spirit, but does not complete the thought (indicated by the dash at the end of v. 12 in NRSV); verse 13 not only shifts from "we" to "you" (plural) but also issues a warning and a promise; verses 14-15 introduce a wholly new idea (sons of God), which in verses 16-17 segues into the theme of solidarity with Christ, using the same sort of language found in 6:4-8. What holds these diverse ideas together is the Spirit.

Had Paul completed the thought in verse 12, he would have gone on to say, "but we are obligated to live according to the Spirit" (AT; perhaps he assumed that the readers would supply the absent clause). Instead, in verse 13 he warrants the obligation with a warning (living according to the flesh leads to death) and a conditional promise: "If by the Spirit you put to death the deeds [*praxeis*, practices] of the body, you will live." Here "by the Spirit" does not imply that the believer uses the Spirit, as if it were a power at his disposal; rather, the phrase refers to the Spirit's enabling power without which one could not "put to death" the deeds of the body—namely, those that result from the operation of the "other law" in the body's "members." That is, the Spirit enables the captured prisoner of war (see 7:23) to terminate the captor's power that is manifest when one lives according to the flesh. But why does Paul speak of putting to death the "deeds of the body" and not the "deeds of the flesh"? Because only the body does deeds; as a domain, "flesh" does not act. (The Vulgate, however, like a few Greek manuscripts, reads, "If then by the Spirit you mortify the deeds of the flesh" [si autem spiritu facta carnis mortificatis].) The life that is promised, like the death that is threatened, refers to one's ultimate destiny. Remarkably, this life is conditional: if you put the (sinful) practices of the body to death, not on your own but "by the Spirit"—that is, if you allow the Spirit to enable you.

Verse 14 characterizes those who are "led by the Spirit of God" as "the sons of God." Paul's use of "children of God" in verse 16 shows that the masculine gender of huioi (sons) is irrelevant. Why, then, does Paul not say "children of God" (so NRSV) in verse 14 as well? Because verse 14 leads up to verse 15, where Paul contrasts the "spirit of slavery" with the "spirit of adoption," thereby creating an untranslatable wordplay between "sons" (huioi) and "adoption" (huiothesia, lit., "son-effecting," an action that makes one a son legally). This imagery is drawn from the well-established practice, provided for by Roman law but not by Jewish law (see Lyall 1969, 459-61), by which one formally and officially designated someone other than physical offspring to be the "son," the heir-designate (for a concise discussion of the practice and procedures, see Nicholas 1979, 76-80). So it is altogether appropriate that the passage ends by pointing out that God's (adopted) children are God's heirs (klēronomoi), indeed "joint heirs [sygklēronomoi] with Christ" (v. 17). The imagery fits Paul's theology because adoption confers on the "son" a new status to which he has no right but which he receives solely because of the father's decision—theologically, adoption is an act of grace.

Understanding the imagery clarifies the flow of thought, whose compact expression needs to be unpacked. First, the internal residence of the Spirit obligates one to live in accord with the Spirit, not the flesh (v. 12), and this entails putting to death the deeds of the body that are contrary to God's will. Those who do so will have true life (v. 13). Second, verses 14-17 state why the basis of this promise too is the Spirit: The resident Spirit is the Spirit of God, God present as effective power, controlling ("leading") the way one lives—that is, it generates obedience. *Third,* assuming that the son obeys the father, "those who are led by God's Spirit are God's sons" (v. 14, AT). Why is that the case? Because the Spirit that is received is the son-making Spirit ("the Spirit of *huiothesia,* adoption"). *Fourth,* the Spirit is evidence for that son status because calling God "Abba" implies that one is a child. Moreover, when the Spirit prompts that exclamation, it joins our human spirit in attesting that we are God's children (v. 16). One might *think* of God as Father, but apart from the Spirit, Paul implies, addressing God this way would be *hybris.* Because it is God's Spirit that prompts one to call God "Father," there can be no doubt that one is a child of God. *Fifth,* because the child is the heir, the adopted children of God are God's heirs—they will receive what is now rightfully theirs. *Sixth,* those who are God's heirs because they have been adopted sons are now joint heirs with Christ, the Son of God. *Seventh,* to be Christ's joint heirs entails suffering jointly *(sympaschomen)* in order to be glorified with him as well—that is, share his resurrected state (v. 17). Whereas 6:6-7 emphasized dying with Christ in the rite of baptism, here Paul speaks of suffering with him as the current form of solidarity that leads to future solidarity in glorification, perhaps in order to point to the next unit, which speaks more fully of the suffering that characterizes the "not yet" of salvation.

Romans 8:14-17 is similar to Gal 4:5-7. There too, Paul, having said that God sent his Son so that we might receive *huiothesia,* goes on to say, "God sent the Spirit of his Son into our hearts, crying, 'Abba!' 'Father!' So you are no longer a slave but a son, and if a son, also an heir, through God" (AT; some manuscripts read "heir of God, through Christ"). Important in both passages is the word "cry" *(krazō,* cry out, shout, shriek). Because this cry is Spirit-generated, the text implies that the community ("we cry") shouts "Abba!" in an emotionally intense worship setting. The use of the Aramaic word *Abba* by Greek-speaking Christians (for whom the word is translated) in both letters shows that this way of addressing God was early, significant, and distinctive of the Christian community. Whether this use of the word was linked to Jesus' own use in Gethsemane (Mark 14:36) is not clear (see

Wenham 1995, 275-80). Since the shout or exclamation is prompted by the Spirit, it is improbable that Paul had in mind Luke's form of the Lord's Prayer, which begins simply, "Father" (Luke 11:2), though Cranfield (1975, 1:400) thinks it "highly likely" that he did.

◊ ◊ ◊ ◊

All references to "flesh" in Romans (except 13:14) that are significant for Paul's theological anthropology appear between 7:5 and 8:13 (in 1:3; 4:1; 9:5, 8 the term refers to physical descent); moreover, only in chapter 8 is flesh contrasted with the Spirit (as it is frequently in Galatians; see Gal 3:2-3; 4:29; 5:15-26; 6:7-8). When one assembles the seventeen references to flesh in Rom 7:5–8:13, it soon becomes evident that while Paul's perspective is consistently negative, the word does not always refer to exactly the same phenomenon; the meaning of each use depends on the phrase in which it appears.

7:5	we were *(ēmen)* in the flesh
14	I am *(eimi)* fleshly
18	the good does not reside in my flesh
25	with my flesh I am a slave
8:3	the law was weakened through the flesh
	the Son was sent in the likeness of sinful flesh
	God condemned sin in the flesh
4	walk according to the flesh
5	live (exist, *ontes*) according to the flesh
	set minds on the things of the flesh
6	the mindset of the flesh is death
7	the mindset of the flesh is enmity toward God
8	those who live (exist, *ontes*) in the flesh
9	you are *(este)* not in the flesh
12	not obligated to the flesh
	not obligated to live according to the flesh
13	live according to the flesh

Since 7:5, 14; 8:5, 8, 9 use some form of the verb "to be," the meaning of all those expressions is virtually identical: They refer to a state or mode of one's existence. This mode is actualized by living or walking "according to the flesh" (8:4, 12, 13).

Noteworthy is the connection between being in the flesh and the mindset of the flesh (mentioned three times in vv. 5-7). To exist according to the flesh is to set the mind on the things of the flesh. This mindset *is already* death (just as the mindset of the Spirit *is* life and peace now, not just after death). The mindset of the flesh is enmity toward God, rebellion against God's law. Together these formulations express Paul's view of the human plight as a *condition* that must be replaced, and that *is* replaced by solidarity with God's own Son, through whose death God condemned sin in the flesh, and by the residence of God's Spirit, whose work will be completed by the resurrection of the body. If "flesh" was the logo that identified prebaptismal existence, Spirit is the logo that identifies the present in which the "already" and the "not yet" of salvation are inseparable. In the next unit Paul will say what that inseparability looks like.

Expecting Redemption (8:18-30): In Romans, the concluding phrase of one unit frequently is the starting point for what will be discussed next (e.g., 4:25–5:1; 6:14-15; 7:12-13; 8:8-9). So here the last line of verse 17 (". . . that we may also be glorified with him") sets up the discussion in verses 18-30, which begins by linking present "sufferings" with future glorification, and ends with glorification (thus framing the unit with an *inclusio*); the unit expresses once again the "not yet" of redemption in light of its "already." Paul first puts suffering in a context that includes the plight of creation from Eden to the Eschaton (vv. 18-25), then speaks of the role of the Spirit during the "not yet" (vv. 26-27) before warranting confidence in God's providence by recalling God's sovereign acts in redemption (vv. 28-30).

Verse 18 functions as a topic sentence for verses 18-25; at the same time, its contrast between present suffering and future glory echoes verse 17 in which the same sequence is emphasized. What are "the sufferings of the present time" *(tou nun kairou)*? Are they simply "our [Christian] present sufferings" (NIV, similarly REB)? Does the "present time" (used also in 3:26) refer to the time between Christ's death and the Eschaton (so Cranfield 1975 and Fitzmyer 1993)? In light of what follows, it is more likely that the phrase is a surrogate for what still remains of "the present age."

If so, then the whole passage is to be understood in light of the Jewish image of the two successive ages, This Age and The Age to Come. Given the utter difference between the two ages, it is understandable that Paul considers the sufferings of this age "not worth comparing with the glory about to be revealed to us" (*eis hēmas*; NIV: "in us"; REB: "for us"). Since this "glory" refers to "being glorified with Christ" in verse 17, the revealing is much more than a disclosure; it is a transforming event, as in Phil 3:21, where Paul writes of expecting Christ who "will transform our humble bodies [NRSV alt.] that they may be conformed to his glorious body." That this revelation of glory is "about to" occur reflects Paul's conviction that the "not yet" will soon end, though here he does not explicitly mention the parousia, the coming of Christ; nor does he do so in the whole letter.

That "the present time" refers to what remains of "this age" is confirmed by verses 19-23, in which Paul includes the whole creation in the expected transformation. In these few sentences Paul implies more than he actually says; therefore, understanding what is explicit requires attending also to what is implicit: Humans are an integral part of creation, so much so that similar verbs are used of both: Creation and believers "wait" (vv. 19, 23, 25), and both creation and believers "groan" (v. 23). It is not surprising, then, that here creation is "personified." Moreover, the groaning of creation reflects the apocalyptic appropriation of Gen 3, according to which Adam and Eve were banished from Eden "to work the ground from which he had been taken" (Gen 3:23, NIV)—ground that God had just cursed. In short, the human condition is inseparable from that of creation. It is just this totalizing of the consequences of Adam that apocalyptic thought expressed by "This Age" and that Paul called "the present evil age" in Gal 1:4. Not to be overlooked, however, is that whereas Gal 1:4 speaks of rescue from "the present evil age," Rom 8:19-25 speaks of creation's redemption, liberation, and participation in the "freedom of the glory of the children of God" (v. 21).

But first Paul speaks of creation's eager waiting "with longing expectation for the revealing of the children of God" (v. 19, AT) because what it yearns for is the same as what believers expect.

This remarkable statement so strongly asserts the inseparability of humans from the rest of creation that Paul could easily have had creation ask what the enslaved self asks in 7:24: "Who will rescue me from this body of death?" Indeed, creation's yearning for liberation "from its bondage to decay" (v. 21) is so great that Paul speaks of it as "groaning in labor pains" (v. 22). This "bondage to decay" is enslavement to death (REB: "the shackles of mortality"), for decay (*phthora* also means corruption, dissolution) is the symptom of death. The assumption that what befell Adam also befell creation, namely, death, goes beyond Gen 3:17-19, where the curse means that only through hard labor will the earth now provide sustenance for Adam and Eve. Paul had already alerted the readers to this view: Through one man, Adam, "sin entered the *kosmos* and through sin, death" (5:12, AT).

In verse 20 Paul interprets God's cursing the ground (LXX: *gē*, earth): "creation was subjected to futility" *(mataiotēti;* NIV and REB: "frustration"); that is, it could no longer be or become what it was intended to be; it could no longer actualize its "nature" for it could not evade or escape the inevitability of its decay. The one who "subjected" creation was neither Adam nor Satan, as has been suggested, but God, who did so "in hope"—that is, with an eye to its eventual liberation and participation in the same future that God's children will enjoy (v. 21). Verse 22 implies that creation's current condition (futility, impermanence, incompleteness) is not "natural" but by definition a self-contradiction that requires a correction, as does the contradiction of the self in 7:25. Although Paul does not actually point this out, he implies that this correction is nothing other than God's rectitude rectifying creation.

Especially important is verse 23. To begin with, here Paul interprets the Spirit as "first fruits" *(aparchē* of the Spirit is not the Spirit's first fruits, for the genitive here is not possessive but epexegetical [explanatory]: It interprets first fruits *as* the Spirit). "First fruits" is a metaphor derived from the requirement that Israelite farmers offer the first of the harvest to God (actually to the priests for their livelihood; Num 5:9; 18:8-19), thereby acknowledging symbolically that the whole harvest, like the land itself, really belonged to God (see Deut 26:1-11). Paul had used "first fruits" imagery before; when he insisted that Christ's resurrection is inseparable from the resurrection of all who died "in Christ," he called *Christ* "the first fruits of the resurrection" (1 Cor 15:20-23). Moreover, since by definition "first fruits" implies that the rest of the harvest, though perhaps not yet fully ripe, is sure to follow, Paul can also say, "all will be made alive in Christ. But each in his own order: Christ the first fruits, *then* at his coming those who belong to Christ." In short, in 1 Cor 15 Paul exploits "first fruits" to support two ideas at the same time: As "first fruits," the singular resurrection of Jesus anticipates in time the resurrection of all the dead in Christ that will follow, and thereby guarantees it.

In Rom 8:22-23 Paul reasons in the same way, this time by applying the metaphor "first fruits" to the Spirit. The anticipatory, forward-looking aspect is expressed in saying that those who "have the Spirit" (a phrase used in v. 9) "expect adoption" (not just "wait for," NRSV), while the solidarity aspect is implied when Paul says that "we ourselves, who have the first fruits of the Spirit," groan along with the whole creation (v. 22). Having the Spirit does not isolate the believer from the unredeemed creation; rather, it reinforces the believer's solidarity *with* the creation. Why? Because calling the Spirit "first fruits" implies that what the Spirit effects now is the beginning, the foretaste, the preview, of the redemption yet to come. In 2 Cor 1:22 Paul had spoken of the Spirit as salvation's *arrabōn*, a pledge, like the earnest money is evidence that the buyer of real estate will complete the sale. (NRSV's "first installment" wrongly implies salvation will be paid off in stages; better is NRSV's "guarantee" in 2 Cor 5:5; REB uses "pledge" in both passages.) In other words, for Paul the presence of the Spirit combines "the already" and "the not yet." One would not distort Paul's point here by saying that what the Spirit is for the Christian, the Christian is for all creation—foretaste and pledge of what is to come.

What is to come Paul calls "the redemption of our bodies" (v. 23)—not release *from* the body but the transformation *of* the body by resurrection. This is the only time he puts it this way, but it is not the first time that he thought this way. In 1 Cor 6:13, he probably shocked those who thought that salvation was for the soul only when he wrote, "the body is . . . for the Lord, and the Lord for the body," because this is exactly what resurrection implies. Over against the old slogan (later emphasized by Gnostics), *sōma-sēma* ("the body is a tomb"), Paul went on to say that the body is the Spirit's temple (1 Cor 6:19). According to the last line of Rom 8:23, "the redemption of the body" is the adopted sonship that believers wait for. But has not Paul said that believers have already received the "Spirit of adoption"? Are they not already God's children by the adoptive presence of the Spirit (8:15)? Does verse 23 contradict what Paul had said only a few lines before? Not really—precisely because the Spirit of adoption/son-making *(huiothesia)* is itself the inauguration, not the completion, of the new status; so the sequence of benefits ends with future glorification. "Putting to death" the "deeds of the body" by the Spirit (v. 13) is a sign that the inauguration has occurred, but the complete "redemption of the body" is yet to come. In short, the tension between verses 15-16 and verse 23 is nothing other than the tension between "the already" and "the not yet."

Understandably, then, Paul writes next about hope, not to define or describe it, but rather to explain why the redemption of the body is something "we wait for with patience" (vv. 24-25). What he says first, however, is not as clear as it might be *(tē gar elpidi esōthēmen)*, as the differing translations show:

NRSV, NASB	"for *in* hope we were saved"
NIV	"for *in this* hope we were saved"
REB	"It was *with this* hope that we were saved"
NJB	"*In hope* we already have salvation"
Moffatt	"We were saved, *with this hope* ahead"
CEV	"And *this hope* is what saves us"

The last is off the mark, for not only does it change the tense of the verb, but it also makes Paul assert what he would never say: that hope is the *means* of salvation. Since Paul uses the noun *elpis* rather than the verb, he evidently has in view what is hoped for, not the hoping itself; this becomes evident in what follows: "Hope that is seen is not hope." That is, here "hope" is the future that is not manifest. So the line could well be rendered, "we have been saved for hope" (for what is hoped for, the object of our hoping). Its not being seen does not count against its reality but for it, because the age to come is not yet here. Chapters 12–15 will show that patient waiting does not imply moral idleness but a life in which the anticipated is made real—precisely as anticipation.

Here (in vv. 26-27), however, Paul addresses one implication of what he had written about living during the "not yet," vulnerable to "the sufferings of the present time" while hoping and waiting patiently for the redemption not manifest—namely, that this existence has not yet fully overcome the "weakness" that marks the human condition as such (see 5:6). But in response, he does not say that one will outgrow this "weakness," that with the Spirit's help and self-discipline one will become an ever "stronger" Christian. Instead, he writes of another role of the Spirit: It "helps" (synantilambanetai, lit., "come to the aid of," as in Luke 10:40). Since Paul could just as easily have written antilambanetai, which means virtually the same (as in Acts 20:35), beginning the same word with the prefix syn- links this word to the four syn-words in verses 16-17 (and in 6:5-8). Consequently, the "likewise" in verse 26 indicates that the Spirit's "coming to help" is comparable to the Spirit's "bearing witness with our spirit [v. 16] that we are children of God" (so also Fee 1994, 576). According to NRSV and NIV, the Spirit "helps us in our weakness," but the text says that the recipient of the help is "our weakness." Paul is not talking about "weakness" as the circumstance in which the Spirit helps us; his point, rather, is that the weakness itself is met by the power of the Spirit. What follows, introduced by "for," explains what Paul means by this help for our weakness. Since verse 26 resumes the "co-witness" of verse 16, which followed the reference to crying "Abba" in verse 15, it is understandable that Paul now talks about the Spirit's help for our weakness in prayer.

Before explaining the help, Paul identifies the weakness: "We do not know *what* we ought to pray for" (NIV); the text does *not* say, "we do not know *how* to pray as we ought" (NRSV and REB). The Spirit does not help one pray better, more effectively. Rather, its help consists in speaking on behalf of ("intercedes") those who do not know what to pray for. How does it do this? "With groans" ("sighs" [NRSV] is too weak), repeating the word used of creation in verse 22 and of believers in verse 23. The "groans" with which the Spirit speaks on our behalf are *alalētois* (lit., "not spoken"; REB: "inarticulate"). Are the groans unspoken because they are unspeakable (NRSV: "too deep for words"), or because they are a form of "tongue-speaking"—uttered sounds that are not spoken words (Fee [1994, 579-85] discusses various possibilities)? Given the recent increase in "Pentecostalism," it is understandable that much attention has been focused on these "unspoken groans"; the focus of the passage itself, however, is in verse 27, which explains why the Spirit's interceding is the effective help for believers who do not know what they ought to pray.

The explanation assumes that the Spirit resides in the self (v. 9). So God "who searches the heart knows the mindset [*phronēma*, as in v. 6] of the Spirit" (AT), because, presumably, the Spirit resides in the heart. Moreover, the Spirit "intercedes," speaks to God on behalf of those who do not know what to pray, and does so in accord with God *(kata theon)*, that is, in keeping with God's will. The Spirit does not need to persuade God on our behalf (as if it were a lobbyist) because the Spirit speaks in accord with God. In other words, Paul apparently says that the Spirit's intercession transforms our ignorant praying into what is in keeping with God's will. When one compares what is said here about the Spirit with 1 Cor 2:9-16, a significant difference becomes evident: Whereas in the present passage the Spirit communicates *to God* on our behalf, there the Spirit communicates *to us*, since the Spirit is the only one that knows "the things of God." In both passages, the Spirit's role in communication overcomes human limitations, whether by revealing the otherwise unknowable things of God to us or by speaking to God on our behalf.

The note of assurance, in the face of sufferings while waiting for redemption, that is struck in verses 26-27 becomes a full chord in verses 28-30, which consist of two sentences, the second (vv. 29-30) explaining the first. The reference to "his Son" in verse 29 clearly implies that the subject of the verbs in this complex sentence is God. But in verse 28 the subject of the verb *synergei* (work together) is not stated and so must be inferred. There are three possibilities: (a) NRSV's preferred translation: "all things"; (b) NRSV's alternative rendering, "God" (preferred by NIV); or (c) the Spirit (REB and Fee 1994, 589-90). Of these, "all things" is the least probable (though preferred by Moo [1996] and defended by Cranfield [1975]); "the Spirit" is possible (because the Spirit has been the major theme in chap. 8); but it is preferable to regard "God" as the subject of all the verbs in this passage, as a number of important manuscripts actually say.

Although "we do not know what we ought to pray for" (v. 26), we do know that "for those who love God, God works all things together for good" (v. 28). Paul now characterizes "those who love God" as "called [*klētois*, see 1:1, 6-7] according to his purpose." Verse 29 then explains what being "called" by God entails: God "foreknew" *(proegnō)* them and "predestined" *(proōrisen)* them "to be conformed to the image of his Son," the intended result of which is Christ as "the firstborn among many brothers" (NRSV: "within a large family"). This compact explanation itself needs explanation because each of its elements carries considerable theological freight. Interestingly, Paul does not find it necessary to explain the hefty concepts; he writes as if they were well understood in Rome even before he arrived to explain them.

Paul's letters use the language of predestination, foreknowledge, and election naturally, without advocating, defending, explaining, or systematizing these concepts. His usage must not be confused or conflated with "determinism"—a comprehensive view that everything is already decided and is simply working itself out in time. His view is rooted in the Old Testament (though neither "foreknew" nor "predestined" is used in the LXX), where it is said, in various ways, that God knows what will happen. Although soothsaying and odd events interpreted as portents from the gods were common in antiquity, Yahweh's knowledge of the future was emphasized. For example, Isa 41:21-24 taunts the gods, daring them to "declare to us the things to come," knowing that they cannot do so. In Isa 44:6-8 God's foretelling the future is evidence that there is no other god. In Isa 46:9-10, God declares, "I am God, and there is no one like me, declaring the end from the beginning." Theologically, God's knowing the future is inseparable from God's reliability in making and keeping promises, a motif that pervades Paul's Bible. When Paul writes of God's "foreknowing" and "predestining," he does so from the same perspective as Eph 1:4, "God chose us in Christ before the foundation of the world"—that is, in eternity. That is, the priority of God's action is not earlier *in* time but prior *to* time. To speak of God's *fore*knowing and *pre*destining is to acknowledge, as faith's confession, that one responds to God's initiative, an acknowledgment formulated in theology as "prevenient grace."

What verses 28-29 emphasize, however, is the goal or purpose of God's prior knowledge and decision—that the recipients of God's initiative (the "called") are to be "conformed to the image of his Son, in order that he might be the firstborn among many brothers" (AT; "within a large family" [NRSV] obscures the allusion to "sons of God" in v. 14, and to "joint heirs with Christ" in verse 17). In addition, v. 29 picks up the motif of solidarity with Christ (6:1-11) and alludes as well to the role of Christ, the counterpart of Adam in 5:12-21. Also, the aim expressed in verse 29 (conformity to Christ) is the counterpart to the purpose expressed in 8:3 (the sending of the Son "in the likeness of sinful flesh")— that is, the Son was sent to be like us so that we might be like him, expressed also in saying that Christ is the oldest Son among the sons (the adopted children) of God. The "conformity" in view here is not to be confused with the disciple's being like the master, but is the result of resurrection, as verse 17 implies and the conclusion of verse 30 confirms. ("Conformed" renders *symmorphous,* another *syn-* word; see v. 17, as well as 6:5, 6, 8.)

Verse 30 concludes the discussion begun at verse 18 by using four verbs of God's saving action, each repeated in the next line— a device ancient rhetoricians sometimes called *klimax,* ladder. The verbs are not a summary of everything God has done, for "sanctified" is absent, as is "freed." Rather, the verbs highlight God's saving acts seen from different angles: two are experienced in time ("called" and "justified"), two occur in eternity ("predestined" and "glorified"). "Glorified" alludes to the hope that is not seen, the redemption of the body (vv. 23-24). Logically, the verbs *seem* to be in temporal sequence, though they are not connected by "then" or "next." Actually, they are all used from the perspective of eternity, in which tenses do not exist by definition. From that perspective, all the past tenses used here are equally "improper." By using the past tenses nonetheless, Paul assures the readers that their glorification, while temporally future, has already occurred in the atemporal mind of God.

◊ ◊ ◊ ◊

"Spirit" is mentioned more often than "flesh," and in 8:2-27 more frequently than in all of the rest of Romans. This clustering suggests that *where* Paul writes of the Spirit is significant for *what* he says about it—namely, that he emphasizes the Spirit where he explains how and why Christian existence differs from prebaptismal bondage to sin and death. Thus his words about the Spirit have a twofold *function*: On the one hand, they provide a basic grounding for moral exhortation, while on the other hand, they provide the essential link between what Paul says about God's liberating act in Christ and the individual person. To put it sharply, if the discussion of emancipation from bondage to sin and death did not include references to the Spirit, Paul's exposition of the Christ-event (including one's participation in it by baptism) could/would easily be dismissed as "just talk," as a "nice idea," without validation in experience. But the Spirit is not just a lively attitude; it is essentially the name for *God's power experienced immediately* (without mediation). The presence of the Spirit both confirms what the gospel announces about God's act in Christ and obligates as well as enables the recipient of the Spirit to live in accordance with the new freedom. What Paul says about the Spirit in Romans does not describe the exceptional Christian, the one who has an unusually intense "religious experience"; rather, this is how it is—for *all* who believe the gospel. Thus Paul's portrayal of the Spirit fits the character of Romans— a theology of mission. That is one reason Romans has no interest in the intramural church problems concerning the Spirit that are addressed in 1 Corinthians. "Spiritual gifts," for example, are not mentioned at all.

God's Love Celebrated (8:31-39)

This paragraph concludes the extended argument begun at 1:16. With 1:16-17 it forms an *inclusio*; it also functions like a peroration in a speech, drawing together motifs already discussed and building a crescendo that sweeps the readers along, partly by combining theology and emotional appeal (see Keck 2001, 90-92), and partly by the rhetorical questions, whose answers draw the readers into a remarkable celebration of confidence, whatever may befall them. The first part of this well-known paragraph is dominated by questions (vv. 31-35), to which the responses get longer and longer; the remainder consists of Paul's bold assertions.

The first question is phrased in a way that signals a turn in the discussion by asking, "What, then, shall we say in response to this?" (AT; lit., "to these things"). Paul is not asking the readers to *talk about* them (NRSV), but to appropriate the import of what he has been saying. The next question shows that the first is not as open-ended as it appears, for like a switch in a railyard, it sets the direction in which subsequent questions move: "If God is for us, who is against us?" God's being "for us" (*hyper hēmōn*, acting on our behalf or for our sake) sums up the thrust of the whole argument since 3:21 (God's righteousness revealed apart from the law) and simultaneously contrasts with 1:18–3:20 (God's wrath is revealed against all human wickedness). The question is designed to elicit an unequivocal answer, which Paul assumes: "No one!"

Whereas the expected "No one!" responds to "Who is against us?" the next question (v. 32) amplifies what is entailed in "If God is for us." By first stating what God has already done, Paul again elicits a response that is appropriate. In referring to what God has done, he focuses on the saving significance of Christ's death as God's act: "He who did not withhold his own Son, but gave him up for all of us. . . ." Paul's language alludes to what he had said before: 3:25 (God "put forward" Christ as a *hilastērion*, sacrifice of atonement); 4:25 (God "handed over Christ"); 5:8 (God's love for us made clear by Christ's dying for us "while we were still sinners"); 8:3 (God's "own Son" was given by God). New here is "did not withhold" *(ouk epheisato)*, virtually identical with a phrase used in Gen 22:12, 16, where God commends Abraham for being willing to sacrifice Isaac: "You did not spare your beloved son." Jewish tradition came to attribute atoning significance to that event, called the Aqedah (lit., the "binding" of Isaac). Some scholars have claimed that Paul alludes to the Aqedah (e.g., Cranfield 1975, Dunn 1988), but others have contested it (e.g., Fitzmyer 1993, Moo 1996), largely because the history of the development of the Jewish tradition itself is not without its problems.

In light of the great thing that God has done—he gave his own Son for all of us—Paul now asks, "Will he not with him also give us everything else?" (lit., "all things"). Again Paul recalls what he had said before, for "with him" summarizes the motif of solidarity with Christ in 6:1-11 as well as "co-heirs" in 8:17; so too, "will give" *(charisetai)* echoes the "free gift" *(charisma,* "begracement"), as well as "the free gift in the grace *[charis]* of the one man, Jesus Christ" in 5:15. Thus the question in verse 32 is based on reasoning from the greater to the lesser: If God has already given us his own Son, will he not also give us everything that goes with that gift? Or, if God has not withheld his own Son, he will not withhold the benefits that flow from that act, will he? To such rhetorically phrased questions the answer is self-evident.

Although the inaugural question, Who is against us? has already elicited an unstated No one, in verses 33-36 Paul returns to the theme of opposition by asking three questions. The first two pertain to the coming judgment when God holds court: Who will accuse? and Who will condemn? This time, however, Paul himself answers each question, though it is not clear whether the answer is a statement or a question that expects a "No!" in reply. Although NRSV, NIV, REB, and NASB assume the former, the latter is more likely (so also Barrett 1957 and Fitzmyer 1993). Thus, instead of "Who will bring any charge against God's elect? It is God who justifies," it is preferable to read, "Who will bring any charge . . . ? God who justifies?" Implied answer: "Impossible!" If one reads the passage this way, Paul continues to elicit the right answer from the reader, a more effective strategy than that of the translations which have Paul state the right answer for the benefit of the readers.

The punctuation affects also the content. Thus in verse 33, if we read, "It is God who justifies," the response implies that it does not make any difference who may be the accuser because God is the judge who justifies (in the sense of acquits). If we read, "God who justifies?" the response implies that it is impossible that the One "who justifies the ungodly" (4:5) will accuse those he has chosen.

In verse 34, the question "Who is to condemn?" is followed by a question (or assertion) about Christ "who died, or rather who also is at God's right hand, who also intercedes for us" (AT). "Or rather" is not a correction but a rhetorical device indicating that what is important here is Christ's resurrection, because the next two clauses depend on the resurrection's having occurred. That the resurrected Christ is "at God's right hand" reflects the widespread early Christian appropriation of Ps 110:1 ("the LORD said to my lord, / 'Sit at my right hand / until I make your enemies your footstool'") to interpret Jesus' resurrection as exaltation (see 1 Cor 15:24-27; Acts 2:33-35; 5:31; Eph 1:20; Col 3:1; Heb 1:3, 13; 8:1; 10:12; 12:2). In antiquity "the right hand" was the special place of honor and authority. The Letter to the Hebrews, which interprets Christ as a high priest in the heavenly sanctuary, also points out that Christ intercedes (Heb 7:25). There is no contradiction between Rom 8:34 (Christ intercedes) and verse 27 (the Spirit intercedes) because Paul has already referred to the Spirit as the Spirit of Christ (v. 9); in 2 Cor 3:17 Paul says flatly, "the Lord is the Spirit." Now, then, if the sentence is an assertion, it answers the question, "Who will condemn?" by pointing out that whoever may condemn, the believer has Christ as intercessor, as the one who "pleads our cause" (REB). But if the sentence is a question, it too elicits the reader's response: "Not at all!" for how could the interceding Christ be the one who condemns?

The third question (v. 35) turns from the heavenly courtroom at the Last Judgment to earthly threats in the present: "Who will separate us from Christ's love?" (AT; "love of Christ" might suggest our love for Christ, which is not Paul's point). The list of seven possibilities is clearly a question (thereby increasing the likelihood that the responses to the first two questions are also questions). Since the letter will be read aloud, rhetorically Paul makes the list *sound* and *feel* long by repeating "or" (so Anderson 1999, 233), thereby intensifying the hearers' emotional involvement (a use of *pathos* to persuade). Except for "sword," each of the dangers was experienced by Paul himself (see 2 Cor 11:26-27; 12:10), yet he does not call attention to it for doing so would deflect the argument. The sequence of dangers is rhetorical; the threat of martyrdom (sword) easily led to the quotation from Ps 44:22 (LXX 43:23), which underlines continuing vulnerability (v. 36). In the psalm itself, these lines refer to the Israelites' repeated devastations; Paul now finds in them language for Christian exposure to sufferings (see v. 18), aptly described ("as it is written" expresses accord, not prediction). He does not mention the help of the Spirit (v. 26), perhaps because doing so would detract from the force of what he says next.

Verses 37-39 are effective rhetorically because in the starkest possible contrast with the utter vulnerability to suffering in verses 35-36, Paul now declares, "We are supervictors" (Fitzmyer 1993), not through our super endurance but "through him who loved us"—namely, through God's love expressed in Christ (v. 39, alluding to 5:8). To express the warrant for the bold declaration, verses 38-39 list nine things that will be unable "to separate us" from God's love in Christ, ending with an *inclusio* corresponding to verse 37. Theologically, the victory is cosmic in scope. Of the nine threats, all but "powers" *(dynameis)* are listed in four pairs of contrasting realities that transcend the historical experiences listed in verse 35. None of the four pairs contrasts malign and beneficial realities; instead, in each pair both items are threats (as are the unpaired "powers"). Each pair refers to a different kind of reality: life-death (the givens of creaturely existence), angels-rulers (heavenly and earthly beings), present-future things (temporal vicissitudes), height-depth (cosmic dimension). Finally, "nor any other created thing" *(oute tis ktisis hetera,* paraphrased as "nor anything else in all creation") removes all doubt: Nothing can separate the recipient of God's love in Christ from the Giver. It is this indestructible bond that convinces Paul that come what may, "we are supervictors," for God's love in Christ is invincible.

The arc of the argument, begun in chapter 1, is remarkable: It begins with God's wrath *against* all human wickedness and ends with God being *for us*—not because God has changed but because of what God has done for us in Christ's death and resurrection. To focus on this concluding passage apart from what precedes it is to short-circuit Paul's thought. More than that, from his angle it is also to pretend that God's being "for us" was not costly, that the Son whom God did not "withhold" was someone other than God's own self-expression. The astounding confidence expressed here is grounded solely in the power of God's love, expressed as God's giving him—that is, the self-involvement of the God who thereby not only rectifies the ungodly (4:5) apart from the law, but also acts to redeem creation from the inevitability (death) that marks its condition. If Paul assumed that this letter would be read through—as is likely—then in composing this peroration he set his argument to music.

THE FREEDOM OF GOD'S SOVEREIGNTY (9:1–11:36)

Paul has insisted that in the Christ-event, and through the import of the gospel, God has kept the promise made in scripture (1:2). And while the gospel is God's power for salvation of all who believe, it is so "for the Jew first" (1:16). Indeed, the insistence that everyone who believes is rectified on the basis of faith rather than by obeying the law does not destroy the law but actually upholds it (3:30-31), because God's rectifying rectitude apart from the law is attested in scripture (3:21-26). Moreover, Abraham himself is the prototype of the sort of faith Paul is talking about (chap. 4).

Nonetheless, there is a problem, made acute by precisely these positive links between the gospel and the Jewish people and their scripture: Already in Paul's day, it was apparent that most Jews were refusing to believe the gospel while more and more Gentiles were accepting it and enjoying its power to save. Given the gospel's rootage in Israel's scripture, would one not expect that Jews would welcome the gospel even more than Gentiles? How is this anomalous situation to be understood? Has something gone wrong? Has Paul misunderstood the meaning of Christ? If not, what is the alternative explanation? Moreover, since the gospel announces the eschatological, definitive act of God, denying the truth of the gospel is more serious than transgressing a commandment. What, then, is the consequence of this refusal? That the Jews' No to the gospel entails God's No to the Jews? Since Paul has already denied that the faithlessness of some nullifies the faithfulness of God (3:3-4), how is one to square the faithlessness of the many with the faithfulness of God? One cannot insist too strongly that while Rom 9–11 is elicited by the need to account for the Jews' No to the gospel, the real problem is the faithfulness of God, for only a faithful God is righteous.

But *whose* problem is being addressed here? That it is Paul's problem is evident by the way he expresses his intense involvement in it three times (at the beginning of each chapter). Less evident is *why* the Jews' No is his problem. After all, he understands himself to be the apostle not to Jews but to Gentiles (which he points out three times: 1:5; 11:13; 15:16); moreover, the leaders of the church in Jerusalem had agreed that taking the gospel to Jews would be Peter's responsibility, not Paul's (Gal 2:7-10). Why, then, does he have so much at stake in the Jews' refusal of the gospel that he devotes almost as much space to this phenomenon as to the liberation from bondage to sin and death in 5:12–8:39? Chapters 9–11 were not set afoot by either a repressed criticism of Peter's unsuccessful mission or by an unstated desire to exonerate him. Rather, the vehemence with which Paul begins (9:1-5) suggests that he knows he has been accused of being a major factor in the Jewish refusal. Not because he took the gospel *to Gentiles,* but because of the *gospel he took*—one that insisted that Gentiles must not be required to become converts to Judaism in order to enjoy the full benefits of salvation in Christ, the Messiah. So one reason the Jews' No is Paul's problem is that law-observant

Christian Jews *made* it his problem by blaming him for preaching a gospel to Gentiles that made it unacceptable to most Jews who were convinced that he dissolved the significance of Judaism. Further, because Paul evidently knew that also the readers knew of this accusation, he used chapters 9–11 to set the record straight. He needed to if he also suspected that his harsh words about the law in his Letter to the Galatians were known (see Martyn 1997, 37-46), perhaps even in Rome.

A second reason for writing these chapters may have been even more important: The likelihood that the Christian Gentiles in Rome were beginning to think that the corollary of the Jews' No to the gospel is God's No to the Jews as a people. In other words, Rom 9–11 is addressed to the beginnings of what is now called "supersessionism"—the idea that the (mostly Gentile) church has replaced Israel as God's people. Indeed, *only* a Christian Gentile would have come to such a conclusion, which Paul delays formulating until 11:1, "Has God rejected his *people*?" Perhaps those who thought this way were appealing to Paul's mission in support of their view (so Campbell 2000, 203-6). Not only do chapters 9–11 deny this, but when Paul explicitly addresses Christian Gentiles (11:13-24), he insists that they are actually being included in Israel. From Paul's angle, it is the Christian Gentiles—more than the Christian Jews—who need to understand the true significance of their own acceptance of the gospel. In other words, Paul not only sets the record straight about his theology; he also sets them straight about theirs. Had he not done so, Paul surely realized, they would misconstrue his plan for the mission in Spain (15:22-24), where there were very few Jews (see introduction, p. 30); they would conclude that he, like God, had written the Jews off.

Whereas the first two reasons for writing chapters 9–11 were grounded in historical circumstances, the third is rooted in what Paul has already written about God in chapters 1–8. As the commentary noted from time to time, those references to God assumed God's otherness, God's freedom to be God and exercise "Godhood" on God's own terms, apart from the law but not contrary to the law. The most astounding, and theology-transforming, of those references does not use the word "God" but simply speaks of "the one who rectifies the ungodly" (4:5). In short, the *theology* in chapters 1–8 is applied to the Jews' No in chapters 9–11. In these chapters, we see what the theology built into 4:5 looks like when applied to Israel and the Gentiles. One can also say that just as 5:12–8:39 probed the dilemma of Jew and Gentile more deeply by viewing it as the human condition, so chapters 9–11 penetrate deeper into the understanding of God by speaking of God's sovereign freedom in both election and salvation.

The underlying theological continuity between chapters 1–8 and 9–11 must not eclipse the literary difference between these two sections of the letter, for chapters 9–11 are a clear unit in which Paul reasons from scripture in a way he had not done since chapter 4. Moreover, in these chapters he draws on Jewish apocalyptic as well as Wisdom traditions (shown by Johnson 1989), and relies heavily on the book of Isaiah, sometimes beyond what he actually quotes (emphasized by Wagner 2003). At the same time, the allusions to chapters 1–8 indicate that chapters 9–11 were written for the letter, and are not simply Paul's previously preached sermon "On the Rejection of Israel" as Dodd (1932, 149) proposed (though Paul may well have reused ideas and formulations). Nonetheless, this section does have many features of a speech (argued in detail by Kim 2000). Looked at this way, the opening paragraph (9:1-5) functions as an *exordium*, while the concluding passage serves as a *peroratio* (11:33-36). The bulk of the discussion falls into three parts: 9:6-29, which emphasizes God's freedom in election; 9:30–10:21, which identifies and corrects the error of the elect regarding righteousness; and 11:1-32, which brings the whole discussion to a head by outlining God's way of saving both Jews and Gentiles.

◊ ◊ ◊ ◊

The Anomaly and the Apostle's Agony (9:1-5)

Having declared triumphantly that nothing "will be able to separate us from the love of God in Christ Jesus our Lord" (8:39), Paul suddenly, and without hint or warning of what is to come, shifts gears and discloses that he would be willing to be separated from God's love in Christ—"accursed and cut off from Christ"— if forfeiting his own salvation would gain that of his own people. These lines function rhetorically as the *captatio benevolentiae*, that part of a discourse designed to win the hearers' favorable disposition toward the speaker and his case. This function does not preclude the possibility that Paul sees himself ready to sacrifice himself as did Moses (Exod 32:32; so Wagner 2003, 45). It is unlikely, however, that Paul implies his people are already cut off from Christ (so Piper 1983, 29). Remarkable is both the vehemence with which verse 1 begins and the two theological warrants adduced to assure the readers that Paul is telling the truth: He speaks "in Christ," and the Holy Spirit confirms his clear conscience (NRSV's "confirms" renders *symmartyrousēs*; the *sym*-prefix indicates joint witness as in 8:16). These nuances are obscured by REB: "I am speaking . . . as a Christian; my conscience . . . assures me that I do not lie." Paul virtually takes an oath, as defined by the *Rhetoric to Alexander*, ascribed to Aristotle: "An oath is an unproved statement supported by an appeal to the gods" (*Ad Alex.* 17).

Paul does not linger with his agony, however, but turns the reference to his people into a recital of their privileged status (vv. 3-5). He does not refer to them as "the Jews," but as "my brothers [NRSV: "my own people"] who are my kindred according to the flesh"—that is, biologically speaking. With "according to the flesh" he distinguishes them from his fictive kinship with believers, whom he addresses simply as "brothers" in 10:1 (see also 1:13; 7:1; 8:12; 11:25; 12:1). He does not say "we are Israelites," but refers to them in third person (*hoitines*, "they are the ones who"), as he does throughout chapters 9–11; despite his ethnic solidarity with them, "we" has become "they." Nonetheless, the designation of his biological kindred as "Israelites" signals the religious significance of the *people* ("Jews" is generally used to emphasize the ethnic contrast with Gentiles). Moreover, instead of writing simply "my kindred according to the flesh, Israelites," he inserted the unnecessary *eisin* ("are"), thus pointing out that despite their current unbelief they *are and remain* Israelites.

As Israelites, they have seven God-given privileges. The list first mentions six nonpersonal realities, then the patriarchs, to which is attached the reference to "the Messiah according to the flesh" (a cross-reference to 1:3 where Paul refers to Jesus as "God's Son, who was born of the seed of David according to the flesh"). Rhetorical considerations, not repeatable in English, govern the sequence of the first six items, all of which are feminine nouns. The first, *huiothesia* (NRSV: "the adoption"; REB: "chosen to be God's sons"), alludes to God's "calling" (and thereby making Israel "my son"; Exod 4:22; Jer 31:9; Hos 11:1-4; see also comment on 8:15-17). REB's "the glory of the divine presence" rightly renders *hē doxa*, the splendor that attends and manifests God's invisible presence (often called "the glory of Yahweh," as in Exod 16:7), and later referred to as the *Shekinah* (lit., "the dwelling"). We have no comparable concept by which to designate the numinous in experience, though artists sometimes portray it as dazzling light (suggested perhaps by Luke 2:9). NRSV uses "the giving of the law" for *nomothesia* (which can also mean "legislation"), thereby implying that Paul has in mind both the law and the Sinai event in which God gave it (REB, however, uses "the law"). "The worship" renders *latreia*; it refers primarily to the cultic activity in the Jerusalem temple (still going on!), not simply to worship in general. Unusual are the plurals "the covenants" and "the promises" (though some manuscripts use singular nouns), and their referents are uncertain. The first six items are a unit, for verse 5 begins afresh: "to whom belong the patriarchs." The Messiah, however, does not "belong" to them; he is "from the patriarchs." This is one place where *ho Christos* clearly means "the Messiah," appropriate in this context. Usually Paul either uses *Christos* without the article or combines it with the personal name Jesus. These seven privileges "belong" to the Israelites because God has given them; later, Paul will allude to them as the irrevocable "gifts and the calling of God" (11:29).

Few passages in the New Testament have generated more discussion than the second half of verse 5 (for details, see Cranfield 1979 and Fitzmyer 1003); indeed, if one understood clearly what it says, one could translate it confidently. Recent versions vary, but print alternative possibilities in the footnotes. At issue is whether Paul says that the Messiah is "God over all" (so, e.g., Moo 1996), or (by using a different punctuation) "the Messiah. May he who is God over all be blessed forever. Amen" (so NRSV footnote). The matter need not be decided, since nothing in the context requires a firm decision (for a detailed discussion, see Harris 1992, 143-72; he concludes that Paul did call Jesus "God").

◊ ◊ ◊ ◊

The seven things that "belong" to the Israelites are stated without any interpretive comment. There is no allusion to the Jew whom Paul taunts for his sense of superiority because he has the law (2:17-24); nor is there any hint either of sin's misuse of the law (7:14-25) or of the law's incapacity to deliver the life it promises (7:10; 8:3). Except for "the patriarchs," the list does not signal topics to be discussed, nor is the list followed by a "therefore." What, then, is its role in the argument? It is quite unlikely that Paul adds the list to the expression of concern for his people in order to elicit "compassion for the Jews" from Christian Gentiles (so Elliott 1990, 263). It is much more likely that by listing these items straightforwardly, as any faithful Jew might do, Paul underlines the anomaly of the Jews' refusal of the gospel all the more.

God's Freedom in Election (9:6-29)

Without explicitly mentioning the Jews' refusal, Paul inaugurates the discussion with a thesis statement (v. 6a) that rejects the wrong inference from the anomaly: "It is not as though the word of God had failed" (REB: "has proved false"). The basis for this bold assertion follows: "For it is not the case that all who are *of* Israel *are* Israel" (v. 6b, AT), thereby pointing to the way Paul will argue his case: by identifying God's word as the reality that determines who really *is* Israel. (The distinction between the two, between the faithless and the faithful who constitute the true people of God, appears often in scripture; it led to the crises that provoked the Maccabean Revolt in 168 BCE, and was emphasized later by the sectarians at Qumran; see the concise summary in Richardson 1969, 21-28.) As supporting evidence, Paul adduces the biblical reports of God's electing the patriarchs (vv. 7-13). Because the reliability of God's word is to be demonstrated, Paul emphasizes what God *said*, beginning with what God said *to* the patriarchs and ending with what God said *about* them in Mal 1:2-3 (v. 13). Paul assumes that the readers, though predominantly Gentile, know the stories in Genesis in which his quotations are embedded; if the Christian Gentile readers had been God-fearers, they would have learned the stories in the synagogues.

But the very emphasis on God's free choice raises the question, Is God unfair? In the next unit (vv. 14-18) Paul responds by asserting God's freedom to choose. This, in turn, provokes a further question: If the identity of Israel really depends on God's choice, "Why does he still find fault?"—that is, How can No-saying Jews be blamed? The third unit (vv. 19-29) contains Paul's response.

The Identity of Israel (9:6-13)

What the thesis statement in verse 6a denies is that God's electing word is now terminated (*ekpeptōken*, perfect tense of *ekpiptō*, which has exactly this meaning in the Hamburg manuscript of the second-century *Acts of Paul*, which reports that a lion's loud roar so shocked the imprisoned apostle "that even Paul broke off [*ekpesein*] his prayer in terror"; quoted from Hennecke-Schneemelcher 1991, 2: 251). By expressing the wrong conclusion so strongly, Paul underscores the right conclusion, expressed in verse 11: "so that the purpose of God might continue to be [*menē*, remain] according to election [*kat' eklogēn*]" (AT). Thus, Paul maintains, if God's purpose continues in a way that is consistent with election, then the fact that only part of ethnic Israel says Yes to the gospel shows that God's word "has not failed." The identity of real Israel has never been determined by lineal descent alone. Because God is consistent, it suffices to show that God's election was determinative in the time of the patriarchs; conversely, if God were inconsistent, for the present nothing could be inferred from how God operated during the time of the patriarchs.

Abraham had two sons, Ishmael by his concubine Hagar, and Isaac by his wife, Sarah. Because Ishmael was born first, Sarah wants to make sure that her son does not come in second when the inheritance is determined, and so insists that Abraham send Hagar and Ishmael packing (Gen 16:1-6; 21:9-10). But God, responding to Abraham's distress over Sarah's demand, tells him to do as Sarah says because "it is through Isaac that offspring [lit., "seed"] shall be named [lit., "called"] for you" (Gen 21:12, NRSV). Why Isaac? Because it was he, not Ishmael, whose birth God had promised (Gen 17:15-19). In verse 8, Paul generalizes: "It is not the children of the flesh [children born by ordinary human means] who are the children of God [an allusion to "sonship/adoption" in v. 4], but the children of the promise are counted as descendants [lit., "seed"]." Verse 9 provides the explicit warrant for this generalization: "For the promise was this very word: 'About this time I [God] will return and Sarah will have a son'" (Gen 18:10, AT). In short, because Isaac, not Ishmael, was promised, Paul infers that just as physical, lineal descent alone did not determine who was Abraham's "seed," so now "not all Israelites truly belong to Israel" (v. 6). Who truly belongs depends on God's decision, expressed in Isaac's case as God's promise. In light of God's word to Abraham, Paul implies, the fact that only a few Jews believe the gospel actually confirms that God's electing, effecting word continues, for this is how God operates: by election (see v. 11b).

This is even more evident in the next patriarchal generation (vv. 10-13). Paul notes that according to Gen 25:23, God told Isaac's wife, Rebecca, that *before* her twins were born, "the elder shall serve the younger," contrary to all custom. Just as God chose Isaac over Ishmael despite their birth order, so now he chose the younger (Jacob) over Esau—in fact God chose Jacob *before* either boy "had done anything good or bad." Why? "So that God's purpose might continue to be according to election" (v. 11), which the next clause explains, "not on the basis of works but on the basis of the One who calls" (AT; Paul uses "call" language to express God's action in choosing, as in 1:1, 6; see comment). Malachi 1:2-3 gives the coup de grace: God says, "I have loved Jacob but I have hated Esau" (the traditional ancestor of the Edomites, often Israel's enemies). In the idiomatic "loved-hated" contrast, "hated" could mean "loved less" (as in Luke 14:26), but Paul understood the quotation to express sharply God's choice and rejection. God's free choice is underscored by noting that the twins had the *same father* (v. 10) as well as by observing *when* God chose Jacob. The reference to "works" shows the theological connection between God's free choice and rectification "apart from the works of the law" (3:28); it is solely God's action that counts. Interestingly, precisely the opposite is asserted by the first-century Pseudo-Philo *Biblical Antiquities*: "And God loved Jacob but he hated Esau because of his deeds" (32:6; Charlesworth 1985, 2:346).

God's Justness (9:14-18)

Paul, aware that what he has just said offends moral sensibility, reverts to the diatribe style and again has the interlocutor state the wrong conclusion as a question ("Is there injustice *[adikia]* on God's part?") so that he can state the truth of the matter. After denying flatly that God is unjust, Paul insists on God's freedom by quoting what God said to Moses and Pharaoh; thereby he tacitly claims that what was true in the time of the patriarchs remained true also at the next stage of Israel's experience with God, the exodus.

Both the question in verse 14 and Paul's response deserve close attention. The question does not challenge Paul's point that it is solely God's choice that determines who constitutes Abraham's "seed" (the people of God). Indeed, precisely its validity evokes the objection, put as question, "Is God to be charged with injustice?" (REB). Even though Paul rejects this as the wrong conclusion, the question is quite understandable from the standpoint of common sense: God *does* act arbitrarily in choosing Jacob instead of Esau before either one could do anything that merited or disqualified him from being chosen. Does not such an act call into question God's fairness, God's impartiality (2:10-11)? Paul has the interlocutor raise the question because he knows it is also the readers' question (and not only those in Rome!). In examining his response, however, one should remember that he is not outlining an essay on God's governance in human affairs, but arguing for the validity of verse 6.

Paul does more than simply reject the question, and he also does less than engage in a discussion of theodicy, for what he says accounts for his rejection of the question of God's injustice. He relies on what God said to Moses in Exod 33:19. God, having refused to let Moses see the divine glory because that would be fatal for Moses, promises an alternative: "I will make all my goodness pass before you, and will proclaim before you the name, 'The LORD' [Yahweh]; and I will be gracious to whom I will be gracious, and will show mercy on whom I will show mercy." By quoting the last part of the reply, Paul tacitly undermines the standpoint of the questioner: Now the interlocutor (and the reader) has no neutral place from which he or she can assess God's justice, but instead is placed before God's sovereign freedom to exercise mercy and compassion as God wills. By definition, mercy and compassion do not occur on the basis of fairness or justice. This is what Paul points out in verse 16: "So it [the identity of the one who receives mercy] depends not on human will or exertion [lit., "on the one who wills or runs"] but on God who shows mercy." In other words, God's choice is not a reward but an act of sheer mercy, expressing God's own character. Wagner (2003, 52-53) rightly observes that Paul's reasoning is especially perceptive since the exchange between God and Moses follows the story of Israel's lapse into idolatry, the worship of the golden calf (Exod 32). Though Paul does not point it out, here too God's self-generated mercy coheres with God's rectitude that rectifies "apart from the law" (3:21).

Verse 17, beginning with "for," provides the warrant for verse 16. (Paul assumes that the readers know that Pharaoh has reneged on his promise to allow the Israelites to leave Egypt.) Paul quotes LXX Exod 9:16 (slightly modified), where God informs Pharaoh of his dual purpose: "I have raised you up for this very purpose: in order to show my power by means of [lit., "in"] you, and in order that my name may be proclaimed in all the earth" (AT). God's sovereign freedom uses even Pharaoh's treachery to disclose God's capacity to achieve his purpose. (In quoting God's dual purpose, Paul anticipates what he will say about the potter making two kinds of vessels [vv. 21-23] as well as for what he will say later about the role the Jews' No plays in the salvation of the

Gentiles in 11:11-12, 28-32.) In verse 18, from God's dual purpose Paul draws the conclusion: God "has mercy on whomever he wills, and he hardens [the heart of] whomever he wills"(AT). (Whereas in common usage, a "hard-hearted" person is one who is indifferent to the needs of others, in biblical usage a person whose heart is "hardened" is one who persists in resisting God's will and so becomes disobedient. Acts 7:56 uses "stiffnecked" to make the same point.)

In Exodus, the repeated references to the "hardening" of Pharaoh's heart are an integral part of the account of the plagues that preceded the exodus; sometimes Pharaoh is said to "harden his heart" (Exod 8:15, 32; 9:34-35), sometimes God hardens it (Exod 9:12; 10:1, 20, 27; 11:10; 14:8). Paul either ignores the former or, more likely, assumes that God is at work also where Pharaoh hardened his heart. In any case, for Paul, just as being the beneficiary of God's mercy does not depend on the action of the recipient (v. 16), so God "hardens whomever he wills" (v. 18), not whoever deserves it (though Pharaoh does!). Precisely, Pharaoh is the means by which God discloses the freedom with which God's sovereignty is exercised. In Isa 10:5-7 God makes a similar claim: "Ah, Assyria, the rod of my anger [against Israel]. . . . But this is not what he [Assyria] intends." Precisely. The same is true of Pharaoh, Esau, and Ishmael. In none of these cases does God's act or choice depend on "willing or running" (v. 16). Paul's conclusion in verse 18 rests squarely on a combination of God's word to Moses and God's word to Pharaoh.

God's Freedom to Act (9:19-29)

The emphasis on God's complete freedom to show mercy or to "harden" anyone's heart generates a problem, expressed in the interlocutor's double question in verse 19: "Why then does he [God] still find fault? For who resists his will?" (AT; RSV, NRSV, REB: "can resist"). Because the second question warrants the first, both raise the same issue: If there is no defense against God's negative decision, how can God hold one accountable for wrongdoing?—that is, How can a just God blame Pharaoh for the wrong that God's hardening made him do? It is one thing for God to choose before Rebecca's twins had done good or bad, but quite another for God to cause bad action for the sake of the Name ("for this very purpose," v. 17, AT). The question does not dispute the validity of combining what was said to the antagonists, Moses and Pharaoh (in quite different contexts: Exod 33:19; 9:16). What it protests is the logical consequence of Paul's conclusion in verse 18; that is, it questions Paul's theology at the core: God's unqualified freedom to act both mercifully and negatively in order to achieve God's purpose. At issue is not *whether* God finds fault but *why*. In other words, the questioner does not protest innocence, but protests being victimized by an arbitrary deity. The problem is the morality of God.

So how does Paul respond? He does not answer the questions! Instead, he denies that the questioner has the right to ask them. Rhetorically, his response begins with an ad hominem counter-question, "But who indeed are you, O man [*anthrōpos*, not *anēr*, male] to talk back to God?"—that is, have you forgotten that you are a mere creature? Paul's response is like that of the book of Job, in which God finally silences Job's complaints by emphasizing the difference between what the Creator can do and what Job can do (chaps. 38–39), and then asks, "Shall a faultfinder contend with the Almighty?" (40:2). Paul then proceeds to emphasize God's *right* to choose by relying on widely used images of the potter and the clay (vv. 20*b*- 23).

Paul's use of this image differs somewhat from uses found in biblical and postbiblical Jewish texts. (a) Paul does not use the potter's work as an image of Israel's utter destruction as does Isa 41:25: "He [Israel's enemy] shall trample the rulers as on mortar, as the potter treads the clay." (b) Nor does he say that God will change his mind if Israel repents, just as the potter reworks the clay (Jer 18:1-10). (c) Nor does he, like the Qumran *Rule of the Community* (1QS 11:22) and *Thanksgiving Hymns*[a] (1QH[a] 1:21; 3:23-24; 4:29; 11:3; 12:26, 32; 18:12), use the image of kneaded clay to express the lowliness of the human being but ignore the potter, because for Paul it is the potter's relation to the clay that carries the argument. (d) Closer to Paul are two passages in the Jewish Wisdom tradition. One is Wis 15:7, part of the polemic against making gods with human hands (as in Isa 44:9-20): "a potter . . . fashioning out of the same clay both the vessels that serve clean uses and those for contrary uses . . . but which shall be the use of each of them the worker in clay decides." The other is in Sirach, which uses the image to say that all God's works "come in pairs," one the opposite of the other: "Like clay in the hand of the potter, to be molded as he pleases, so are all in the hand of their maker, to be given whatever [form] he decides" (Sir 33:13).

In verses 20-21 Paul apparently combines the imagery found in these Wisdom texts with words taken from Isa 29:16, where Israel is accused, "You turn things upside down! Shall the potter be regarded as the clay? Shall the thing made say to its maker, 'He did not make me'; or the thing formed say of the one who formed it, 'He has no understanding'?" (see also Isa 45:9). With this passage in mind, Paul asks, "The thing molded will not say to the molder, 'Why did you make me like this,' will it? Or does not the potter have a right over the clay, to make from the same lump one vessel for honorable use and another for common use?" (NASB). In this way, Paul continues to insist on God's freedom to choose and right to choose. As Johnson (1989, 148) rightly observes, up to this point "Paul has said nothing to which a non-Christian Jew might take exception." It is the application of the imagery to the Jews' No and the Gentiles' Yes (vv. 22-29) that is noteworthy.

Paul proceeds gradually in order to lead the readers to his conclusion. First, he poses a seemingly hypothetical, nonthreatening question concerning two kinds of objects made by the potter ("What if . . . ?"), but it soon becomes apparent that the question is not at all speculative but is rather his way of talking about God's way of bringing about a people consisting of both Jews and Gentiles (v. 24). In support, he appeals to a number of biblical quotations (vv. 25-29); they are more than proof texts, for each of them also carries the argument forward.

Modern translations of verses 22-24 are clearer than Paul's Greek text, partly because (a) the passage begins with an "if" clause (the protasis) but lacks a clear "then . . ." (the apodosis), and partly because (b) it is not self-evident whether the participle *thelōn* (at the beginning of v. 22), which qualifies the whole sentence, has a causative force (as in NRSV: "What if God, desiring to show . . .") or a concessive force (as in NASB: "What if God, although willing . . ."). The translators also face a text problem: If they translate the majority of manuscripts that begin verse 23 with "and," then Paul writes of *two* parallel purposes of God, one negative (wrathful, v. 22), the other positive (merciful and salvific, v. 23). But if they use the minority of manuscripts that omit "and," then Paul subordinates the negative purpose (showing wrath) to the positive one (disclosing salvation), as in REB (God has "tolerated vessels . . . for destruction, precisely in order to make known . . . glory"); like translators, exegetes disagree. The interpretation here regards "willing" as causative, not concessive, and retains the "and."

The passage is awkward. Verses 22-23 are a question without an answer; verse 24 is loosely attached, though it states the point Paul is aiming for. So it is easier to follow his thought by omitting "what if . . . ?" and to read the passage as a series of three assertions: (a) God desired "to show his wrath *and* to make known his power" (v. 22, alluding to God's dual purpose in the quotation from Exod 9:16 in v. 17). If this reference to power includes God's saving power in the gospel (as in 1:16; 1 Cor 1:18; 1 Thess 1:5; 2:13), then here God's salvific power is contrasted with God's destructive power (wrath).

(b) In order to show the wrath, God patiently put up with those objects that were "readied for destruction" (NRSV: "made for"; REB: "tolerated vessels that were objects of retribution due for destruction"). This reference to God's "patience" *(makrothymia)* may allude to the context of God's word to Pharaoh (Exod 9:16) quoted in verse 17. In verse 15 God says to Pharaoh, "For by now I could have stretched out my hand and struck you and your people . . . and you would have been cut off from the earth. But this is why *I let you live*: in order to show my power," and so forth (AT). If Paul has this passage in mind, then God's "patience" interprets the reason God let Pharaoh live momentarily, though still destined for destruction. "Destruction" is a harsh destiny, but this sort of language fits the reference to God's wrath (v. 22) and recalls the apocalyptic horizon of Paul's thought. Still, Paul does not actually say that the pots facing destruction are unbelieving Israel, perhaps because in 11:16, 25-26 he will say that "all Israel will be saved" (so also Wagner 2003, 72-78).

(c) The negative expression of God's patience with the "objects of wrath" actually serves God's positive aim: "to make known the riches of his glory for the objects of mercy, which he has prepared beforehand for glory." And who are they? The believers, to whom Paul refers as "us," the ones "whom he called [picking up "not on the basis of works but on the basis of the One who calls" in v. 12], not *from* the Jews only but also *from* the Gentiles" (v. 24, AT). Here, God's call "from" Jews and Gentiles is an important detail that underlines God's continuing election by selection. Their being "prepared beforehand" resonates with what Paul had said in 8:29-30 about God's foreknowing and predestining the believers. The quotations that follow show that in this whole chapter Paul is *not* talking about predestination or double predestination with respect to an individual's salvation, though this chapter later became the quarry from which those doctrines were extracted and hewn. He is talking about groups of people. (Piper [1983, 52, 183] and Moo [1996, 603] insist that Paul *is* talking about the eternal destinies of individuals within Israel.)

In support of the claim in verses 23-24 that the "objects of mercy" are those whom God has "called" from both Jews and Gentiles, Paul now cites four biblical passages, two from Hosea and two from Isaiah (vv. 27-29). The reference to "seed" in verse 29 creates an *inclusio* (bracket) with the "seed" mentioned in verse 7 (not visible in NRSV, which translates "seed" as "descendants" in verse 7 and as "survivors" in verse 29, putting "descendants" in the footnote). The *inclusio* signals that this thought unit is now completed. It began in verse 7 (not all of Abraham's children are his "seed") and ends by identifying the "seed" as the "remnant."

The quotations themselves constitute a carefully constructed argument in verses 25-26. *First,* what Paul gives as quotations from Hosea actually combine in verse 26 the words of Hos 1:10 (LXX 2:1) with his own interpretation of Hos 1:6, 8-9 in verse 25. According to Hos 1:6, God told the prophet to name his daughter Lo-Ruhamah ("Not Pitied"); in verse 8 God told him to call the next child Lo-Ammi ("Not My People"). Both names express God's judgment on Israel, the northern kingdom. In Hos 1:10 this judgment is to be reversed: "And in the place where it was said to them, 'You are not my people,' there they shall be called sons of the living God" (AT of LXX). Whereas Hosea's words originally referred to Israel, Paul applies them to Christian Gentiles (who were "not my people" to begin with). That is why in the first line of the quotation in verse 25 Paul states this reversal in his own words: "those who were not my people I will call 'my people.'" He evidently assumes this reversal changed also Lo-Ruhamah ("Not Pitied") to Ruhamah ("Pitied"), but for some reason replaced the language of pity with that of love: "And her who was not beloved I will call 'beloved.'" *Second*, both his own formulation (v. 25) and the inference about "not beloved" / "beloved" (v. 26) use the word "call," so that the entire passage (vv. 25-26) emphasizes God's "call" in two senses: to name and to elect. In verse 24, "called from" refers to the election of both Jews and Gentiles. This "call" language expresses God's sovereign, defining, transforming act, imaged as an oral event, God's speech. When Paul writes, "Those who were not my people I will *call* 'My People,'" he means that in giving Christian Gentiles this new name God is actually *making* them "My People," because for Paul God's speech is effective; it achieves what it articulates. Today, students of language identify this use of language as "performative." (It is often illustrated by referring to the wedding ceremony in which "I pronounce you husband and wife" legally makes them married.) *Third*, the climax of the Hosea citation is the promise that Gentiles will be called God's sons (NRSV: "children of God"), thereby giving them a share in the "sonship" (*huiothesia*, "adoption") that belongs to Israel (9:4) because it was given to Israel (see, e.g., Exod 4:22; Jer 31:9; Hos 11:1). For Paul, Hosea's words refer to Christian Gentiles because Hosea used the future tense ("will call," "shall be called"). What God promised through Hosea (recall the language of 1:2!) has for Paul become a historical fact—evidence that God's word has not been terminated.

In verses 27-28 Paul uses an abbreviated form of Isa 10:22 to characterize the situation of Israel (the objects of wrath, v. 22).

For the prophet, the "remnant" motif expressed hope for Israel beyond the disaster of the exile: a remnant *will return* (see also 28:5; 37:4, 31-32; just as Hosea gave his children names that expressed his message, so Isaiah had named one of his sons Shear-Yashub ["A Remnant Shall Return"], Isa 7:3). Since the LXX of Isa 10:22 had replaced the Hebrew "shall return" with "will be saved," Paul saw in this text a prediction that the minority of Israel (the Jewish Christians) *would* accept the gospel. Paul's view of the "remnant" is *not* negative (as NRSV, NIV, and REB imply by inserting "only" into v. 27) but positive (so also Meyer 1988, 1156). The current situation, which prompted this discussion, causes anguish for Paul but not despair, because Isaiah's remnant prefigured the remnant situation in Paul's day, and so suggested hope. Just because most Jews say No to the gospel, one must not infer that "the word of God has failed" (v. 6, AT). In short, in order that salvation may come to the Gentiles, Paul implies, God now patiently endures most Jews' No to the gospel (the objects of wrath, v. 22)—a point to which Paul will return in chapter 11, especially 11:11-12, 25-31. Indeed, this is also what Paul sees in the last line of the quotation in verse 28: "For the Lord will accomplish his *word*" (AT; NRSV: "execute his sentence"). God not only speaks, but also turns the word into event. God's word effects what it says. Paul learned this from his Hebrew scripture, where *dabar* often means both word and event.

The last quotation (v. 29), also from Isaiah (1:10), shows just how pivotal the remnant motif is: were it not for this small minority (the "seed"), which bears the hope of the future, God's people would have been destroyed completely as were Sodom and Gomorrah, the abiding symbols of complete devastation wrought by the wrath of God. Paul is not really interested in Sodom and Gomorrah; he might have omitted this reference, but he retains it because it underscores both the importance of the "seed" and God's graciousness in preserving it. (In 11:5 he will say, "So too at the present time there is a remnant, chosen by grace.") As already noted, because Isaiah uses "seed" to refer to the remnant, adding this quotation rounds out the whole discussion that began by pointing out that not all of Abraham's offspring are his "seed" (v. 7). The sorting out that began with Isaac and Ishmael, that was repeated with Jacob and Esau, and that was to be actualized in Isaiah's remnant, has occurred again in Paul's own day in the emergence of another remnant—the Jewish Christian minority. Consequently, Paul argues, one cannot say that God's word is ended; to the contrary, its persistence is evident precisely in this repeated distinction between biological Israel and "Israel."

◊ ◊ ◊ ◊

The more one recognizes that in Rom 9–11 Paul is struggling to make sense of a particular historical phenomenon—the refusal of the gospel by most Jews who, he was convinced, should have embraced it—the more evident it is that his reading of the situation is rigorously and consistently theological. He eschews explaining the Jews' response in empirical terms, just as he does not engage the reasons they may have given for their No. He is not talking *to* them. Instead, he relies on a particular way of reading scripture to talk to Christian Gentiles *about* Israel and God's relation to Israel. Nor does he link the Jews' refusal of the gospel either to his own pre-conversion rejection of it or to the Palestinian Jews' resistance to Jesus' mission and message. He does not blame anybody for the Jews' No, not even "the god of this age" as he had done in 2 Cor 4:4. Had he gone down any of those roads, he would have abetted the very attitudes that he is trying to thwart. Instead, he interprets the situation by putting it in the largest possible framework—the freedom and sovereignty of God, expressed in God's election.

Paul's theological argument speaks of God on the basis of God's ways as attested in scripture. Paul eschews all speculation about the nature of God but, in accord with 4:5 ("the one who rectifies the ungodly"), concentrates on what God says and does. God is the caller (vv. 12, 24, 25), the lover and the hater (v. 23), the shower of mercy (vv. 16, 18). God has a dual purpose for Pharaoh whom he "raises up" to achieve it (v. 17); God hardens (v. 18), still finds fault (v. 19), wills to show wrath (v. 22) and make known his power (v. 22) and the amplitude of his glory (v. 23); he saves a remnant (v. 27) and retains the "seed" for the future (v. 29). What has occurred in Israel's history—be it weal or woe—is the result of what God has done and said, for God's will prevails (v. 19). The God characterized here is neither a bystander nor a motivator, but a purposeful actor whose sovereignty, exercised in freedom, must be taken seriously. If Paul got it right . . .

The Error of the Elect (9:30–10:21)

Having emphasized the role of God in electing Israel and in preserving a remnant, Paul now emphasizes Israel's responsibility for not finding the righteousness of faith. He first says that Israel misunderstood the rectitude it sought (9:30–10:3) before he explains how the law's own rectitude is achieved by faith in Christ as proclaimed in the gospel (10:4-13). Because Israel has heard the gospel, its continued refusal amounts to disobedience (10:14-21).

◊ ◊ ◊ ◊

Rectitude Misunderstood (9:30–10:3)

The image of the potter allowed Paul to emphasize God's role as the one who chooses. In turning to Israel's responsibility, he uses a different image—the racetrack, suggested by the quotation of Isa 28:16 (in v. 33), which speaks of Israel "stumbling." Thus he invites the readers to visualize Gentiles and Jews as two runners, one of whom reached the goal, while the other did not. The anomaly lies in the fact that the runner who "attained" the goal, the Christian Gentiles, did not even "strive" (diōkōn, pursue, run for, press on) for the goal, while the runner "who did strive" for it, unbelieving Israel, did not arrive at it. In 11:11 Paul will return to the image of the race, saying that while Israel "stumbled" it did not "fall"—an important distinction left unsaid in 9:30-33, where mentioning it would have detracted from the seriousness of the "stumbling." What Paul says about Israel in 9:30–10:3 has been central to recent debates about Paul's view of Judaism.

Having characterized the Gentiles as those "who did not strive for righteousness," he hastens to add, "that is, righteousness through faith" (ek pisteōs). In 2:14-16 he had pointed out that

Gentiles without the law nonetheless do "what the law requires." That righteousness/rectitude, however praiseworthy (see 2:10), he now points out, is not the rectitude that Christian Gentiles "attain," for *this* rectitude comes from faith or trust in response to the gospel. The morally upright Gentiles in 2:14-16 did not "strive" for *this* rectitude; it was attained by faith. *These* Gentile runners reached the goal, but not because they ran better than other Gentiles. Were they lucky? "By no means!" Paul would say, because (using the language of v. 16) reaching this goal "depends not on human will or exertion [*trechontos*, running!], but on God who shows mercy." This is the way God, who like the potter making what he wills of the clay, actually works: God really does justify the ungodly (4:5), for he "has mercy on whomever he chooses" (9:18).

But where does that leave Israel, with all those privileges (vv. 2-5)? Had Paul wanted simply to contrast unbelieving Israel with believing Gentiles, he could have written, "Gentiles who did not strive for righteousness attained it, but Israel who did strive for righteousness did not attain it." Perhaps that is what he meant to say. What he actually wrote, however, is somewhat different: "But Israel, *diōkōn* [striving for, pursuing] the law of righteousness, did not arrive at the law" (AT). This rather cryptic formulation contains several ambiguities. (a) Does Paul mean, "Israel, *by striving* for the law of righteousness, did not arrive at the law," thereby blaming the striving itself for the failure to arrive? Or does he mean to say, "Israel, *although striving*," did not arrive, thereby suggesting that the effort was unsuccessful because it was made in the wrong way? The latter is preferable. (NRSV, REB, NIV bypass the problem by using an active verb!)

(b) What does Paul mean by the vexing phrase, "the law of righteousness," the object or goal of Israel's striving? (NRSV rewrites the text: "the righteousness that is based on the law," as if Paul had written *dikaiosynēn ek nomou* instead of what he did write, *nomon dikaiosynēs*. NRSV also replaces "did not arrive at the law" with "did not succeed in fulfilling that law," as if not arriving there were failure to obey it completely.) "The law of righteousness" (used only here) probably means the law that promises or leads to righteousness (for a discussion of options, see

Das 2001, 242-47). In any case, it is a goal that Israel runs toward but does not reach. "Legalism" is not the Israelites' problem. The reason Israel did not reach the goal is stated in verbless verse 32: their striving was not "on the basis of faith, but as if it were based on works"—that is, their effort was based on the wrong assumption that the goal could be reached by doing what the law requires rather than on the basis of faith ("faith" is mentioned thirteen times in 9:30–10:21). Clearly, Paul views Israel's error from the standpoint of "faith" as one's trustful reliance on what God has done in Christ; he is not implying that nonbelieving Jews had no faith at all. Paul then explains this error: "They stumbled over the stumbling stone," just like scripture (v. 33) says: "See, I am laying in Zion a stone of stumbling and a rock of offense, and the one who believes in it [ep' autō] will not be shamed" (AT).

No known text, however, says exactly what Paul cites. What he gives as scripture is based on LXX Isa 28:16 where God promises, "See, I will place for the foundations of Zion a stone, a costly, chosen, prized cornerstone for its [Jerusalem's] foundations, and the one who believes on it [only LXX has "on it"] will not be put to shame" (AT). Paul omits all of the positive qualities of the stone and replaces them with the negative character of the stone—"a stone of stumbling and a rock of offense" (NRSV: "a stone that will make people stumble, a rock that will make them fall"); this negative portrayal is probably derived from LXX Isa 8:14: "If you will trust in him [God] he will be a sanctuary for you, and you will not come against him as a stumbling stone nor as a fallen rock" (AT). By replacing the foundation stone with a stumbling stone, the quotation makes God the instigator of Israel's stumbling, though not the efficient cause. Since 1 Pet 2:6-8 uses these two Isaiah passages, as well as Ps 118 (LXX 117):22, to speak of Christ, some scholars have inferred that Paul is using a compilation of "stone" passages that had been assembled by others for Christian preaching (see also Mark 12:10; Acts 4:11; Eph 2:20). But 1 Pet 2:6-8 does not say that God placed the stumbling stone in Israel's path, and the imagery of Ps 118 is absent from Romans. It is more likely that Paul himself combined these passages and reworded them in doing so (see also Davis 2002, 120-30 and Wagner 2003, 131-34).

But what did Paul regard as the stumbling stone? Most interpreters confidently assert that it is Christ, as do recent translations: whoever "believes in *him* will not be put to shame," though the footnotes in NRSV and REB have "whoever trusts in *it*" (*ep' autō* can be either masculine or neuter). But Meyer (1980, 64) has insisted that this stone must refer to the law (see also his commentary); Gaston (1987, 129) claimed that it is the gospel contained in Torah, the gospel of the inclusion of Gentiles, and Davis (2002, 142-45) thinks Paul is deliberately ambiguous, and that the stone is a polyvalent symbol of the law, the Messiah, and the Gentiles (similarly Meeks 1991, 115). Indeed, since Christ has not been mentioned since the reference to the Messiah in verse 5, an abrupt allusion to Christ here would be surprising. If the stumbling stone is indeed the law, then Israel's stumbling against it occurred by pursuing the law in the wrong way, as if righteousness were reachable on the basis of works rather than by faith. Then, too, Israel's mistake here anticipates 10:3—Israel, being "ignorant of God's righteousness and seeking to establish its own, did not submit to God's righteousness" (AT). Had Israel pursued the law of righteousness on the basis of faith, it would have achieved the goal, and would not be "put to shame" by stumbling on the track while Christian Gentiles got to the goal, the rectitude that comes from faith. Thus, in verses 30-33 Paul actually exposes a *double anomaly*: The Christian Gentiles attained what they did not strive for, and the nonbelieving Jews did not attain what they did strive for.

Before continuing his diagnosis of Israel's error, Paul tells his readers ("brothers") that he prays for the salvation of Israel (10:1). Then, in order to make the diagnosis all the more serious, he affirms that "they have a zeal for God" but immediately qualifies it: "but it is not *kat' epignōsin*" (lit., "according to knowledge"; NRSV: "enlightened"; REB: "ill-informed"). With this comment Paul begins to explain why Israel's pursuit of the law that leads to righteousness was done in the wrong way. Not a word is uttered against the zeal itself. What Israel needs is neither less nor more zeal but correct understanding, true knowledge of God's righteousness, God's rectifying rectitude. And that entails understanding how, in light of Christ, God's righteousness differs from rectitude based on obeying the law. In writing about unbelieving Israel's zeal for God, Paul knew what he was talking about, for in Phil 3:5 he characterized his own pre-Christian life as follows: "with respect to the law, a Pharisee; with respect to zeal, persecuting the church; with respect to righteousness actualized in the law, blameless" (AT). Likewise, he wrote the Galatians that he had been "far more zealous of the traditions of my ancestors" (AT) than his peers until God revealed his Son to him so that he might "proclaim him among the Gentiles" (Gal 1:14, 16).

In verse 3 Paul explains what he means by claiming that Israel's "zeal for God" is driven by misunderstanding. The explanation is constructed and phrased with care. It begins with two participial clauses whose chiastic rhetorical balance (participle + object; object + participle) defies translation into acceptable English. The first clause states what Israel did not understand ("not knowing the righteousness of God") and so clarifies the zeal that is out of step with true knowledge. The second clause states the obverse of the first: "seeking to establish their own" (i.e., righteousness; some manuscripts supply the missing word). Both clauses interpret Paul's statement in 9:32 that Israel pursued the law as if righteousness depended on "works" rather than on "faith," on the one hand; on the other, they account for the main point, stated at the end of verse 3: "They did not submit to the righteousness of God" (AT). Verses 4-13 explain what Israel should have understood; verses 14-21 hold Israel accountable for not submitting to God's rectifying rectitude.

The phrasing of verse 3 is so succinct that recent translations (and commentators) introduce words to make clear what Paul said but which are not warranted. Thus, RSV, NRSV, and NIV have Paul write, "the righteousness that comes from God" (ek theou), reflecting the long-standing view that here Paul is writing about righteousness that God gives, confers, or imputes to the believer, as in Phil 3:9. There he contrasts "a righteousness of my own that comes from the law" (ek nomou) with "the righteousness from God [ek theou] based on faith." But precisely the pivotal "from" (ek) is absent from verse 3 where Paul writes tēn tou theou dikaiosynēn ("the righteousness of God"). The fact that ek appears in verse 5 ("the righteousness that comes from the law"*[ek tou nomou]*), where it is contrasted with "the righteousness that comes from faith" (*ek pisteōs*, v. 6), does *not* mean that in verse 3 "the righteousness of God" means the same thing, but indicates that Paul's argument has moved from "God's righteousness" as God's saving action to a consideration of two kinds of human rectitude, one based on law, the other on faith. Only the latter entails submission to God's righteousness as God's activity. Israel's "not knowing about God's righteousness" (NASB) does not mean that Israel did not know *that* God was righteous; rather, what it did not know is that God's rectitude rectifies all who believe. Paul's phrasing indicates that here, as in 9:30-32, he assumes his readers have not forgotten what he had said before (in 3:21-31, his last prior use of "the righteousness of God"; see comment)—namely, that God's act in Christ discloses God's rectifying rectitude apart from the law. In other words, "the righteousness of God" in verse 3 and "righteousness of [*ek*] from faith" in 9:30 are abbreviated allusions to 3:21-31, where Paul proclaimed that God's rectitude rectifies all, Jew and Gentile alike, who believe the gospel. Israel does not know this is the true character of God's righteousness, since it is disclosed only when the news of God's eschatological act in Christ is believed and understood; because Israel does not believe or understand this, it seeks, wrongly, to establish its own rectitude by obeying the law ("as if [that could be done] on the basis of works," 9:32, AT).

What, then, is "their own righteousness" that they are seeking to establish? Since this phrase sets up the rest of the passage that builds toward the emphasis on salvation by faith for *all* (four times in vv. 11-13), it is likely that "their own righteousness" is contrasted with the righteousness "for *all* who believe." In other words, the phrase refers to the righteousness that distinguishes Jew from Gentile (so also Dunn 1988, 2:595). It was commitment to this righteousness that kept Israel from reaching the goal of the law in Christ: "righteousness for all who believe."

When Paul characterizes this refusal as, "they have not submitted to God's righteousness," he is stating *his* interpretation, not that of the refusers. The unexpected verb "submitted" shows that here God's righteousness is not simply an attribute (like God's holiness), but God's saving action in Christ that, apart from the law, rectifies every believer's relation to God. Given God's definitive (eschatological) act in Christ, pursuing righteousness/rectitude as if it were the result of law-obedience amounts to resisting God's act in Christ; such refusal is an act of insubordination. This is especially painful to Paul because he knows that it expresses "zeal for God." Though he understands what Israel does not, he is not gloating, for he writes with "great sorrow" (9:2).

◊ ◊ ◊ ◊

Theologically, it is important to see the relation between 9:31-32 and 10:3. According to 10:3, Paul's people, though zealously devoted to God, did not understand God's righteousness/rectitude, and according to 9:31-32 they did not reach the goal of the law of righteousness because they pursued it wrongly, as if righteousness resulted from "works." According to the former, their error was theological; according to the latter it was anthropological (they misread their own striving). Given Paul's understanding of God's rectifying rectitude, the two misunderstandings are two sides of the same coin, and inevitably so, for either one leads to the other. Paul clearly is interpreting the situation of those Jews who say No to the gospel. But does not his insight pertain also to those Gentile Christians who, despite their zealousness for Christ, assume that their rectitude is the result of their earnest striving to be righteous?

Faith's Rectitude Explained (10:4-13)

The standpoint from which Paul interprets Israel's erroneous quest for righteousness appears abruptly and functions as the thesis statement of the unit (as did 9:6a): "For Christ is the end [telos] of the law for righteousness to everyone who believes" (NASB). This assertion is so compressed that modern translators have deemed it necessary to restate what they think Paul meant. Already in 1935 Moffatt rendered it as: "Now Christ is an end to law, so as to let every believer have righteousness."

RSV   "For Christ is the end of the law, that every one who has faith may be justified."

NRSV/NIV   "For Christ is the end of the law so that there may be righteousness for everyone who believes."

NEB   "For Christ ends the law and brings righteousness for everyone who has faith."

NEB alt.   "Christ is the end of the law as a way to righteousness for everyone who has faith."

REB   "For Christ is the end of the law and brings righteousness for everyone who has faith."

NJB   "But the Law has found its fulfilment in Christ so that all who have faith will be justified."

CEV   "But Christ has made the law no longer necessary for those who become acceptable to God by faith."

The pivotal term is *telos*, commonly translated as "end," which is equally ambiguous. Some interpreters (e.g., Dunn 1988, Käsemann 1980, Williams 1980, 284) hold that *telos* means *termination*; others (e.g., Cranfield 1979; Fitzmyer 1993; Badenas 1985, 79; Hays 1989, 76) insist it means *goal*, while still others (e.g., Achtemeier 1985, 168; Westerholm 2001, 233-34) think it means *both* termination and goal. A number of considerations, cumulatively, persuade this interpreter that by *telos* Paul means goal, consummation, or object/purpose of effort. (a) Badenas (1985, 46-47) has demonstrated that this is the consistent meaning of the word in ancient Greek, and cites a line from Plutarch's *Amatorius* 75E that is an exact parallel, including the word order and lack of verb and article: *telos gar epithymias hēdonē*, "for the object [or goal] of desire is pleasure." It certainly does not mean that pleasure is the termination of desire. (b) "Goal" is consonant with the image of the footrace in 9:30-32, for *telos* was used to refer to the goal line. (c) Were Christ the termination of the law, one would need to explain why in 9:4 Paul includes "the giving of the law" as one of Israel's privileges, without hinting that the privilege has been terminated. (d) It would be virtually a flat contradiction were Paul to say that God's word has not failed (9:6) and then claim that Christ terminated the law. (e) Badenas (1985, 104) notes that in Rom 9–11 all references to the law are positive.

Although it is customary to translate verse 4 as "For Christ is the end of the law . . . ," Paul's sentence begins, "For the end of the law is Christ," indicating that the accent is on the identity of the law's *telos*, not on a predication of Christ (so also Badenas 1985, 112). To specify the law's *telos* as Christ is to assert that its purpose, its intent, the goal toward which it is oriented, that in which its inherent character is actualized, is an event called Christ; the statement does not mean that Christ fulfilled the law perfectly.

The most serious distortion of the assertion occurs when it is extracted from its context and abbreviated into a slogan, "Christ is the end of the law!" The statement must be understood as a whole, or it is not understood at all. Moreover, it is especially important to see that verses 5-13 explain what verse 4 means: verses 5-10 by emphasizing "believe," and verses 11-13 by accenting "*all* who believe" ("all" is mentioned five times: vv. 4, 11, 12 [twice], 13). That verse 4 is explained in verses 5-13 is shown by the fact that Paul's interpretation of scripture in these verses picks up all the key terms in verse 4 except *telos* itself: law, righteousness, all, believe, Christ.

Paul's explanatory warrant for verse 4 in verses 5-13 itself relies on his explanation of four quotations of scripture, which in turn are explained by the gospel message whose content is Christ. In developing verses 5-13, he varies his procedure: in verses 5-6 he gives his interpretation *before quoting* scripture; in verses 6-8 he quotes key lines *before interpreting* them in a midrashic mode ("that is . . .") like that found also in various Dead Sea Scrolls (see Fitzmyer 1993). In verses 11-13 his own interpretation bridges two more quotations, each of which begins with "and." The fourfold use of "all" in verses 11-13 ties the conclusion to the "all" in verse 4, thus creating an *inclusio* that indicates the conclusion of the thought unit, while also setting up the next step in the argument (vv. 14-21).

Since "the goal of the law is Christ for righteousness for all who believe" (AT), Paul begins his supporting argument by quoting Moses, pointing out that what Moses is talking about is "the righteousness that comes from the law" *(ek tou nomou)*: "the person who does them [the commandments] will find life in them" (AT; REB: "Anyone who keeps it shall have life by it"; NRSV sounds banal: "the person who does these things will live by them"). That is, Moses promises that one will find life by obeying the law. This promise became standard Israelite and Jewish thought. Ezekiel repeated it in order to indict Israel for ignoring it (Ezek 20:11, 13, 21); Sir 17:11 calls knowledge of God "the law of life" (the life-giving law). Philo quotes Lev 18:5 and adds, "So then the true life is the life of him who walks in the judgments and ordinances of God" (*Congr.* 16). Jesus, replying to "What must I do to inherit eternal life?" pointed to the law and said, "Do this and live" (Luke 10:25-28). Indeed, in Rom 7:10-11 Paul too referred to "the very commandment that promised life," though he then explained that "it proved death for me," not because it was flawed but because of sin's deceptive power.

Paul does not say that the promise is false or outdated, nor does he imply that Christ is the doer of the law who receives life (as some have proposed; e.g., Cranfield 1979; Stowers 1994, 309). Instead, he juxtaposes and interprets another word from Moses, actually a combination of a line from Deut 9:4 ("Do not say in your heart") and a modified form of Deut 30:11-14. This exegetical move invites scrutiny.

Paul cites only a few lines from Deut 30:11-14, but he apparently has the whole passage in view. Here Moses, before promising that "if you obey the commandments . . . then you shall live and become numerous" (v. 16), insists that the law is not too difficult to obey (the italicized words are used by Paul):

> Surely, this commandment . . . is not too hard for you, nor is it too far away. It is not in heaven, that you should say, "*Who will go up to heaven* for us, and get it for us so that we may hear it and observe it [lit., to do it]?" Neither is it beyond the sea, that you should say, "Who will cross to the other side of the sea for us, and get it for us so that we may hear it [LXX: "and make it audible for us"] and observe it [lit., to do it]?" No, the word is very near to you; it is in your mouth and in your heart [LXX inserts "and in your hands"] for you to observe" [lit., to do it]. (NRSV)

In Rom 10:7, however, crossing the sea has been replaced with "who will descend into the abyss?" This substitution of "abyss" is not arbitrary, for Fitzmyer (1993) notes that in the LXX "*abyssos* often refers to the 'deep sea, depths of the sea' in contrast to sky and earth (Deut 8:7; Pss 33:7; 77:17); in time it also developed into the name for the netherworld or Tartarus (Ps 71:20; Job 41:23-24)." Also in the New Testament the word refers to the underworld (Luke 8:31; Rev 9:1-2, 11). Perhaps Paul is responsible for "the abyss" here, for it is not in the LXX. In any case, this substitution allows Paul to see in the line an allusion to Christ's resurrection (from the subterranean realm of the dead).

In having faith-grounded righteousness speak, Paul again relies on a form of *prosōpopoiia* (so Stowers 1994, 309). The import of doing so should not be missed. Since this righteousness is the rectitude that the Gentiles attained (*hē de ek pisteōs dikaiosynē* is the same as *dikaiosynēn de tēn ek pisteōs* in 9:30), the saving result itself proclaims that the Christ-event has happened, using Moses' own words to say so. Because the law's *telos* is Christ, what Moses promises in writing—life—is announced as near because the Christ-event has occurred; faith-based righteousness itself bears witness to it.

Noteworthy is the implication of verse 6—Christ has already come down. What does Paul have in mind here? He evidently visualizes the event of Christ as having a descent-ascent pattern like that in Phil 2:6-11 and John 6:62; bringing "Christ down" does not allude to the "Second Coming" (so Dunn 1988). By referring to Christ's incarnation (bringing Christ "down") and resurrection, Paul points to the Christ-event as a whole, marked by these transitions into and from the phenomenal world (just as in 1:3-4). Moreover, since Christ is the goal of the law, what Moses inferred from the givenness of the law—the nearness of the word (it is "near you, on your lips," and so forth)—Paul identifies as the result of the happenedness of the Christ-event: The near word is now the proclaimed "word of faith" (v. 8, "the word that elicits faith"). Paul does not preach faith; he preaches Christ in a way that calls for faith.

Behind both Phil 2:6-11 and Paul's interpretation of the "descent" of Christ lies the way Wisdom was regarded in Jewish thought. For example, in Sir 24 Wisdom claims she "came from the mouth of the Most High" (v. 3) and also asserts a cosmic sweep:

> Alone I compassed the vault of heaven
> And traversed the depths of the abyss. (v. 5)

Also noteworthy is Sir 24:23, which says Wisdom is the law of Moses. Even though Baruch was written somewhat later than Romans, it shows how Deut 30:11-14 was used to speak of Wisdom:

> Who has gone up into heaven, and taken her,
>   and brought her down from the clouds?
> Who has gone over the sea, and found her,
>   and will buy her for pure gold?
> No one knows the way to her,
>   or is concerned about the path to her. (Bar 3:29-31)

But God "gave her to his servant Jacob. . . . Afterward she appeared on earth / and lived with humankind" (Bar 3:36-37); a few lines later, we read, "She is the book of the commandments of God. . . . All who hold her fast will live, / and those who forsake her will die" (4:1). In short, Jewish Wisdom theology provided the conceptual framework for Paul's use of Deut 30:11-14 to speak of Christ (so also Suggs 1967, 308-11; Hays 1989, 80-81), though Paul does not actually equate Christ and Wisdom here.

Decisive for the interpretation of the passage is the relation between verse 5 and verse 6; unfortunately, Paul is not clear. So one must decide whether verse 6 (and what follows) *complements* verse 5 or states a sharp *contrast* with it (as NRSV, NIV, and REB imply by beginning verse 6 with "But"). Paul, however, did not write the usual word for "but" *(alla)*; he used *de*, which can combine continuation with distinction without making a contrast, as in Titus 1:1: "Paul, God's slave and *[de]* Christ's apostle." In fact, the same complementary use of *de* occurs in verse 10, where it clearly does not mean "but." At issue is whether what faith-derived righteousness says is a christological *alternative* to what Moses says or a christological *appropriation* of it. If the law's termination is Christ, then one must render *de* as "But." If the law's *telos* is indeed Christ, then *de* means "but also"; the latter is the more likely (so also Stowers 1994, 309; Wagner 2003, 162).

In verses 9-10 Paul speaks of confession before he speaks of faith because he is interpreting the "near word" in verse 8 (quoted from Deut 30:14) as the preached gospel, and so follows the biblical sequence, "in your mouth" and "in your heart." He points out that "if with your mouth [NRSV: "lips"] you make the confession, *Kyrios Iēsous* [Jesus is Lord], and with your heart believe that God raised him from the dead, you will be saved" (AT). Why is this the case? "Because," Paul continues, now reversing the sequence (a chiasm): "With the heart one believes for [to attain] righteousness, and with the mouth one makes the confession for [to attain] salvation" (AT). This "believe for righteousness" is simply the "righteousness that comes from faith" spelled backwards. So too, in verse 10, "righteousness" and "salvation" are not stages but virtually synonymous, as in Ps 71:15 (LXX 70:13; "my mouth will proclaim your righteousness, all day long your salvation," AT) and especially in the book of Isaiah (e.g., "my righteousness [NRSV: "deliverance"] will be forever, and my salvation for all generations," AT of LXX Isa 51:8; see also Isa 46:13; 51:5). "Jesus is Lord" is widely regarded as an early Christian confession used in baptism; Paul refers to it also in 1 Cor 12:3.

The apostle has more to say. In verses 11-13 he supports his claim in verse 10—believing yields righteousness and confession leads to salvation—by appealing to the logic of two passages of scripture when juxtaposed. (a) In verse 11 he cites Isa 28:16, which he had already quoted in 9:33 ("whoever believes in him [or it] will not be put to shame"). In the earlier context, the accent was on "believes"; here it is on "whoever," and so Paul *adds* "everyone" (*pas*, all) at the beginning of the quotation so that it now reads, "everyone who believes." Not being "put to shame" is a deliberate understatement *(litotēs)*, meaning "vindicated, affirmed," perhaps implying (for Paul) the positive verdict at the

Last Judgment. Verse 12 draws the conclusion: "Everyone" means "there is no distinction between Jew and Greek, for [omitted by NRSV] the same Lord is Lord of all," and so forth—reasserting what was said in 3:22 and paraphrasing 3:29-30 (see comments). Here Paul does not indicate whether "Lord of all" refers to God (as in 9:5) or to Christ, whose lordship is confessed in verse 9. Paul need not specify one or the other because the status of the resurrected and exalted Jesus as Lord does not compete with the lordship of the one God, but expresses it, as in Phil 2:9-11. There God, by resurrection, "highly exalted him and gave him the name [Lord] that is above every name"—God's own name; moreover, the cosmic acclamation, "Jesus Christ is Lord," is "to the glory of God the Father." For Paul, the lordship of the one God and the lordship of Christ are distinguishable but not separable, for God's lordship is now exercised through the lordship of Christ.

Paul clinches his exegetical argument by citing part of Joel 2:30-32, which predicts that on the "terrible day of the LORD" (v. 31) "everyone who calls on the name of the LORD shall be saved." Even though Paul's interest here in salvation for "everyone" probably accounts for his by-passing Joel's reference to the horrendous day, Paul might nonetheless have it in mind, since he mentions the wrath of God more frequently in Romans than in any other letter (see comment on 1:18). If so, the future tense ("shall be saved") would allude to the Eschaton. But since Paul is not expounding the nature of present Christian existence but calling attention to the way it comes about, the future tense might simply express the logical outcome, as in *Pss. Sol.* 6:1: "Happy is the man whose heart is ready to call on the name of the Lord . . . he will be saved." The common OT expression, "call on the name of the LORD," became usable in various contexts, as in 1 Cor 1:2, where it simply designates Christians.

◊ ◊ ◊ ◊

Today's readers often find Paul's use of scripture in verses 5-8 to be misuse and arbitrary, for he turns Moses' words about the law's promise of life into assertions about Christ and the gospel. But

Paul's reading of Deuteronomy is no more arbitrary than the assertion that the *telos* of the law is Christ; in fact, his interpretive moves are the logical inference from that assertion. Without Paul's understanding, Christian teaching and preaching about Christ readily becomes its own form of bringing Christ up "from the dead" (from the past), an attempt to make him "relevant." But as Paul sees it, God has already done so in the eschatological event of Christ's resurrection which, by definition, made him definitive for all. Unless Paul concluded that God's resurrecting Christ entailed repudiating the law, he could scarcely avoid saying that the *telos* of the law is Christ, the resurrected one. What other *telos* could the law have? Accordingly, the near word that Moses talked about must now be the near word of faith; Moses' word is neither historical background nor "the last word" but the anticipatory word.

Error as Disobedience (10:14-21)

Having explained how righteousness and salvation come to all who believe the gospel and call on the Lord's name, in verses 14-21 Paul interprets as disobedience Israel's refusal to "submit to God's righteousness" (v. 3), proclaimed in the faith-eliciting gospel. He first spells out more clearly how faith is elicited (vv. 14-17), thereby showing what he means by "the word of faith that we proclaim" (v. 8). Then he raises two considerations that might excuse Israel's refusal, only to dismiss them by quoting scripture (vv. 18-21). At the end of the chapter, Paul returns to the contrast between Christian Gentiles and non-believing Israel stated in 9:31-33. Here, too, his reasoning is sometimes elusive and his thought allusive—the former because he does not state the logic by which he moves from one step to another, the latter because in using scripture he alludes to more than he says.

Picking up the words of Joel 2:32 that promise salvation to all who call on the Lord's name (v. 13), Paul now spells out the conditions that precede this "calling on the Lord" (vv. 14-15); to do so, he uses a series of questions that work backward from the "call." Each question's final word generates the next question (a rhetorical device called *klimax* [ladder], used also in 8:29-30). Since the self-evident answer to each question is, "They cannot," one can reformulate Paul's point as assertions: They cannot call on the name if they do not believe; they cannot believe unless they hear; they cannot hear if there is no proclaimer (or herald); they cannot proclaim unless they are sent (to do so). The final assertion is similar to what Epictetus says about the true Cynic philosopher—that he is a herald sent by the gods (*Discourses* 3.22.70). Paul, of course, alludes to the apostles (the word means "sent ones"), sent by God. At this point (v. 15a), he might well have stated his conclusion: "So faith comes from what is heard" (v. 17); instead, he quotes Isa 52:7, which mentions "those who bring good news," and observes, "But not all have obeyed the good news," an allusion to Israel's refusal to "submit" to God's righteousness (v. 3). To support his observation that "not all have obeyed the gospel" he quotes Isa 53:1. Since NRSV, like most translations, is clearer than what Paul actually wrote, here too one must attend to the details of the Greek text.

The first detail requiring attention appears in the second question (v. 14b), which NRSV renders as, "And how are they to believe *in one of whom* they have never heard?"—as if the italicized words translated *eis hon hou ouk ēkousan*. The text, however, does not have *eis hon* ("in one") and so says literally, "believe *one* whom they have never heard." Thus Paul does not say that people cannot believe in Christ if they have not been informed *about him*, but rather that they cannot believe because they did not hear *him* (so also Cranfield 1979)—that is, Christ speaking through the apostles' proclamation, as the third question assumes, "And how are they to hear [him] without a proclaimer?" (AT). In other words, faith is really elicited by Christ himself, who is present and active in human proclamation, which to be sure also informs the hearer about Christ. This understanding of Christian preaching accords with what Paul had written to the Corinthians; there, in explaining the apostles' preaching, he said, "God is making his appeal through us" (2 Cor 5:20). So too, he had told the Thessalonians that "when you received the word of God that you heard from us, you accepted it not as a human word but as what it really is, God's word, which is also at work in you believers" (1 Thess 2:13). The first readers of Romans will not have known that Paul had written this way before, but they may well have remembered that at the beginning of the letter he had asserted that the gospel *is* the power of God, not information about God's power (see comment on 1:16). Paul's view of Christian preaching recalls that of the Old Testament prophets, who saw themselves as the human vehicles through whom God spoke (see, e.g., Isa 37:22; 44:6; Amos 3:1-2; Mic 5:10).

Although the second detail also involves translation, this time of the quotation of Isa 52:7 in verse 15, the larger question concerns what Paul intends to convey by quoting it at all. First the details. The word commonly rendered "beautiful" can also mean "timely"; but "the timely feet" is as strange as "the beautiful feet." The quotation is taken from Isa 52:7-10, which celebrates the end of Israel's Babylonian captivity as God's return to Zion (Jerusalem), and ends with the declaration that "all the ends of the earth shall see the salvation of our God." Since Paul surely planned what he would say before dictating to Tertius, he probably had the conclusion of Isaiah's oracle in mind even though he quoted only a modified form of its opening line. In fact, in verse 18 he quotes Ps 19:5, which speaks of words that went "to the ends of the world." Since he understands these "words" to refer to the gospel, what interests him in the line from Isaiah is the proclamation of "good news" expressed in the participle *euangelizomenōn* ("those who bring good news," *euangelion*). The expression "How beautiful are the feet" is a *synechdochē*, a rhetorical figure in which the part stands for the whole; here, then, "feet" stands for the messengers who come. Paul's point can be paraphrased: "How beautiful is the sight of those who bring good news." Having clarified the meaning of this declaration, we can now attend to its function. Rhetorically, it is an *apostrophē* (lit., a "turning away"), which momentarily abandons the argument in order to comment on its content—here, celebrating, from the standpoint of the recipients of the message (as "bring" indicates), the arrival of proclaimers. Such a celebrative outburst, Paul implies, occurs when the good news has been heard, thereby implying that all the forementioned conditions needed for calling on the Lord's name have been met.

What is celebrated in verse 15*b* sets up the poignant observation in verse 16: "But not all have obeyed the good news" (the *euangelion*). Given the emphasis on believing, one expects Paul to have written "not all believed." He used "obeyed" partly because he engaged in wordplay: The Greek word for "obey" *(hypakouein)* is clearly related to the word for "hear" *(akouein)*, like "harken" is related to "hear." Moreover, for Paul, believing the gospel entails allowing oneself to be shaped by it, and that means submitting to it (in 1:5 he wrote of "the obedience of faith"; see comment). By using "obey," then, Paul alludes to Israel's refusal to "submit to God's righteousness" (v. 3). While rhetorically, "not all" is either a *litotēs* (deliberate understatement) or a *meiosis* (an amelioration) as in the "some" of 3:3, here it echoes, negatively, what Paul had said about the "remnant" in 9:27 and also anticipates what he will say about it again in 11:5. Since "not all" = "some," Paul alludes to the minority of Christian Jews (who did "obey" the gospel), while at the same time he calls attention to the majority that did not. This disappointing outcome, which generated the whole discussion in chapters 9–11, was foreseen in Isa 53:1, which Paul now quotes according to the LXX: "Lord, who has believed our message?" Implied answer: "Only some." By quoting Isaiah, Paul implies that the current situation accords with that of the prophet. For Paul, Isaiah's "our message" refers to the word of the "sent" ones (the apostles) who "proclaim the word of faith" (v. 8). Because Isa 53:1 is part of the Song of the Servant, whose suffering brings redemption, perhaps Paul tacitly alludes to the gospel as the early Christian interpretation of Jesus as the Suffering Servant. The allusion is possible, though neither evident nor necessary.

The third translation detail requiring scrutiny appears in verse 17 and has two aspects. Just as "calling on" in verse 14 picks up the same word in verse 13, so verse 17 picks up the last words of the quotation in verse 16: "our message" (*akoē*, that which is heard, reflecting *akouein*, "hear"). NRSV recognizes this, and translates *ara hē pistis ex akoēs* as "So faith comes from what is heard, and what is heard [*hē de akoē*] comes through the word of Christ." But because some think that the first *akoē* means the act of hearing, NIV (as well as REB and NASB) translates: "faith comes from *hearing* the message, and the message is heard through the word of Christ." It is unlikely, however, that Paul would give *akoē* two meanings in the same sentence. One must also decide whether the genitive "of Christ" refers to the content of what is heard (objective genitive) or to its origin (subjective or "authorial" genitive). Probably the latter is correct: "The word of Christ" refers to Christ's word, namely, the word that, according to verse 14, one must hear from the living Christ himself if one is to believe in him. So one may translate verse 17 this way: "So faith comes from the message, and the message comes through Christ's word that occurs when the apostles proclaim the gospel."

In verses 18-21, Paul relies on the diatribal style to voice two excuses for Israel's refusal, only to reject them and to bring this discussion to its climax. The first excuse ("Have they not heard?" v. 18) responds to verse 16 and means, "They haven't really heard, have they?" The particle *mē* at the beginning of the question indicates that a negative reply is expected: "No, they haven't." Prefaced by *menounge* ("on the contrary," as in 9:20), this question is rebuffed by Ps 19:5 (not actually identified as a quotation): "Indeed they have" (NRSV). The second excuse ("Did Israel not understand?" NRSV) also means, "Israel did not understand, did it?" and is refuted by quoting Moses (Deut 32:21) and Isa 65:1-2. Thus Paul cites scripture to argue that Israel has no excuse.

In verse 18, the appropriateness of using lines from Ps 19:5 (LXX 18:4) is not self-evident, for it says, "Their voice has gone out to all the earth, and their words to the ends of the world." But Paul's own plan for a mission in Spain (15:28) shows that he knew that the gospel had not yet gone "to the ends of the world" (*oikoumenē*, the known inhabited world); moreover, what the psalm itself celebrates is the heavens' witness to God's glory (Ps 19:1-6) and the perfection of God's law (vv. 7-13). How can Paul use this psalm's words to refer to gospel preaching? Even if Paul's use of these lines is an exuberant exaggeration (somewhat like 1:8), the basis for using this psalm as evidence of the worldwide Christian preaching of Christ's word remains somewhat unclear. Still, his point is not that the Jewish apostles' mission to Jews is "now finished" (so Munck 1987, 96); rather, because the *telos* of the law is Christ, wherever the law has gone, its *telos* too has gone, for Christ is not foreign to the law. (Did Paul think it a coincidence that in the LXX the superscription for Ps 18 is *eis to telos*?) So Israel is accountable for refusing the gospel, seen as its disobedience (the result of thinking that righteousness was the result of works [9:32] and of not knowing that God's rectitude rectifies [10:3]).

Understandably, in verse 19 the interlocutor tries to excuse Israel by asking whether Israel might not have understood what it heard. Rather than insisting that it did, Paul lets Moses and Isaiah make the point for him. Moses' words are from Deut 32 ("The Song of Moses"), which contrasts God's goodness with Israel's infidelity. Indeed, Deut 32:20 calls the Israelites "sons in whom there is no faithfulness" (*pistis*, Paul's word for "faith"). Paul ignores this accusation, perhaps because Isaiah's word at the end of the chapter will characterize Israel's faithlessness even more effectively. In any case, he quotes Deut 32:21, God's response to Israel's infidelity: "I will make you jealous of those who are not a nation," and so forth—for Paul, the Gentiles who accept the gospel. That is, Paul implies that this jealousy shows that Israel did understand. In 11:13 he will pick up this reference to Israel's future jealousy.

Whereas Moses spoke of the future, Paul takes Isaiah's words (vv. 20-21) to refer to the present anomaly, which he had stated in 9:30-31—the believing Gentiles, who had not striven for faith-derived righteousness, "have attained it," whereas Israel "stumbled." To use Isaiah to make this point again, Paul first applies to the Gentiles what the prophet had said about Israel, "I have been found by those who did not seek me," and so forth (Isa 65:1), and then points out (in v. 21) that the next quotation does apply to Israel: "But of Israel he says, 'All day long I have held out my hands to a disobedient and contrary people'" (Isa 65:2). Not to be missed is that this quotation expresses both Israel's enduring obstinacy and God's persistent "Nevertheless," thereby setting the stage for chapter 11.

◊ ◊ ◊ ◊

Running through the discussion of Israel's error is the note of tragic reversal: Gentiles reached the goal of righteousness even though they did not pursue it, while Israel pursued it but did not reach it (9:30-31); Israel has zeal for God but, not understanding God's rectifying rectitude, refused to submit to God's action (10:2-3). Israel indeed heard but did not heed the gospel (10:16-18), though Gentiles did. As a result, this people will be jealous of the Christian Gentiles who are not a people. God has been "found" by those Gentiles who did not seek God (restating 9:30-31), while Israel remains "a disobedient and contrary people" to whom God keeps stretching out his hands (10:21). By pointing out these unfortunate outcomes, Paul is implicitly celebrating the freedom of God's Nevertheless! for not only does the positive response of the Gentiles accord with God's plan for them, but also God's outstretched hands toward disobedient Israel suggests that ultimately God's posture will not be in vain. In fact, in light of the portrayal of Israel's error, the ultimate achievement of God's purpose (to be revealed in chapter 11) is all the greater. The freedom of God in election (chap. 9) coheres with the freedom of God's patience in chapter 10, and above all with the freedom of God's mysterious mode of fidelity in chapter 11. At the same time, Paul holds Israel accountable for its error; indeed, he must, since by his lights Israel rebuffed the news that the *telos* of the law has occurred in Christ. Yet Paul does not "solve" the logical problem created by the tension between God's sovereign freedom in election and Israel's accountability for its misunderstanding. Nor does anyone else in the Bible—or beyond it, for that matter.

God's Freedom as Fidelity (11:1-32)

Having ended both chapters 9 and 10 with the contrast between believing Gentiles and nonbelieving Israel (9:30-33; 10:20-21), Paul now explains how God uses the situation to achieve salvation for both. Thereby Paul confirms the assertion with which he began, "It is not as though the word of God has failed" (9:6, AT). The chapter has four units: verses 1-12 respond to the harsh portrayal of Israel at the end of chapter 10 by explaining God's way with Israel; verses 13-24 explain how God relates believing Gentiles to Israel; verses 25-32 complete the argument; the peroration in verses 33-36 celebrates the awesome otherness of God's ways, and forms the counterpart to 9:1-5.

◊ ◊ ◊ ◊

God's Way with Israel (11:1-12)

Paul's thought moves in three steps. First, he rejects the inference that God has "rejected his people." As evidence, he uses both himself and the precedent of Elijah to claim that now too there is a believing minority in Israel, a "remnant chosen by grace" (vv. 1-6). Next (vv. 7-10), he turns to the unbelieving majority, using scripture to characterize it with the harshest language in the whole discussion. Then, in verses 11-12 he again states an inference that must be rejected, and looks ahead to the fullness of Gentile salvation.

The opening question formulates sharply the issue that has propelled the whole discussion since 9:1. The "I ask" (lit., "I say") suggests that here (as in v. 11) the interlocutor is Paul himself. The customary translations, "Has God rejected his people?" imply that Paul is asking an open-ended question, but the particle *mē* (used to signal that a negative reply is expected) shows that Paul really asks, "God has not rejected his people, has he?" (Some manuscripts read "the inheritance" *[klēronomian]*, which Wagner [2003, 222] prefers.) The wording of the question is taken from Ps 94 (LXX 93):14: "For the Lord will not reject [Paul: "has not rejected"] his people, and his inheritance he will not forsake" (AT). The first clause is identical with part of 1 Sam 12:22 (LXX: 1 Kingdoms), where Samuel reassures the people, "The Lord will not reject his people for the sake of his great name" (AT), despite Israel's insistence on having a king, though God is their king (1 Sam 12:12). Perhaps Paul saw in Israel's current refusal to submit to God's righteousness and attempt to establish its own (10:3) a repetition of Israel's earlier action (so also Wagner 2003, 223-24). In any case, to the words taken from scripture Paul adds "whom he foreknew," thereby applying to Israel what he had said about Christians in 8:29-30 (the only other time he used "foreknew," *proegnō*). Thus, by rejecting the idea that God has rejected Israel,

Paul sets in motion the whole subsequent discussion in which he argues that exactly the opposite is the case. Who needs to hear this? Not Jews, Christian or non-Christian, but Christian Gentiles who are misinterpreting the widespread Jews' No to the gospel.

In the latter half of verse 1, Paul refers to himself as "an Israelite, a descendant of Abraham," as evidence that God has not rejected the *people*. He can use his own ethnic identity to argue this way because, as throughout chapters 9–11, he is not thinking of individual Jews and Gentiles but of both as groups. Israel *as a people* cannot be rejected if there are Israelites who are not rejected. Paul is not the exception that proves the rule (that Israel is rejected), because *as* a believer he *is* an Israelite (*is* is emphasized in Greek), a specific instance that demonstrates that God has not rejected the people. Adding "whom he foreknew" underscores God's constancy: The One who on his own initiative chose Israel (and chose Jacob over Esau) has not responded to Israel's unbelief by rejection. Paul had made the same point at 3:3-4.

Next Paul reminds the readers of the Elijah story, which he takes as biblical evidence that God has not rejected the *people*, for Elijah too was part of the faithful minority. In verses 2-4 Paul refers to 1 Kgs 19, which reports that Elijah, having slain the prophets of Baal, fled from their patron Jezebel, who had vowed to kill him. In verse 3, modifying 1 Kgs 19:14, Paul cites the refugee's complaint: "Lord, they have killed your prophets and demolished your altars; I alone am left, and they are seeking my life" (AT). Paul ignores the last clause; his interest is in "I alone am left," because this complaint evokes "the divine reply" (NRSV for *ho chrēmatismos*, oracular announcement), "I have kept for myself seven thousand who have not bowed the knee to Baal" (1 Kgs 19:18; LXX: "you will keep seven thousand," and lacking "for myself"; other differences between LXX and Paul are noted by Moo 1996, 676 nn. 25-26).

Paul exploits this segment of the Elijah story in several ways. (a) Then, as now, neither individual is a solitary exception; both situations actually show that the bond between God and Israel has not been severed by the action of the majority. Elijah and the seven thousand anticipate Paul and the current minority, the Christian

Jews. (b) When Paul introduces Elijah, he asks, "Or do you not know what the scripture says in the Elijah story, how he speaks to God against Israel?" (AT). By appealing to what they know, Paul expects the readers to agree that "in just the same way . . . a 'remnant' has come into being" (REB). For Paul, "remnant" does not refer simply to what is left over (as in a fabric shop) but to the enduring part that survives disaster and so assures the future. Thus Paul uses God's rebuke of Elijah's complaint "against Israel" to rebuke the Christian Gentiles who also complain against Israel when they think that God has rejected his people. (c) By mentioning "remnant" Paul recalls 9:27-29, where he quoted Isaiah's words about a saved remnant; this distinction between the remnant and the others recalls also 9:6 ("not all Israelites truly belong to Israel") because empirical Israel is not flatly identical with the real Israel, which is always determined by God's free choice. Paul had signaled this emphasis on God's prior action by changing "You will keep seven thousand" (LXX) to "I have kept for myself seven thousand." God's prior action accords with God's foreknowledge in verse 2. (d) With the observation, "So too at the present time there is a remnant, chosen by grace" (v. 5), Paul in effect asks the readers to focus not on the nonbelieving Jewish majority but on the believing minority whom God has elected. If the readers get the point, they will understand the minority not as evidence that God has *rejected* his people as a whole but that God remains faithful to them through the remnant. (e) In verse 6 he links both remnants to his major theme: "If it is by grace, it is not on the basis of works, otherwise grace would not be grace" (AT), for by definition, grace is unmerited favor. This accent on grace-not-works puts into theological language the significance of God saying, "I have kept for myself . . ."; that is, the Christian Jewish minority exists because of God's action, not because of its achievement.

But if the remnant exists because God chose it "by grace," where does that leave the majority that was not chosen? Was their not being chosen also the result of God's act? This is precisely the question that Paul addresses in verses 7-10. To do so, in verse 7 he applies to Israel as a whole the same distinction that he had made between Israel and the Gentiles in 9:31 (non-striving Gentiles "attained" righteousness but striving Israel did not). Now he asserts three points: (a) Israel (as a whole) did not "obtain" (= "attain") what it was seeking; (b) those who did "obtain" it are the elect (= the remnant chosen by grace; REB: "the chosen few"); (c) the rest "were hardened" (by God), consistent with 9:18: "So then he has mercy on whomever he wills, but hardens whomever he wills" (AT). What is implicit in "were hardened" (Israel's No) becomes explicit in the quotations in verses 8-10: Israel's refusal is God's doing.

> He gave them a spirit of stupor
> eyes so that they do not see and
> ears so that they do not hear
> until this very day. (AT)

Despite the introductory phrase "as it is written," no biblical text actually says this. The "quotation" makes its point by changing and combining selected words and phrases from several LXX passages (italicized):

Isa 29:10   "The Lord has made you drink with *a spirit of stupor,* and he will close their eyes."

Deut 29:3   "The Lord God did not give you a heart to understand, and *eyes* to see and *ears* to hear *until* this *day.*"

Isa 6:10   "The heart of this people has been made dull [lit., "fat"], and their *ears* have become hard of hearing, and they have closed their *eyes,* lest they see with their *eyes* and *hear* with their *ears* and understand with their heart and turn, and I will heal them." (AT)

Paul, following the lead of Isa 29:10 (which emphasizes God's action), changed Deut 29:3 (which says what God did *not* do) into saying what God *has* done, and in this way explains what he means by saying "the rest were hardened" in verse 7.

Paul was not alone in attributing the Jews' lack of understanding to God's action. According to Mark 4:11-12 Jesus used Isa 6:9-10 to explain that he used parables *so that* outsiders would not understand him (according to Matt 13:13-15 he used parables *because* they did not understand); in John 12:37-40 the evangelist sharpens Isa 6:10 to explain why they were "*not able* to believe" despite the "signs" that Jesus had done: "He [God] has blinded their eyes, and hardened their heart so that they might not see with their eyes and understand with their heart, and turn, and I will heal them" (AT). There is no evidence that Paul relied on the traditions in the Gospels or that the Evangelists were influenced by Paul.

In verse 9, Paul quotes David's curse on his enemies in Ps 69 (LXX 68):22-23 and adds "and a trap" to the first line:

> Let their table become a snare and a trap,
> a stumbling block and a retribution for them;
> let their eyes be darkened so that they cannot see,
> and keep their backs forever bent.

What Paul understands by "their table" is not clear. Is it the altar in the Jerusalem temple (so, e.g., Dunn 1988), or the "table" in the Roman church, which was arguing over dietary matters addressed in chapter 14 (so Minear 1971, 78-19)? Or did Paul include the first line simply because without it the second would make little sense? It is the second line that interests him because it refers to the "stumbling block," a cross-reference to the quotation of Isa 28:16 in 9:33 (see comment). What Paul understood by the "bent backs" is not clear either. In any case, both 9:31-33 and 11:8-10 emphasize that the unbelieving part of Israel stumbled over what God has done. Even though Paul's thinking expressed in these quotations in verses 8-10 is harsh, it would have been even more harsh had he gone on to quote the next verses in Ps 69, namely, verses 24-28, in which the psalmist asks God to pour out wrath on the poet's enemies, cause their habitation to become desolate, compound their iniquity, "not let them come into your righteousness," blot out their names from "the book of the living and prevent their names from being written" with the righteous (AT).

Because verses 8-10 are adduced in support of the assertion that the nonelect were hardened *by God*, Paul takes the quotation in verse 9 to imply that God has now done what David asked God to do to his (David's) enemies. However, translating *dia pantos*

(v. 10) as "forever" (NRSV, NIV, NASB, NJB) instead of "continuously" or "unceasingly" (REB) implies that God's action in Paul's time continues endlessly into the future—an inference that has legitimated the pernicious notion that Jews are perpetually suffering because they did not become Christians. But Paul goes on to argue that the plight of the currently "hardened" part of Israel will *not* be forever. The present unbelieving part of Israel has not caused God to annul the whole people's election; rather, in the future God will annul the present unbelief of the "hardened" part, so the whole people will be saved (11:26).

After the harsh quotations in verses 9-10, Paul returns to the imagery of the footrace (in 9:32-33) and denies vigorously that the "hardened" have "stumbled so as to fall" (v. 11). The runner who stumbles is not excluded from the race; rather, God uses just this "stumbling" by the majority to achieve the divine purpose. To express this, Paul uses strong contrasting theological language: "through their trespass [NRSV: "stumbling"] salvation has come [a verb must be supplied] to the Gentiles, so as to make the 'hardened' [lit., "them"] jealous" (AT). By calling the nonacceptance of the gospel "their trespass" *(paraptōma)*, Paul restates the refusal to "submit" to God's righteousness (10:3), which had interpreted Israel's mistaken way of pursuing the law that leads to righteousness (9:31-32). Nonetheless, that "trespass" is not wholly disastrous, for God uses it to save the Gentiles, which in turn is to make the refusers "jealous." This jealousy too is God's act, for in 10:19 Paul had quoted Deut 32:21 in which God (through Moses) said, "*I* will make you jealous of those who are not a nation" (Gentiles). Since Paul is using the scripture to interpret the current situation, he shows no interest whatever in explaining the psychodynamics of this jealousy. Nor does he explain *how* it is that unbelieving Israel's "trespass" is the means by which salvation has come to Gentiles. He is reflecting on what has actually happened and will happen.

The book of Acts does, interestingly, have Paul turn to the Gentiles because the Jews in Pisidian Antioch "were filled with jealousy" when they saw Gentiles listening to him (Acts 13:44-48). But because Acts nonetheless reports that Paul continued going first to synagogues (17:1, 3, 10, 17; 18:4; 19:8), many scholars regard Paul's words in Acts 13:46-47 as the author's (later) view of what happened repeatedly in Paul's mission. But more important is the difference between Acts 13 and Rom 11: In the former, the Jews' jealousy accounts for their rejection of Paul and his turn to the Gentiles, but in the latter the Jews' jealousy prompts them to change their negative attitude toward the gospel, for Rom 11:12 looks ahead to the salvation of all Israel (v. 26).

Verse 12 argues from the lesser to the greater: If X is true (as it surely is; see below), then how much more is Y true (the same argument was used in 5:10, 15, 17). In such reasoning, the accent falls on Y. In verse 12, by doubling the X clause ("Now if their stumbling [lit., "trespass"] means riches for the world, and if their defeat means riches for Gentiles"), the Y clause is especially underscored. The X clauses assume that God has "hardened" Israel to bring salvation to Gentiles, expressed as "riches" *(ploutos)*—the abundant gifts of salvation that flow from God's own abundance (9:23: "the riches of his glory") and that God bestows on all who call on the Lord's name (10:12). Since Paul is talking about Gentiles and Jews, "world" means the Gentile "world." To interpret the "trespass" the second X clause speaks of Israel's *hēttēma* (NRSV: "defeat"; REB: "falling short"; NASB: "failure"; NIV: "loss"); but since this *hēttēma* is contrasted with "riches" accrued to Gentiles, NIV's "loss" is preferable. In other words, God has used Israel's "loss" to "enrich" the Gentiles. Seen as a whole, verse 12 asserts that while God's use of Israel's "trespass" to bring salvation to Gentiles is itself marvelous (the two X clauses), it is even surpassed by what the Y clause envisages: the *plērōma* (fullness) of Israel—that is, the ultimate salvation of all Israel, not simply of the present remnant. (NRSV renders *plērōma* as "full inclusion"; REB as "their coming to full strength.") The rift within Israel, announced at 9:6, will not be permanent.

To summarize: Paul celebrates the marvelous ways of God: God uses "hardened" Israel's "trespass" (= not "attaining" what it seeks [v. 7] = not obtaining righteousness though pursuing it [9:31] = seeking to establish its own rectitude because it does not know that it is God's rectitude that rectifies [10:3]) to bring salvation to Gentiles, and to make a people out of the motley Gentiles who now are "not my people" (9:25; 10:12). But *even greater* is God's overcoming the hiatus between the "hardened" Israel and the "remnant" (the current Christian Jews) so that Israel will no longer be divided but "full," complete. Paul's conviction that God has not rejected Israel, and the apostle's commitment to "his people" will be expressed even more strongly, and more fully, in verses 25-32. But first, Paul must explain to Christian Gentiles the meaning of the salvation that has come to them in light of God's way with Israel.

◊ ◊ ◊ ◊

It is much easier to *look at* Paul's wrestling with the meaning of his people's responses to the message of God's act in Jesus than it is to look *with him* at the unexpected phenomenon itself. Western Christian Gentiles find it difficult to empathize with his agony despite recent scholarship's emphasis on his "Jewishness," on the one hand, and the emergence of identity consciousness among women and minorities, on the other. What is most difficult, however, is thinking *theologically* about the phenomenon he had in view. But not because Christian Gentiles are reluctant to talk about God! The difficulty is centered rather in the reluctance of many Western Christians to speak, as Paul did, about God as the active Reality who accounts for the phenomenon—and to do so by studying scripture. The latter difficulty is intensified by calling Paul's scripture "the Hebrew Bible"—not simply because he quoted scripture in Greek while we read it in English and not Hebrew, but also because giving it this name distances it even more from Christian Gentile sensibility. But the more deeply the Christian faith is rooted among non-Jewish peoples around the globe, the more urgent is the task of appropriating Paul's legacy by pondering theologically the significance of the fact that Africans, Asians, and Polynesians are learning to call Abraham "our father" (4:12).

God's Way with the Gentiles (11:13-24)

Even though Paul has been instructing his predominantly Gentile readers all along, at verse 13 he pointedly says, "I am speaking to you Gentiles"—that is, what follows pertains particularly to *you*. And what is that? That the Christian Gentiles' salvation is inseparable from that of Israel! It occurs neither alongside Israel's salvation nor in its place, but by participation in it, like the grafting of a wild olive branch into a cultivated olive tree. In short, Paul argues that there can be no valid "Gentile Christianity" apart from Israel, precisely because "God has not rejected his people" (v. 1). Somehow, he implies, ultimately they are saved together or not at all. The task of what follows (vv. 25-32) is to explain this "somehow."

The first thing Christian Gentiles must understand is how Paul's own mission to Gentiles is related to God's way with Israel (vv. 13-14). Remarkably, he says that precisely as the Gentiles' apostle, "I glorify my ministry if somehow I might make my flesh jealous and save some of them" (AT). By "glorify" Paul probably means, "I make the most of my ministry." By translating *ei pōs* ("if somehow") simply as "in order to," NRSV substitutes Paul's motivation for his uncertainty about the desired result. Here REB's paraphrase is preferable: "yet always in the hope of stirring those of my own race to envy" (mentioned in v. 11 and 10:19). Even though Paul sees himself as God's instrument in evoking this jealousy, he pointedly expects that only "some of them" will be saved—and not necessarily through his own work. He insists, in other words, that he is devoting his energies to Gentiles because, like God, he has not given up on Israel. Peerbolte (2003, 197) is surely right: Paul is not disclosing his long-held strategy or revealing his ulterior motive for going to Gentiles. Rather, verses 13-14 are required by the thrust of the argument on the one hand, and his projected mission to Gentiles in Spain on the other. With this self-interpretation, he relates his own (often misunderstood) vocation to both God's clear will and God's mysterious way of achieving it.

In verses 15-16 Paul resumes celebrating the eventual inclusion of the "hardened" part of Israel in the whole people of God. At verse 12, as noted, he began to advance his argument by using a series of "if . . . then . . ." assertions ("then" must be supplied); now he resumes this mode of reasoning (vv. 15, 16 [twice], 17, 18, 21, 24). In none of these instances does the "if" call into question the truth of what follows; rather, in each case, the "if" clause says something so evident that it need not be validated, and so states something *from which* Paul can argue (as in v. 6). In verse 12 and verse 24 this mode of argument is combined with another: "If X, then how much more Y" (the content of v. 15 suggests that this mode of reasoning is implied here as well). In other words, these "if . . . then . . ." statements are the rhetorical equivalent of "since . . . therefore . . ." assertions.

Verbless verse 15 continues the thought of verse 12: "If their [the "hardened" part of Israel] rejection *[apobolē]* is the reconciliation of the world, what will be their acceptance *[proslēmpsis]* but life from the dead?" (AT). The "if" clause restates "the riches of the world" and "the riches of the Gentiles" that result from God's use of the "trespass" of the "hardened" part of Israel. Since Paul continues to speak of God's action, "their rejection" means their rejection by God, now contrasted by their "acceptance" by God, not their rejection/acceptance of the gospel. In speaking of their "rejection" Paul is not asserting what he had denied in verse 1; he is using this harsh word for rhetorical reasons, in order to contrast strongly the present and the envisioned future. That future is so remarkable that it can be characterized as "life from the dead"—not an allusion to the general resurrection at Christ's parousia, when the remnant's massive enlargement will occur. Paul's real concern here is the radical, transforming reversal that Israel's "acceptance" will entail.

After noting how radical the transformation of the hardened part of Israel will be, in verse 16 Paul sets the stage for verses 17-18, the olive tree analogy. The logic of verse 16 is simple and straightforward: What is true of the part is true of the whole. Therefore, Paul implies, when the "fullness" of Israel is actualized, there will be no difference between the present remnant of Israel (= the "first fruits") and the "hardened." In light of verses 7-15, verse 16 implies that this unification will be achieved only by

God's amazing freedom to reverse the present. The No of the "hardened" in no way precludes the Yes of God. Here "first fruits"(*aparchē*) refers to Num 15:17-21 (see comment on 8:23). Nowhere, however, does the Old Testament say that giving the first fruits to God (actually to the priests) makes holy what is not given; rather, giving the part to the Holy One makes *it* holy, and so differentiates it radically from the retained non-holy, even though it represents the whole. But Paul emphasizes precisely the opposite: The holiness of the part implies the holiness of the whole. Paul makes this surprising turn because for him "first fruits" symbolizes the currently believing remnant, which is part of the whole Israel (Moo [1996], oddly, thinks "first fruits" refers to the patriarchs). Because both the remnant and the hardened are part of the same dough, what is true of the part is ultimately true of the whole as well. (Thus the "first fruits" imagery is a comment on the "fullness," the *plērōma* in v. 12.) Were that not the case, then by believing the gospel, Jews would forfeit their relation to Israel, and conversely, the current cleavage in Israel would be permanent even after its "hardened" part is saved. Here, too, what Paul says about the dough in verse 16 anticipates what he will say in verse 26: "All Israel will be saved."

The rest of verse 16 uses the same logic but changes the imagery: "If the root is holy, then the branches also are holy"— that is, what is true of the root is true also of the branches, for they are one tree. In referring to the holy root, Paul seems to allude to a particular known image, namely, Abraham as the "root" of Israel (so Philo, *Her.* 279), as Cranfield (1979), Moo (1996), and Fitzmyer (1993) also think. The root and the branches are "holy" because they belong to God, not because they have achieved moral perfection. The reference to the tree sets up the analogy of the olive tree that follows (vv. 17-24), according to which this tree includes wild olive branches that *became* part of the tree by being grafted into it—namely, the Christian Gentiles.

The apostle is often accused of shoddy thinking in what he says about the olive tree because, being a city man, he does not understand grafting. But his surprising statements about grafting "a wild olive shoot" into the tree are as essential, and as appropriate, to his overall argument as the surprising twist he gives to "the first fruits." His theological argument is not controlled by what occurs in the olive grove but by the subject matter, which by definition is improbable. Yet precisely this improbability is central to Paul's point. This is why scouring ancient literature to show that what he writes about grafting does accord with at least some current practice is largely irrelevant.

In the analogy, the main thought moves in three steps, each beginning with "If . . ." (vv. 17, 21, 24). While also these "if . . ." clauses state what Paul regards as undoubtedly true (as in vv. 12-16), here the inferences are more varied: In verse 17, the "if . . ." clause is the basis of a prohibition (v. 18); in verse 21 it leads to a warning; in verse 24 it is part of the reasoning from the lesser to the greater. Remarkably, the prohibition in verse 18 ("Do not boast over the branches") rests on a double "if . . ." clause that formulates Paul's basic point as if it needed no argument, as being self-evidently true: (a) "Some of the branches have been lopped off" and (b) "you [sg.], a wild olive, have been grafted in among them" (REB; the sudden switch from third person plural to second person singular is probably used to intensify the rhetorical effect by accosting the individual hearer). The prohibition clearly has in view Christian Gentile arrogance, whether already known to Paul or anticipated. In verse 18 Paul goes on to modify his prohibition: "If you do boast, remember that it is not you that support the root, but the root that supports you." Getting this relationship right is an essential part of the whole argument. This "support" restates the latter part of verse 17: The grafted branch has "come to share the same root and sap as the olive" (REB). That is, it is permissible for Christian Gentiles to be proud of being incorporated into Israel so long as they recognize that the benefits of salvation they enjoy are derived from, and are contingent on, their inclusion in the tree that is nourished by the root—namely, by God's election of Abraham (chap. 4) and by God's continued undeserved election of the patriarchs (9:6-13). Because Paul's olive tree image calls for Christian Gentile inclusion in Israel, "a Gentile church . . . as an equal co-partner *alongside* Israel" (so Gaston 1987, 149, italics added) is precisely what Paul does *not* want.

Inclusion, however, is *not* replacement. The grafted wild olive shoots do not take the place of the severed branches (so also Donaldson 1997, 179)—though, unfortunately, this is precisely what NRSV (like RSV) has Paul say when it translates *en autois* as "in their place" instead of "among them" (so rightly NASB, NIV, REB). Had Paul asserted that the severed branches were replaced, he would have written *anti autōn*. Not to be overlooked is that *some* of the branches were lopped off, not all; here "some" = "the rest" that God "hardened" (v. 7). Those not cut off are the Christian Jews.

Does Paul create a logical tension with some of his own assertions? This appears to be the case when verse 20 explains that the branches "were broken off by unbelief *[tē apistia]*, but you stand by faith" (*tē pistei;* AT), for this appears to make human activity decisive, whereas 9:16 claims that what matters is not "human will or exertion" but God's sheer mercy. The rest of verse 20, however, shows that the tension with 9:16 is more apparent than real, for in verse 20 Paul is not correcting 9:16 (nor has he forgotten it), but undermining the Christian Gentiles' propensity to "become proud," so he urges "fear" (NRSV: "stand in awe"), the signature of faith. Whoever sees a tension between these two passages assumes (wrongly) that for Paul faith is a matter of exertion, of striving. More serious is the image of the branches that were "cut off," for this severance suggests that God has indeed rejected (at least this part of) his people (11:1). But this tension too is more apparent than real, because given the image of the tree, lopping off branches is the appropriate metaphorical equivalent of the "hardening" of part of Israel.

Paul mentions "fear" in order to show that the Gentile's "standing" must not be taken for granted, and to indicate that "standing" is not risk-free, as verse 21 makes clear: "For if God did not spare the natural branches [as he surely did not], he will not spare you either" (NIV; NRSV translates those manuscripts that include *mē pōs*: "*perhaps* he will not spare you"). It is not God's capriciousness that makes the Christian Gentile's "standing" insecure but the possibility that this Christian's faith will prove to be transient. As a Gentile, this person has no inherited, indelible, covenant-based relation to God but is a graftee who has come into this inheritance by faith (by *pistis*); therefore, loss of faith or trust puts this person in the same situation as that of the natural branch that was broken off by *apistia* (v. 20). Verse 22 reinforces this observation by insisting that the Christian Gentile reader take note of both God's "kindness and severity"—to those who "fall" God is severe, but you, believing Gentile, benefit from God's kindness, "provided you continue in his kindness; otherwise you also will be cut off." Paul could hardly have emphasized more strongly the importance of the believer's continued reliance on God's kindness. Verse 23 makes exactly the same point with regard to the severed branches: if they cease their unbelief *(apistia)*, God will graft them too into the tree, for God has the power to do so. God's kindness is as effective as God's severity.

Verse 24 both summarizes Paul's use of the olive tree analogy and looks ahead to the resolution of the issue that generated the whole discussion from 9:1 onward. The "how much more" indicates that verse 24 argues from the lesser to the greater in order to underscore God's power to reinstate the severed branches. Because the lesser is itself a marvelous event—the inclusion of Gentiles—the regrafting of the severed branches into their proper place is even greater. Really? Is not what is "contrary to nature" (the grafting of the wild olive branch) greater than the restoration of what is "according to nature" (NRSV: "natural branches")? Not in this case, writes Paul, because here too the theological content is not controlled by what olive growers can do. Here regrafting the cut branches is even more marvelous than grafting the wild olive shoot into the cultivated tree, because the former entails overcoming Israel's active resistance, whereas the latter does not. Verse 24, in other words, restates what Paul had already said in verses 11-12.

◊ ◊ ◊ ◊

What Gaston (1987, 143) said about 11:11-13 is even more true of the olive tree: "The language is rhetorically artful but tantalizingly vague." Clear, of course, is Paul's insistence that by faith Christian Gentiles are incorporated into Israel. But exactly what does that mean? Everything depends on the sort of inclusion Paul has in mind, which he did not spell out, however, because that was not the issue here as it was in his Letter to the Galatians. There he was adamant: Male Gentile believers must not be required to be circumcised—that is, become proselytes, actual members of the Jewish people. What Paul now asserts about Abraham—that he is the "father" of "all who believe without being circumcised" (4:11)—shows that also in Romans he did not envision Gentile inclusion through conversion to Judaism. In this letter he does not argue this point (as he had in Galatians), for he simply assumes it. Since Paul's discussion is theological rather than ecclesial, matters of policy and practice are left aside here. Important theologically are two things: that the included remain Gentiles, and that the graftees remain as dependent on the root (God's grace in electing Abraham) as the rest of the tree. The combination of these two emphases generates important questions for Gentile Christian theology. Accepting them as an essential dimension of Christian self-understanding is itself a sign that Romans is more than an artifact from early Christianity, but part of the Christian canon.

The Mystery of God's Way with All (11:25-32)

This paragraph concludes the discussion that began at 9:1 as well as the relentless theological argument that commenced at 1:18. So Paul sometimes paraphrases what he has said before; he also states implications not made explicit previously. By not developing ideas but simply stating them, the passage is rhetorically more effective. After the Holocaust and in light of all the issues it raised, and continues to raise, about the relation of the Jewish people to Christianity, what Paul says here about the future salvation of "all Israel" propels this paragraph into the center of conversations between Jews and Christians, and among Christians too. Understandably, debates among Christian exegetes have been particularly vigorous. The issues in those debates cannot be rehearsed here, but many of them are nonetheless present, silently standing in the wings and noting the interpretation of what Paul says and does not say.

Verse 25 begins with the formulaic "I want you to know" (lit., "I do not want you not to know," as at 1:13), which signals that what Paul is about to say is especially important—here, the core teaching, supported by scripture (vv. 25-27). In light of this core, Paul then restates how the "disobedience" of *both* Jews and Gentiles functions in the achievement of God's purpose (vv. 28-31). Precisely in the face of Gentile immorality grounded in idolatry, and of Israel's refusal, the last word is God's mercy for all (v. 32). Appropriately, when in chapter 12 Paul takes up the theme of the rectitude of the redeemed, he begins by referring to "the mercies of God."

What Paul wants his "brothers and sisters" (as in 10:1) to know is "this mystery," a teaching that is neither self-evident nor inferable from observed phenomena, but must be revealed (as in 16:25; 1 Cor 2:7; 4:1; 13:2; 14:2; 15:51). Here, *mystērion* (as in apocalyptic thought going back to Dan 2:17-18) is the destined future now disclosed, as in the *Habakkuk Commentary* from Qumran: "For all the ages of God reach their appointed end as he determines them in the mysteries of his wisdom" (1QpHab 7:14; Vermes 1995, 344). Paul does not say how he came to know the mystery he is about to share. There is no reason to think it was revealed to him shortly before he dictated this passage, as has been suggested. Before giving the content of the mystery, however, he first tells the readers why he is disclosing it: to forestall their being "conceited" (NIV; NRSV: "claim to be wiser than you are"; REB: "to keep you from thinking yourselves wise"). Paul's wording *(par' heautois phronimoi)* may allude to Prov 3:7: "Do not be wise in your own eyes" *(phronimoi para seautois)*. In any case, precisely because the Christian Gentiles are beneficiaries of God's "hardening" part of Israel, they should not look down disdainfully at the unbelieving Jews (repeating v. 18), but gratefully acknowledge the awesome capacity of God to achieve the divine goal.

The mystery has four interconnected elements, each of which has generated arguments about the precise meaning. First, Israel's "hardening" (alluding to v. 7) is not permanent but temporary, lasting only as long as necessary—"until the full number *[plērōma]* of the Gentiles has come in" (v. 25). Into what? Paul does not say! Some (e.g., Dunn 1988, Moo 1996) suggest that Paul thinks of the kingdom of God or eternal life because Jesus is reported to have spoken of entering (eternal) life in Mark 9:43 or the Kingdom (Matt 5:20; Mark 9:47), but this is unlikely since Jesus was talking about something quite different. Others have understood Paul to be alluding to the biblical and early Jewish vision of the Gentile nations coming to Zion—sometimes to worship the one true God, sometimes bearing gifts that enrich the nation (e.g., Isa 2:2-4; 40:14; 60:5-22; Tob 13:11)—in response to God's restoration of the nation from exile. Indeed, Sanders (1983, 171) claimed, improbably, that Paul's whole mission must be understood in this light. Donaldson (1997, 187-97), however, rightly rejects such an allusion here. In light of the foregoing image of the olive tree, Paul probably understands the Gentiles "coming in" as their entering the people of God—not expected of the nations. Not clear is whether the "full number" implies that there is a Gentile quota, a preset number of Gentiles, that must be filled (so Moo 1996, 719), or whether Paul thinks more generally of the completion of God's goal for Gentiles. What *is* clear is that Paul says neither *when* nor *how* this completion is to occur in relation to the end of the "hardening" of Israel. By using the same word *plērōma* for Gentiles in verse 25 as for Israel in verse 12, Paul implies that there will be "no difference" between them in the completedness of their salvation, just as there is "no difference" between them now in sin (3:22-23; see also 10:12).

Second, Israel's hardened state was not total but *apo merous tō Israēl,* a phrase that can mean either "a partial" hardening (NASB, REB, and Gaston 1987, 143) or a hardening of "part of" Israel (NRSV). The latter is the more probable, for it distinguishes nonbelieving Israel from the Christian Jews, who by definition are not among the hardened. Saying that a hardening "has come upon" a part of Israel is the same as saying "the rest were hardened" (v. 7). God is as much at work in this "hardening" as in the hardening of Pharaoh's heart (9:17-18).

Third, the referent of "all Israel" is not problem-free. Paul began the whole discussion declaring that it is not the case that all who are *of* Israel actually *are* Israel (9:6), because Israel is really constituted by God's election, not simply by lineal descent. Does he now say, in effect, that "all who are of Israel are Israel," destined to be saved, in keeping with the later rabbinic dictum, "all Israel has a share in the life to come"? Since "all Israel" represents *kol Yisra'el* (used 148 times in the Old Testament, as Fitzmyer [1993] notes), it is likely that here Paul does envision ethnic Israel as a whole (not every Israelite) as destined for salvation. Paul does not thereby retract what he had said in 9:6, because, we may infer, he distinguishes the phenomenon "Israel" in history (based on election) from the Israel that will be saved on the day of salvation. This Israel may also be the olive tree into which the *plērōma* of the Gentiles have been grafted, joining the regrafted Jews, though Paul does not say so because he is not explaining *who* will be saved, but the *manner* in which Israel will be saved.

Fourth, that the content of the mystery is the manner in which Israel will be saved is stated in the opening words of verse 26: *kai houtōs*, which clearly means "and in this way" (NRSV's "and so" is ambiguous at best). REB, however, shifts the focus from God's *modus operandi* to an explicit *sequence*: "Once that has happened [the entry of the Gentiles], the whole of Israel will be saved." Though sequence is implied when Paul says that "hardening" has happened to part of Israel *until* the Gentiles have "entered," the accent does not fall on the sequence itself, but on the temporary hardening that has befallen part of Israel—like an extended pause during which God's purpose for Gentiles is actualized. Since God, being faithful despite Israel's faithlessness (3:3), has not rejected his *people* (11:1), the ultimate salvation of Israel does not need to be explained; what needs explanation is how that destiny can be squared with the majority of Israel's current stance toward the gospel, particularly in light of the Gentiles' acceptance of it. The "hardening until" is Paul's theological explanation of what is happening in history, an explanation intended to inhibit Christian Gentile arrogance. But whenever interpreters make sequence (the logical implication of Paul's "until . . .") the primary subject matter, Paul's thought is pushed out of focus and unwarranted inferences follow. For instance, Byrne (1986) thinks that Paul reverses the biblical expectation of the nations coming to Zion (see above):

there, first the nation's redemption, then the Gentiles' arrival; here, first the Gentiles, then Israel. Others detect a reversal from "the Jew first" in 1:16 to "Israel last" in 11:25-26—assuming that the primary meaning of "first" is temporal.

Because Paul takes hardened Israel's current status seriously, he finds the manner of Israel's salvation to be in accord with scripture, namely Isa 59:20-21 and Isa 27:9. The Hebrew of the former is rendered by NRSV as follows:

And he will come *to Zion* as Redeemer,
to those in Jacob who turn from transgression. . . .
And as for me, this is my covenant with them, says the LORD. . . .

The LXX, however, reads as follows:

And the Redeemer will come *for the sake of [heneken] Zion*
and he will turn away ungodliness *[asebeias]* from Jacob
And this will be my covenant with them, says the Lord. (AT)

Paul's quotation, "the Redeemer will come *from Zion*," agrees with neither the Hebrew nor the Greek nor with any other ancient text, though the "from Zion" motif is attested elsewhere in the LXX (for details, see Wagner 2003, 280-86); Paul's last line modifies LXX Isa 27:9 ("Therefore the sin of Jacob will be taken away") to read, "when I take away their sins." For Paul, the sins that will be removed are not submitting to God's rectifying rectitude (10:3), being "a disobedient and contrary people" (10:21), and "unbelief" (*apistia*; 11:20; see also v. 23).

Problematic is what Paul says about the Deliverer (for various views, see Fitzmyer 1993, 618-20). (a) Assuming that the Deliverer is Christ, as many do, the problem concerns Paul's understanding of the first line of his quotation: "Out of Zion will come the Deliverer." Paul does not claim that what Isaiah looked forward to has occurred in the mission of Jesus or in the gospel coming from Jerusalem. Since Paul looks forward to the future removal of Israel's sins as the antidote to its present situation, does the coming of Christ the Deliverer refer, then, to the parousia (so, e.g., Kim 2000, 139, but rejected by Wright 2002, 689)? If that is what Paul wanted to say, the "Zion" whence he will come must refer to the heavenly Jerusalem (as in Gal 4:26; see Martyn 1977, 440; the image is found also in Rev 3:12; 21:2). (b) Or is God the coming Deliverer (remembering that apart from 9:5 and 10:17 Christ is not mentioned in chaps. 9–11)? Indeed, nothing in the quotation in verses 26-27 clearly refers to Christ. Moreover, the Old Testament regards the earthly Zion as God's dwelling place (see, e.g., Pss 9:11; 50:2; Joel 3:17). The view that the Deliverer is God rather than Christ has become a significant factor in the much debated claim that Paul envisages God saving Israel without faith in Christ—a view hard to square with 11:23. (c) Actually, Paul probably regards the Deliverer as God, though the apostle does not think of God's salvific action apart from the Christ-event (so also Wagner 2003, 297, agreeing with Sanders 1983, 194).

When Paul itemized Israel's privileges in 9:4-5, he spoke of them as Israel's possessions (NRSV: they "belong to" Israel). Now, in verse 29, he declares flatly, "The gifts and the calling [= election] of God are irrevocable." Thereby he states unambiguously the nonnegotiable conviction on which his whole discussion of Israel rests (in keeping with 3:3). It is just this conviction that both requires and enables him to explain to haughty Christian Gentiles how God's faithfulness, God's self-consistency, is squared with the refusal of the gospel by the majority of Jews. As his argument progressed, it became more and more dialectical, claiming in 11:11, 13-14 that God uses Israel's negative response to achieve the positive goal for Gentiles. Now, in verses 28-31, with rhetorical skill, he formulates God's ways in the sharpest contrasting terms to tell the arrogant Gentiles that, in God's mysterious mode of faithfulness, their own salvation is intertwined with Israel's refusal of the gospel.

In verse 28, Paul abruptly juxtaposes two contrasting perspectives, both valid, on the hardened part of Israel, then in verse 29 states the basis for both perspectives: "for irrevocable are the begracements [charismata, REB: "gracious gifts"] and call [klēsis] of God" (AT; "irrevocable" begins the statement as its most important word). These verses too have been formulated with rhetorical considerations in mind: Not only are the contrasting terms for hardened Israel ("enemies" and "beloved") enhanced by using them in identical constructions ("according to . . . for the sake of . . ."), but the sharpness of the contrast also makes their shared warrant (v. 29) all the more important.

According to verse 28, the unbelieving Jews can be viewed from the gospel perspective and the election perspective. The former looks at *their present action* and so views them as "enemies" (a severe term chosen to emphasize its opposite, "beloved," used in 9:13). The latter perspective looks at them in light of *God's action*, and so views them as "beloved." Moreover, each perspective puts the unbelieving Jews in the context of God's purposes. In the gospel perspective, they are "enemies for your sake" *(di' hymas)*; that is, you Christian Gentiles are the beneficiaries of their hostility (restating v. 19, which in turn is a restatement of v. 11). In the election perspective, Israel is "beloved for the sake of the patriarchs" (AT of *dia tous pateras;* "their ancestors" [NRSV] is too vague and too general)—that is, God does not walk out on the promises made to the chosen patriarchs. How does Paul know this? Because "the begracements and the calling of God are irrevocable." God keeps faith with the patriarchs. If the election perspective is valid, the Christian Gentiles should grasp that the temporary "hardening" (v. 25) is really for their sakes, and so abandon their haughty attitude toward unbelieving Jews (see comment on 11:5).

But how can the same group (the "hardened" part of Israel) be both God's "enemies" and God's "beloved"? Is this not a logical contradiction? Not really, at least not according to verses 30-31, for which verse 32 provides the warrant: "For God has imprisoned all in disobedience so that he may be merciful to all." That is, God's mercy (like God's impartial justice) treats Gentiles and Jews in *the same way* (all are "imprisoned" in disobedience), but *not at the same time*. God's mercy is treated here not as a timeless attribute or as an undifferentiated disposition, but rather as a mode of activity that uses specific, historical forms of human disobedience to achieve God's goal. Thereby the logical contradiction—created in the first place because "enemies" and "beloved" are registered as antinomies in the human mind—is dissolved when historical considerations are brought on board. Here Paul's rhetorical prowess has produced terse formulations of *contrasts* expressed as historical *reversals* ("once . . . now . . .") that are placed within a syntactical construction that emphasizes *similarity* ("just as . . . so also . . ."). In fact, the text has a double reversal, one *within* Gentiles and hardened Israel, the other *between* them.

Past	Agency	Now
As with Gentiles		
disobeyed	Israel's disobedience	received mercy
So also with Israel		
disobeyed	Gentiles' (received) mercy	received mercy

What the chart displays, verse 32 says: "God has imprisoned all in disobedience so that he may be merciful to all."

The Christian Gentiles' prior disobedience was portrayed in 1:18-31; 6:20-21. Hardened Israel's current disobedience refers to the refusal to submit to God's rectifying rectitude (10:3), to its being "a disobedient and contrary people" (10:21), to the olive branch "broken off because of unbelief" (11:20); it also anticipates the "ungodliness" and "sins" that must be removed from Jacob (vv. 26-27). It is this very disobedience, Paul claims, that God used to bring salvation to Gentiles. At no point, however, does he provide an empirical explanation of how God did so, or speculate on how salvation would have come to Gentiles had Israel accepted the gospel. Rather, he reflects on what has actually happened, and interprets it as God's freedom and power to use the Jews' disobedience.

Having pointed out (v. 30) that God used Israel's disobedience, verse 31 turns the coin over and now speaks of the Christian Gentiles' role in God's showing mercy to Israel. Unfortunately, verse 31 is not as clear as verse 30, partly because a number of important manuscripts do not have "now" in the concluding phrase, and so read, "in order that they too may receive mercy"

(REB); other manuscripts read, "in order that . . . they too may *now* receive mercy" (NRSV, NIV). That this "now" expresses a sense of imminence ("now at any time"), as Moo (1996, 735) thinks, is not evident. Less evident is the view advanced by Wright (1991, 249-50) who, while rightly insisting that in verses 25-26 Paul is not talking about sequence, contends that verses 25-26 concern the *process* by which all Israel is being saved now, and so he infers that Paul envisages "a steady flow of Jews into the church." Though this language is not repeated in the commentary (2002), Wright continues to insist that the salvation of Israel is not to be an event at the End, but is going on now. The textual uncertainty of the "now" suggests caution in interpreting this verse.

More important is what Paul said about Israel's disobedience in relation to Christian Gentiles. Just as verse 30 specifies whom Gentiles had disobeyed (God, using the dative case), so also verse 31 identifies what Israel disobeyed by using the dative case: *tō hymeterō eleei,* literally, "your mercy" (viz., "the mercy you received"). Translations, however, as well as exegetes, understand the phrase somewhat differently (e.g., NRSV: "they have now been disobedient in order that, *by the mercy* shown to you"). This translation not only ignores the parallel structure but changes the point. The apostle probably said exactly what he meant to say: Israel "disobeyed" the mercy that the Gentiles received ("disobeyed" is used because of the parallel structure)—namely, God's rectifying rectitude apart from the law, to which Israel did not "submit" (10:3).

The identical way in which God responds to the disobedience of both Gentile and Jew disallows the much-discussed claim that Paul envisions the salvation of Israel apart from Christ (so also Wagner 2003, 298, who also notes that it was some form of "realized eschatology" that opened the door to Christian supersessionism). Given Israel's election and its privileges (9:4-5), their form of disobedience differs from that of the Gentiles, but in the last analysis disobedience characterizes both. To paraphrase 3:23, "there is no distinction, since all have disobeyed," there is no distinction in salvation either, for God is merciful to all, and on the same basis: God's sending his own Son while all were disobedient sinners (8:3-4). The impartiality of God in salvation is the obverse of the impartiality of God in judgment, and both aspects are grounded in the freedom of God to be the One who rectifies the ungodly (4:5). Further, had Paul thought that all Israel would be saved apart from Christ, he would have implied that for Israel, Jesus is not the promised Messiah after all.

Understanding what Paul is saying in this paragraph requires most Christian Gentiles to flush out of their minds what they assume Paul is talking about, namely, the "conversion" of Jews to "Christianity" (a word Paul did not know, and which is problem-laden in any case), and their entry into the predominantly Gentile church. From Paul's angle, it is not Jews who do the "entering" but Gentiles, the wild olive shoots grafted into Israel, yet without becoming converts (proselytes) to Judaism. As Paul sees it, Gentiles abandon their religion when they accept the gospel (1 Thess 1:9-10), but observant Jews who accept it do not change religions but reconfigure the religion they already have. Together, both groups constitute something new, a new "people" united by a shared conviction about the Christ-event as God's eschatological act. Given what has happened since Paul, what he envisioned cannot be actualized now; what can, perhaps, be achieved is nonetheless important: a more truly Pauline understanding of the significance of God's indelible covenant with the people of Israel for the authenticity of the faith of Christian Gentiles. Such an achievement requires much more than tactful "Jewish-Christian dialogue," important as that is; it requires sustained, serious theological work by both faithful Jews and faithful Christian Gentiles.

God's Awesome Ways Celebrated (11:33-36)

Paul now steps back and comments on the import of his argument for what it implies about the human understanding of God. This poetic passage does not add theological content (ideas or doctrines) to what Paul has already said about God; rather, it expresses his keen sense that in disclosing the mystery of God's dealings with Israel and the Gentiles he has glimpsed the magnitude of God's awesome otherness. He celebrates God's greatness not only in light of chapters 9–11, but also in response to what has been said about God since 1:16. Lacking any reference to Christ, the passage resolutely concentrates on God. Its thought moves in clear steps: It begins with an apostrophe celebrating the depth of God's riches, wisdom, knowledge (not *our* knowledge of God!), and ways (v. 33); then it uses scripture to articulate the contrast between God and humans (vv. 34-35), and finally it confesses that God is the beginning and end of everything, before ending with a formulaic doxology (v. 36). This movement of thought is matched by careful attention to rhetorical considerations, not evident in translation For instance, verbless verse 33 falls into four lines, each ending with a word whose last vowel has the same sound *(ou)*; verses 34-35 also have four lines, but ask three questions, "Who . . . ?" The careful poetic construction (obscured in NRSV) suggests that Paul appropriated (without change) a liturgical tradition developed in the Greek-using synagogues (for a discussion of details, see Johnson [1989, 164-74], who calls it a "Wisdom hymn").

By speaking of the *depth* of God's riches, wisdom, and knowledge, Paul recognizes that God's "judgments" (decisions affecting human affairs) are "unsearchable" (i.e., they cannot be explored) and that his "ways" are "inscrutable" (i.e., they are beyond human capacity to track). Thus he admits that despite his best efforts to explain God's ways, he knows only partly (see 1 Cor 13:9, 12 for a comparable admission). Given the depth of God, one cannot see to the bottom of God's ways. In beginning with that, the unit recognizes that this is the first thing that theology must say—and remember.

The "For" with which the three questions in verses 34-35 begin shows that they function as the warrant for verse 33. The first two questions quote LXX Isa 40:13, which differs from the Hebrew. The third question might be formulated under the influence of Job 41:3 (modified). The implied answer to all three questions is, "No one!" The first question ("Who has known the mind of the

Lord?") follows naturally from verse 33: Given the depth of God's wisdom and knowledge, no one has really known the Lord's mind, nor has anyone been "his counselor"—though many do not hesitate to tell the Lord what to do and not do. The implied negative answer to the third question rejects the notion of "exchange" or recompense between God and the worshiper, expressed by the Latin formula, *do ut des* (I do, so that you [God] do); verse 35 reminds the reader of what Paul had said in 4:4, "Now to one who works, wages are not reckoned as a gift but as something that is due" (AT). Verse 35, in other words, reasserts Paul's insistence that everyone depends on God's inexplicable grace; no one makes a deal with God.

Whereas verses 33-35 draw on biblical thinking about God, the first line of verse 36 appropriates Stoic language (characterized by the emphasis on prepositions) to laud the biblical God, as Philo too had done. Well-known is the comparable formula found two centuries later in Marcus Aurelius's *Meditations* 4.23: "All things come *from* you, all things exist *in* you, all things are destined *for* you." Instead of "all things exist in you" (which blurs the distinction between Creator and created), Paul has "all things are *through* you," an allusion to the idea that God creates *through* or *by means of* Wisdom (as in John 1:1-3). Thereby Paul celebrates God as the origin, continuing means, and destiny of everything that is (similarly 1 Cor 15:28). Perhaps because Romans is theocentric, Paul does not mention Christ as the mediator of creation as he does in 1 Cor 8:6, "For us there is one God, the Father, from whom are all things and for whom we exist, and one Lord, Jesus Christ, through whom are all things and through whom we exist" (see also Col 1:16-17).

◊ ◊ ◊ ◊

In appropriating this poetic piece to conclude the discussion of God's mysterious ways, Paul invited the readers to view the subject matter from the angle of biblical and postbiblical Wisdom theology, which emphasized the hiddenness of God's wisdom. He also revealed his own wisdom by recognizing that he has not unraveled the mystery of it all. Yet, by including the Stoic-like formula in verse 36, the passage also acknowledges something not to be overlooked—that the faithful God is One who must be reckoned with, for there is none other than this Other. In a way, the whole passage is the stone against which theology stumbles when it claims too much, when it forgets that the Reality called "God" is a mystery, when it neglects the task of showing why it is a mystery—one too deep to be fathomed but which must be acknowledged, gratefully.

DAYBREAK ETHOS (12:1–15:13)

In Rom 12:1–15:13 Paul focuses attention on certain hallmarks of the emergent Christian ethos that is to take shape now that "the night is far gone, the day is near" (13:12). Some interpreters regard the whole section as Paul's general counsels, appropriate for Christians in various places, while others try to relate it to the specific problems that divide the believers in Rome. The latter effort has been more successful in interpreting 14:1–15:6(7) than in tying chapters 12–13 to the Roman scene. More important, 12:1–15:13 are to be related to chapters 1–11, though the coherence is largely implicit—perhaps because Paul assumes that the recipients will hear the letter read through and so will not have forgotten what he has already said. In any case, this part of the letter consists of three sections of unequal length, each with its own characteristics. (a) 12:1–13:14 calls attention to important features that should characterize the community's ethos. (b) 14:1–15:6 deals with intramural disputes over Christian freedom and obligation. (c) Verses 15:7-13 not only concludes the section but also ties it to the grand horizon of the whole letter; these verses function as the peroration of the whole discourse.

The Community's Transformed Ethos (12:1–13:14)

After the opening paragraph sets the stage (12:1-2), Paul launches into a series of exhortations that pertain to the internal life of the Christian community and to its overall relation to the surrounding world (12:3-21). Then 13:1-7 suddenly counsels the appropriate stance toward "governing authorities," including the payment of taxes. Next, 13:8 resumes addressing the intramural life of the community. Though Christ is mentioned only near the beginning (12:6) and end (13:14), these references actually frame substantively what lies between them, as do the eschatological notes sounded in 12:2 and 13:11-14. Apart from the discussion of civil authorities in 13:1-7 and the eschatological horizon in 13:11-14, the exhortations are not argued but clustered around general topics.

◊ ◊ ◊ ◊

Worship and Transformation (12:1-2)

This brief introductory paragraph combines two remarkable exhortations that together express the mandate that the subsequent exhortations spell out more fully. The first says what the readers are to do ("present your bodies as a living sacrifice"); the second, using two contrasting passive imperatives, says what is to happen to them: "Do not be conformed . . . but be transformed." (The injunctions in vv. 1 and 2 are linked with "and"; they are not just juxtaposed, as in NRSV, NIV, and REB.) The initial word *parakalō* conveys more than a request; it expresses strongly an appeal that is important and urgent (used again in 15:30; 16:17; see also 1 Cor 1:10; 4:16; 2 Cor 2:8; 10:1; Phil 4:2; Phlm 10); "implore" (REB) too readily suggests supplication, but Paul is not begging the readers to do as he says. Rather, he is exercising his apostolic vocation to bring about "the obedience of faith" (1:5), evident from the way he continues in verse 3: "For by the grace given to me I say . . ." (repeated in 15:15). Paul has emphasized God's mercy repeatedly, though using a different word (see 9:16 and especially 11:30-32); now it is the basis on which he makes his appeal.

What does Paul imply by beginning the passage with "therefore"? The word usually signals that what follows is the right inference from what has just been said. But how are the exhortations that follow the consequence of celebrating God's awesome ways in 11:33-36? Actually, the reference is to God's showing mercy to all in 11:30-32. Although some interpreters take "therefore" loosely, simply as a way of continuing the discourse, it should be taken seriously, indicating that the exhortations are his response to God's mercy, which the whole argument thus far has delineated. In effect, these chapters call the readers to a mode of life that is the opposite of that described at the beginning of the letter (so Furnish 1968, 101-6).

Paul's "Therefore" is significant also because it discloses that, for him, appropriate conduct is precisely not an afterthought, loosely attached to what "really matters" (theology), but the obverse of the same coin. That Paul can write chapters 12–13 without using the "righteousness" terminology, especially important in chapters 1–5 and 9–11, must not eclipse the fact that chapters 12–13 make concrete the righteousness/rectitude that results from God's rectifying the ungodly (4:5). In fact, these chapters are Paul's own commentary on 6:13: "No longer present your members to sin as instruments [lit., "weapons"] of wickedness, but present yourselves to God as those who have been brought from death to life, and present your members to God as instruments of righteousness." Although the verb "present" appears in both passages, in 12:1 it is part of cultic imagery, for *parastēsai thysian* (present/offer sacrifice) is a well-documented nonbiblical expression that Paul's largely Gentile readers would have recognized as soon as they heard it read (see references in Cranfield 1979, 598 n. 4).

What may well have jarred them, however, is being enjoined to offer their "bodies as a living sacrifice." By using "bodies" Paul urges them to offer their actual, physical, phenomenal selves, as REB recognizes: "offer your very selves," for here "body" means self, the whole person, as in "somebody." The entire self is to be offered to God, "who did not spare his own Son, but gave him up for us all" (8:32, REB). In other words, this self-offering is the beneficiaries' *response* to God's own self-giving. Understandably, then, Paul makes his appeal "in view of God's mercy" (NIV).

Three words characterize the sacrifice: living, holy, and acceptable. A "living" sacrifice is ongoing, steadily manifest in daily life (thereby eliminating the chasm between the sacred and the profane); the import of "living" will be made concrete in the exhortations that follow. A sacrifice is "holy" because it is dedicated to God and blemish-free; "holy" compresses into one word what Paul had said in 6:19, "For just as you once presented your members as slaves to impurity [*akatharsia*, the opposite of holiness] and to greater and greater iniquity, so now present your members as slaves to righteousness for sanctification [being made holy]" (see also 6:22). A sacrifice that is "acceptable" does not simply meet minimum requirements (getting a C-), but is literally "well-pleasing" *(euareston)* to God; it is worthy of divine approbation. A life well-pleasing to God is not subject to God's wrath against all human wickedness (1:18), though not beyond God's judgment (see 14:10).

This offering of oneself to God Paul calls your *logikēn latreian*, for which there is no exact English equivalent. *Latreia* is usually translated "worship," but the word refers to cultic activity or duty in the service of God (Moffatt: "that is your cult, a spiritual rite"); its Latin equivalent was *religio* (so Betz 1991, 337). In 9:4 Paul had used the word to refer to cultic worship in the Jerusalem temple; in 1:9 he used the verb *latreuō* to speak of his own mission. More important here, however, is the use of the verb in 1:25 to characterize idolatry: "they have exchanged the truth of God for a lie [spelled out in v. 23] and have offered reverence and worship [*elatreusan*] to created things instead of to the Creator" (REB; NRSV: "worshiped and served"); as a result, "God gave them up in the lusts of their hearts to impurity [*akatharsian*, the opposite of holiness], to the degrading of their bodies" (v. 26, AT). In other words, what Paul calls for is the reversal of the situation portrayed in chapter 1; the offering of the body selves *to God* the Creator is the mandatory sign that salvation has indeed come to Gentile believers (11:11). This salvation-manifesting worship is more oriented to the future (as 15:7-13 will show) than the past; it does not envision a restoration of the primordial situation that was destroyed by the lapse into perverted religiosity characterized in 1:21-23 (so also Betz 1991, 338).

But what does Paul mean by characterizing the readers' *latreia* as *logikē*, and what makes it so? NRSV's alternative translation "reasonable" is better than its preferred rendering, "spiritual," which implies a worship that is inward; the word implies also more than "mind and heart" (REB). Since *logikos* is the adjectival form of *logos*, reason, the point here is not the inward contrasted with the external aspects of religious activity, but the contrast with irrational, foolish worship—precisely the sort of worship that emerged when humans did not honor God as God or give thanks but "became futile in their thinking, and their senseless minds were darkened" and so began worshiping sundry visible images instead of the invisible Creator (1:20-23). What makes the mandated worship "reasonable" is not so much the inbuilt rationality of the actor (as Byrne [1996, 363] translates it: "the worship you owe as rational beings") as its being the expression of the proper, understandable, restored correlation between creature and Creator. In short, this *latreia* is honoring God as God. The alternative implied is not Jewish worship in the temple but what Paul saw as the unreasonable, foolish religions of the Greco-Roman world. CEV appears to intuit Paul's point: "That's the most sensible way to serve God." Paul's implied critique of surrounding religiosity is based not on philosophical reflection on the origin and nature of religious practices, but on "the mercies of God"—the merciful acts that have already rescued the Gentile readers from the folly of their former cultic worship (see 1 Thess 1:9). Clearly, Paul's "reasonable worship" has nothing to do with "rational religion" as the Enlightenment understood it. Nor is he tacitly dismissing various acts in corporate worship, like hearing scripture, praying, singing, or participating in the rites of baptism and Eucharist.

The second exhortation in verse 2 has both negative and positive aspects: "Do not be conformed . . . but be transformed." It has a stated goal as well: discerning God's will. What Paul here proscribes and prescribes together explicate the self-giving in verse 1, on the one hand, and provide the basis for developing the new ethos according to God's will, on the other. Whereas verse 1 clearly has in mind Christian Gentiles, verse 2 pertains especially to Christian Jews, who—like the interlocutor in 2:17-18—may be inclined to continue their pre-Christian confidence that they already *"know his will* and determine what is best" because they have learned the law. (Esler [2003, 310], however, thinks verse 1 pertains to Jews, verse 2 to Gentiles.) In addition, this complex introductory exhortation tacitly prepares the way for Paul's counsels aimed at the arguments in Rome over observing dietary laws and special days (chaps. 14–15). The present tense of both imperative verbs suggests that not being conformed but being transformed is to be as ongoing as being a "living sacrifice."

Paul evidently assumes that he need not explain "this age" (*aiōn*, NRSV: "world"), used only here in Romans, but found also in 1 Cor 1:20; 2:6, 8; 3:18; 2 Cor 4:4, and characterized as "the present evil age" in Gal 1:4. The expression is derived from Jewish apocalyptic thought, where it is paired and contrasted with "the age to come," the wholly new state of affairs that will be the God-given solution to what the whole of history has become. Paul, however, never speaks of "the age to come," probably because for him it has already dawned; instead he speaks of "new creation" (2 Cor 5:17; Gal 6:15), by which he does not mean that "a new heaven and a new earth" have displaced the old, as in Rev 21:1, but a newness that is already beginning to restore creation to its right relation to the Creator. In proscribing ongoing conformity with "this age" Paul acknowledges that it continues; but since its time is running out (13:11) conformity to it is no longer unavoidable; already one can, and so must, live out of the future that is dawning. Making this nonconformity actual entails a transformation, one that is not achieved by one's willpower but, as the passive "be transformed" implies, is the work of God in renewing the mind, creating a new mentality. For Christian Gentiles, the renewed mind replaces the "debased mind" to which "God gave them over" (1:28, AT). In effect, 12:1-2 restates 6:2: "How can we who died to sin go on living in it?" (see also 6:11-12; 8:5-8).

The purpose of this transformation is the new ethos, one that now conforms to God's will, which can, and therefore must, be "discerned"—NRSV's and REB's rough rendering of *dokimazein*, better translated by NIV as "test and approve." This nonconformity to "this age" is not an end in itself nor simply a manifestation of "alienation" rooted elsewhere, but the requisite prelude to the real end, doing God's will, which is not self-evident so long as "this age" has not yet run its course. Nor does Paul say that by renewing the mind one becomes a more astute interpreter of the law. While God's will must be detected and tested, it can be characterized as "what is good and acceptable [*euareston*, see above] and perfect." Paul does not require perfection; he does, however, make his readers responsible for the pursuit of God's perfect will. He also does more: He goes on to spell out what he understands that will entail.

◊ ◊ ◊ ◊

Paul does not launch his exhortations by referring to Jesus, but what the apostle says here is consistent theologically with the theology at the core of Jesus' message as Mark formulates it: "The time is fulfilled, and the kingdom of God is drawn near. Repent, and believe in the gospel" (Mark 1:15, AT). What Jesus calls for is repentance *(metanoia)* in response (more explicit in Matt 4:17) to God's reign, which "is drawn near" (perfect tense!) because of God's action. Repentance does not bring the Kingdom closer; rather, by a changed life it acknowledges what God has already done. Paul strikes the same note when he warrants his appeal by pointing to "the mercies of God." He does not, of course, mention *metanoia* (only at 2:4 does he use the word in Romans). But when the Hebrew word *shûb* (turn) was translated as *metanoia* (lit., "change of mind"), the accent implicitly shifted to a transformed outlook, a changed mentality that governs the way one lives. Substantively, then, Paul's call for a transformation by the renovation of the mind is his equivalent of Jesus' call for *metanoia*. Likewise, even though Paul mentions the kingdom of God rarely (in Romans only at 14:17), the injunctions that follow 12:1-2 sketch the kind of life that should flow from responding to God's mercies, definitively expressed in the Christ-event (5:6-11). The whole of Romans, then, is essentially a statement of what God has done, and its consequences—some of which are instantiated in 12:3–15:13.

Mandates for the New Ethos (12:3-21)

Although the believers in Rome assembled in various house churches (see chap. 16), the exhortations are addressed to the entire community. Paul first emphasizes the mindset that is appropriate for the community in which there are diverse gifts (vv. 3-8) before turning to various matters, especially nonretaliation (vv. 9-21). While the passage seems like a string of commands and prohibitions, close attention to details suggests that each unit has its own rationale.

◊ ◊ ◊ ◊

Verses 3-8 begin by restating the basis on which the exhortations rest. English translations obscure, probably for stylistic reasons, what the letter's recipients would have *heard*: that verse 3 begins similarly to verse 1 (in both, the verb comes first):

v. 1 "I appeal . . . through the mercies of God"

v. 3 "I say   through the grace given to me" (AT)

Verse 3 clearly recalls Paul's apostolic authorization expressed at the beginning of the letter: "We [viz., "I"] have received grace and apostleship to bring about the obedience of faith among all the Gentiles . . . including yourselves" (1:5-6). Now Paul sees himself fulfilling this task by identifying the hallmarks of this obedience. By referring to his authorization as "the grace given to me" he says much more than CEV: "I realize how kind God has been to me" (as if that would have authorized his exhortations), and somewhat less than REB's "By the authority that the grace of God has given me," and even less than Moffatt's translation: "In virtue of my office." Moreover, in verse 6 he does not exalt his own authority but instead speaks "according to the grace given to *us*." Exhorter and exhorted alike are recipients of God's "begracements" (*charismata*), just as in 1:1 he is a "called" apostle writing to those who are "called" (1:6). The whole paragraph concerns proper differentiation in practice of what is given to all.

Apparently recognizing that proper differentiation depends on each person's attitude, Paul first addresses the danger of haughtiness in "every one of you" (NIV), whatever your ethnic identity, gender, or social status. To do so, he emphasizes a way of thinking, a mindset, by using a form of *phronein* four times: "Do not think of yourself more highly [*hyperphronein*] than you ought to think [*phronein*] but think [*phronein*] sensibly [*eis to sō-*

phronein]" (AT; the related noun *sōphrosynē*, prudence, moderation, was long recognized as one of the four cardinal virtues). By
accenting *phronein* as a primary result of receiving God's begracement, Paul alludes to what he had written before about the *phronēma* (mindset) of those who belong to Christ and live by the Spirit
(8:5-8), though he mentions the Spirit here only at verse 11. Here
the accent is on the mentality for which each person is responsible, first of all with regard to oneself, in keeping with the renewed
mind's discerning God's will.

But what is the criterion of sensible self-understanding, marked
by "sober judgment" (NRSV)? Unfortunately, Paul's answer—the
remainder of verse 3—is far from clear: "as God has measured the
measure of faith to each" (AT). "Measured" translates *emerisen*
(to divide, distribute, apportion, allot [NRSV: "assign"]), not simply "give" (NIV), and fits the theme of differentiation that governs
the whole paragraph. The noun *metron* can mean either an instrument for measuring (a meter) or the amount measured out, the
allotment. If Paul uses it in the latter sense, CEV gets it right:
"Measure yourself by the *amount* of faith that God has given
you." But does Paul think that God distributes faith in various
quantities? Probably the genitive ("of faith") is used appositional-
ly, just as "sign of circumcision" in 4:11 means "sign that is circumcision"; in other words, Paul means "measure that is faith."
Paul's point is not that God ladles out differing amounts of faith
by which each person is to view oneself (that criterion for self-
measurement would produce precisely what Paul seeks to avoid:
pride!); rather, the criterion of a realistic self-affirmation is faith—
knowing that one's relation to God is a matter of trust in the one
who "rectifies the ungodly" (4:5).

The "for" at the beginning of verses 4-5 (omitted by NIV)
announces the warrant for verse 3: The diverse believers are like
one body with many parts. The sentence *compares* the human
many-membered body with the many-membered community;
it does not say that the community *is* the body of Christ, as CEV
has it: "We each are part of the body of Christ"; that is what
1 Cor 12:27 says: "You *are* the body of Christ and individually
members of it" (see also Col 1:24). The comparison between a

community and a human body consisting of diverse organs had become a commonplace by Paul's time and was especially useful for urging unity in civic affairs (see Mitchell 1991, 157-64). So it is not surprising that Paul, writing to a somewhat anarchic church in Corinth, would insist that all the various gifts are from the same Spirit "for the common good," and that diversity is so essential that no one, like no organ, can say, "I have no need of you." He also maintained, in effect, that the church as Christ's body is not a motley aggregate of organs, but a living organism, some of whose organs are more important than others; indeed, he ranked them (see below). Precisely because Paul had addressed 1 Cor 12–14 to a particular situation in a church he had founded, it is important not to conflate what he said in that letter with what he now writes to the Romans (so also Fee 1994, 605); here Paul adapts what he had said before without simply repeating himself.

For one thing, in Romans Paul does not develop the body image as in 1 Cor 12; he simply points out that in the one body "individually we are members one of another." This remarkable mutuality, we may infer, is the result of being baptized into Christ (6:3), which Paul may allude to in saying that "we, who are many, are one body *in Christ*" (not one body *of* Christ). In addition, while verses 6-8, like 1 Cor 12:27-30, also conclude the discussion by listing the divine gifts, in Romans Paul neither ranks them nor uses the same list. Indeed, even within 1 Cor 12 the "manifestations of the Spirit" listed in verses 7-10 differ from those listed in verses 28-29 (see below). Evidently Paul is neither identifying the gifts so that the Romans may know what they are, nor ranking them so that the readers know their respective standing in the community, but rather is using the variety of gifts to make concrete what it means to be "members of one another" precisely because, like the body, "not all the members have the same function." "In Christ" this diversity is not something to be overcome but to be treasured and actualized rightly.

Verses 6-8, however, contain a syntactical difficulty that affects how one understands what Paul says. These verses begin "having differing begracements [*charismata*, gifts of grace] according to the grace given to us," but they have no active verb. Dunn (1988,

2:725) therefore argues that these verses continue the sentence begun at verse 4 and so *describe* how the gifts are actually functioning, but the vast majority think that verse 6 begins a new sentence that Paul fails to complete, and that one must supply the implied missing verb, namely, an exhortation, as in NIV: "If a man's gift is prophesying, let him use it. . . ." The context makes Dunn's interpretation unlikely. Paul is not describing; he is urging that each gift be actualized in a particular way, in keeping with the nature of the gift.

Paul mentions seven begracements that were "given to *us*." The first two are abstract nouns (prophecy, service), the next five refer to specific doers (the teacher, etc.). Paul's letters being the earliest Christian writings, the desire to learn from them as precisely as possible the nature of early church leadership is understandable, but the desire is frustrated, in part at least, by the variations in his three rosters of gifts (modifying NRSV):

1 Cor 12:7-10	1 Cor 12:28-29	Rom 12:6-8
utterance of wisdom	apostles	prophecy
utterance of knowledge	prophets	ministry
faith	teachers	the teacher
gifts of healing	deeds of power	the exhorter
miracle working	gifts of healing	the giver
prophecy	forms of assistance	the leader
discernment of spirits	forms of leadership	the compassionate
various tongues	various tongues	
interpretation of tongues		

(Whereas all these lists reflect the various functions that begraced persons had, the shorter [and later] list in Eph 4:11 names specific offices: apostles, prophets, evangelists, pastors, and teachers— all being the gifts of Christ, not of the Spirit.) Although Paul had not yet been to Rome, he assumes that the Romans will know what he is talking about. We, however, should not assume that Paul knows that these "begracements" were as divisive in Rome as in Corinth.

By prophecy Paul does not mean soothsaying or some form of clairvoyance, but articulate, intelligible, inspired speech that benefits the assembled community; in 1 Cor 14 Paul carefully explained why understandable prophetic utterance is superior to glossolalia (speaking in "tongues"): The latter requires an interpreter before it benefits the church. Even so, the prophet's speech does not have automatic authority, for the others are to "weigh what is said" (v. 29); the prophets are not mantics controlled wholly by the Spirit, but rather "the spirits of prophets are subject to the prophets" (v. 32). The whole discussion in 1 Cor 12–14 is Paul's response to the problems generated by an over-emphasis on prophecy and tongue-speaking. Even though Rom 12:6-8 also begins with prophecy, Paul neither contrasts it with tongue-speaking (not even mentioned!) nor explains its proper role, but is content to say that it is to be exercised "in proportion to faith" *(kata tēn analogian tēs pisteōs)*, an unusual phrase. The word *analogia* is not used in the LXX and only here in the New Testament; it means right relationship, and here probably means something like "according to the right relation to God that is [or, is determined by] faith." The gift of prophecy is not a license to innovate but power to explicate the faith given to all. Even though the phrase is used only with regard to prophecy, there is no evident reason to conclude that it does not pertain also to the other gifts of grace.

Next, Paul mentions "ministry" *(diakonia)*, not "the ministry" as a distinctive vocation in the modern sense; his word means "service" (NIV). While the word is associated with waiting tables (as in Acts 6:2; REB: "assist in the distribution"), no evidence suggests that Paul has this function in view here, or that the word means "gift of administration" (REB). Nor is much gained by suggesting that Paul refers to the (unspecifiable) activities of a "deacon" *(diakonos)* like Phoebe (16:1). Paul's point is that the one who received the begracement of serving should serve. He is not saying that those who serve should be servile servants; he is urging each person to do what the gift of grace gave one to do. Likewise, the one who was given the gift of teaching (compressed into "the one who teaches") should teach. Guessing what is taught to whom, or whom the exhorter is exhorting about what, detracts from hearing what Paul is saying.

Paul's last three exhortations in verse 8 differ, for now he specifies *how* each gift is to be actualized. Here, too, it is difficult to know just whom he has in mind, as the varying translations show. In verse 8, who is *ho parakalōn* (participle of the same verb used in verse 1)? Is he "the exhorter" (NRSV)? One who "encourages" (NIV, NJB, CEV), or "counsels" (REB)? Who is *ho metadidous*? "The giver" generally (NRSV), the one who is "contributing to the needs of others" (NIV), the one who gives "to charity" (REB), "the philanthropist" who shares personal wealth (Fitzmyer 1993)? Or does this person give out the pooled resources of the community? Whatever giving by whoever to whomever Paul has in view, the giving is to be done *en haplotēti* (lit., "with simplicity or sincerity," that is, with no ulterior motives; NRSV: "in generosity"; REB: "without grudging"). Finally, who is *ho proistamenos* (NRSV: "the leader")? The phrase was used for officials and administrators; Paul used it in 1 Thess 5:12 (NRSV: "those who have charge of you"; REB: "your leaders"). Since the related noun *prostatēs* refers to a benefactor or patron (used of Phoebe in 16:1), here Paul may well refer to the person who functions as a patron looking after the well-being of the community, and for this reason is "the leader." This person is to act *en spoudē* (eagerly, devotedly, conscientiously; NRSV: "in diligence"; REB: "lead with enthusiasm"). Who is *ho eleōn* (lit., "the one who shows mercy")? Is it "the compassionate" who, according to Cranfield (1979), tends the sick and cares for the aged and disabled? Or simply the one who helps "those in distress" (REB)? This person is to do so *en hilarotēti*, gladly or cheerfully.

Prophecy, service, teaching, and exhortation pertain to the specific activities that build up the community assembled in several house churches, but no less gifts of grace are uncompromised giving, diligence in patronage, and deeds of mercy done cheerfully. Noticeably, verses 6-8 are completely free of the sort of regulations that appear later in 1 Tim 5:1-22; Titus 1:5-9; 2:1-10 (see Bassler 1996, *ad loc.*). Paul envisions a community in which diverse begracements are not yet routinized into "offices" but are expressed spontaneously, freely, and problem-free. What he envisions in verses 6-8 makes concrete his admonition not to be haughty (vv. 3-5), which in turn is the first consequence of the transformation that is to occur when the mind is renewed (v. 2).

Whereas verses 3-8 concentrated on the exercise of seven begracements for the well-being of the whole community, verses 9-21 pertain to all readers. Remarkably, verses 17-21 insist on non-retaliation and prohibit vengeance—prompting one to wonder whether this disproportionate emphasis reflects Paul's experience with churches or his knowledge of conditions in the Roman house churches. In any case, Paul's counsels echo what he says elsewhere in Romans, as well as in his other letters. They also appear to draw on a variety of traditions without explicitly quoting any of them (only scripture is quoted, v. 19), including Hellenistic Jewish Wisdom (emphasized by Walter Wilson 1991), Stoic motifs (similarities are emphasized by Troels Engberg-Pedersen 2000, 265-77, 285-91; differences by Esler 2004, 106-23), and perhaps orally circulating Jesus traditions, though Jesus is not mentioned (David Wenham 1995, 250-52). Unconvincing, however, is the idea that Paul is drawing on an "Essene homily" (so David Flusser 1997, 78-82). Seen as a whole, verses 9-21 do not develop an argument; they rather assemble and cluster diverse materials that go beyond verses 3-8 in specifying the kind of ethos that should characterize the community.

Verses 9-21 have several literary features that are worth noting. (a) At verse 14 there is a shift in style. From here on we find mostly imperative verbs, whereas in verses 9-13 there are no verbs at all but only participles, which translators render as imperatives. (The "imperatival participle" has generated considerable debate, conveniently summarized by Fitzmyer [1993].) If that rendering is correct, the whole passage consists of commands and prohibitions. (b) This generalization should not, however, be taken for granted, since the opening line (v. 9a) has neither verb nor participle, but consists of three words: *hē agapē anhypokritos*, to which translations give an imperatival force (NRSV: "Let love be genuine"; REB: "Love in all sincerity"). Still, the words can also be a declarative statement: "Love is genuine." Whether this is correct (so Esler 2003, 316-18) or not, this opening line seems to function as the umbrella over what follows, even though the word "love" is not repeated (in v. 10, NRSV's "love one another" translates a different word). This may be Paul's way of signaling that what follows first celebrates the qualities of genuine love (vv. 9*b*-13) before verses 14-21 prohibit its opposite, retaliation and vengeance. (c) However one regards verse 9*a*, the rest of the passage is framed by two couplets that contrast good and evil.

v. 9*b*	Abhor the evil *[poneron]*
	cling to the good
v. 21	Do not be defeated by the evil *[hypo tou kakou]*
	but defeat the evil with the good (AT)

Everything in between can be regarded as instantiating this contrast.

Within the frame are eight diverse admonitions that follow one another staccato-like in a 3-2-3 structure (vv. 10-12), then three couplets (vv. 13-15), followed by an exhortation against haughtiness (v. 16), and the prohibition against retaliation (the only one supported by scripture, vv. 17-20). The combination of similarities and variations enhances the passage's rhetorical effectiveness, especially when heard. Because the subtle skill with which the passage is crafted cannot be reproduced in English, translations sometimes connect the unconnected and sometimes resort to paraphrase (especially REB in v. 10*a*: "Let love of the Christian community show itself in mutual affection").

The couplet in verse 9, using the plural participle *apostygountes* (abhor, hate) sounds like a maxim: "Abhor the evil, cling to the good" (AT), similar to Amos 5:15 ("Hate evil and love good"), *T. Benj.* 8:1 ("run from evil . . . cling to goodness and love"), the Qumran *Community Rule* ("that they may abstain from all evil and hold fast to all good," 1QS 1:5, Vermes 1995, 70), and *m. Aboth* 2:12-13, which reports that Johanan b. Zakkai first asked, "Which is the good way to which a man should cleave?" then, "Which is the evil way from which a man should keep himself?"

These similarities suggest that the couplet draws on the Jewish moral teaching of the Two Ways, taken up by some early Christian writers. If the Christian Gentiles in Rome had attended synagogues before accepting the gospel, they may well have learned this Two Ways tradition, and so would have recognized Paul's brief allusion to it, as would his Jewish readers.

The eight admonitions in verses 10-12 have a markedly similar structure. Rhetorical considerations apparently determined the sequence; the first three participles end in *-oi*, the next five in *-ontes* or *-ountes*. The following wooden translation may convey the brusque style; it takes the initial article in the dative case (*tē* or *tō*) to mean something like, "regarding" or "with respect to" (here abbreviated as re:):

tē (re:) brotherly love toward one another, [be]	devoted
tē (re:) honor,	one another preferring
tē (re:) zeal, eagerness	not hesitant, not indolent
tō (re:) the Spirit	enflamed
tō (re:) the Lord,	serving
tē (re:) hope,	rejoicing
tē (re:) tribulation,	patiently enduring
tē (re:) prayer,	persisting, being assiduous

The first three (brotherly love, honor, zeal/eagerness) pertain to interpersonal relations; the last three (hope, tribulation, prayer) concern life between "the already" and the "not yet" of salvation. (In the middle two [v. 11] it is likely that *pneuma* refers to the divine Spirit, and that in v. 11*b* the preferred text reads *kyriō* [Lord], not *kairō* ["the opportune time," NRSV alt.].) Verses 10-12 emphasize the kinds of persons the community members are to *be*; none of them specifies what they are to *do*. The concern here is not *whether* they are to do what is listed, for that is assumed; the accent falls rather on the *manner* in which these relationships and deeds are to be expressed.

Unfortunately, despite the sophistication with which the rest of the chapter assembles various admonitions and prohibitions, the structure of verses 13-21 is ambiguous because the principle that governed their sequence is not always evident. Fortunately, however, the content—and the issues it raises—can be understood without a convincing analysis of the structure. Indeed, lacking an argument, these verses are a chain of individual injunctions, juxtaposed by word or thought association. Even if the whole is greater than the sum of the parts, each part can also stand on its own.

Whereas verses 10-12 emphasize how appropriate deeds are to be done, the couplet in verse 13 begins a series of admonitions that says *what* is to be done and not done. Verse 13 itself urges solidarity with persons in particular circumstances, privation, and shelter.

> Share *[koinōnountes]* [with] the needs of the saints
>
> pursue *[diōkontes]* hospitality. (AT)

Wisely, Paul did not specify which needs should be met by sharing; historians, of course, wish he had. The widely attested mobility of early Christians made hospitality an important feature of the Christian movement and contributed significantly to its unity and sense of "group identity." According to Acts, Paul and his companions relied repeatedly on hospitality: Philippi (16:15); Thessalonica (17:7); Corinth (18:1-2, 7); Malta (28:7); Rom 16:23 implies the same at Cenchreae. Also, parts of his letters commend traveling associates (see Rom 16:1-2; 1 Cor 16:10-11, 15-16; Phil 2:25-30; in Phlm 22 he asks for hospitality for himself). The letters assume that the courier who brought them would be received hospitably (for a discussion of hospitality, see Malherbe 1983, chap. 4).

Another form of solidarity is commanded in verse 15: "Rejoice with the rejoicing, weep with the weeping" (AT), which also sounds like a maxim. Whereas its second line is similar to Sir 7:34 ("Do not avoid those who weep, but mourn with those who mourn") and is not altogether different from Epictetus, who *allowed* such solidarity in certain circumstances ("Where a man may rejoice with good reason, there others may rejoice with him," *Discourses* 2.5.28), the last line of verse 15 diverges from the Stoic ethos, which prized imperturbability *(ataraxia)*. Compared with that ideal, what Paul urges in verse 15 can be read as a sign of being no longer conformed to this age (v. 2).

Apart from verse 15, verses 14-21 now specify the kinds of things the readers are to *do and not do*. Verse 14 urges them to bless, not to curse persecutors; neither is a mere wish, for both call on God to bring weal or woe. The antithesis of blessing and curse is as early as Deut 11:26-28, where Moses says, "See, I am setting before you today a blessing and a curse: the blessing, if you obey . . . and the curse, if you do not obey" (restated as life and death in Deut 30:15; Jer 21:8). But whereas Moses offers a choice, Paul commands the one and prohibits the other: "Bless the persecutors . . . and do not curse [them]"; he does not, like Moses, go on to spell out the consequences of doing the one or the other. Paul differs also from *T. Jos.* 18:2: "And if anyone wishes to do you harm, you should pray for him, along with doing good, and you will be rescued by the Lord from every evil." Paul allows for no extenuating circumstances. The command and the prohibition are unequivocal, absolute, as in apodictic law (which is devoid of "If . . . then . . ."). The relation of Paul's words here to the teaching of Jesus is complex (see Thompson 1991, 96-105). What Paul says differs more from Matt 5:44-45, which states both consequence and warrant ("Love your enemies and pray for those who persecute you, so that you may be children of your Father in heaven"), than from Luke 6:27-28, which lacks them. The historical relationships between these forms of the tradition are opaque because the Gospels appropriated the saying from Q, which has its own historical problems, and which Paul might not have known (see Allison 1982). In any case, Rom 12:14 also insists on the positive response to persecution ("bless" is repeated for emphasis). Paul had included persecution *(diōgmos)*, as well as martyrdom, in the list of dangers that cannot separate the believer from Christ's love (8:35-36); here he commands positive action toward the persecutors, thereby going beyond both nonresistance and nonretaliation, as did Jesus, as well as Paul himself in 1 Cor 4:12: "When reviled, we bless; when persecuted *[diō komenoi]*, we endure."

Verse 16 reverts to the theme emphasized in verse 3. Recent translations, however, conceal the threefold use of some form of *phronein* (think in a certain way, have a mindset, a *phronēma*) used four times in verse 3. Both verses urge a unity that expresses a shared mindset (not to be confused with thinking identical thoughts!), which verse 16 spells out more fully, though less than clearly. The prohibition *mē ta hypsēla phronountes* literally means "do not set your minds on lofty *things*" but the required alternative *tapeinois* (lowly) can be either neuter or masculine (lowly things or lowly people); NRSV prefers "the lowly" (people) and puts "humble tasks" in the footnote. Pivotal, of course, is the imperatival participle *synapagomenoi* (lit., "led away" as in Gal 2:13), which can also mean "associate with." So NRSV has Paul say, "Do not be haughty, but associate with the lowly." NJB tries to express the sequence (neuter followed by masculine): "Pay no regard to social standing, but meet humble people on their own terms"; similarly REB: "Do not be proud, but be ready to mix with humble people." Perhaps "Do not claim to be wiser than you are" alludes to Prov 3:7, "Do not be wise in your own eyes."

Verses 17-21 prohibit retaliation and vengeance. The imperative not to "repay evil for evil" appears in Paul's earliest letter (1 Thess 5:15), and may echo Jesus' more vivid teaching in Matt 5:39-41: "Do not resist an evildoer. But if anyone strikes you on the right cheek, turn the other also; and if anyone wants to sue you and take away your coat, give your cloak as well; and if anyone forces you to go one mile, go also the second mile." Interestingly, what Paul commands appears in *Joseph and Aseneth* (the Greek legendary account of Joseph and Pharaoh's daughter) as a description of behavior that is appropriate to Jews: "And we are men who worship God, and it does not befit us to repay evil for evil" (23:9 [Charlesworth 1985, 2:240]; restated in 28:5; 29:3; see also 28:10). Already Prov 20:22 had forbidden retaliation.

Noteworthy in verse 17 is the alternative to retaliation: "Take thought [*pronooumenoi*] for what is noble [*kala*] in the sight of all" (a paraphrase of LXX Prov 3:4, used of Paul himself in 2 Cor 8:21). In REB the alternative to retribution is "Let your *aims* be such as all count honorable" because it gives full weight to the *pro* in *pronooumenoi* ("take *fore*thought"). Jesus' alternative to retaliation is a different kind of *act* (turn the other cheek), but in verse 17 Paul's alternative is a *disposition* oriented toward what *everyone* ("all") deems "noble" (*kala*, beautiful, fine, defect-free, good), not just fellow Christians (as in 1 Thess 5:15). That Paul means "all Christians" because *kala* refers to the gospel (so Cranfield 1979 and Moo 1996) is quite unlikely. By contrasting retaliation with a disposition toward the commonly recognized good, Paul tacitly acknowledges that the impression Christians make on others is important for the reputation of the gospel; he also suggests that a renewed mind should value as good what is deemed good by everyone, Christian or not. Evidently not being conformed to this age (v. 2) does not require total rejection of all the values in the culture. Still, there is a tension between what Paul implies here and what he said about the idolatrous Gentiles in 1:21-32; Paul either ignores the disparity, was not aware of it, or was using here a traditional teaching with a more positive outlook.

In verse 18 the counsel to "live peaceably with all" (not just all believers) restates the alternative to the consequences of retaliation—animosities—and apparently is placed here by word association ("all" repeats the "all" in v. 17). That verse 18 draws on Jesus' word in Mark 9:50 ("be at peace with one another") is doubtful—unless one assumes, as does Moo (1996, 785), that Jesus' word also concerns outsiders rather than the disciples. In any case, "If it is possible, so far as it depends on you" shows that Paul recognizes that being at peace with *all* is not in the hands of Christians only, and that even they will find peaceable relations to be a challenge.

Verses 19-21 are more than an elaboration of verse 14; they also bring to a head Paul's mandates concerning the house churches' relation to society at large. The readers are "beloved" not by Paul but by God (see 5:8; 8:39). *Because* they know themselves *loved* by God through what God has already done, they are liberated from the widely sensed necessity to avenge themselves, free to give way to *God's* prerogative, expressed as "leave room for the wrath [of God]," presumably at the coming Judgment (as in 1 Thess 1:10). The prohibition against vengeance appears in scripture:

"You shall not take vengeance . . . against any of your people, but you shall love your neighbor as yourself. I am the LORD" (Lev 19:18). Sirach 28:1 observes, "The vengeful will face the Lord's vengeance, for he keeps a strict account of their sins." Various forms of Judaism continued the prohibition. *Testament of Gad* 6:7 urges forgiveness even of the one who persists in wrongdoing, adding, "and leave vengeance to God" (Charlesworth 1983, 1:816). The hymn that concludes the *Community Rule* found at Qumran includes these lines (1QS 10:17; Vermes 1995, 85):

> I will pay no man the reward of evil;
> I will pursue him with goodness.
> For judgment of all things is with God
> and it is He who will render to man his reward.

In this whole legacy, vengeance is forbidden, not because it is morally destructive, but because it pre-empts the role of God. Paul supports his point by quoting a version of Deut 32:35, "Vengeance is mine, I will repay, says the Lord" (the first clause agrees with the Hebrew, the second with the LXX; neither has "says the Lord"). What Paul insists on is quite different from Aristotle's observation: "To take vengeance on one's enemy is nobler than to come to terms with them; for to retaliate is just, and that which is just is noble; and further, a courageous man ought not to allow himself to be beaten" (*On Rhetoric,* 1.9.24).

In verse 20 Paul commands positive, helpful acts in response to one's enemies, quoting LXX Prov 25:21-22. The quotation is useful because it makes vivid the positive response to the enemies; to ask, "What if the enemies are not hungry or thirsty?" is to miss the point, profoundly. What Paul, and Proverbs before him, had in mind in saying that by deeds of kindness one heaps "burning coals" on the enemies' heads has eluded a convincing explanation for centuries (see Klassen 1963 for extended review, Fitzmyer 1993 for a summary). Given the frustrations that mark the history of interpretation here, a prudent student will avoid insisting that any proposed interpretation is the right one, lest one fulfill Sir 27:25a: "Whoever throws a stone straight up throws it on his own head." It suffices to note that the context, especially verse 21, indicates that Paul regarded the expression as a positive result of deeds of kindness. Not a word is said about the response that might be expected from the beneficiary of the positive acts. In terms of "ethics," Paul's command is not prudential but deontological—that is, verse 20 is not a wise strategy to change the opponent; it is simply one's obligation.

According to verse 21, Christians are not to accept evil passively, but rather to respond to it by doing good, thereby instantiating their nonconformity to "this age" (v. 2). One should not take this injunction for granted, as if it were a motto (though it sounds like one), for defeating evil with good is precisely the work of God. Paul has the audacity to urge the readers to do as God does—precisely in response to evil. According to Matt 5:44-45 Jesus did so too.

◊ ◊ ◊ ◊

It is instructive to ponder chapter 12 as a whole. Noteworthy is the sequence in which verses 3-21 proceed to make concrete the discernment of God's will (v. 2). After beginning with the mandated criterion of faith, Paul concentrates on intramural relationships and attitudes before looking outward to include even the persecutors. In doing so, he starts with the individual (twice in v. 3). At the same time, this individuality (expressed in differentiated begracements in vv. 6-7) is what links each to the other—"members *of* one another," so that each has a stake in the well-functioning of the other. Not until that reciprocity of each in the other has been pointed out does Paul commence expressing his exhortations that use plural forms (beginning at v. 9). Envisioned here is the individual *in a* community not conformed to "this age" because its mind, its mentality, is being made new. A different ethos is to be formed, one that apparently knows nothing of either "self-help" or "self-fulfillment." What is to be fulfilled is rather God's will.

Noteworthy also is the way the exhortations combine specificity and open-endedness, suggesting that the various specific injunctions do not constitute a code but are a series of channel markers guiding the readers as they discern what God's will actually calls for in detail. Not surprisingly, then, few of the admonitions are warranted by Paul's own reasoning. To discern the details of what accords with God's will, the renewed minds are expected to think—and to do so in response to "the mercies of God."

Submission to Governing Authorities (13:1-7)

It is not the opaqueness of this passage that has distressed and divided interpreters but its clarity—its plain, unqualified call for submission to "governing authorities." Why did Paul write such a paragraph, one unlike anything found in his other letters? Indeed, some have found it so out of step with his overall thought that they concluded that he did not dictate it and that someone added it later (for the arguments, see Walker 2001, 221-31). Most scholars, however, have rejected the interpolation hypothesis, primarily because no manuscript of Romans lacks these verses; an interpolation would have been made so soon after the letter was written that all subsequent copies contained it. Instead of adjudicating the arguments at the outset, we will first examine the passage, then comment on it as a whole before discussing attempts to account for it.

To begin with, the literary context itself shows that Paul is *not* outlining his view of "the state"; the paragraph is part of his *exhortations* that begin at 12:1. Nonetheless, no "therefore" links it to chapter 12; verses 1-7 are a self-contained unit. It begins abruptly, and is linked to verse 8 only by word association (see below). The content of verses 1-7 interrupts the discussion of love begun at 12:9 and resumed in 13:8-10. Still, the passage is not wholly without links to its context. The counsels in 13:1-7 make concrete what 12:18 urges: "If it is possible, so far as it depends on you, live peaceably with *all*"—that is, by submitting to the governing authorities, paying taxes, and honoring *all* who deserve it. In addition, Paul's insistence that the Roman believers are not to avenge themselves but to "leave room for the wrath of God" (12:19) coheres with his comment in verse 4 that the authority is God's servant to "execute wrath on the wrongdoer," perhaps God's wrath as well as the government's (so Yoder 1972, 200). One should be alert to both continuities and discontinuities between our passage and its immediate context.

The passage begins and ends with general mandates, the first to be heeded *by* all, the last concerning the obligation *to* all. The bulk of verses 1-5 explains why submission is warranted; verses 6-7 make this injunction concrete. That the whole unit is an argument is shown by the fact that it uses *gar* (for, because) seven times (vv. 1, 2, 4 [three times], 6 [twice]). Noteworthy also is the fact that the exhortations in verses 3-4 address the individual (using second person singular), whereas those in the surrounding verses use second person plural. Whether this shift to and from diatribal style is substantively significant is not self-evident.

The opening mandate is an unequivocal command: "Let every person [lit., "soul"] be subject to the governing authorities" (NRSV). No "if it is possible, so far as it depends on you" (12:18) qualifies this obligation. Understanding *what* is commanded requires attending to the reason *why* it is commanded, stated as a fact in the rest of verse 1. To express this reason Paul exploits various nuances of the verb *tassō* (to order, arrange, put in place), beginning with the comand *hypotassesthō* (put under, submit). All are to put themselves under "the governing authorities" because they are *tetagmenai* (perfect participle of *tassō*)—that is, they are put in place by God (NRSV; REB: "instituted"; NIV, NASB: "established"; NJB: "appointed"; CEV: God "puts these rulers in their places of power"). In short, the text commands all readers to put themselves under the established authority structure that God established. Although verse 4 will acknowledge that the authorities have recourse to "the sword," here the basic warrant for submission is not political (their power) but theological: God's actualized will, here expressed both negatively ("there is no authority except from God") and positively: "those authorities that exist have been instituted by God." Submission entails accepting and acknowledging what is given instead of resisting it. Similarly, 10:3 says that Israel has not "submitted [*hypetagēsan*, from *hypotassō*] to God's righteousness"—did not accept and acknowledge that God's rectitude rectifies. That also 13:1-7 entails accepting the result of God's act is evident in verse 5, which speaks of "the necessity *[anagkē]* to be subject" (AT; *anagkē*, the constraint flowing from the nature of things, is not to be confused with fate *[heimarmenē*, not used in New Testament], an inescapable destiny not rooted in the nature of things but imposed on them). Nonetheless, though submission is obligatory, the text also implies that everyone is an agent who is accountable for submitting to or resisting the authorities in place.

Who are they? Paul calls them *exousiai hyperechousiai* (NRSV, NIV, NJB: "governing authorities"; REB: "the authorities in power"). All these translations agree that Paul refers to political authorities of unspecified rank. Wholly fanciful is the notion that he is asking Christian Gentiles in Rome to "subordinate themselves to the *institutional* requirements" of the synagogues (so Nanos 1996, chap. 6; his italics). Others have claimed that Paul is referring to the cosmic powers that operate through earthly (political) figures—a view now widely rejected (the arguments for and against this view are well summarized by Cranfield 1979, 2:657-59 and Moo 1996, 795-96), but which persists among those who see the same view in 1 Cor 2:8. There Paul writes that the "rulers *[archontes]* of this age" would not have "crucified the Lord of glory" had they understood God's hidden mystery. Many scholars regard these "rulers" as Roman authorities, while others maintain that they are both cosmic powers and their Roman agents—an unconvincing view (see Carr 1981, chap. 5). Actually, because Rom 13:3 also mentions "the rulers," probably both 1 Cor 2:8 and Rom 13:3 refer to human rulers only (in v. 3 REB uses "governments" instead of "rulers"). In other words, instead of relying on a questionable interpretation of 1 Cor 2:8 to interpret Rom 13:1-3, one should read 1 Cor 2:8 in light of Romans.

All believers are to submit to the *exousiai* because authority *(exousia)* itself is *from* God, since those authorities that exist have been put there *by* God, and because they function in the service *of* God. The readers are to submit to the authorities, irrespective of their motives or machinations. Paul could hardly have been more explicit: submit to "the system" in place because God put it there. And while it is Roman authorities that are in view without being mentioned, Paul's eye is on the civic authority structure as such.

Paul apparently implies that it is part of the created order (contrary to Yoder [1972, 203], who claims God did not "ordain" the authorities but "put them in order," or "lined them up with his purpose"). Here the legitimacy of government is derived not from "the consent of the governed" but from the act of God; consequently, the "consent of the governed" is the right response to what God has done, not to what Rome has achieved or to its ideology of power.

What Paul says in verse 1 may be original in its formulation but not in its substance. Bruno Blumenfeld (2001, 244), for example, quotes the Pythagorean Diotogenes, "God gave rule" *(hagemonian, sic)* to the king. Paul's near contemporary, Dio Chrysostom, also said that kings "derive their powers and their stewardship from Zeus" (*First Discourse on Kingship,* 45). Paul, of course, knew that scripture too said that kingship comes from God, not only Israel's kingship (as in 2 Sam 12:7-8) but also that of its conqueror, Babylon (Jer 27:4-7). The book of Daniel emphasizes repeatedly that God gives kingship to whomever he pleases (Dan 2:21, 37-38; 4:17, 25, 32; 5:21). Sirach 17:17 declares that the Lord "appointed a ruler for every nation"; so too Wis 6:1-3, addressing the kings of the world, says, "your dominion was given you from the Lord, and your sovereignty from the Most High." The *Letter of Aristeas* has a Jewish sage tell the king, "You are really a king, God having granted you authority as your manner deserves" (*Let. Aris.* 2:19; Charlesworth 1985, 2:27). In 4 Macc 12:11, even the tyrant, "most impious of all that are wicked," received his kingdom from God. In verse 1, then, Paul formulates in universal, generic terms what was a commonplace, as well as what he learned from scripture and inherited from Judaism. Remarkable is not the divine origin of the authorities' authority but the unqualified obligation that Paul finds implied in that origin.

Verses 2-5 explain the implications of verse 1, beginning with the unavoidable: Since God has put the governing authorities in place, "whoever opposes [*ho antitassomenos,* continuing the wordplay already noted] the authority is in opposition [perfect tense of *anthistēmi,* be against] to what God has installed [*diatagē,* what is ordered, put in place; from *diatassō*] and the opposers [*hoi anthestekotes]* will be condemned [lit., "will receive judgment on themselves"]" (AT). REB makes Paul say even more: "It follows that anyone who rebels against authority is resisting a *divine insti-tuition*"; but installation by God does not make the installed "divine." Paul does not say that those who oppose the authority oppose *God*, but oppose God's deed. Nor does he speak of oppo-sition to persons, thereby tacitly distinguishing the person from the office. Verses 3-5 probably imply, but do not actually say, that the condemnation will come from the governing authorities (called "rulers" *[archontes]* in v. 3).

Verse 3 warrants the warning in verse 2 by explaining the role of the rulers: They "are not a terror to the good work *[tō agathō ergō]* but to the bad" (NRSV: "good conduct"; NIV: "for those who do right"; REB modernizes: "Governments hold no terrors for the law-abiding but only for the criminal"). Verse 3 assumes that the rulers are fair, that they will not punish those who do what is good. First Peter 3:13-17, written later, is more realistic: "Now who will harm you if you are eager to do what is good? But *even if you do* suffer for doing what is right, you are blessed. . . . For it is better to suffer for doing good . . . than to suffer for doing evil" (the precedent of Christ follows).

As noted, in verses 3-4 Paul addresses an individual (four verbs use second person singular: wish, do, will have, fear), as in a dia-tribe: "Do you wish to have no fear of the authority? Then do the good *[to agathon]* and you will have praise from it" (AT). Whereas those who oppose the rulers live in fear of their punish-ing power, the one who does the good expects their praise. What Paul urges now goes beyond submission and staying out of trou-ble; he commends doing "the good work." In verse 4 he states the basis for this counsel: The authority is "God's servant for you [*soi*, second person singular] for the good" (AT; the few manuscripts that omit *soi* generalize: "God's servant for the good"). But what is "the good work/deed"? Is it simply "good conduct" as in NRSV? And does Paul really expect governing authorities in Rome, a huge city, to notice the good behavior of an individual and respond with praise? That seems implausible, though not for Bruce Winter (1994, chap. 2).

Winter notes that both literary and epigraphic evidence shows that it was widely assumed and asserted that one of the ruler's functions was to publicly praise those who did good deeds for the city and punish the lawless—precisely the alternatives that appear in verses 3-4. He also notes that Paul's phrase "do the good" *(to agathon poiei)* appears in inscriptions honoring benefactors who provided things like baths, paved streets, or public games. So Winter (assuming the change to second person singular is not stylistic) thinks Paul addresses any individual who has sufficient means to provide "the good work" (a public benefaction), and promises unequivocally that the ruler would acknowledge it with public praise. Significant as the terminological evidence in itself is, Winter's interpretation does not comport easily with the concerns of the passage as a whole.

Paul supports his promise that the ruler will praise the doer of "the good work" and punish the one who does "the bad" by pointing out that the governing authority "does not bear the sword in vain" because it is "the servant of God to execute wrath on the wrongdoer." The phrase "bear the sword" is not used by any other ancient writer. It does not refer to the *ius gladii* (the power of the sword), which in Paul's time only provincial governors could use against Roman citizens in the army (Sherwin-White 1978, 9-11). Nor is it clear that it refers to Rome's war-making power to put down rebellion (so Borg 1973, 217). Paul appears to use the phrase to refer generally to Rome's law-enforcement power, including the police (for the notorious role of secret police and spies, see Friedländer 1965, 1:221-22). Paul is neither legitmating nor advocating capital punishment; he simply reminds the readers that the governing authority does have the power to punish. But in doing so, he is quick to add that it is God's servant "bringing retribution on the offender" (REB for *ekdikos eis orgēn*, lit., "the avenger for wrath"; NIV: "an agent of wrath to bring punishment on the wrongdoer"). As noted, what Paul said here about the authority comports with 12:19-20, whose language belongs in the same semantic field: "Do not avenge *[ekdikountes]* yourselves but leave space for the wrath [of God]" (AT). Invisible, earth-transcending power does operate through governing authority, but that power is God's, not that of the cosmic powers some have detected in verse 1 (see above). Paul's concern is not *how well* he acts but *that* he acts as God's instrument (whether or not he knows he is God's instrument).

That God acts through human agents agrees with what was said about Pharaoh in 9:17, and with what God proclaims in Isa 10:5-7:

> Ah, Assyria, the rod of my anger—
> the club in their hands is my fury!
> Against a godless nation [Israel!] I send him,
> and against the people of my wrath I command him. . . .
> But this is not what he intends,
> nor does he have this in mind.

In Jer 42:10 God calls Nebuchadnezzar "my servant," and Isa 45:1 even calls Cyrus God's "anointed" (Messiah). Just as none of these rulers or empires understood themselves to be God's agents (though doubtless claiming the approval of their gods) yet were God's servants nonetheless, so Roman rule serves God's justice whether or not it intends to—not because of *what* that rule is (Rome's *imperium*) but because of *who* the sovereign God is. The deity that Paul is talking about is, of course, neither the goddess Roma nor Zeus but the holy One who is against all human wickedness (1:18).

Verse 5 adds that submission is necessary "also because of conscience." The previous reference to the role of conscience (2:15) suggests what is meant here: the self-knowledge of the person who acknowledges the role of governing authority in the purpose of God, or perhaps more simply, "knowledge of the good" (Blumenfeld 2001, 394). That is, since for Paul "conscience" refers to the ability to assess morally what is done, "because of conscience" implies that the reader—who understands that the authorities serve God—knows that he or she is accountable to God for one's relation to them. In verse 5 the warrant that underlies the necessity to submit is both external (threat of punishment) and internal (conscience). Verse 5 does not envisage refusal to submit as "an act of conscience" in the modern sense ("civil disobedience"). Still, the nonviolent who allow themselves to be arrested and jailed for acts of civil disobedience do heed Paul's counsel to submit to the governing authority "because of conscience"—but in a different sense.

"For the same reason" (v. 6) introduces another inference from verse 5 and makes the theme of submission concrete by using the fact that the readers *are paying* the *phoros* (tax) as evidence that they are already submitting to the authorities. (While the word *teleite* ["pay"] can be an imperative, the "for" shows that here it is used in the indicative.) The *phoros* was a tax levied on *subject persons* (as in Luke 20:22; in Mark 12:14 it is called the *kensos*, poll tax), including tribute required of conquered rulers (as in 1 Macc 8:4). The very act of paying the *phoros* expressed submission. Those to whom this tax is paid too are God's servants, indeed of a special kind: They are God's *leitourgoi* (for which there is no adequate English equivalent; NRSV: "servants"; NIV and REB paraphrase: "the authorities are in God's service"). A *leitourgos* was a public official whose duties originally had overtones of sacral significance (Fitzmyer 1993: "cultic minister"; in 15:16 Paul uses the word to characterize his own work). Precisely as assiduous collectors of this tax, these functionaries are God's public servants, doing their "sacred duty" whether or not the tax is fair or its collectors honest.

Verse 7 concludes the discussion with a complex imperative that repeats what verse 6 said about tax payment and then goes beyond it as well: "Pay to all what is due *[tas opheilas]* them" (REB: "Discharge your obligations to everyone"). *Opheilē*, like *opheilēma*, can refer to a financial obligation (as in Matt 18:32) or to a social obligation (as in 1 Cor 7:3, where NRSV renders it "conjugal rights"); the Matthean version of the Lord's Prayer uses the plural metaphorically: "Forgive us our debts" (Matt 6:12). Paul takes advantage of the dual meaning by using it first to refer to two financial obligations, then to two social ones. The former makes mandatory the payment of the *phoros* mentioned in verse 6, and adds to it another tax, the *telos* (taxes on things like custom duties, tolls [as in Matt 17:25], salt [as in 1 Macc 10:29], and so forth; here NRSV translates it as "revenue," REB as "levy"). Since there were many such taxes—for example, poll taxes on all adults under sixty-five, sales tax, inheritance tax (5 percent), tax on the sale of slaves (4 percent) and on the manumission of slaves—Paul may have used *telos* to refer to all such taxes that people may have tried to avoid.

More important is the fact that he insists on paying taxes at all. His words about taxes are not "mere rhetorical commonplaces" (Elliott 1994, 223), for such an injunction is absent not only from comparable exhortations in 1 Tim 2:1-3; 2 Tim 3:1-2; 1 Pet 2:13-17, but also from Jewish and Greco-Roman texts. Indeed, because tax payment is the only specific thing that Paul urges (twice!), some have detected here the issue that triggered his writing the whole paragraph (see below). Blumenfeld (2001, 391) claims that Paul's exhortations about taxes are his "most vocal consent to the existing political regime."

The second pair of obligations is social: *phobos* ("fear"; NRSV flattens: "respect") and *timē* ("honor"). In this context, those who are owed fear are probably the "rulers" in verses 3-4; whether, or in what way, those to whom honor is due differ from those who ought to be feared is not clear. Paul's society emphasized honor— the public acknowledgment of someone's merit or meritorious deeds (see Moxnes 1988, 207-18). In a context in which honor was sought, often competitively, withholding honor would have been tantamount to contempt. With the necessity of submission to the authorities (a legal obligation) goes the obligation to honor all who deserve it (a moral obligation). Having urged intramural honor (12:10), Paul now extends it to those outside the community, to those who have a right to expect it.

Remarkable as the content of the passage is, one should not overlook what it does *not* say (the silences are significant even if one regards the passage as an interpolation). Seen as a whole, two things are notably absent: a specific reference to the Roman Empire itself, and any mention of Christ, together with the vocabulary of salvation.

Though the letter was sent to believers in Rome, neither the city nor its role as the center of imperial power is even alluded to; nor is the emperor (Nero, then still popular) mentioned. Nor is a word said, or implied, about Rome's achievements (e.g., pacification of warring peoples and of the seas, the roads that Paul surely used, the pervasiveness of Roman law, etc.) or their cost in blood (emphasized by Wengst 1987; for a detailed nonpolemical yet unromantic portrait see Petit 1976). The Roman Empire, whether as a whole or in any of its particulars, is not evaluated, neither denounced nor celebrated. (For an overview of early Christian attitudes toward Rome, including Paul, see Alexander 1992, 835-39.) Rome is simply treated as a given, apparently expected to continue indefinitely. As Yoder (1972, 202) notes, "nothing in the text . . . justifies the concept of just rebellion."

Nor is there any evident interest in the general well-being of Rome. Paul does not urge the readers to pray for the emperor or his government, as does the "Paul" of 1 Timothy: "First of all I urge that supplications, prayers, intercessions, and thanksgivings be made for everyone, for kings and all who are in high places" (2:1, AT)—though even here the motivation is not civic but ecclesial: "so that we may lead a quiet and peaceable life in all godliness and dignity" (1 Tim 2:2). Nonetheless, Christians who heed the exhortation of 1 Timothy are concerned for the health of the government; there is no such concern in Rom 13:1-7. Further, much of Paul's life was spent in western Asia Minor, especially in Ephesus, where the emperor cult was enjoying rising popularity and was an integral part of communal life (so Price 1984, 80, 102, 108); Paul could not have been unaware of its processions and temples (Price offers a map of the 180 communities where such temples were built). Yet our passage breathes not a whiff of this worship. Submission to the authorities is required not despite who the emperor and his priesthood claim he is (for example, *Sotēr* [Savior], *Kyrios* [Lord], *Patēr* [Father]) but because God has put them in place. Paul would surely have known the stories of the Maccabean martyrs, yet Paul gives no hint of the "God *or* Caesar" issue. Nor is there any connection made between the authorities in verses 1-7 and the persecutors mentioned in 12:14.

In short, when one views what is said in these verses together with what is not said, one is struck by its pragmatic, minimalist character. In light of the authority structure that God has put in place, Paul offers straightforward, sound advice to those who must cope with it. And while his interpretation of the authorities is thoroughly theological, he does not "theologize" about God's relation to the emperor or the empire. What is especially noteworthy is that he doesn't even refer to the righteousness of God.

What makes the silence about Christ noteworthy is not just the absence of the name itself but the fact that the passage takes no account of the significance of the Christ-event as a whole, whose eschatological significance, certified by resurrection, was decisive for Paul's whole theology and mission. (Cranfield [1979], arguing that the passage does not lack Christology, resorts to what was in Paul's mind—the implications of what Paul had said earlier about Christ.) The absence of Paul's eschatological perspective is a major reason that James Kallas (1965) regards the passage as an interpolation. Paul does, of course, go on to say that "salvation is nearer to us now than when we became believers" (13:11, AT). But the import of this conviction for the counsels in verses 1-7 is implicit retroactively; the counsels themselves do not mention it.

What 13:11-14 does warrant is renouncing the desires of the flesh, not a positive attitude toward the authorities; there is nothing here comparable to the influence of the imminent coming of Christ on 1 Cor 7:11-14: "The appointed time has grown short; from now on, let . . . those who deal with the world [live] as though they had no dealings with it. For the present form of this world is passing away." Instead, in 13:1 Paul writes as though the authorities that have been put in place by God will stay in place; 13:11-14 does not show that the present status of the powers "is not permanent" as Elliott (1994, 224) claims. Even if the two references to "the wrath" (vv. 4, 5), as well as to the "judgment/condemnation" (v. 2), refer to God's wrath/judgment as well as that of the authorities, the readers would not have understood these words as allusions to what Paul had written a few years before: the day of the Lord will come unexpectedly, "when they say, 'There is peace and security' [persistent themes of Roman ideology], then sudden destruction will come upon them" (1 Thess 5:2-3). Nor would the readers have surmised that Paul had written that "the rulers of this age," who ignorantly "crucified the Lord of glory," are "doomed to perish" (1 Cor 2:6-8). It is *our* knowledge of Paul's eschatology, and the eschatological horizon of the rest of the letter, that permits (requires?) one to read verses 1-7 in keeping with that perspective. Otherwise, taken by themselves, these verses read as if Paul had written them before he became an apostle. Indeed, Byrne (1996, 386) reckons with the possibility that Paul adapted "instruction circulating in Hellenistic-Jewish diaspora communities."

The absence of a christological grounding makes it quite unlikely that the passage restates Jesus' word about paying taxes to Caesar (Matt 22:15-22; Mark 12:13-17; Luke 22:20-26). The only word common to these passages and verses 1-7 is *apodote* ("pay"). More important, whereas Jesus distinguished what belongs to Caesar from what belongs to God, and so refused to say that paying the tax with Caesar's coin was unlawful, our passage urges that taxes be paid because those who collect them are God's servants. Jesus neither said nor implied that Caesar or his procurators were God's agents (see also Thompson 1991, 111-20).

The more the peculiar character of verses 1-7 emerges into view, the more pressing become the questions, Why did Paul write it? How do its content and tone fit into the thought and purpose of Romans as a whole? Does Paul view the governing authorities so positively that Blumenfeld (2001, 292) can claim—hopefully with tongue in cheek—that Romans might be virtually a contribution to a Festschrift for Nero?

Attempts to explain why Paul dictated verses 1-7 emphasize either (a) Paul's positive experience with Rome, (b) the role of the passage in the purpose of the letter, or (c) the historical circumstances of the readers—though frequently these factors are combined. Running through all explanations is the (presumed) need to distance Paul's own view from the history of tyranny—especially in the previous century—in which all too often Paul was claimed as its warrant. No explanation is problem-free; all suffer from the lack of convincing evidence. This is particularly evident in the first explanation.

A century ago, writing at the height of the British Empire, Sanday and Headlam (1895, 370) wrote confidently of Paul's "fascination" with Rome, claiming also that in writing verses 1-7 he was "thinking of a great and beneficent power which had made travel for him possible . . . under which he had seen the towns through which he passed enjoying peace, prosperity and civilization" (xvi). Half a century later, John Knox (1954, 599-600) was sure that Paul "found himself often thanking God" for the benefits of the empire, including "the protection which Roman magistrates gave him when he was threatened by mob violence." But Paul never mentions such protection, and even Acts reports only one such incident (Acts 19:21-41); the Romans rescued him from the Jerusalem mob (21:27-36) *after* Paul wrote this letter. Dodd (1932 , 202) saw in the positive attitude toward Rome an expression of 2 Thess 2:6-10 because he regarded its reference to the Restrainer, who holds back lawlessness until the parousia, to be Paul's allusion to Rome—ignoring Paul's criticism of the "Peace and Security" slogan in 1 Thess 5:2-3 noted above. Moreover, the identity of "the Restrainer" is as uncertain as the genuineness of 2 Thessalonians.

Decades ago, Minear (1971, 88), while insisting that the whole of Romans addresses the tensions in chapters 14–15, admitted that he was "unable to find particular reasons in the Roman situation" that account for this passage. Since then, others have claimed to have found them. But they have not been successful either. Thus Philip Towner (1991, 149-69) claims that Paul was facilitating his mission by encouraging readers to do good in society in keeping with the household code tradition (Col 3:18–4:1; Eph 5:22-33; Titus 2:1–3:8; 1 Pet 2:13-17), which emphasized adherence to acceptable mores (similarly Johnson 1997, 186). Yet none of these codes is found in the undoubtedly genuine letters of Paul. More important, the connections between Paul, authorities and taxes, household codes, and Spain are transferred from the mind of the scholar to the mind of Paul. Similarly, when Käsemann's commentary claims that Paul is coping with "enthusiasm," it transfers his understanding of the situation in Corinth to Rome. Another effort (Byrne 1996, 386-87) is more suggestive: These verses continue Paul's self-presentation begun in 1:1-17— that is, Paul shows that he will not arrive as a potential agitator. True as this may be, one wonders why Paul would have bypassed the opportunity to at least allude to such concerns when he resumed his self-presentation in 15:14. Least successful is Elliott's view: After claiming that Romans is Paul's "intifada" against Rome's ideology (1994, 190, 215), he says that in verses 1-7 Paul "means simply to keep members of the ekklesia from making trouble in the streets" (223). If so, as an "intifada" Romans self-destructs in verses 1-7.

Often those who focus on the readers' circumstances point out that the believers, a powerless minority grouped in a number of house churches, had no way to influence Rome's governance anyway; consequently, Paul was simply being realistic. (Insofar as this observation, true as it is, masks a desire to excuse Paul for not encouraging modern Christian participation in civic affairs, it manifests a patronizing attitude toward the apostle.) Borg (1965, 365-74) proposed a more particular circumstance, one especially important for recently returned Christian Jews in Rome: Paul urges the readers not to be caught up in the rising anti-Roman passions in Judea, of which the Christian Jews in Rome were surely aware. "Participation in Israel's cause would defeat a central purpose of the gospel"—the unity of Jews and Gentiles—because it would expose the Christian community in Rome (consisting of both Jews and Gentiles) to anti-Jewish reaction. But plausible as this may be, nowhere does Romans show any awareness of fervent Jewish nationalism in either Judea or Rome. Another particular circumstance has been proposed—the problem of taxes in Rome. According to Tacitus (*Annals* 13.50), in 58 CE Nero, responding to persisting complaints, reorganized that part of the tax structure pertaining to indirect taxes and sought to curb the abuses of the tax collectors. Since Romans was written just before that change, Paul allegedly urged all the Roman believers to pay the taxes, lest refusal to do so threaten the church; besides, the world still needed "a state authority to regulate it so that it did not prematurely [before the Judgment] sink into chaos" (so Friedrich et al. 1976).

◊ ◊ ◊ ◊

Doubtless, efforts to account historically for this notorious paragraph will continue—and properly. But if the history of schol-

324

arly endeavor here shows anything, it is that the passage will be more successful in thwarting a convincing explanation than the experts in achieving it. But such a bleak prospect is not without its value, for it suggests that Robert Frost's couplet often applies also to scholarship:

> We sit in a circle and suppose,
> The Secret sits in the middle and knows.

That being said, something else must be said as well: Precisely because this passage resists historical explanation deemed convincing by the majority of scholars, interpreters are discouraged from tying it so tightly to its unique first-century setting that it can be ignored as irrelevant in the twenty-first. Indeed, being part of Paul's extended exhortation, it can stimulate unusually serious thought about the character of actual Christian life in a world where there *are* authorities to cope with, as well as about the character of God in light of the Christ-event. What makes such theological effort significant is the disconcerting fact that while this paragraph addresses believers, neither its view of the authorities nor its mandates are uniquely "Christian." Nor is there a word suggesting that Christians are to submit to those authorities with whose "politics" they agree or whose moral integrity they respect. Perhaps the passage is theologically significant because it exists at all, expressing an obligatory stance marked by neither hatred toward civil authority (as in Rev 13) nor by adulation of its power—a sign that one's mind has indeed been made new (12:1-2).

The Obligation to Love (13:8-10)

Readers who are distressed by the content and tone of verses 1-7 may be relieved to find the content of verses 8-10 more congenial because its validity seems self-evident. In any case, this paragraph too begins abruptly; no "therefore" signals that it continues the thought of verses 1-7, though superficially verse 8 is linked by word association (*opheilete*, "owe") to verse 7, which speaks of *tas opheilas* ("the things owed"; NRSV: "what is due"). Materially, however, it resumes the discussion of love begun at

12:9. Whereas 13:1-7 concerns the readers' external relationships (to civil authorities), verses 8-10 return to their intramural relationships and now speak of the relation of law to love (*agapē* is used five times); it also sets the stage for chapters 14–15 where Paul addresses their quarrels over law observance. Rhetorically, verses 8b-10 resemble an enthymeme (a rhetorical syllogism as a form of argument) that warrants the imperative in verse 8a: "To love one another is your only obligation" (AT).

◊ ◊ ◊ ◊

According to verse 8, the one thing that is obligatory for all believers is mutual love (see also 1 Thess 4:9-10). Being no longer "under the law but under grace" (6:15) does not mean that one is freed from all obligation, for as 8:3-4 pointed out, God acted in Christ "so that the just requirement of the law might be fulfilled [*plērōthē*; related words are used also in 13:8, 10] in us." Now, in the last explicit discussion of the law in Romans, Paul says what that fulfillment actually entails: mutual love. Surprising (and significant) is the reason why such love is the sole obligation: "for the one who loves [present participle] another has fulfilled [*peplērōken*, perfect tense] the law," has already actualized it. (REB shifts the focus: "has met every requirement of the law," as does CEV: "If you love others, you have done all that the Law demands.") Mutual love is *not* the alternative to obligatory law-fulfillment but its mode; mutual love is the way requisite obedience to the law is actualized.

Although mutual love among believers is emphasized also by other New Testament writers, only Paul grounds its obligatoriness in the fulfillment of the law. In John 13:34 Jesus calls mutual love "a new commandment," and then makes his own love for the disciples the basis for their obligation to love each other (so also 15:12). First Peter 1:22 traces the Christians' mutual love to the salvation they have received; similarly, in 1 John the obligation to love is grounded in God's salvific act in Christ: "Since God loved us so much, we also ought to love one another" (1 John 4:11; see vv. 7-12 as a whole). Paul would not contest such statements, but he has his own point to make.

To support the claim that "the one who loves another has fulfilled the law," verse 9 selects four commandments from the "second table" of the Decalogue (abbreviated from Deut 5:17-20; some manuscripts add the fifth, "do not bear false witness"). The phrase "and any other commandment" shows that these four are treated as representative and so suffice for the unstated minor premise of the enthymeme: The law prohibits doing wrong to the neighbor. (In keeping with 1:24; 6:12; and especially 7:7-12 [see comments], "you shall not desire" is a more appropriate rendering of *ouk epithymēseis* than "do not covet," especially since the next paragraph warns against the "desires *[epithymias]* of the flesh"; see also Gal 5:16-17; 1 Thess 4:4-5.) "Summed up" translates *anakephalaioutai* (to bring to a head, add up a column of figures), which in Eph 1:10 means "recapitulate." Jewish sages too stated the point of the law's 613 commands; best known is Hillel's formulation: "That which you hate do not do to your fellows; this is the whole law; the rest is commentary." A few years after Paul, Rabbi Akiba said that Lev 19:18 is "the greatest principle in the Torah" (quoted from Dunn 1988, 2:778).

But what reasoning is at work in juxtaposing the four explicit prohibitions and the love command? The answer is stated in verse 10a: "Love does not do evil [*kakon*, used at 12:21] to the neighbor" (AT). That is, what the representative prohibitions are designed to prevent is achieved by love (see also 1 Cor 13:4-7). *Ergo:* "the fulfillment of the law is love" (AT). Paul did *not* write what REB has him say: "Love *cannot* wrong a neighbor."

But even so, does the rest of verse 10 really follow: "*Therefore* love is the fulfillment of the law" (AT)? Is Paul defining love as not doing wrong to the neighbor? Since not doing the prohibited bad falls short of doing the good, how can doing no wrong be an act of love that fulfills the law? Does not love entail more than that? A closer look is called for, beginning with the translation of the last line: "Therefore love is the fulfillment [NRSV: "fulfilling"] of the law." Actually, Paul is not explaining what love is, but what constitutes the fulfillment of the law. It is not love that needs explanation here but law fulfillment. That is why the last line should be translated, "The fulfillment of the law is love." Thus the argument of verses 8-10 is clear: (a) Your sole obligation is mutual love because the one who loves the other (*heteros* implies "the one who is other" not simply someone else) has fulfilled the law. (b) Why is this true? Because the law is summed up in the love command. (c) Therefore the actualization of the law occurs in love.

That Paul alludes to Jesus' teaching without saying so is possible but no more evident here than in 12:14-21, especially since no Gospel has Jesus say that these four prohibitions are summed up in Lev 19:18. What we do find are the following: (a) In Mark 10:17-31, Jesus, answering, "What must I do to inherit eternal life?" quotes the prohibitions against murder, adultery, theft, false witness, fraud, and the obligation to honor parents. While Matthew and Luke generally agree, only Matthew adds the command to love the neighbor (Matt 19:18-19; Luke 18:20). (b) In Mark 12:28-34, Jesus responds to the question about the chief commandment by combining Deut 6:4-5 (the Shema plus the obligation to love God totally), and the love command in Lev 19:18. (The parallel in Matt 22:36-40 is somewhat different.) If Paul knew any or all of these Jesus-traditions (including the Golden Rule, Matt 7:12; Luke 6:31) he thoroughly restated them (for a full discussion, see Thompson 1991, 121-40). Not to be overlooked in any case is the significance of *how* he tries to persuade the readers: not by citing the authority of Jesus, but rather by reasoning—that is, by asking the readers to come to the same conclusion as he by following the logic of an argument.

◊ ◊ ◊ ◊

When this brief paragraph is taken seriously, it challenges illusory assumptions about love. Read apart from its context, it can easily encourage the illusion that what Paul has in mind coincides with the commonly accepted understanding of love as a positive sentiment, a kindly disposition. Whoever already knows what love is will readily read the text as a confirmation rather than summons. Then the assertion that the fulfillment of the law is love will be welcomed with relief, especially by Christian Gentiles who conclude that love has replaced the "legalism" of the law. Love as sentiment seems both easier and more positive than obeying commandments. But the text does not replace the law with love. It claims that the law is actualized in love; what is actualized in love is not a disposition but the law.

The text challenges one to think deeply about Paul's understanding of love, here expressed as an argument that takes its beat from the Decalogue, and only part of it at that. Evidently the text concentrates on interpersonal relations because it continues the same emphasis found in 12:3-21. But for just this reason, attention is drawn to the mandate that opens this paragraph, for it concentrates every obligation among the believers on reciprocal love. In effect, verses 8-10 function as the foundation on which 12:3-21 rests. While we know what Paul had written about love in all his previous letters, those who first heard Romans did not. But surely Paul expected what he says here to be intelligible and cogent on its own terms, without reference to what he had written elsewhere, and consistent with what he had written in Romans up to this point. In short, this passage sends us back to "the mercies of God" (12:1-2), which in turn sends us back to 5:8-11, as well as to passages like 7:4-6 and 8:4. What is paramount exegetically is what Paul says about love in *this* letter.

The Wake-up Call (13:11-14)

This brief paragraph concludes the general counsels in chapters 12–13 by emphasizing the moral imperatives of the moment, seen in light of impending salvation.

Also, verses 11-14 both amplify the note struck at 12:2 ("Do not be conformed to this age," AT) and together with 12:1-2 create a bracket around chapters 12–13. The thought of the paragraph flows swiftly, using one image after another as it combines brief instruction with exhortation. Similar to verses 11-14 is 1 Thess 5:1-11, where the same themes are found. But whereas the latter is preceded by Paul's fullest portrayal of the parousia (1 Thess 4:13-18), verses 11-14 allude to it only obliquely; they focus on the moral obligations of the present *kairos* (meaning-laden time, not excluding *chronos,* calendrical time).

The abrupt beginning *(kai touto eidotes ton kairon)* has been translated variously because the meaning of the initial words *kai touto* is not clear:

NRSV:	Besides this, you know what time it is
NJB:	Besides, you know the time has come
NIV:	And do this, understanding the present time
NASB:	And this do, knowing the time
REB:	Always remember that this is the hour of crisis
CEV:	You know what sort of times we live in

Of these, REB best suggests the meaning of *kairos,* while CEV mistakenly implies that Paul expresses cultural criticism. The rest of verse 11, however, manifests the main point clearly: It's the daybreak of the New Age, "high time for you to wake out of sleep" (REB). Were Paul's readers in Rome shocked to be told to wake up? Not necessarily, for they probably understood the imagery.

Sleep was used widely as a metaphor for being uncomprehending, unready, unresponsive, preoccupied with the wrong things. Moreover, since being dead was often spoken of as being asleep (as in 1 Thess 4:13), both sleep and death could be used as metaphors for moral desuetude (as in Rev 3:1-2: "You are dead. Wake up, and strengthen what . . . is on the point of death"; and Eph 5:14: "Sleeper, awake! Rise from the dead, and Christ will shine on you"). Philo compared the person intoxicated with folly to "sleepers with the eyes of his soul closed, unable to see or hear aught that is worth seeing or hearing," for that sleep "robs the mind of true apprehension" (*Somn.* 2.160, 162). Waking up, accordingly, could be used to express enlightenment or conversion. Thus Philo speaks of Abraham's abandoning polytheism as "opening the soul's eye as though after profound sleep" (*Abr.* 70). So too, when Antiochus urged Eleazar to eat pork, he said, "Will you not awaken from your foolish philosophy, dispel your futile reasonings?" (4 Macc 5:11). Understandably, staying awake was an image for being alert to moral and spiritual dangers (as in Eph 6:18; 1 Thess 5:6), especially in light of the Lord's sudden coming (as in Mark 13:35-37; Rev 16:15).

According to verse 11, although the readers "know what time it is," Paul tells them anyway: Time to wake up! Why? "Because our salvation is nearer now than when we first believed" (NIV); it is not we who draw nearer to salvation (so Fitzmyer 1993); rather, it is the day of salvation that is coming toward us. The time of the "not yet" is growing shorter. Indeed, "the night is far gone; the day is near" (v. 12). In the remainder of verse 12 as well as verse 13, the image of the impending daybreak suggests the contrast between darkness and light, which in turn suggests the contrast between two modes of life, the one to be rejected, the other to be appropriated. This, apparently, is what responding to the wake-up call entails. To express both the rejection and the appropriation, Paul introduces yet another image: taking off (NRSV: "lay aside") one set of clothes and putting on another (REB has "throw off," translating a different verb used in a few important manuscripts). To be "put aside" (NIV) are "the works of darkness," a metaphor for all wrongdoing; some of these "works" are identified in the short vice list in verse 13.

But instead of urging the readers to put on "the works of light" Paul speaks of putting on "the armor [*hopla*, "weapons"] of light" (v. 12), thereby suggesting that the readers are to get ready for battle. The appropriate moral life will be a struggle. (CEV ignores the imagery: "We must stop behaving as people do in the dark and be ready to live in the light.") In 6:12-13 Paul had used the imagery of weaponry to depict the moral life before and after baptism: "No longer present your members to sin as *hopla* [NRSV: "instruments"] of wickedness, but present . . . your members to God as *hopla* of righteousness." Paul's purpose in neither Rom 6:12-13 nor Rom 13:12 requires him to identify specific weapons, such as sword, spear, or dagger (instruments for aggressive action), though "*hopla* of righteousness" suggests armament that facilitates assertive action. Ephesians 6:10-17, however, urges readers to "put on the whole *panoplian* of God," and then refers to the belt, breastplate, shoes, shield, and helmet—most of which defend the wearer from assault. In Rom 13:12 the "armor of light" probably is to be worn for both offensive and defensive action, as the exhortation and prohibitions that follow suggest.

The imagery of replacing one type or quality of clothing for another does not imply that the change is merely external; rather, it expresses the idea of substantial change (on the assumption that one's attire made visible one's identity or status). This idea was useful as imagery for various kinds of changed identities or traits. Thus *Pseudo-Philo* says God told Joshua to take the deceased Moses' "garments of wisdom and clothe yourself, and with his belt of knowledge gird your loins, and you will be changed and become another man." And when he did so, "his mind was afire and his spirit was moved" (*L.A.B.* 20:2-3; Charlesworth 1985, 2:329). In 1 Cor 15:53-55 Paul appropriates this imagery to say that at the End "we will all be changed," for the perishable body must "put on immortality" (see also 2 Cor 5:1-5). In Rom 13:14 he will urge the readers to clothe themselves with Christ (see below).

In verse 13, the general, positive exhortation to live (lit., "walk") properly (*euschēmonōs*, "decently") is contrasted with six prohibited vices, paired:

> NRSV: not in reveling and drunkenness
> NIV: not in orgies and drunkenness
> REB: no drunken orgies
> CEV: don't go to wild parties or get drunk

> NRSV: not in debauchery and licentiousness
> NIV: not in sexual immorality and debauchery
> REB: no debauchery or vice
> CEV: vulgar or indecent

> NRSV: not in quarreling and jealousy
> NIV: not in dissension and jealousy
> REB: no quarrels or jealousies
> CEV: Don't quarrel or be jealous

Of these, only "quarreling" *(eris)* appears in the vice list in 1:29-31, but all of them are included in the longer list in Gal 5:19-21, where they specify the "works of the flesh" (though Gal 5:19 uses *porneia* ["fornication"] instead of *koitē*, sexual promiscuity, debauchery). Whereas quarreling and jealousy *(eris* and *zēlos)*, being the opposite of mutual love and love of neighbor (vv. 8-9), fracture the community, the other vices manifest a dissolute mode of life; perhaps quarreling and jealousy come last in verse 13 because they are manifest in the disputes Paul will address in a moment (chaps. 14–15).

More significant is the seeming tension between the injunction to abandon the other four vices and 6:20-21, where Paul implies that the readers have already done so when they began to live a different kind of life: "When you were slaves of sin, you were free in regard to righteousness. So what advantage did you then get from the things of which you now are ashamed?" (see also 7:5). The tension, however, is only apparent, for in chapter 6, which emphasizes the sharp contrast between life before and after baptism into Christ, Paul also writes, "Therefore, do not let sin exercise dominion in your mortal bodies, to make you obey their passions" (6:12, followed by the obligation to be weapons for righteousness, mentioned above). Just as 6:12 warned against the "passions"(*epithymiais*, "desires"), so 13:14 ends on the same note: "Make no provision for the flesh, to gratify its desires"— which NJB paraphrases: "Stop worrying about how your disordered natural inclinations may be fulfilled." In short, both Rom 6 and 13:11-14 express, each in its own way, the already/not yet character of present Christian life by insisting on moral obligation.

In verse 14, Paul returns to the image of changing clothes, but now urges the readers to "put on the Lord Jesus Christ." They are to actualize what occurred in their baptism "into Christ Jesus" (6:3) as in Gal 3:27 where Paul wrote, "As many of you as were baptized into Christ have clothed yourselves with Christ" (see also 1 Cor 12:12-13). When verse 14 continues, "and make no provision for the flesh," and so forth, it implies that this treatment of the flesh will be the result of being clothed with Christ, as in CEV: "Let the Lord Jesus Christ be as near to you as the clothes you wear. *Then* you won't try to satisfy your selfish desires." In any case, those who heed verse 14 will "behave properly, as people do in the day" (v. 13, CEV). Remarkably, neither in this paragraph, nor in all of chapters 12–13, does Paul refer to the power of the Spirit vis-à-vis the flesh, emphasized in 8:1-17. But this absence of the Spirit from our paragraph must not be exaggerated, because for Paul, the Spirit is the means by which the Risen Christ exercises his power over those who are "in" him.

◊ ◊ ◊ ◊

For understanding Paul's apocalyptic eschatology, this passage is significant in two respects. First, since Romans was his last letter (assuming that Philippians was written before he arrived in Rome, probably from Ephesus), it clearly shows that there is no weakening of his conviction that God's salvific work would be completed soon, even though he does not actually mention Christ's parousia. More important exegetically, however, is noting the assumption that underlies the imperatives that he connects with that expectation: One must be prepared morally. The logic of the passage precludes any slackening of moral rigor because the impending day of salvation will solve all problems anyway. To the contrary, precisely because salvation is nearer now, it is all the more urgent to actualize "the already," for by definition, Christian existence is anticipatory. The passage assumes that a diminished moral urgency, precisely when the anctipated is nearer, is the mark of *apistia*, unbelief as infidelity.

The more clearly one grasps Paul's way of thinking, however, the more difficult it is to think with him, for centuries later it seems that salvation is more distant, not closer. If one does not try to repristinate the early Christian expectation of Christ's imminent coming, one can affirm that the faithful life, clothed with Christ, is and remains a life marked by anticipation, one that knows the "not yet" precisely when daring to make the "already" actual.

Disputes Over Freedom (14:1–15:6)

Paul now begins to address an issue whose capacity to destroy the Christian community in Rome should not be underestimated: what to do when there is deep disagreement over daily practices pertaining to food and drink, as well as special observances—all rooted in customs sanctioned by religion. Stated conceptually, the issue concerned the nature and scope of freedom—not freedom from cosmic powers like sin and death, but from religious practices deemed an essential aspect of group identity (for a suggestive sociological analysis of the conflicts, see Esler 2003, chap. 14). Since such matters were especially important for Diaspora Jews, one can readily envision the conflicts that emerged between Jewish Christians and Gentile Christians in Rome. While Jewish food laws were central in the conflict, it is noteworthy that not a word is said about Jews and Gentiles until the summation in 15:7-13. Thereby Paul averted exacerbating the tensions in terms of ethnic identities. The precise details of the quarrels in Rome, their roots and ramifications, remain somewhat obscure because Paul did not need to inform the addressees about their quarrels; today's readers, however, must infer both the details and the larger picture from Paul's response.

Paul does not explain why he discusses the readers' attitudes toward these matters so much more fully than their attitudes toward the governing authorities in 13:1-7. Most readers today would reverse the proportions. Presumably, the controversies were so important for Paul because he knew they were significant in Rome, though he does not disclose how he knew it. Nor does he identify the individual disputants by name (as in Phil 4:2)—noteworthy in light of the many names in chapter 16; instead, he refers to them as "the weak in faith" and "the strong." While he openly includes himself in the latter group only at 15:1, his whole discussion avoids simply advocating their position. Probably there were others not yet polarized between these two groups, as Minear (1971, 7-17) argued. More important is Minear's insistence that the evidence points not to a single congregation in Rome but rather to multiple house churches with differing styles—a view more plausible than the claim that there were two congregations that Paul wanted to unite in "a single 'Paulinist' congregation" (so Watson 1986, 97-98), though of course he did want all readers to "see things his way." Whatever the disputants may have said to each other (and to themselves) in justifying their positions, Paul approaches the situation from *his* perspective, sketched in chapters 12–13, though no "therefore" explicitly connects this discussion with those chapters.

The mandate to "welcome" (14:1) inaugurates not only the whole discussion but also its summation in 15:7-13. It is likely that 14:1-12 has *primarily* "the weak" in view, 14:13-23 "the strong"; 15:1-6 begins by addressing "the strong" but soon pertains to *all* readers, as does the summation in 15:7-13. Inevitably, what pertains to one group cannot be separated from what pertains to the other (as the contrast "weak" and "strong" itself implies), for it is the attitude of each toward the other that Paul must deal with.

Paul's Perspective (14:1-12)

Remarkable is the way Paul inaugurates the whole discussion: He begins with the imperative (implicitly addressed to "the strong"): "Welcome those who are weak in faith" (quite implausible is the claim that this is only a rhetorical device inviting all readers to think they are "weak in faith"; so Sampley 1995, 47). Thus he signals his solution (in 15:7 expanded to include both groups) before stating the problem, first identified as diet (vv. 2-4), apparently because this was more divisive than "days" (v. 5). His own perspective begins to emerge in verse 6, where he acknowledges the theological integrity of the diverse practices by relating the practitioners to the Lord. After expanding the christological aspect of his perspective (vv. 7-9), he undermines the attitudes of both groups by reminding them that each person will be accountable to the judgment of *God* (vv. 10-12), not to each other. Paul apparently expects his perspective to give leverage to his arguments because all of its elements are noncontroversial.

◊ ◊ ◊ ◊

What probably was controversial, however, is the designation "the weak in faith," as well as "the strong." Paul did not explain these designations because he apparently knows they are already being used in Rome. "The weak in faith" (better: "the weak with respect to faith") is clearly not a self-designation but the contemptuous epithet used by "the strong" to express their disdain for the scrupulous vegetarians (who also conscientiously respect certain days). The language of verse 14, together with that of verse 20, shows that the vegetarians eschewed meat lest it fail to be kosher. (That concern differentiates them from those who today choose a vegetarian diet for other reasons, such as animal rights or personal health.) All the vegetarian Christians in Rome need not have been Jews, for some Gentiles too avoided meat, though for different reasons (conveniently summarized by Talbert 2002, 314). What "the weak" called themselves is not known. It is unlikely that the Christian Jews among them called themselves "the circumcision" and labeled the nonobservant "the uncircumcised," as Marcus (1989, 73-81) proposed.

While the Torah specified which animals may and may not be eaten (see Lev 11; 17:10-16), it nowhere commands a vegetarian diet. The book of Daniel does, however, indirectly commend it by reporting that Daniel and friends insisted on such a diet in a pagan environment (Dan 1:3-17; similarly Jdt 12:1-2). Josephus reports that Jewish priests detained in Rome ate only figs and nuts (*Vita* 14). Philo reports that a Jewish ascetic group in Egypt, the Therapeutai, were vegetarians (*Contempl.* 4:37). Even though *T. Reu.* 1:8-10 reports that Reuben expressed his repentance by abstaining from wine and meat or "pleasurable food," Paul's letter offers no basis for inferring that "the weak" in Rome were vegetarians as a sign of their repentance (so Boring et al. 1995, 388). Later, the Christian Jews who produced the *Gospel of the Ebionites* said that John the Baptist had been a vegetarian: "his food was wild honey, tasting like manna, like a cake in olive oil" (so Epiphanius, *Against Heresies* 30.13.14; compare Mark 1:6). According to Eusebius, citing Hegesippus, Jesus' brother James (the leader of the Jerusalem church in Paul's time) "drank no wine or strong drink, nor did he eat flesh" (*Hist. eccl.* 2.23:5). The extent of such asceticism among Jews is unknown.

What matters for Paul, however, is not *who* the vegetarians in the Roman church were, but why, as Christians, they were vegetarians at all. While he does not give *their* reasons (they were known to the readers), he recognizes, albeit implicitly, that for them this diet was not a matter of preference but of obedience to the law, and perhaps also a way of avoiding disobeying it unintentionally because one could not be sure the meat had not been offered first to the gods before being sold in the markets. These vegetarians were scrupulous about their diet because they were serious about their religion. They did not consider themselves "weak with regard to faith" but steadfastly obedient; the

Christian Jews among them would have thought it outrageous to conclude that believing Jesus was the Messiah released them from the dietary rules that distinguished them from pagans. (One can only speculate why there is no hint that circumcision was also an issue. Or did Paul simply ignore it because after writing Galatians he did not want to get into *that* issue again?)

"The strong," on the other hand, "ate all kinds of food" (REB), either because as Christian Jews (like Paul) or former "God-fearers," they believed themselves *no longer* subject to any food taboos, or because as Gentiles they refused *to begin* living by Jewish food laws now that they accepted the gospel. In 15:1 he identifies with them ("we who are strong"), perhaps knowing that they had already identified with *him* because they had learned his position on such matters (e.g., "Certainly food will not bring us into God's presence: if we do not eat, we are none the worse, and if we do eat, we are none the better," 1 Cor 8:8, REB; for the similarities and differences between 1 Cor 8–10 and our passage, see introduction). Had they learned his views from his former associates, Prisca and Aquila, who were now back in Rome (16:1-3 in light of Acts 18:1-3)? Or were "the strong" relying on a bowdlerized version of his teaching? Had their use of him made him a controversial figure even before setting foot in Rome? It is not difficult to imagine various scenarios because in such situations multiple factors are often at work. Be that as it may, Paul could expect neither a broad-based welcome nor support for his mission in Spain (15:22-33) unless he quelled the quarrels. In any case, he addresses "the strong" vigorously, and in his opening line makes *them* responsible for welcoming "the weak."

Verse 1 reveals not only the practices of the two groups but also what is going on as a result, though its language is not as precise as one might wish. After urging "the strong" to "welcome the weak with respect to faith" (AT), he adds *mē eis diakriseis dialogismōn* (NRSV: "not for the purpose of quarreling over opinions"; NIV: "without passing judgment on disputable matters"; REB: "without debate about his misgivings"; CEV: "Don't criticize them for having beliefs that are different from yours"; NJB: "but do not get into arguments about doubtful points"). Instead of agreeing to disagree, apparently each group is trying (with limited success) to show why the other is wrong. Paul's remark indicates that the disputants were part of the same house church. What Paul forbids in verse 3 exposes the situation: Those who eat meat "despise" the vegetarians, and the vegetarians "pass judgment" (NIV: "condemn") on the carnivores (v. 4). Dunn (1988, 2:803) notes the difference between the contempt of "the strong" and the judging by "the weak" and infers that the latter are acting as judges because they claim to know what will befall the others at the coming Judgment. Paul's rejection of both attitudes makes concrete what he had said in 12:3 about a realistic self-understanding.

If this is the situation Paul has in view, his opening line is all the more remarkable: "The strong" are to welcome (receive, accept into their circle or household) precisely those who are passing judgment; the judged are to welcome the judges. On the other hand, "the weak" are to cease judging "the strong," for God has welcomed *them* (lit., "him"). Although interpreters commonly assume that this clause refers to God's welcome of both, the fact that verse 4 continues the objection to judging implies that the emphasis falls on "them"—"the strong." (CEV, while theologically correct, misunderstands the argument: "After all, God welcomes everyone.") Thus, the vegetarians are in effect undoing the welcome that God extended to those who eat anything they wish. Understandably, Paul goes on to confront "the weak."

In verse 4a, Paul's rhetorical, diatribe-style question needs no answer, for its formulation deftly exposes the vegetarians' absurd assumption that they have the right to judge someone else's household slave *(oiketēs)* as if he were accountable to *them*, not to his own master (here *kyrios* means "master," though simultaneously suggesting "Lord"). While the imagery of "stand" or "fall" probably means simply to have or lose approval, it also connotes disaster, as the use of "fall" in verse 20 suggests. Also by inserting "and stand he will" before pointing out that "the Lord [some manuscripts: "God"] is able to make him stand," Paul rebukes "the weak" for assuming that their verdict finally matters.

At verse 5, Paul uses a wordplay on "judge" to mention another matter of controversy: "days." However, verse 6 shows that he regards "days" as simply another form of the same issue (as the disputants probably did too). Many interpreters plausibly think verse 5 refers to the Sabbath, and probably other Jewish holy days (like the Day of Atonement) as well, but that inference does not square easily with Paul's rather vague characterization of the issue: whether one day is "better" (NRSV) than the next. To observant Jews Sabbath observance is not a value judgment but an obligation. The fact that he does not name any particular "day" suggests that for him it does not matter *which* day is deemed religiously special or sacred. What matters is that "each one should be fully convinced [*plērophoreisthō*, used in 4:21 of Abraham's confidence in God] in his own mind" (NIV; CEV: "But each of you should make up your own mind"). That, of course, is what they had already done, and so caused the controversy in the first place! In effect, Paul urges them to agree to disagree—perhaps easier to do with regard to days than to diet.

Especially important are verses 6-9, for here Paul puts the Roman situation within a perspective that undergirds his whole counsel: The practice of each is to be respected because it is done "in honor of the Lord" (NRSV "to the Lord," *tō kyriō*). Moreover, both those who eat (meat) and those who do not eat it "give thanks to God"—perhaps an allusion to saying "grace" at mealtime, a Jewish practice adopted by Christian Gentiles. Paul implies that in giving thanks Christian Gentiles overcome what he regarded as the root cause of Gentile sinfulness: the refusal to honor God as God or "give thanks to him" (1:21).

The unusual expression "to the Lord" recalls 6:11, where the readers are urged to consider themselves "dead *to* sin and alive *to* God"—that is, respond obediently to one or the other. Verses 7-8 explain what Paul means by this expression. The phrases in verses 7-8 are carefully balanced, with the decisive point coming last:

For	none of us	lives	to himself,
and	none	dies	to himself,
for	whether	we live, we live	to the Lord
and	if	we die, [we die]	to the Lord,
for we are the Lord's. (AT)			

Because we belong to the Lord, our existence is oriented to him and derives its validation from him, because that is what his being Lord entails for us. Indeed, his sovereignty over us was the purpose of the Christ-event: "that he might be Lord of both the dead and the living" (v. 9). In referring to Christ's resurrection, Paul here replaces his usual "and was raised" with "and lived again" *(ezēsen)* in keeping with "we live," thereby expressing a fundamental motif of Christology—the solidarity of the Savior and the saved. Behind the idea of belonging to the Lord lies 1 Cor 6:20; 7:23, "You were bought with a price" (see also 1 Cor 3:23). The import of verses 6-9 should not be missed: Paul has shifted the discourse from the *deeds* to the status of the *doers* and its consequences—the transformation that results from a renewed mind (12:1-2).

Since both groups belong to the Lord of the living and the dead, their contentious behavior toward one another is totally inappropriate, especially since their common Lord makes them siblings (v. 10). Moreover, the present parity of those who are the Lord's will be manifest in the future, for "we all will stand before the judgment seat of God" (some manuscripts have "of Christ," as does 2 Cor 5:10). That being the case, to judge or despise one's fellow believer is to forget who will give the real verdict on both. In support of this reminder, Paul quotes scripture (v. 11). His inference from the quotation ("So then") is given in verse 12: "Each of us will give an account of himself to God" (AT). The quotation is part of LXX Isa 45:23, from which Paul omits "righteousness will come out of my mouth, and my words will not be turned away" (is it in his mind nonetheless?); he also replaces "I swear by myself" with "As I live, says the Lord," a common Old Testament oath formula. The Christ hymn in Phil 2:6-11 too appropriates part of Isa 45:23 to express the cosmic Lordship of Christ (vv. 10-11), but in our passage "the Lord" refers to God (except for those manuscripts that read "judgment seat of Christ" in v. 10). Although *exhomologēsetai tō theō* can mean "will confess to God" (NIV), here the expression probably means "shall give praise to God" (NRSV; NJB: "give glory to God"; CEV: "praise my name"; see BDAG *s.v.*[4]). Together with "every knee shall bow to me," God pledges that all persons will acknowledge and celebrate God's sovereignty before the judgment seat. Since that is how it will be, "Why do *you* act as if you were the judge, as if you too were not going to be judged? What gives you the right to hand down verdicts on God's behalf?"

In a mere dozen verses, Paul puts the contentious situation in a perspective that doubtless diverged markedly from the perspectives of both "the weak" and "the strong." Instead of adjudicating the merits of their positions, he reminds them not only of what was common to them both because of what God had done in Christ, but also of what they all will face because of what God will yet do. Thereby he also undermined the self-assurance with which each group dealt with the other. But Paul has just begun; in verses 13-23 he will build on this foundation.

The Responsibility of "the Strong" (14:13-23)

The passage has two parts, "so then" *(ara oun)* marking the transition from verses 13-18 to 19-23. As "judge" was a key word in verses 1-12, so some form of "stumble" is pivotal in this word to "the strong" (vv. 13, 20 [twice]). Substantively, the exhortation in verses 13-18 is reinforced by the restatement in verses 19-23.

◊ ◊ ◊ ◊

The responsibility of "the strong" is the responsibility of the free—of those who eat what they wish and ignore special days because they understand themselves to be emancipated from obligatory observances. But they do not, apparently, live or worship in conventicles of the like-minded; were that the case, they could simply go their own way and ignore the scrupulous observants. Instead, both are members of the same faith community, perhaps even of the same house churches where a common meal—the context of the Eucharist—may have been eaten. In such a setting, how are "the strong" to exercise their freedom in ways that do not exacerbate the tensions with "the weak" brother or sister?

Are they to inhibit, if not forfeit, their freedom in order to create space in which "the weak" are free to be scrupulous in matters important to them? Although Paul does not mention "freedom" here (or in all of chaps. 12–15), as Meyer (2000, 1071) notes, the exercise of freedom was the central issue for "the strong"; substantively, also for Paul, understanding freedom properly was pivotal, lest its misuse fragment the community. To avoid this, he repeatedly used "one another" in the admonitions (12:4, 10, 16; 13:8; 14:13, 19; 15:5, 7). Had Paul made "freedom" an explicit topic, the discussion would have led to a consideration of one's rights (as it did in 1 Cor 9), for assertions of freedom often express themselves in claims to "rights." And that, presumably, was at the center of the self-image of "the strong." But Paul is not interested in nourishing their "rights"; it is their responsibility, what they "owe," that is his concern.

The range of meaning of *krinein* (to judge, pass judgment, determine, decide, condemn, find fault) allows Paul to link verses 13-23 to verses 1-12 with a wordplay for which there is no ready English equivalent. So NRSV renders verse 13 as, "Let us therefore no longer pass judgment [*krinōmen*] on one another, but resolve [*krinete*, second person plural] instead never to put a stumbling block or hindrance in the way of another [lit., brother]." What does Paul mean by "stumbling block" here, and how might "the strong" put one in the way of a fellow believer? What does he want "the strong" not to do, and why does he want them not to do it? Are they not to do anything that is positive?

The imagery implied in this metaphor shows that he is not speaking of a mere irritant, for "stumbling block" (*proskomma*, something one strikes the foot against, an obstacle), like "hindrance" (*skandalon*, trap, enticement, offense), implies a danger to the runner (as in another context, 9:32-33). So Paul is urging "the strong" not to endanger the brother or sister. That would occur if "the strong" were to induce "the weak" to eat meat despite not being convinced that eating it is permissible. Doing so would violate their faith-grounded commitment. Having pointed out that "those who abstain [from meat] abstain in honor of the Lord," Paul now proceeds to insist that "the strong" must respect the vegetarians for *their* sake, even though—strictly speaking—their concerns are not warranted. But "the weak" are convinced that they *are* warranted, and their convictions must not be violated. Not because the vegetarians are "sensitive" folk who are easily offended, but because their convictions too are rooted in faith. That is why in verse 14 Paul not only says that they are wrong ("nothing is unclean [*koinon*, common] in itself") but that "it *is* unclean for anyone who *thinks* [*tō logizomenō*, who reckons, considers] it is unclean" (restated positively in v. 20: "Everything is indeed clean").

The radical—indeed, revolutionary—character of this assertion should not be overlooked. In his Pharisee days, Paul would never have said such a thing. For one thing, it puts an astounding premium on the individual's judgment. In addition, it tacitly grants the individual the right to be wrong, and insists that such a person is to be respected. The story in Acts 10:9-16 shows that Paul's contemporary Christian Jews would not have shared his view. But the Christian Paul is fully confident that he is right: "I know and am persuaded in the Lord Jesus" (even if the law says otherwise). What, then, is it about "the Lord Jesus" that persuades Paul that nothing is "unclean in itself"?

Was it something Jesus had said or done? In Mark 7:15 Jesus says, "There is nothing outside a person that by going in can defile, but the things that come out are what defile." Later he explains this riddle: the things that enter a person by mouth actually enter (only) the stomach and pass on, but do not defile the real person; what do defile the person are the vices that come out of the heart. Here the Gospel writer inserts his own comment: "Thus he declared all foods clean" (Mark 7:19; Matt 15:17-18 omits this comment). In other words, while Jesus himself was not discussing which food is "clean" or "unclean" but what defiles a person as a moral agent, Mark saw an implication in what he said: If nothing one eats defiles, then no food is "unclean" and all foods are "clean." Since Mark was probably written a decade or more after Romans (and perhaps in Rome), it is more likely that Mark's comment reflects Paul than that Paul's comment reflects Mark. Moreover, just as Mark 7:19 is the evangelist's comment, so "but it is unclean for anyone who thinks it is unclean" is Paul's comment, not part of the christological warrant itself. Probably, then, Paul claims to be persuaded, neither by Jesus' own words, nor by a private disclosure from the Lord, but by the meaning of the Jesus-event, in accord with 7:4: "You have died to the law through the body of Christ," and with 3:21, according to which God's act in Christ occurred "apart from the law." In any case, the warrant for Paul's declaration is not pragmatic (if you see it my way, you'll get along better), but *christological*, in keeping with the rest of the passage.

If "the strong" ignore the sensibilities of "the weak" and persist in eating what they wish, their assertion of freedom will have four consequences, stated in verses 15-17. (a) The brother or sister is *lypitai*, "distressed" (NIV) or "outraged" (REB), not necessarily "injured" (NRSV). (b) "The strong" are then "no longer walking according to love" (a clear reminder that love is the one thing that Christians owe one another, 13:8); that is, "the strong" are defaulting in their obligation. (c) They actually ruin those "for whom Christ died" (restated in v. 20 as the destruction of God's work)—not because "the weak" are upset but because they "go along" with "the strong" while still unconvinced. Their convictions are violated, and their integrity is shattered. (d) That which is "the good" for "the strong" will be "spoken of as evil" (lit., "blasphemed"; CEV paraphrases: "Don't let your right to eat bring shame to Christ"). Though Paul does not say who will denounce their action, it is more likely that he has in view the outraged "weak" than "outsiders" who will "gain a low opinion" of the community (so Dunn 1988, 2:821-22). "Blaspheming" the "good" (the freedom of "the strong") is precisely what happens when "the weak" pass judgment on them. For each of these foreseeable consequences, Paul holds "the strong" responsible (and accountable to God).

In verse 17 he identifies what both groups, by their behavior toward one another, are actually doing: They are reducing the kingdom of God to "food and drink," as if *that* were what it amounted to, rather than "righteousness and peace and joy in the Holy Spirit" (was the copyist who added "and asceticism,"an ascetic himself?). This is one of the few times that Paul mentions "the kingdom of God" (see also 1 Cor 4:20; 6:9, 10; 15:50; Gal 5:21; 1 Thess 2:12 alludes to it). Here "kingdom of God" serves as a comprehensive term for salvation, to be achieved fully at the parousia (as in 1 Cor 15:24); but here, as in 1 Cor 4:20, the accent is on its present expressions: righteousness, peace, and joy, recalling Rom 5:1-2. These are the *ways* one serves Christ ("thus" in v. 18)—precisely the opposite of causing the ruin of those for whom Christ died. The servant of Christ who lives in accord with these three traits is "acceptable to God" (in the minds of "the weak" a major consideration) and "has human approval" (the alternative attitude to despising the vegetarians, v. 3).

Having emphasized what the readers are not to do, at verse 19 Paul turns to what they ought to do, but in verses 20-21 reverts to prohibitions, clarifying and reinforcing verses 13-18. Of the three signs of salvation, Paul asks the readers to "pursue the things that make for peace and build up the common life" (lit., "one another," as in REB; this admonition recalls 12:18). He does not ask them to pursue what makes for righteousness, probably because that is what "the weak" thought they were doing already; joy, on the other hand, is not something one pursues anyway, especially since it is a fruit of the Spirit (so also Gal 5:22). Paul need not spell out what "makes for peace" and mutual upbuilding because chapter 12 had already done so. "Upbuilding" (*oikodomē*, act of building, constructing, or maturing, "edification") is a metaphor for developing or maturing the community, which in 1 Cor 3:9 Paul calls a building. His concern to build up the community of faith appears repeatedly in his letters to the Corinthian church, also deeply divided (1 Cor 10:23; 14:12, 26; 2 Cor 12:19); in 1 Thess 5:11, as here, building up the church is the responsibility of all.

Verse 20 says more explicitly what was assumed in verses 13-15. But verse 21 goes far beyond what was said there: what is really good (*kalos*; REB: "right"; NIV: "better"; CEV: "best") is to avoid *"anything* that makes your brother or sister stumble"—to violate their own convictions in order to avoid embarrassment. Is Paul giving "the weak" veto power over the freedom of "the strong"? Is he urging "the strong" to "sacrifice their freedom based on their correct knowledge" (Talbert 2002, 319)? *No!* He is urging them to *exercise* their freedom—here, as the freedom to forego victory over "the weak." Only those who know they are free to eat anything (v. 2) are also free *not* to eat anything for their relation to God does not ride on matters of "food and drink." That being the case, Paul continues, "As for *you*, the faith that you have, keep to yourself before God" (Moo's translation, showing that "you" is emphatic in the Greek sentence). Here "faith" *(pistis)*—trust or confident reliance—shades into "conviction" without losing its general meaning for Paul: complete reliance on God in response to the gospel.

With an eye on "the weak" who "fall" (v. 20) when they eat meat despite thinking it is wrong before God, in verse 22 Paul caps his word to "the strong" who know they are right: "Blessed is the man who does not condemn *[krinōn]* himself by what he approves" (NIV; flattened by REB: "Anyone who can make his decision without misgivings is fortunate"). The word "approves" *(dokimazei)*, not accidentally, alludes to what 12:2 said is the goal of a renewed mind: to *"dokimazein* [NRSV and REB: "discern"; NIV: "test and approve"] the will of God." The person who does not condemn himself for what he approves has "a clear conscience," even though Paul does not use the word, since for Paul "conscience" is the faculty by which one assesses one's own conduct (see 2:15; 13:5; 1 Cor 4:3). The beatitude does not make one's self-assessment the real criterion of what to do or not to do; it rather recognizes that the absence of self-condemnation confirms that the decision made "in honor of the Lord" (v. 6) is valid because it expressed faith in God.

In verse 23 Paul turns to "the weak" and formulates the perspective within which the whole passage was developed. Especially provocative is the last clause: "for whatever does not proceed from faith *[ek pisteōs]* is sin." As Matera (1996, 204) notes, Paul does not mean that whatever is not based on faith in Christ is sinful; he is talking about *pistis* as conviction unalloyed with doubt or hesitation—though this conviction is inseparable from *pistis* as reliance on God's rectifying rectitude manifest apart from the law (3:21-25). Still, since Paul had insisted that love is the one thing Christians owe one another (13:8), one wonders why he did not say that whatever is not from love is sin. Precisely because what he did say is aimed at the controversy over observances, it is the most radical understanding of sin in the New Testament, because its function is to inhibit the believer from continuing to understand sin as transgression. For the believer, it is not the law that finally identifies what is sin, but acting on a basis other than faith. Where one's life grows out of faith in God's mercies, there is freedom for scrupulous observance and for nonobservance as well.

At this point, some manuscripts add what is found in 16:25-27 (see below).

◊ ◊ ◊ ◊

To understand Paul's perspective one must see how two themes here are related: the remarkable emphasis on the individual's judgment, and the pervasive concern for the community's upbuilding. What holds together the mandate not to put a stumbling block in the way of "the weak" and the beatitude pronounced on those who "have no reason to condemn themselves because of what *they* [themselves] approve"? From what standpoint does Paul affirm simultaneously the freedom of "the weak" to regard some food as unclean though it is not, and the freedom of "the strong" to eat whatever they wish because they are right in holding that "everything is indeed clean"? The observation that God's kingdom concerns "righteousness and peace and joy in the Holy Spirit" does not really disclose Paul's standpoint because these traits do not account for Paul's actual counsel. It is also unlikely that his standpoint resembles that of the Stoics, namely, he regarded days and diets as *adiaphora*, indifferent, unimportant. Although Paul himself may have regarded them as such, saying so in that situation would have been patronizing. Rather, the standpoint from which he affirmed the freedom of both "the weak" and "the strong" to be true to themselves, while also insisting on the well-being of the whole, was remarkable for its simplicity: *Being right is not the most important thing.* Where being right prevails, we "live to ourselves" (v. 7). Where self-actualization is the paramount good, one must prevail. And then the good ends up being "spoken of as evil" (v. 16). The well-being of the fellow believer—even "the weak with regard to faith"—is more important than being right.

The Outcome and the Outlook (15:1-6)

Paul now states the outcome of what he has been saying since 14:1. The thought flows rapidly, from the obligation of "the strong" to the christological warrant which itself is warranted by scripture (v. 3), to the rationale for this use of scripture (v. 4), to the concluding "prayer wish" for the unity of the readers in glorifying God—an allusion to worship that recalls 12:1-2. Beginning the paragraph with *opheilomen* (we owe, we are obliged) lifts what follows from prudent strategy for achieving more harmony to the level of moral obligation, here grounded in the precedent set by Christ.

◊ ◊ ◊ ◊

Paul first states the obligation positively ("We strong ones *[hoi dynatoi]* are obligated to bear the weaknesses *[asthenēmata]* of the not-strong [the *adynatoi*]"), then crisply states what doing so means: not pleasing ourselves. Noticeably, he not only discloses that he identifies with "the strong" but now does not call those who differ "the weak with regard to faith" (14:1, AT). Now he refers to their convictions and practices as their "weaknesses" that "we strong ones" are obligated to "bear" (*bastazein*, carry). Since an *asthenēma* can refer to weakness, illness, or limitation, it is not surprising that recent translations differ in conveying what Paul is asking: NRSV: "put up with the failings of the weak"; REB: "accept as our own burden the tender scruples of the weak"; NJB: "bear with the susceptibilities of the weaker ones"; CEV: "we should be patient with the Lord's followers whose faith is weak." All of these translations convey a patronizing, condescending attitude—precisely what Paul wanted to avoid. What Paul is really after is closer to Gal 6:2: "Bear *[bastazete]* one another's burdens, and in this way you will fulfill the law of Christ." In other words, it is obligatory for "the strong" to share the "weaknesses" of "the not-strong" by not pleasing themselves, but by pleasing the neighbor for the neighbor's good, for upbuilding *(oikodomē)* the community (v. 2). By speaking of "weaknesses" Paul shifts the focus from persons to their incapacities, to their inhibitions, their inability to be fully convinced that all victuals are indeed "clean" (14:20). To share that inability is to be free to forego eating meat and drinking wine, which cause the inhibited fellow believer to stumble (14:21); it is to acknowledge that what this brother or sister does is done "to the Lord" just as "the strong" eat and drink to the Lord (14:6), even though they do not agree with each other's practices. Where these "weaknesses" are accepted and borne, the vegetarians are no longer despised, and perhaps the nonobservant cease to be condemned because they no longer "please themselves" and so stroke their self-image by showing how right they are. In pleasing the neighbor (v. 2) instead of themselves, they obey the love command quoted in 13:9-10 and so demonstrate that they too fulfill the law, actualized in love, even if they do not heed its dietary requirements.

Verse 3 is a fine instance of Paul's ability to say a lot in a few words. The initial "for" indicates that what Christ did not do ("please himself") is the warrant for the readers not pleasing themselves either; this warrant makes it more difficult for the readers to evade the injunction in verse 2. Moreover, the word *kai* (here "even" as in NIV, REB, CEV, rather than the usual "and") emphasizes his example: "for *even* the Christ. . . ." (The text uses the article ["the Christ"], perhaps indicating that here Paul uses "Christ" as a title [the Messiah], thereby making the example all the more significant.) Theologically, what Christ did not do is the obverse of what he did do: He died for the brother or sister (14:15; see also Gal 2:20: "loved me and gave himself for me").

To support this claim, Paul refers not to anything found in the Gospels but to a quotation from Ps 69:9 (LXX 68:10): "The insults of those who insulted you [God] have fallen on me"—that is, the hostility toward God is borne by the speaker (who in v. 7 had just said, "It is for your sake that I have borne reproach"). Romans is the earliest Christian text to quote this psalm (Rom 11:9-10 quoted vv. 22-23), but parts of it came to be associated with various elements of the Passion story (compare Ps 69:21*b* with Mark 15:36 and John 19:28; Ps 69:4 with John 15:25; v. 25 is quoted in Acts 1:20 in connection with Judas's death). According to John 2:17, 22, when Jesus "cleansed" the temple, the disciples remembered the first half of verse 9 ("zeal for your house will consume me"), the second part of which Paul quotes here. The psalm itself laments the plight of the righteous sufferer who looks to God for deliverance from his foes, who made him bear the insults really aimed at God. Paul, however, ignores the lament character of the psalm. Instead, he interprets the line "the insults of those who insulted you" as evidence that "the Christ did not please himself"; he assumes that "did not please himself" interprets the willingly accepted misdirected insults (does Paul allude to the taunts hurled at the crucified Jesus? see, e.g., Mark 15:29-32). He also assumes that "did not please himself" fits the known demeanor of the Christ. Does he also assume that the speaker *is* Christ (so, e.g., Hays 1993, 122, 132)? Paul's argument does not require this inference. What the argument does require is agreement that the quoted lines fit an already known image of Christ's demeanor and so can validate him as the paradigm of not pleasing oneself.

This is the first time Romans uses a christologically interpreted line from scripture for an exhortation, so verse 4 justifies this move. Its comprehensive sweep (*"whatever* was written"), however, goes beyond what is needed here; perhaps it was an independently formed hermeneutical principle, either adduced by Paul himself or perhaps added by a later hand (suggested by Keck 1990, 125-36; rejected by Hays 1993, 122-36). Be that as it may, verse 4 is somewhat similar to what Paul had said about the moral import of scripture in 1 Cor 10:11; there he said that Israel's lapse into idolatry (see Exod 32:1-6 and Num 25:1-9) and the consequences occurred "as an example" and were written "as a warning for us" (REB; NRSV: "to instruct us"). Here, verse 4 generalizes: Anything in scripture was written "for our instruction so that . . . we might have hope," presumably the "hope of sharing the glory of God" because of God's love in our hearts (so 5:1-5). Just how scripture functions in relation to this hope is not as clear as REB makes it: "in order that through the encouragement they [the scriptures] give us we may maintain our hope with perseverance." Better is NRSV, which retains the text's two parallel phrases: "so that by [our] steadfastness *and* by the encouragement *[paraklēsis]* of the scriptures we might have hope." Elusive is the precise meaning of *paraklēsis* here, as it is also in 12:8. Does it mean "exhortation," "comfort" (as in 2 Cor 1:6-7), or "encouragement" (as in 1 Cor 14:3)? Does a choice matter?

The "prayer wish" in verses 5-6 picks up *hypomonē* (steadfastness, endurance) and *paraklēsis* from verse 4, and speaks of God as the source of both. The formulaic expression "the God of . . ." appears elsewhere in such passages, sometimes mentioning hope (15:13), sometimes peace (15:33; 1 Thess 5:23). What Paul asks for in verse 5 is the unity of the community, literally "that you may have the same mindset *[to auto phronein]* toward one another." Paul is not asking God to effect agreement between the two groups, but to bring about the harmony that can occur when each pleases the neighbor for the well-being of the community (v. 2), which is "in accordance with Christ" (as v. 3 said). Paul recognizes that actualizing what he envisages for the community will be the gift of God. The ultimate goal (v. 6) is the glorification of God by the community that is unified (*homothymadon*, "with one mind," used by Paul only here but frequently in Acts to characterize the earliest congregation in Jerusalem: e.g., Acts 1:14; 2:46; 4:24).

◊ ◊ ◊ ◊

The whole discussion, from 14:1 on, has been aimed at the admonition in this paragraph. Throughout, Paul has both dealt respectfully with the entrenched positions and, more important, has put both the convictions and those who hold them in a framework that is consistent with the gospel. It is not accidental, then, that the core of this paragraph is in verse 3, which explicitly combines "Christology and ethics." In exhorting the quarrelsome believers to please one another instead of pleasing themselves because even the Christ did not please *him*self, he makes concrete what he had urged at 13:14: "put on the Lord Jesus Christ," that is, live enveloped by Christ as one is surrounded by one's cloak. The fact that Paul never quotes Jesus (all the more significant if he did know relevant sayings of Jesus) shows that what is decisive for him is what Christ *did*: He "died and lived again, so that he might be the Lord of both the living and the dead" (14:9). Consequently, because "we are the Lord's" (14:8), "we do not live to ourselves" (14:7), and so must not "please ourselves" just as Christ did not, but instead are to "please our neighbor" and thus avoid causing "the ruin of one for whom Christ died" (14:15). In short, for Paul, Christology—what one believes about Christ—is inseparable from how one lives, first of all with one's fellow believers who draw differing conclusions from their allegiance to the same Lord (14:6). What is built into Paul's discussion here is found also in Phil 2:1-13, where the "Christ hymn" is cited as the warrant for the mandate to "look not to your own interests, but to the interests of others."

The Grand Horizon (15:7-13)

Only verse 7 links this paragraph to the conflict in Rome (the Greek text begins with *dio*, therefore, so then), but actually the content of verses 8-12 discloses the horizon against which Paul's treatment of the conflict is to be seen—the role of Christ in overcoming the hiatus between Jews and Gentiles, yet without obscuring or erasing the differences between them. That horizon includes the entire discourse part of the letter, begun at 1:16. The paragraph does not summarize the argument; it states the grand horizon of Paul's theology in this letter. (The epistolary framework resumes at v. 14.)

Interestingly, while the overall content of verses 8-12 is unique, the motifs of verses 1-6 are repeated in verses 7-13, even in sequence:

exhortation	vv. 1-2	7
Christ	3a	8-9a
scripture	3b-4a	9b-12
hope	4b	13
praise of God	6	9-11

The paragraph combines four kinds of material: exhortation and its soteriological warrant (v. 7); christological assertion (vv. 8-9a);

four quotations from scripture (vv. 9*b*-12); and the concluding "prayer wish" (v. 13).

◊ ◊ ◊ ◊

Having emphasized unity in verse 6, it is not surprising that in verse 7 Paul now urges all readers to welcome "one another." This mutual welcome is to be extended "for the glory of God," mentioned in verse 6. Appropriately, God's welcome (v. 3) is now replaced with that extended by Christ, for the theme of the paragraph is Christ's role in God's purpose. Appropriate also is the comparison between the way the readers are to welcome one another and Christ's welcome ("just as"), for already in verse 3 Christ's not pleasing himself is the warrant for the mandate to please the neighbor instead of oneself. By saying that the christomorphic welcome is "for the glory of God," Paul also anticipates verses 8-10, where glorifying God is spoken of as praise.

Although the "for" in verse 8 indicates that verses 8-12 provide the warrant for the mandate in verse 7, the thought of verses 8-9 itself is complex (see Keck 1990, 85-97). That verses 8-9*a* formulate an allusion to what Paul had said earlier in the letter is more explicit in REB ("Remember . . .") than in Paul's own "For I tell you," which is more than "in my opinion." It has the force of a solemn pronouncement. The real difficulty, however, is centered on the relation of verse 8 to verse 9*a*, because the syntax is awkward (the sentence runs through verse 12). Comparing translations exposes the problem. (a) In NIV Paul tells the readers that "Christ has become a servant of the Jews [lit., "the circumcision"] . . . to confirm the promises made to the patriarchs so that the Gentiles may glorify God." Here there is *one* purpose/result of confirming the promises—Gentiles glorifying God; this subordinates God's purpose for Israel to the purpose for Gentiles. (b) Whereas NIV ignores the *de* at the beginning of verse 9, NRSV and REB render it as *and*; now Christ's servanthood has *two* purposes: "that he might confirm the promises . . . *and* in order that the Gentiles might glorify God." While this translation is preferable to that of NIV, "and" does not indicate how the Gentiles' praise results from Christ's being a servant of the *Jews;*

the purposes are simply parallel. (c) Wagner (1997, 481-82), seeing an ellipsis in verse 9, supplies the words that make Christ's role clear for both Jews and Gentiles, and also produces a perfectly balanced statement:

> The Christ has become
> > a servant of the circumcision
> > > on behalf of the truthfulness of God
> > > in order to confirm the promises . . .
> > and [a servant] with respect to the Gentiles
> > > on behalf of the mercy [of God]
> > > [in order] to glorify God.

This way of reading the text emphasizes the pivotal role of the Christ throughout, for in the last line it is he who glorifies God, not the Gentiles.

In verse 8, Paul does not say what Christ *became* (so REB, as in a few manuscripts) but what he "has become" and now is (perfect tense)—"servant of the circumcised" (assuming the genitive, represented by *of*, is possessive, and so means the group to which he belongs, not those whom he serves). The perfect tense implies that as a result of a past event (particularly the resurrection) Christ has become and now is a servant (*diakonos*, not *doulos*, slave) "on behalf of [*hyper*, "for the sake of"] the truth of God"—that is, to manifest God's truthfulness (as in 3:7 where it is associated with God's righteousness; in short, "the truth of God" refers to God's faithfulness). Although "in order to" can mean either purpose or result, here the latter is preferable, for the text does not speak of Christ's intention. As a result of what occurred in the Christ-event, the patriarchal promises are confirmed—namely, the promise to Abraham "that he would inherit the world" (4:13), or become "the father of many nations" (4:17). To confirm a promise is to make it firm, valid, reliable, by actualizing it. (The infinitive *bebaiōsai* in v. 8 echoes the adjective *bebaios* in 4:16: "in order that the promise may . . . be guaranteed" [NRSV; REB: "valid"].) In other words, because of what Christ has become, the patriarchal promises are ratified, not ignored or dissolved, for God has not abandoned his people (11:1).

According to Wagner's translation of verse 9, Christ has become also "[a servant] with respect to the Gentiles." (Wagner regards the unexpected accusative *ta ethnē* as an accusative of respect.) The difference between Christ's having become a servant "*of* the circumcised" (i.e., he belongs to them because he was one of them) and a servant "with respect to the Gentiles" (to whom he does not belong) is significant: Whereas for the circumcised the servant Christ expresses God's truthfulness/faithfulness, "with respect to the Gentiles" he expresses God's sheer mercy (in accord with 9:25-26). As a result, the circumcised are assured that the promises are valid, and the Gentiles are the beneficiaries of God's mercy. (Since God is merciful to all [11:32], the distinction is a matter of emphasis.)

Remarkably, Paul claims that precisely this view of Christ's servant role agrees with four quotations from scripture (vv. 9*b*-12), each carefully distinguished from the others, not simply juxtaposed as in 3:10-18. Paul first quotes the last line of Ps 18:49 (LXX 17:50, virtually the same as 2 Sam 22:50). Then in verse 10 he cites Deut 32:43 (though the wording agrees exactly with no known text; see Fitzmyer 1993); in verse 11 he quotes Ps 117:1, and in verse 12 he quotes Isa 11:10 according to LXX (which differs from the Hebrew). Although all three parts of the Hebrew Bible (Law, Prophets, Writings) are represented, both the sequence of the quotations and the fact that there are four of them suggest that this is incidental if not accidental. What matters for Paul is that the word *ethnē* (Gentiles) occurs in all four quotations—the only word that does.

Pivotal for understanding Paul's use of these quotations is whether the initial words of verse 10 are to be translated as "and again he says" (so NRSV) or as "again *it says*" (so NIV; REB has simply "and again"!). If the former, then both verse 10 and verse 11 can be understood as also the words of the "I" in verse 9*b*, namely, of Christ (not of Paul himself, as Käsemann [1980] thought). Reading the quotations in verses 9*b*-11 as the words of Christ, however, invites one to decide whether Paul thinks Christ foretold what he would do before the incarnation (so Keck 1990, 93) or whether this is "Christ's post-resurrection discourse" (so Hays

1993, 135). But if one agrees with NIV, then such questions become moot. The interpretation here adopts NIV (so also Moo 1996).

The one complex sentence in verses 8-12 should be seen as a whole, and that implies taking seriously the disproportionate emphasis on Christ's significance for Gentiles, which is said to be in accord with scripture, particularly the first three quotations (vv. 9b-11). Moreover, if the infinitive "to glorify" in verse 9b indeed refers not to Gentiles but to Christ (so Wagner 1997), then it is likely that it (like "in order to confirm" in v. 8) expresses the achieved result rather than intentional purpose. On this basis, the first three quotations support the assertion in verse 8: Christ, being a servant with respect to the Gentiles on behalf of God's mercy, glorifies God. Seeing this allows one to see also how verses 8-12 undergird the imperative in verse 7: "Welcome one another [Christian Jews and Christian Gentiles alike] as the Christ has welcomed you for the glory of God." Accordingly, each of the first three quotations emphasizes the praise of God.

Moreover, the rationale that governs the sequence of the first three quotations is now clearer: (a) Ps 18:49 ("Therefore I will confess you among the Gentiles, and sing praises to your name," AT) comes first because it confirms the claim that with respect to the Gentiles (v. 9), Christ glorifies God. (b) Next, consistent with Christ's welcoming both Jews and Gentiles (v. 7), verse 10 summons Gentiles to join Israel in the praise of God. Such praise is precisely what Paul desires for the Romans in verse 6. (c) What verse 10 envisages for the current believers in Rome, verse 11 universalizes: "All you Gentiles" and "all peoples" are to praise God, presumably with God's people. This way of understanding Christ's role coheres with his role as the New Adam, through whom "the grace of God and the free gift of the one man, Jesus Christ, abounded for the many"—that is, for the whole lot (5:15, AT). The universal praise of God—from the circumcised who celebrate the confirmation of the promises, and from the Gentile recipients of God's mercy—is the sign that God's purpose is achieved through Christ's twofold servant role.

The significance of the fourth quotation (in v. 12)—the only one referring to the author—also comes into sharper focus. In addition to forming an *inclusio* with verse 8, it accounts for Christ's dual role. Whereas the Hebrew text of Isa 11:10 says, "The root of Jesse shall stand as a signal to the peoples; the nations shall inquire of him" (NRSV), Paul cites the LXX, which identifies Jesse's root as "the one who rises to rule the Gentiles; in him the Gentiles shall hope" (perhaps an allusion to Isa 42:4; 51:5). Since "the root of Jesse" (probably the "shoot" that comes from the root, as in Isa 11:1) is Jesse's son David, by quoting this line Paul expresses Christ's Davidic Messiahship (and so accords with "the Christ" in verse 7) and thus supports the claim that the promises were confirmed in him. Paul probably understood "rises to rule" as a reference to Christ's resurrection, through which he began his cosmic rule as Kyrios. This allusion to Christ as the Davidic figure corresponds to 1:3-4. In both passages, it was the resurrection that distinguished Jesus as Son of God with power (here expressed as "rule") from simply being of David's seed. In both passages, what Jesus once *became* is completed by what he *has become and now is*. It is as the resurrected and preached Christ that he confirms the promises, and, through the Gentiles' response, glorifies God.

In keeping with the reference to the Gentiles' hope in Christ, the concluding "prayer wish" emphasizes hope, asking that "the God of hope" (the source and/or ground of hope) fill the readers "with all joy and peace in believing" so that they may "abound in hope by the power of the Holy Spirit." If Paul's prayer is answered, peace and joy and hope will replace condemnation and condescension in Rome.

◊ ◊ ◊ ◊

The olive tree analogy in 11:17-24 clarified who Gentile believers are by viewing them as wild olive shoots grafted into Israel; 15:8-13 also clarifies who they are in relation to Israel: co-participants in the praise of God. But God is not a generic deity, but the One who keeps promises made, whose mercy is actualized in resurrecting Jesus so that he is now the one in whom Gentiles hope. Gentiles who praise this God have been freed from their illusions about God that resulted from not honoring him "as God" and not giving thanks to God (1:21-23). According to the logic of verses

358

8-9*a*, this would not have happened had the Christ not belonged "to the circumcised," for only a member of this people can be the one through whom Gentiles join Israel in the praise of God. Christ's Messiahship is a necessary, but not sufficient, condition for this role. Only when he is the one in whom Gentiles hope do they "rejoice *with* his people."

THE MESSENGER:
BETWEEN PAST AND FUTURE (15:14-33)

Having ended the discourse part of the letter, in the second part of the epistolary framework Paul now resumes the discussion of his vocation, begun at 1:8. Just as a brief word there about the readers (v. 8) is followed by a fuller statement about the apostle's relation to them, so here a short expression of confidence in the readers (v. 14) is followed by a discussion of Paul's relation to them. But now Paul not only explains that once again his trip to Rome is delayed (see 1:13), but he also discloses, for the first time, two additional matters of great importance: That he has unfinished business in Jerusalem, and that he expects Rome to be a stopover on his projected trip to Spain. He also shares his apprehension about what might befall him in Jerusalem. A brief benediction (v. 33) signals the end of the discussion. The section has two units, verses 14-21 and verses 22-33, closely related.

The Completed Mission in the East (15:14-21)

If Romans is the earliest Christian theology of mission (see p. 33), this paragraph, together with 1:1-15, is its complement— a brief theology of the missioner. It is not, however, Paul's earliest theological interpretation of his lifework, but the last we have from him (assuming Philippians had been written before). Whereas his previous reflections on his vocation were generated by controversies with congregations he had founded, here his remarks are destined for a cluster of Christian groups whose internal disputes he has just addressed. His remarks here are not programmatic; they are more backward-looking than forward-looking.

Moreover, as part of his self-presentation they highlight how he wants the readers to view his work. So, then, what sort of self-image is projected (and not projected) here?

Just as in 1:8-15 he wrote positively about the recipients before talking about himself, so here he begins by affirming their positive qualities: They are "full of goodness, full of all knowledge [!], and able to instruct one another" (v. 14, AT)—a clear alternative to the way they are acting, according to 14:1, 10, 13. Rhetorically, this positive note functions as a *captatio benevolentiae* (as do 1:8 and 9:1-5).

Perhaps aware that the positive characterization of the readers in verse 14 might prompt some of them to ask, "Why, then, did you write such an assertive letter?" Paul explains why he wrote "rather boldly," either "on some points" (NRSV, NIV) or "at times" (REB)—namely, to remind them of his God-given mission (vv. 15-16). Earlier he had identified himself as an apostle (1:1, 5), indeed "the apostle of the Gentiles" (11:13, AT); but here he uses terms with well-known sacral meanings: He is a "minister" (*leitourgos*, one engaged in official duties with sacred significance) for the Gentiles, functioning "in the priestly service of the gospel of God," so that "the offering of the Gentiles may be acceptable, sanctified [hallowed] by the Holy Spirit." This "offering" *(prosphora)* does not refer to the money collected from the Gentile churches (see vv. 25-27) but to the Gentiles themselves, as in REB: "It is my priestly task to offer the Gentiles to him as an acceptable sacrifice." The image of people as an offering to God is found in Isa 66:20, where the prophet foresees a time when the widely dispersed Jews will be transported "as an offering to the LORD . . . to Jerusalem." If Paul had this imagery in mind, he transformed its referent so that now "the offering" is not the Diaspora Jews but the Christian Gentiles. Peerbolte (2003, 248) rightly notes that this is a new idea, found nowhere else in his other letters. An offering that is "acceptable" does not merely meet minimum requirements; its quality elicits warm approval, for it has been hallowed by the Holy Spirit.

Having given an overview of his mission, in verses 17-21 (one long, awkward Greek sentence), Paul calls attention to certain aspects of it. He writes first of his pride in his "work for God" (is he responding to negative rumors like that in 3:8?), then he underlines his conviction that he has been Christ's instrument "to win obedience from the Gentiles," a restatement of 1:5 (see comment). It is neither clear nor important whether he refers to three means ("by word and deed, by the power of signs and portents, and by the power of the Holy Spirit," as in REB) or whether "signs and wonders" simply makes "deed" more concrete. In the New Testament, "signs and wonders" (REB: "portents"; NIV: "miracles") are often mentioned as marvelous events that attest the truth of the message (as in Acts 2:22 [Jesus' deeds]; 2:43 [the apostles' deeds]) because they are evidence of God's power. For Paul, these events of power corroborate the gospel, which is God's power to save (1:16; see comment).

Behind Paul's reference to "signs and wonders" lies his struggle with opponents in Corinth (he writes from the city's nearby port), disclosed in 2 Cor 10–13; there he reminds the Corinthians that "the signs of a true apostle [his opponents are "false apostles" in 2 Cor 11:13] were performed among you with . . . signs and wonders and mighty works" (2 Cor 12:12). Whereas Acts reports numerous miraculous deeds by Paul (Acts 14:8-10; 16:16-18; 20:9-12; 28:1-6, 8-9) and one that occurred for his benefit (16:25), Paul's own letters never mention any specific miraculous deed. Since traveling teachers who performed miracles were well-known phenomena at the time, the marvels that marked Paul's mission did not make him distinctive; they made him part of a general type. What made him distinctive, in his eyes, was Christ's working through his (unspecified) weakness (2 Cor 11:30; 12:1-10) rather than through his own powers.

The arc of his mission (v. 19)—"from Jerusalem and as far around as Illyricum" (modern Albania and up the Adriatic coast)—has generated considerable discussion because neither Acts nor Paul's letters give any indication that he had been that far northwest of Corinth. Even more strange is the reference to Jerusalem, since in Gal 1:22 he says he was not known to the churches in Judea (contrast Acts 9:29). Equally obscure is what he means by "fulfilling [*peplērōkenai*, perfect tense] the gospel of

Christ," even if the odd Greek phrase is rightly translated as "fully proclaimed" (NRSV, NIV) or as "completed the preaching" (REB). Since it was Paul's practice to start churches in major centers from which the faith would be spread by others to surrounding areas, here he might simply mean that he has met his goal of evangelizing the region without actually going to all its parts himself, for in verse 23 he claims "there is no more room" for him to continue his mission. In any case, verses 20-21 show that he thinks he has finished his task in the northeastern quadrant of the Mediterranean, and now must move on. If he cannot be the first to elicit faith (the "naming" of Christ probably refers to both his preaching and the confessional response to it), he will not be second, advancing a predecessor's work (building on "someone else's foundation"). He must be on the frontier, a pioneer. One has the impression that he is not only a "called apostle" (1:1) but "a driven one" as well. (NRSV's "ambition" renders *philotimoumenon*, which in the ancient honor/shame culture was used of persons who vied for the honor of doing the most for the city.)

In writing to the Roman Christians, however, there is no need to rehearse his experiences, because his eye is on the result of his work, which in verse 21 he sees as actualizing the words of LXX Isa 52:15 (in Isaiah, "him" refers to the servant; here it refers to Christ). Although 10:16 had quoted Isa 53:1 (the very next verse after 52:15), which leads into the portrayal of the suffering servant, Paul never actually identifies that servant with Christ (though 15:8-9 may allude to it). Perhaps he expects the readers to take the hint and make the identification themselves (so Hays 1989, 63). By pointing out that he is bringing "the gospel of Christ" to those who have not heard it before, Paul invites the hearers to recall that at 10:20 he had quoted Isa 65:1 to make the same point about Gentiles; he also preparesthe readers for what he is about to say regarding his projected mission in Spain.

◊ ◊ ◊ ◊

In this passage, Paul takes responsibility for shaping the readers' view of his mission; that is, he wants them to see him as Christ's sacral servant of the gospel, especially for Gentiles. Here, neither the relation of believing Gentiles to Israel, nor his role in evoking the "jealousy" from unbelieving Jews (see 11:14) is mentioned. Nor does he remind the readers that churches had come into being as a result of the gospel, though perhaps "what Christ has accomplished through me" (v. 18) alludes to that aspect of his work. Paul wants the Romans to see that it is the gospel and the grace he received (v. 15) that define him and his work. Only after he has projected this image does he go on to say what he has in mind for the future.

Now to Spain Via Jerusalem and Rome (15:22-33)

This passage, coupled with inferences drawn from the reference to Prisca and Aquila in 16:3-5 in light of Acts 18:1-1, 24-26, continues to be an important source from which scholars try to reconstruct the setting in which Paul wrote this letter (see introduction, p. 29). Indeed, the historical interrelatedness of Jerusalem, Rome, and Spain is reflected also in the way the passage itself shuttles back and forth between these three places on Paul's mind.

Just as Paul did not identify any of the "signs and wonders" that were part of his mission, so now in verses 22-24 he does not disclose what for many years had often prevented him from going to Rome—though verse 19 implies that it was his need to "complete" his work in the East (alluding to the offering?). He does not say that Satan prevented the trip (as in 1 Thess 2:18), or that the Spirit blocked his way (as Acts 16:6 reports). Rather, verses 28-29 imply that he regarded his trip to Jerusalem as the most recent factor that interfered with his travel plans. Interestingly, Acts reports that while in Ephesus Paul not only "resolved in the Spirit" to go to Jerusalem but that he also had said, "After I have gone there, I must also see Rome" (Acts 19:21). If the author of Acts knew of Paul's desire to go to Spain, he did not mention it here because his story of Paul ends in Rome (as did Paul's life, according to tradition); besides, would Acts have implied that the Spirit foresaw a trip to Spain if it did not occur?

In 1:13-15 Paul did not mention Spain, but simply wrote of his desire to "reap some harvest among you as I have among the rest of the Gentiles" and of his eagerness to "proclaim the gospel" in Rome. The difference between that passage and this one is not as great as some have alleged, for the "harvest" expected may well have included, in Paul's mind, the support he hopes to receive from the Romans, to which he now alludes in 15:24 ("sent on by you"—i.e., with your help). Apparently he does not regard preaching the gospel in Rome as building "on someone else's foundation" (v. 20). Of course he will preach the gospel when he arrives; he will not have come to "see the sights." Aware of the risk that going to Jerusalem involved, he evidently expects God to respond favorably to his (and the readers') prayer for the success of his Jerusalem journey (vv. 30-31). He could not foresee, of course, that the Jerusalem trip would delay his arrival in Rome even more—over two years, according to Acts 24:27—or that when he did arrive, he would be a prisoner.

In verses 25-27 he explains why he is going to Jerusalem: He will be "ministering to the saints" (for Paul's use of "saints," see 1:7) by transmitting the funds collected from his churches in Macedonia and Achaia. Noticeably, Galatia is not mentioned, though 1 Cor 16:1 says he had told those churches how to gather the funds. Evidently that effort failed. All scholars recognize that the fund was a major factor in Paul's mission; it is mentioned in 1 Cor 16:1-4 and Gal 2:10; and 2 Cor 8 and 9 are devoted to it (for a complex reconstruction, see Martyn 1997, 220-28; Joubert [2000] interprets it in light of Greco-Roman assumptions about gift exchange).

In verses 25, 31 Paul interprets the collection as his "ministry" (diakonia). He does not explain the origin of this collection—that about a decade before, at the "council in Jerusalem" where his gospel and his apostleship had been affirmed, the only stipulation was that they (the church in Antioch) would "remember the poor," which he later told the Galatians, "I was eager to do" (Gal 2:10). Considerable discussion has been generated by the way Paul refers to the recipients of the money: "the poor among the saints." It is unlikely that "the poor" here refers to the honorific self-designation used by the believers in Jerusalem; rather, the phrase refers to the destitute in the Christian community (see Keck 1965, 100-29; 1966, 54-78; for the impact of regional famines at the time when Paul agreed to the offering, see Joubert 2000, 107-13).

Recent translations, determined to be clear, have Paul write more specifically about money than he actually does; NIV and NJB have "make a contribution"; NRSV has "share their resources"; REB reads "raise a fund"; CEV goes farthest: "I am now on my way to Jerusalem to deliver the money . . . collected." What Paul actually wrote, however, was more allusive and suggestive: "Macedonia and Achaia were pleased to make *koinōnian* for the poor" (v. 26), which might be translated as: "were pleased to establish a rather close relation with the poor" (see BDAG). Since *koinōnia* usually refers to a close relationship as well as fiscal partnership or sharing, Paul's phrase implies that he does not view the money as a mere donation (as do those manuscripts that in 15:31 read "my gift-bearing" instead of "my ministry"). That Paul does not misrepresent the attitude of the Macedonians and Achaians (they were "pleased" to contribute) is evident from what he had written about them in 2 Cor 8:1-4; 9:1-5.

Earlier, when Paul encouraged the Corinthians to complete the fund, he wrote of it as establishing a certain parity or equality *(isotēs)* between givers and receivers: "Our desire is not that others might be relieved while you are hard pressed, but that there might be equality . . . your plenty will supply what they need, so that in turn their plenty will supply what you need. Then there will be equality" (2 Cor 8:13-14, NIV). Paul's interpretation to the Romans makes a similar point (v. 27), this time more concretely: the Gentiles have come to share *(ekoinōnēsan)* the Jerusalemites' spiritual things, and so they are obligated *(opheilousin)* "to be of sacred service *[leitourgēsai]* to them in material things" (AT). This is not a legal obligation but a moral one, expressing gratitude for the benefits of the gospel, in keeping with the reciprocity ethos that marked the patron-client relationship in antiquity. CEV makes this reciprocity explicit: "This is something they really wanted to do. But sharing their money with the Jews was also like paying back a debt, because the Jews had already shared their spiritual blessings with the Gentiles." In short, according to verse

27, the givers are receivers and the receivers are givers. That is what "making *koinōnia*" really means.

In verses 28-29 Paul resumes writing of his travel plans after completing his ministry in Jerusalem. His unusual expression in verse 28—literally, "have sealed to them this fruit"—has been paraphrased in various ways (NRSV: "have delivered to them what has been collected"; NIV: "have made sure that they received this fruit"; CEV: "have safely delivered this money"). Since seals were used to authenticate documents and to identify the source of what is transmitted (especially tenant farmers' produce), Paul apparently uses the word to say that he will certify that the collection indeed expresses the *koinōnia* of the givers.

Paul could have put the concluding benediction (v. 33) at the end of verse 28. Had he done so, however, we would never have learned of his apprehension about his journey to Jerusalem, an apprehension so deep that he urges the readers to join him in praying for his safety—not in travel to the Holy City but in surviving enemies upon arriving. The first readers, no less than today's, may have been surprised by this passage, for up to this point nothing that Paul had written about Jews or Jerusalem even hinted that he was not welcome there. Nor does he explain now, not even by a single phrase, why he thinks his life will be endangered. He seems to assume that the readers do not need to be informed about the hostility against him. In any case, he does not hesitate to ask for their prayers on his behalf. Near the beginning of the letter, Paul reported his prayers for them (1:9-10); now he asks for theirs. The seriousness of his request is disclosed in his use of *synagōnisasthai*, to struggle with, contend or fight alongside (used only here in the whole Greek Bible). Paul is not asking simply for "earnest" prayer (NRSV) but for participation by prayer in his own struggle *(agōn)* with his opposition.

In specifying what the readers should pray for, Paul mentions two things: that he be "rescued from the unbelievers in Judea" and that his *diakonia* be acceptable to the saints (the Jerusalem church as a whole, not just the poor in it). For historians, the possibility that the offering would be refused is a significant clue to the deterioration of Paul's relation to the Jerusalem church, headed by James the brother of Jesus. Important here is recalling that according to Gal 2:9-10, it was James and the other leaders who had asked the Antioch church (represented by Barnabas and Paul) to "remember the poor" in the first place. If now, nearly a decade later, the money would be refused, Paul's whole Gentile mission, and the construal of the gospel on which it was based, would be repudiated. Paul's language implies that the Jerusalem "saints," fellow believers though they are, identify more strongly with their fellow Jews, unbelievers though they are, than with Paul, the Jewish apostle to the Gentiles. The silence in Acts implies that after Paul was arrested, the Jerusalem church apparently lifted not a finger on his behalf. Ironically, Paul was *indeed* "rescued from unbelievers"—by the Roman authorities (Acts 21:30-36).

Paul concludes the epistolary framework with a "prayer wish" (v. 33), as he had the discourse part in 15:13. There he used "the God of hope"; here he uses "the God of peace" (repeated in 16:20), as in Phil 4:9; 2 Cor 13:11 ("God of love and peace"), and 1 Thess 5:23. In 1 Cor 14:33 he pointedly reminded the Corinthians that "God is a God not of disorder but of peace." As in "God of hope," so in "God of peace" God is acknowledged as the source of peace, understood not just as the absence of conflict but as *shalom*.

◊ ◊ ◊ ◊

While Acts reports in great detail what occurred when Paul arrived in Jerusalem, it says nothing about the offering (nor does it mention the offering as Paul's reason for going to Jerusalem). Acts reports that though Paul was welcomed "warmly" when he arrived, the next day he agreed to James's proposal to counter the hostility of Christian Jews, all "zealous for the law"—namely, to pay the costs of releasing four men from their special vows. When the plan miscarried and a riot ensued, Paul was taken into protective custody (Acts 21:17-36). Later, defending himself before the Roman governor (24:17), he said he had come "to bring alms to my nation"—the sole possible allusion to the offering. It is probable that the offering was rejected. What Paul thought then is wholly unknown. What became of the money also remains unknown. What is evident is that the rationale for the offering stated in Rom

15:26-27 does not account for *Paul's* determination to take the offering to Jerusalem, nor does it disclose what was actually at stake for him—and for the Jerusalem church: the legitimacy of his apostolic standing and interpretation of the gospel. For him, by contributing to the needs of the poor Christian Jews, the Gentile churches acknowledge that they are part of one church, not a "Gentile Christianity," a breakaway movement, or parallel option. Theologically, Paul was right, even though the offering that expressed his conviction failed historically.

CONCLUDING CONCERNS (16:1-27)

Paul's letter has a surprise ending—chapter 16, consisting mostly of greetings. It is not the greetings as such that are surprising (all of Paul's letters except Galatians conclude with greetings), but the great number of them—especially in a letter to a Christian community he has not yet seen. Indeed, these greetings have prompted some scholars to argue that chapter 16 was not part of the letter sent to Rome but was added later—a view now generally abandoned (see introduction, p. 27). Chapter 16 contains also other surprises—the commendation of Phoebe (vv. 1-2) and the abrupt warning in verses 17-20, which stands between Paul's own greetings in verses 1-16 and those from his associates in verses 21-24. As we will see, it is likely that both verses 17-20 and the unusually long doxology in verses 25-27 were added to what Paul sent to Rome.

It would have been rather tactless of Paul to explain why he greets so many persons. One can only guess his reasons for doing so. Not a word links any of the persons named with either "the weak" or "the strong" in chapters 14–15, or with his plans for Spain. Instead of guessing Paul's motives, it is more productive to note carefully what he says and probably assumes. The chapter discloses important information about Paul's lifework, early Christianity, and the readers in Rome. Although his characterizations of the persons named become ever shorter, the names themselves suggest significant aspects of the Christian community's makeup. (See Lampe 2003 for details, analyses, and inferences from the names.)

About Phoebe (16:1-2)

The chapter begins with what is in effect a letter of recommen-
dation for Phoebe, who presumably took the letter to Rome and
read it to the assembled believers there. Brief letters of recom-
mendation were commonly provided for travelers in order to facil-
itate their activity upon arrival in unfamiliar settings (see Acts
18:27 for an example; for a discussion of the practice, see Agosto
2003, 101-33). Since the effectiveness of such a letter depends on
the standing of the writer, we can infer that Paul assumes that his
commendation will count in Rome, where he has many friends
and former associates, who themselves may have been respected
by the believers there. Indeed, Paul may have greeted so many persons in order to provide Phoebe with as many potential helpers as
possible once they welcomed (or received, *prosdexēsthe*) her as a
fellow believer "as is fitting for the saints" to do (see 12:13, where
hospitality is mandated).

◊ ◊ ◊ ◊

Paul's commendation ignores all biographical data and high-
lights instead Phoebe's role in the church at Cenchreae, a seaport
on the eastern side of the narrow isthmus a few miles northeast of
Corinth. "Our sister Phoebe" was "a *diakonos* [masculine noun]
of the church"; the first use of "church" in the whole letter does
not refer to the readers. Although Paul used *diakonos* frequently
(of governing authority, 13:4; of Christ, 15:8; of himself and his
associates, as in 1 Cor 3:5), only in Phil 1:1 does it clearly refer to
an office in the church (NRSV: "deacons"). In 16:1 the word
probably refers generally to one who serves the needs of the community (not by waiting tables!); she may have been "a leader"
(CEV), but to call her "a deaconess" (NJB) is anachronistic. More
important is what else Paul says about her: "She has been a *pro-
statis* of many and of myself as well." The word surely means
more than "a good friend" (REB), for it appears to be the Greek
equivalent of the Latin *patrona*, one who "came to the aid of others, especially foreigners, by providing housing and financial aid
and by representing their interests before local authorities" (Moo

1996, 916; for a discussion of the nature of patronage and its role in Paul's mission, see Lampe 2003b, 488-523). Acts 16:14-15, 40 suggests that Lydia served as Paul's patron in Philippi. Phoebe, then, was a "benefactor," from whose generosity Paul too benefitted (Gaius was another; 16:23). Like Lydia and Gaius, Phoebe had financial resources; what sort of business took her to Rome is not indicated. By making her role in the church a reason to welcome her in Rome, Paul, in effect, says, "She deserves it." Having assisted travelers like Paul, she should now be given assistance herself. Nothing more is known of her.

Paul's Greetings (16:3-16)

Paul greets twenty-six individuals, twenty-four of whom are named, plus an indefinite number associated with certain named persons (see vv. 10-11, 15). One house church is specified (v. 5), two are clearly implied (vv. 14-15), and probably two others as well (vv. 10-11)—five in all. Since the passage refers to a house church at the beginning (v. 5) and alludes to two of them at the end (vv. 14-15), it is possible that Paul names the greeted persons house church by house church. Since it is unlikely that verse 16 ("Greet one another with a holy kiss") addresses only the group mentioned in verse 15, Paul probably envisions an assembly of all the persons greeted; if so, he eschews mentioning the name of the person whose dwelling was large enough for such a gathering.

Whenever possible, Paul says something positive about the persons greeted; otherwise, he simply states the names of those about whom he probably knew little. The number of people that Paul had come to know elsewhere but who are now in Rome is quite remarkable: Prisca and Aquila, Epaenetus, Andronicus and Junia, Ampliatus, Urbanus, Stachys, Apelles, Persis, Rufus and his mother—nearly half of those named. The names indicate that the community consisted of Gentiles and Jews, though in some cases the ethnic identity is uncertain. There is no allusion to the return of previously expelled Jews (see Acts 18:1-3). Women are prominent in the lists. Names commonly used for slaves or former slaves appear frequently (at least nine, according to Lampe 2003, 183); two prominent households (Aristobulus and Narcissus) are also mentioned. Whether the diversity of those greeted reflected also the diversity of the whole Christian community (or communities) in Rome is not known.

◊ ◊ ◊ ◊

First to be greeted are Prisca and Aquila (vv. 3-5), whose role in scholars' efforts to reconstruct the historical setting of Romans was discussed in the introduction (see p. 29). According to Acts 18:1-3, this couple—recently expelled from Rome—arrived in Corinth where Paul lived with them while working with Aquila, a fellow Jewish tentmaker, from Pontus (the Anatolian province on the south side of the Black Sea). Later, when Paul departed for Jerusalem, they accompanied him as far as Ephesus (18:18-19), where they won to the faith the learned and eloquent Apollos (18:24-26; his subsequent role in Corinth is glimpsed in 1 Cor 1:11-13; 3:1-9). Now they are back in Rome, where they host a house church (Acts does not say whether they had done so in Corinth or Ephesus). It is not clear why Paul mentions Prisca (Priscilla in Acts) first; nor is there any evidence that Paul had sent them to Rome in advance of his own planned visit. (For a reconstruction of Aquila's trade, travel, and socioeconomic status, see Lampe 2003a, 187-95.) Given their prior association with Paul, it is understandable that he calls them his coworkers *(tous synergous mou)* in Christ. More important, he wants the readers to know that they "risked their necks for my life," though we can only guess where or when this was. (The riot in Ephesus is an unlikely candidate since Paul was not present at the riot; see Acts 19:21-41.) For their daring action, not only Paul but "all the churches of the Gentiles" too are grateful, for had their intervention on his behalf failed, his mission to the Gentiles may well have been cut short.

Greeted next is Epaenetus (v. 5), the "first convert in Asia" (presumably in Ephesus, the provincial capital). He may have accompanied Prisca and Aquila when they returned to Rome, and might have been part of their house church in Rome. In characterizing him as "my beloved" Paul implies that he had become his dear friend and perhaps associate in spreading the gospel. The same can be inferred for Ampliatus (v. 8) and Stachys (v. 9), for they too are Paul's "beloved." On the other hand, whether Mary's (v. 6) labors on behalf of the gospel were done in Rome or in the East depends on whether Paul wrote *eis hymas* ("for you"; some manuscripts have *en hymin*, "among you") or *eis hēmas* ("for us"). Even though most manuscripts read "for you," the fact that all other persons greeted in verses 3-10*a* (from Prisca through Apelles) were known to Paul before they came to Rome suggests that also Mary had "worked very hard for us" (AT) before going to Rome. If, on the other hand, Paul refers to her work in Rome, one wonders why he thought he must remind the readers of her work. Although a number of manuscripts call her *Mariam*, on the assumption that she was Jewish, *Maria* is a well-attested Roman name; Paul does not call her a "kin" *(syngenē)* as he does Andronicus, Junia, and Herodion. The character of her "work" cannot be inferred from the verb *ekopiasen*, used of her activity and of several others, all women (v. 12). The verb connotes hard labor, wearying toil (as in Acts 20:34-35; 1 Cor 4:12; Eph 4:28), but Paul also uses it regularly to speak of various activities, including teaching and preaching (see, e.g., 1 Cor 15:10; 16:16; Phil 2:16; 1 Thess 5:12); 1 Thess 1:3 speaks of "the labor *[kopos]* of love."

The greeting in verse 7 is especially significant. First of all, although RSV, NIV, NASB, NJB, and CEV say that Andronicus's partner was Junias (allegedly an abbreviation of Junianus), no such name existed; apparently Junias was invented in order to avoid the implications of the name Junia (so NRSV, REB), commonly used for women—namely, that like Prisca and Aquila they are a husband-wife team (evidence is discussed by Fitzmyer 1993, 737; Moo 1996, 921-12; and summarized by Lampe 1991, 223). It is what Paul goes on to say that discloses why it is important to get the name right (a few manuscripts call her Julia): "They are *episēmoi* [outstanding, prominent] *en tois apostolois.*" This does *not* mean what CEV says: "They are highly respected *by* the apostles," but rather "they are prominent *among* the apostles." Here "apostle" is used generically ("emissaries"); that is, like Paul they moved from place to place, spreading the gospel (like Peter and his wife? [see 1 Cor 9:5]). Perhaps for this reason Prisca and Aquila are not called "apostles": They hosted a congregation.

Andronicus and Junia too were Jews *(syngeneis)*, not necessarily Paul's "relatives" (in 9:3 the word means "kinfolk"). At some point, they were his "fellow-prisoners."

More important historically, they "were in Christ" before Paul became a believer; since his "conversion" occurred no later than 35 CE, this couple was part of the Christian community virtually from the start (perhaps in Jerusalem or Damascus?). Verse 7 says just enough to remind us of how fragmentary is our information about earliest Christianity. So too, the words Paul uses to characterize Ampliatus, Urbanus, Stachys, Apelles, Tryphaena and Tryphosa (sisters?), and Rufus imply that he had come to esteem them because of their activities in support of his mission. Had he said even a bit more about them, our understanding of his life-work would be clearer.

The same is true, perhaps for different reasons, of those greeted in verses 10b-11. Herodion is also a *syngenē* (probably not a relative), perhaps a freedman who, as customary, took the name of his former owner, somehow a member of the Herod family. If correct, this would explain why Herodion is mentioned after "those who belong to the household of Aristobulus" (NIV), who may have been the grandson of Herod the Great (and rival of his brother, Herod Agrippa I); Aristobulus had been "brought up in the court of Claudius Caesar" (Josephus *Ant.* 19.9.2 [360]; 20.1.1 [9]), and with others tried to prevent Gaius (Caligula) from having a statue of himself erected in the Jerusalem temple (*Ant.* 1878.4, 273). Paul does not greet Aristobulus, who was dead at the time, but those in his household (lit., "who belong to him") who were believers. (Why CEV has Paul greet "Aristobulus and his family" is not clear.) Similarly, Paul does not greet "Narcissus and others in his family, who have faith in the Lord" (CEV) but "those who belong to the household of Narcissus who are in the Lord" (NIV). If this Narcissus was the freedman who had been Claudius's secretary, Paul did not greet him either since he had been forced to commit suicide when Nero came to power. If these identifications are probable, then they provide valuable evidence that the Christian faith had penetrated two households of the upper social strata in Rome, though not those strata themselves.

Paul greets these believers even though he can name only one of them, Herodion.

Rufus (v. 13) probably was a Gentile whom Paul got to know somewhere in the East. There is no apparent reason to identify him with one of the sons of Simon of Cyrene who was compelled to carry Jesus' cross (Mark 15:21). That Rufus's mother was "mother" also to Paul suggests that he benefitted from their devotion to him, and perhaps from their hospitality, though it is hard to visualize anyone "mothering" Paul. The formulation of verse 14 implies that these five named persons, together with an unspecified number of "brothers with them," constituted a distinct house church; the same is true of verse 15.

As elsewhere (1 Cor 16:20; 2 Cor 13:12; 1 Thess 5:26), Paul asks the readers to greet one another with "a holy kiss" (v. 16). A century later, Justin (*1 Apol. 65*) regards the kiss as a part of the liturgy: "At the conclusion of the prayers we greet one another with a kiss. Then, bread and a chalice containing wine mixed with water are presented" for the Eucharist. There is no evidence that already Paul envisioned this practice.

When Paul adds, "All the churches of Christ [the only time this expression appears in the New Testament] greet you," he probably speaks on behalf of the churches that he had founded.

◊ ◊ ◊ ◊

The number of Paul's former associates who are now in Rome is quite remarkable and provides evidence for the mobility of those touched by the apostle's vocation. It also implies that these people had sufficient means to travel. Not to be overlooked is that Paul greets also persons in Rome whose faith he has learned about, even though he does not (cannot?) mention their names. That he greets them all accords with his mandate that they should welcome one another, and to greet each other with the holy kiss. Nor should one miss the import of the greeting from "all the churches of Christ" (v. 16*b*), even if Paul is doing the greeting on their behalf. The fact of the greeting is an aperture through which we glimpse the sense of solidarity that marked the early Christians who, though unacquainted with each other, understood themselves to be part of a reality neither confined nor confinable to the little house church where they gathered. However much they disagreed, these believers were becoming a people.

Warning and Assurance (16:17-20)

Both the location of this paragraph and its content are unexpected, whether one holds that it is from Paul or from a later editor. Accounting for it requires proposing unverifiable historical hypotheses, whose persuasiveness depends on their capacity to account for the whole phenomenon. While judgments about its genuineness are divided, it is important to read the text carefully first. The paragraph consists of several parts: the warning and its warrant (vv. 17-18), the assurance (vv. 19-20*a*), and the "grace wish" (v. 20*b*), which is absent from some manuscripts; some have a similar "grace wish" at verse 24 (some "grace wish" appears at or near the end of Paul's other letters, 2 Cor 13:13 being the most elaborate).

◊ ◊ ◊ ◊

Verse 17 begins with the same words that Paul had used in 15:30 *(parakalō de hymas)* and similar to those in 12:1: "I exhort you." The readers are to do two things: (a) *skopein* certain people ("watch out for" [NIV, CEV] is better than "keep an eye on" [NRSV, REB]); the word has a more positive meaning in 2 Cor 4:18 ("look at") and Phil 3:17; (b) *ekklinete* ("turn away from, shun, avoid") them. Merely being alert to troublemakers is insufficient; they are to be avoided as well. Although the warrant for this double action is spelled out in verse 18, it is anticipated already in the two ways their actions are characterized in verse 17: They create *tas dichostasias* ("the dissensions"; REB: "stir up quarrels"; CEV: "cause trouble") and *ta skandala* ("the offenses"; REB: "lead others astray"; NIV: "put obstacles in your way"). The use of the definite articles *(tas, ta)* suggests that the author has specific, known controversies and offenses in view, just as "those who . . ." implies particular persons, not just "anyone who . . ." or "in case someone. . . ." Whoever they are, their actions are "contrary to the teaching *[tēn didachēn]* you have learned" (NIV). Somewhat similar language was used at 6:17 (see comment). Here the accent falls not on what is preached and believed, but on what

is taught and learned, a body of right teaching, as in later texts like
2 Tim 3:14-17; *Mart. Pol.* 10:1 ("if you wish to learn the *logos* of
Christianity"); *Diogn.* 1:1 ("learn the religion of Christianity"). In
the New Testament it is Acts that portrays Paul as the teacher of
Christianity (see Acts 15:35; 18:11; 20:20; 28:31). The language
of verse 17 suggests that the author sees the theological substance
of the Christian faith to be at stake.

Instead of identifying the dangerous ideas or explaining why they
are dangerous, the author resorts to two *ad hominem* comments, the
first about their praxis ("smooth talk and flattery"), the second about
its results: The hearts of the simple-minded are deceived. Obviously,
both the troublemakers and their followers would have rejected this
characterization and would have had their own characterizations
of the author. But that need not imply that the author's warning was
misplaced. In any case, by accusing them of "smooth talk and flattery"
the author regards them as con artists who mislead the unwary (the
akakōn, "those without guile, the innocent").

But who are the troublemakers? Presumably, they claim to be
some kind of Christians; the assertion that "such people do not
serve our Lord Christ" (used only here) is not a neutral description but a polemical accusation designed to delegitimate their
authority. The charge that what they really serve is "their own
belly" (NRSV, REB: "appetites") delegitimates them even more. In
Phil 3:18-19 Paul's invective against unspecified opponents, who
he says "live as enemies of the cross of Christ," includes the accusation, "Their god is the belly; and their glory is in their shame;
their minds are set on earthly things." But this passage does not
really help identify the troublemakers in our verse 18. It is wholly
improbable that those who serve "their own belly" are "the
weak" for whom food laws were highly important (see chap. 14),
for Paul had urged "the weak" and "the strong" to welcome one
another (15:7), not for "the strong" to avoid "the weak."
Unfortunately, this vivid epithet for self-promotion, though contrasted with serving Christ, does not disclose what these people
said that is contrary to what the readers have been taught (or by
whom). This whole invective discloses more about the author's
views than about theirs.

In verses 19-20 the author abruptly speaks confidently of the readers' reputation: their "obedience is known to all" (echoing 1:8, "your faith is proclaimed throughout the world," as well as 15:14). Nonetheless, he wants them "to be wise in what is good and guileless [*akeraious*, "unmixed," hence pure and innocent] in what is evil." (REB's "expert in goodness, but innocent of evil" is better than NEB's "experts in goodness but simpletons in evil," probably reflecting the Vulgate's *simplex* for *akeraious*.) The expression sounds like a motto, as does Matt 10:16: "wise as serpents, innocent as doves."

No less abruptly comes the assurance in verse 20: "The God of peace will shortly crush Satan under your feet." Nowhere else in the whole Christian Bible (or in second temple Jewish or other early Christian texts) is there such a promise. Remarkable is not the promised destruction of Satan (see Rev 20:10) but that Satan will be subjected to the readers—and soon! Nor should one overlook the paradox: the God of *peace* will *crush* Satan (the paradox itself recalls that of Rev 5, where the conquering Lion of Judah [Christ] is the Lamb that has been slaughtered). Although the assurance is an independent statement, perhaps drawn from or alluding to a lost apocalypse, perhaps the author used it to promise that the readers will triumph over Satan's agents, the troublemakers.

Whether the paragraph was an integral part of what Paul sent to Rome or a later addition is really a matter of deciding how best to account for its existence at just this point. Serious difficulties are generated by regarding it as the work of Paul, making it highly probable that it is a later addition: (a) Apart from the allusion to opposition to Paul in 3:8, Romans is generally free of the sort of polemic that marks verses 17-18. Even if Paul's insistence in 9:1-3 that he remains concerned about Israel suggests that he is being accused of the opposite, that misunderstanding has no echo in this paragraph. (b) Given the concern of "the weak" for dietary observances, "their own belly" could only cause confusion. (c) It is difficult to regard the paragraph as a last-minute warning, as has been suggested: As Paul was concluding the letter, he learned that the troublemakers had arrived (or were about to arrive), and so hastily added this warning to alert the readers to the imminent danger. (d) Integrating what is implied by the reference to Satan into the thought of the rest of the letter, which never mentions Satan, requires too much exegetical dexterity to be convincing. (e) There is no reason to think that Paul wrote just this paragraph in his own hand, as he did in 1 Cor 16:21 and Gal 6:11. (f) Before verses 17-20 were inserted, the greetings in verses 21-23 had followed naturally after verse 16 ("All the churches of Christ greet you"). Now, however, the transition is awkward at verse 20: "The grace of our Lord Jesus Christ be with you," which normally marks the end of Paul's letters, is followed by more greetings.

Whereas it is difficult to fit our paragraph into Romans, it sounds like a number of later writings with similar warnings. Indeed, what our paragraph warns against, Acts has Paul himself predict in his farewell to the elders at Ephesus: "Keep watch. . . . I know that after I have gone, savage wolves will come in among you. . . . Some even from your own group will come distorting the truth in order to entice the disciples to follow them" (Acts 20:28-30). Something like that situation is combated by the author of Ephesians: "We must no longer be children, tossed to and fro and blown about by every wind of doctrine, by people's trickery, by their craftiness in deceitful scheming" (Eph 4:14). Colossians 2:4 says, "I tell you this [the mystery of God in Christ] so that no one may deceive you by fine-sounding arguments," in 2:8 called "hollow and deceptive philosophy, which depends on human tradition . . . rather than on Christ" (NIV). Second Thessalonians 2 warns against a God-sent (!) "powerful delusion" (v. 11) and also urges readers to "stand firm and hold fast to the traditions that you were taught by us" (v. 15); later it says, "Take note of those who do not obey what we say in this letter; have nothing to do with them" (3:14). While this evidence loses its force if Paul wrote these three letters, similar warnings are found in the Pastoral Epistles (whose deutero-Pauline character is generally assumed). Right off, Timothy is told that he had been left in Ephesus "so that you may teach certain people not to teach any different doctrine, and not to occupy themselves with myths and endless genealogies that promote speculation" (1 Tim 1:3-4, AT; see also 4:7; 6:3-5, 20-21; 2 Tim 2:16-19). Likewise, 2 Tim 2:23 urges, "Have nothing to do with stupid and senseless controversies; you know that they breed quarrels" (see also 4:3-4). Since ideas are encountered through the people who hold and advocate them, these letters too urge the reader to avoid people whose ideas are divisive and corrupting. To be sure, also Paul relied on *ad hominem* invective against his opponents (see especially 2 Cor 11:3-6, 13-15; Gal 3:1; 6:12; Phil 3:17-19), but he did not counsel avoidance. Since no manuscript lacks this paragraph, it must have been added before Paul's letters were compiled.

Whoever added verses 17-20 to the text understood the difference between disputes over dietary observances and disputes over matters contrary to what believers have "learned" as Christian teaching. The author also recognized the difference between believers whose disagreements occur "in honor of the Lord" (14:6) and disagreements with those whose behavior indicated— at least to him—that they were not serving Christ but "their own belly." Where common loyalty is not acknowledged, serious debate is impossible, making avoidance a prudent policy.

Greetings from Associates (16:21-24)

No one knows why Timothy sends greetings now, for he does not appear as a co-author of the letter (1:1) as he does in 2 Cor 1:1; Phil 1:1; 1 Thess 1:1; Phlm 1; nothing is gained by imagined scenarios (e.g., he was not present when Paul began the letter but arrived before it was finished). Here Timothy is characterized as Paul's coworker, as are Prisca and Aquila, as well as Urbanus (vv. 3, 9). The other three—Lucius, Jason, and Sosipater—are Paul's fellow-Jews *(syngeneis)*, as are Andronicus and Junia and Herodion. It is unlikely that Lucius *(Loukios)* is Luke *(Loukas)*, the traditional author of Acts and the Gospel, mentioned in Col 4:16. Since "Sosipater" is the longer form of "Sopater," it is likely that this Christian Jew is the Sopater from Beroea who accompanied Paul to Jerusalem (Acts 20:4). Less likely, though possible, is the suggestion that Jason is the man who hosted Paul in Thessalonica (Acts 17:5-7, 9), since he is not among Paul's traveling companions in Acts 20:4.

Whereas the four persons mentioned in verse 21 were Paul's companions and associates in the East, the three named in verses 22-23 were locals in Cenchreae or Corinth. Although 1 Cor 16:21 and Gal 6:11 indicate that Paul took the pen from the scribe, only here (v. 22) does the scribe identify himself as a fellow believer. Though Paul was producing the letter to the Romans at Cenchreae, it is possible that his current host Gaius (v. 23) is the one he had baptized in nearby Corinth (1 Cor 1:14). In any case, since "the whole church" at Cenchreae meets in his house, he must have been a man of some means.

Erastus too would have had significant resources, for he was "the *oikonomos* of the city." Exactly who he was and what his responsibilities were have been discussed at length. It is unlikely that this Erastus, given his standing in the city, was the one Paul sent with Timothy from Ephesus to Macedonia (Acts 19:21-23). More important, in any case, is his status as a public official. Was he "the city treasurer," as most translations say? Or something like our "city manager"? Or was he "the city's director of public works," as in NIV? The thorough discussion by Winter (1994, 180-97) shows Paul's *oikonomos* was the Greek equivalent of the Latin *aedile*, a person elected for a one-year term following a campaign for office marked by promises of benefits to the city. Perhaps Paul's Erastus was the man memorialized in a mid-first-century inscription found at Corinth. It reads: "Erastus laid the pavement [nineteen meters square] at his own expense in return for his aedileship." Clearly, he was quite wealthy (though perhaps a freedman), as was Paul's Erastus; he would have been among the "not many" who were "powerful" (1 Cor 1:26). As *aedile* he would have been responsible for public buildings (as NIV sees) and the fiscal affairs of the city. But would the required public oath in the name of the gods and emperor have precluded a Christian Erastus from becoming an *aedile*? Winter surmises that if Erastus was a Jew, he might have been excused from it.

Doxology (16:25-27)

These verses are either absent or appear at various places in the text: after 14:23; after 15:33; after 16:24; after both 14:23 and

16:24; after both 14:23 and 15:33. Most exegetes regard them as a later addition, and they are treated as such here (see n. 2 in Moo 1996, 936-37). In its present position, the doxology's opening lines recall the beginning of the letter, thus forming an *inclusio* with 1:6. The passage is one of seventeen doxologies in the New Testament, of which Eph 3:20-21; 1 Tim 6:16; and Jude 24-25 most resemble Rom 16:25-27. Though varying widely, their basic structure is constant: "To X [usually God; in 2 Tim 4:18, Christ] be Y [usually glory; in 1 Pet 5:11, power] forever. Amen." Usually doxologies require the reader to supply the missing verb "be"; consistently, the final word is "Amen." Doxologies are formalized liturgical expressions of praise, which point away from the speaker to the one praised.

In this prolix doxology, the content is conveyed by both language and structure.

> To the one with power to strengthen you
>   according to my gospel and
>   [according to] the proclamation of Jesus Christ,
>   according to the revelation of the mystery,
>
>   silenced for eternal times
>   but manifested now
>   through prophetic writings
>   according to the command of the eternal God,
>
>   for the obedience of faith,
>   for all the Gentiles
>   made known,
>
>   to the only wise God
>   through Jesus Christ
>   to whom [be] the glory forever. Amen. (AT)

Several features are worth noting. (a) The three "according to" *(kata)* phrases state the norm by which God's power is understood (see below). (b) "Silenced . . . made known" as a whole explains the revealed mystery in verse 25; (c) "manifested now" is elaborated by the next two phrases (referring to the prophetic writings and God's command) but the following two phrases ("for the obedience of faith" and "for all the Gentiles") qualify "made known." (d) "To whom" is awkward (some manuscripts omit it; see NRSV footnote); it probably refers to "the only wise God," not to "Jesus Christ."

◊ ◊ ◊ ◊

God's power *(dynamis)* was an important aspect of the letter's argument (see 1:16, 20; 4:21; 9:17, 22; 11:23; 14:4) but only here does it refer to God's capacity to "strengthen" the readers, to make them strong in their faith commitment (as in 1:11, where Paul sees himself as the mediator of "some spiritual gift" that will strengthen them). Later New Testament passages also speak of being "strengthened" in light of the perilous future (2 Thess 3:1-3; Jas 5:7-8; 1 Pet 5:8-10; Rev 3:1-3), but here an explicit reference to the future is absent; a more general stabilization or "upbuilding" may be in view.

God's power to make the readers strong accords *(kata)* with three things: "my gospel," the proclamation *(kerygma)* of the gospel, and the revelation of "the mystery." In 2:16 Paul had referred to Judgment Day, when "according to my gospel" God will judge all secrets (see comment). "My gospel" is not Paul's own invention but "the gospel of God" concerning the Son (see 1:1-4). Here "my gospel" is specified as the proclamation whose content is Jesus Christ (not Jesus' own message). The *kata* ("according to") in verse 25 implies that God's strengthening is consistent with the way God brings strength out of weakness (2 Cor 11:8-10), which accords with God's action through the cross. Here that event is called "the revelation of the mystery" *(apokalypsin mystēriou)*.

The rest of verse 25, together with verse 26, explains this mystery, first by saying *how* it occurred, then by stating its *purpose*. But verse 25 also makes explicit *what* is implied in saying that the mystery is an apocalypse, a revelation or a disclosure, an unveiling: It was *chronois aiōniois sesigēmenou*, an unusual phrase rendered as "kept secret for long ages" (NRSV); "hidden for long ages past" (NIV); "the divine secret kept in silence for long ages" (REB); "For ages and ages this message was kept secret" (CEV).

The passive form of the participle indicates that it is God who kept the matter from being known. In 11:25 Paul had used "mystery" to speak of God's strange way of achieving the salvation of all (see comment). This doxology, however, emphasizes the contrast between being previously unknown and its present manifestedness (*phanerōthentos,* used also in 3:21).

What the doxology has in view accords with the probably deutero-Pauline Col 1:26 ("the mystery that has been hidden throughout the ages and generations but has now been revealed to his saints") and in the clearly post-Paul Ephesians: "In former generations this mystery was not made known to humankind, as it has now been revealed to his holy apostles and prophets" (3:5; see also v. 9). A similar emphasis on the disclosure of the previously hidden appears also in other deutero-Pauline texts (2 Tim 1:9-10; Titus 1:2-3) as well as in 1 Pet 1:20—a similarity that suggests that the doxology too was written later in Paul's name. In any case, here what "mystery" connotes is not the character of the gospel (as being "mysterious," ultimately unfathomable) but something quite different: Only in history is the gospel new; its substance existed "for long ages" before being unveiled. From the author's point of view, that is precisely what makes the kerygma utterly reliable; it does not emerge from historical developments but is unveiled in history when God wills it.

Two phrases characterize this present manifestation: It occurred "through the prophetic writings" and "according to the command [*epitagēn*] of the eternal God." Neither phrase is characteristic of Paul's language. The former refers to the scriptures of the synagogue. It is not evident why the doxology asserts that the "mystery" was made manifest through scripture instead of (or in addition to) through Christ. Paul normally points out that what he is saying accords with scripture ("as it is written"), not that revelation came *through* scripture. Even if the doxology was written after Paul's letters began to circulate as a collection, the "prophetic writings" do not include his letters. Nowhere else does the New Testament speak of "the eternal God" (though 1:20 alludes to the idea). That the disclosure occurred according to "God's command" underscores that it was the result of God's free, sovereign act. The creator of the doxology used the language, including word order, that virtually repeats what Paul had said in 1:5 about the purpose of his apostleship: "to bring about the obedience of faith among all the Gentiles." Thus the doxology tacitly gives glory to God for Paul's lifework. Not to be overlooked is that in 1:5, as here, the text refers to all *ethnē*, Gentiles (though Jews would be included if the word meant "nations," which is far from obvious). There is no evident place here for the salvation of all Israel (11:26).

Verse 27 now specifies to whom the glory is to be ascribed— "the only wise God" (echoing Sir 1:8, "one is wise"). While Paul writes of God's wisdom in 1 Cor 1:21; 2:7, he does not characterize God as "wise," as do 4 Macc 1:12 ("to the all-wise God") and those manuscripts of Jude that at verse 25 read "to the only wise God our Savior" instead of "to the only God our Savior" (similarly at 1 Tim 1:17 many manuscripts read "only wise God"). That glory is to be ascribed to God "through" Christ accords with giving thanks through him (7:25), which is to say that the ascribing of glory in view here is contingent on appropriating the meaning of the Christ-event.

As with the other letters of Paul, Romans too has a *subscriptio*, a scribal comment about the writing of the letter. Here, some manuscripts say that Romans was "written from Corinth"; one says it was written "through Phoebe the deacon" (implying that Tertius was her slave or freedman?); others that it was written "through Tertius but sent through Phoebe." The subscriptions are not printed in our Bibles.

◊ ◊ ◊ ◊

The sheer size of this doxology shows that it is not a mere afterthought, even if it was added. As it stands, the editor made it Paul's last word to the readers—but not only the original recipients, for the editor understood himself to be readying the letter for repeated use in the church. In effect, then, the doxology provides a hermeneutical guide to the way the letter is to be read and reread. Not surprisingly, then, it juxtaposes "my gospel" and "the proclamation of Jesus Christ." In 3:21 Paul had written that God's righteousness is manifested (*pephanerōtai*, perfect tense);

now, in looking back while readying the text for the future, the doxology uses the participle of the same word *(phanerōthentos)* to express the definitive character of what is "now disclosed." Thus the doxology invites the reader to read Romans again, and again—as an act of praise.

SELECT BIBLIOGRAPHY

FREQUENTLY CITED COMMENTARIES

Achtemeier, Paul J. 1985. *Romans*. IBC. Atlanta: John Knox. A theologically alert interpretation that helps teachers and preachers understand the major themes of Romans.

Byrne, Brendan, SJ. 1996. *Romans*. SP. Collegeville, Minn.: Liturgical Press. Its "Notes" provide much important information about relevant ancient texts; its "Interpretation" section discusses the theological content with an eye on Paul's rhetoric.

Cranfield, C. E. B. 1975, 1979. *The Epistle to the Romans*. ICC. 2 vols. Edinburgh: T. & T. Clark. A classic reference work providing an exhaustive discussion of grammatical and philological aspects of the Greek text and taking account of ancient as well as modern interpretations.

Dunn, James D. G. 1988. *Romans*. WBC. 2 vols. Dallas: Word Books. An exhaustive commentary based on the Greek text; it separates technical matters ("Comment") from the "Explanation," which emphasizes positively the Jewish heritage in Paul's thought; includes extensive bibliographies.

Fitzmyer, Joseph A., SJ. 1993. *Romans*. AB. New York: Doubleday. An excellent resource for philological details, especially those pertaining to the Dead Sea Scrolls; includes a summary of the theology in Romans as well as full bibliographies.

Käsemann, Ernst. 1980. *Commentary on Romans,* translated and edited by Geoffrey W. Bromiley. Grand Rapids: Eerdmans. A landmark interpretation by the most significant interpreter of Paul since Bultmann. Theologically provocative, it repays careful study, though the extensive bibliographical references in parentheses make reading difficult.

Moo, Douglas. 1996. *The Epistle to the Romans*. NICNT. Grand Rapids: Eerdmans. A thorough commentary providing full discussions of alternative interpretations as well as philological matters; more readable than Cranfield and more concise than Dunn.

Talbert, Charles H. 2002. *Romans*. Smyth and Helwys Bible Commentary. Macon, Ga.: Smyth and Helwys. Engagingly written, inviting format; emphasizes the formal structure of each unit; actually quotes ancient sources,

Greco-Roman as well as early Jewish; relates Paul's thought to classic theological issues.

Wright, N. T. 2002. "The Letter to the Romans." NIB. 10:393-770. Nashville: Abingdon. A significant, eloquently stated interpretation that emphasizes only the biblical and early Jewish dimensions of Paul's thought; its "Reflections" comment on the current import of Romans.

OTHER WORKS CITED

Achtemeier, Paul J. 1997. "Unsearchable Judgments and Inscrutable Ways: Reflections on the Discussion of Romans." In *Pauline Theology IV: Looking Back, Pressing On*, edited by E. Elizabeth Johnson and David M. Hay, 3-21. Atlanta: Scholars Press.

Agosto, Efrain. 2003. "Paul and Commendation." In *Paul in the Greco-Roman World: A Handbook*, edited by J. Paul Sampley, 101-33. Harrisburg/London/New York: Trinity Press International.

Alexander, Loveday C. A. 1992. "Rome, Early Christian Attitudes to." *ABD* 5:835-39.

Allison, Dale C. 1982. "The Pauline Epistles and the Synoptic Gospels: The Pattern of the Parallels." *NTS* 28:1-32.

Anderson, R. Dean, Jr. 1999. *Ancient Rhetorical Theory and Paul*. Leuven: Peeters. Rev. ed.

Aune, David E. 1991. "Romans as a *Logos Protreptikos*." In *The Romans Debate*, edited by Karl P. Donfried, revised and expanded ed. 1991, 278-96. Peabody, Mass.: Hendrickson.

Badenas, Robert. 1985. *Christ the End of the Law: Romans 10.4 in Pauline Perspective*. JSNTSup 10. Sheffield: JSOT Press.

Balch, David L., ed. 2000. *Homosexuality, Science, and the "Plain Sense" of Scripture*. Grand Rapids: Eerdmans.

Barrett, C. K. 1957. *A Commentary on the Epistle to the Romans*. New York: Harper & Bros.

———. 1994. *Paul: An Interpretation of His Thought*. Louisville: Westminster/John Knox.

Bassler, Jouette M. 1982. *Divine Impartiality: Paul and a Theological Axiom*. SBLDS 59. Chico, Calif.: Scholars Press.

———. 1996. *1 Timothy, 2 Timothy, Titus*. ANTC. Nashville: Abingdon.

Bayes, Jonathan F. 2000. *The Weakness of the Law: God's Law and the Christian in New Testament Perspective*. Carlisle, UK: Paternoster Press.

Betz, Hans Dieter. 1991. "Christianity as Religion: Paul's Attempt at Definition in Romans." *JR* 17:315-44.

———. 1995. "Transferring a Ritual: Paul's Interpretation of Baptism in Romans 6." In *Paul in His Hellenistic Context*, edited by Troels Engberg-Pedersen, 84-118. Minneapolis: Fortress.

Black, C. Clifton. 1984. "Pauline Perspectives on Death in Romans 5–8." *JBL* 103:413-33.

Black, Matthew. 1993. *Romans*. NCB. London: Marshall, Morgan and Scott.

Blumenfeld, Bruno. 2001. *The Political Paul: Justice, Democracy and Kingship in a Hellenistic Framework*. JSNTSup 210. Sheffield: Sheffield Academic Press.

Boers, Hendrikus. 1994. *The Justification of the Gentiles: Paul's Letters to the Galatians and Romans*. Peabody, Mass.: Hendrickson.

Borg, Marcus. 1973. "A New Context for Romans xiii." *NTS* 19:205-18.

Boring, M. Eugene, Klaus Berger, and Carsten Colpe, eds. 1995. *Hellenistic Commentary to the New Testament*. Nashville: Abingdon.

Bornkamm, Günther. 1963. "The Letter to the Romans as Paul's Last Will and Testament." In *The Romans Debate*, edited by Karl P. Donfried, revised and expanded ed. 1991, 16-28. Peabody, Mass.: Hendrickson.

Brooten, Bernadette J. 1996. *Love Between Women: Early Christian Responses to Female Homoeroticism*. Chicago: University of Chicago Press.

Byrne, Brendan, SJ. 2000. "The Problem of *Nomos* and the Relation with Judaism in Romans." *CBQ* 62:294-309.

Campbell, Douglas A. 1992. *The Rhetoric of Righteousness in Romans 3:21-26*. JSNTSup 65. Sheffield: JSOT Press.

———. 1994. "Romans 1:17—A *Crux Interpretum* for the *Pistis Christou* Debate." *JBL* 113:265-85.

Campbell, William S. 2000. "Divergent Images of Paul and His Mission." In *Reading Israel in Romans: Legitimacy and Plausibility of Divergent Interpretations,* edited by Cristina Grenholm and Daniel Patte, 174-86. Harrisburg: Trinity Press International.

Carr, Wesley. 1981. *Angels and Principalities: The Background, Meaning and Development of the Pauline Phrase* hai archai kai exousiai. SNTSMS 42. Cambridge: Cambridge University Press.

Charlesworth, James H., ed. 1985. *The Old Testament Pseudepigrapha*. 2 vols. Garden City: Doubleday.

Das, A. Andrew. 2001. *Paul, the Law and the Covenant*. Peabody, Mass.: Hendrickson.

Davis, Stephan K. 2002. *The Antithesis of the Ages: Paul's Reconfiguration of Torah*. CBQMS 33. Washington, D.C.: The Catholic Biblical Association of America.

Dihle, Albrecht. 1982. *The Theory of Will in Classical Antiquity*. Berkeley: University of California Press.

Dodd, C. H. 1932. *The Epistle to the Romans*. MNTC. New York & London: Harper & Bros.

Doeve, J. W. 1953. "Some Notes with Reference to *Ta Logia tou Theou* in Romans III 2." In *Studia Paulina in Honorem Johannis de Zwaan*, edited by J. N. Sevenster and W. C. Van Unnik, 111-23. Haarlem: Bohn.

Donaldson, Terence L. 1997. *Paul and the Gentiles: Remapping the Apostle's Convictional World*. Minneapolis: Fortress.

Donfried, Karl P. 1991. "False Presuppositions in the Study of Romans." In *The Romans Debate*, edited by Karl P. Donfried, revised and expanded ed. 1991, 102-25. Peabody, Mass.: Hendrickson.

————. ed. 1991. *The Romans Debate*, revised and expanded ed. Peabody, Mass.: Hendrickson.

Dunn, James D. G. 1980. *Christology in the Making: A New Testament Inquiry into the Origins of the Doctrine of the Incarnation*. Philadelphia: Westminster.

————. 1997. "Once More: *Pistis Christou*." In *Pauline Theology IV: Looking Back, Pressing On*, edited by E. Elizabeth Johnson and David M. Hay, 61-81. Atlanta: Scholars Press.

Elliott, Neil. 1990. *The Rhetoric of Romans: Argumentative Constraint and Strategy and Paul's Dialogue with Judaism*. JSNTSup 45. Sheffield: JSOT Press.

————. 1994. *Liberating Paul: The Justice of God and the Politics of the Apostle*. Maryknoll, N.Y.: Orbis.

Engberg-Pedersen, Troels, ed. 1995. *Paul in His Hellenistic Context*. Minneapolis: Fortress.

————. 2000. *Paul and the Stoics*. Edinburgh: T. & T. Clark/Louisville: Westminster/John Knox.

Esler, Philip F. 2003. *Conflict and Identity in Romans: The Social Setting of Paul's Letter*. Minneapolis: Fortress.

————. 2004. "Paul and Stoicism: Romans 12 as a Test Case." *NTS* 50:106-24.

Fee, Gordon D. 1994. *God's Empowering Presence: The Holy Spirit in the Letters of Paul*. Peabody, Mass.: Hendrickson.

Fitzgerald, John T. 1992. "Virtue/Vice Lists." *ABD* 6:857-59.

Fitzmyer, Joseph A., SJ. 1993. "The Consecutive Meaning of *eph hō* in Romans 5.12." *NTS* 39:331-39.

Fortna, Robert T., and Beverly R. Gaventa, eds. 1990. *The Conversation Continues: Studies in Paul and John in Honor of J. Louis Martyn*. Nashville: Abingdon.

Fredrickson, David E. 2000. "Natural and Unnatural Use in Romans 1:24-27: Paul and the Philosophical Critique of Eros." In *Homosexuality, Science, and the "Plain Sense" of Scripture*, edited by David L. Balch, 197-222. Grand Rapids: Eerdmans.

Friedländer, Ludwig. 1965. *Roman Life and Manners under the Early Roman Empire*. London: Routledge & Kegan Paul. 4 vols. (Orig. published 1907.)

Furnish, Victor Paul. 1968. *Theology and Ethics in Paul*. Nashville: Abingdon.

————. 1970. "Development in Paul's Thought." *JAAR* 38:289-303.

————. 1990. "Paul the Theologian." In *The Conversation Continues: Studies in Paul and John in Honor of J. Louis Martyn*, edited by Robert T. Fortna and Beverly R. Gaventa, 19-34. Nashville: Abingdon.

———. 1993. "'He Gave Himself [Was Given] Up . . .': Paul's Use of a Christological Assertion." In *The Future of Christology: Essays in Honor of Leander E. Keck*, edited by Abraham J. Malherbe and Wayne A. Meeks, 109-21. Minneapolis: Fortress.

Gagnon, Robert A. J. 1993. "Heart of Wax and a Teaching That Stamps: *TYPOS DIDACHĒS* (Rom 6:17*b*) Once More." *JBL* 112:667-87.

———. 2001. *The Bible and Homosexual Practice: Texts and Hermeneutics.* Nashville: Abingdon.

Gamble, Harry, Jr. 1977. *The Textual History of the Letter to the Romans.* SD 42. Grand Rapids: Eerdmans.

Gaston, Lloyd. 1987. *Paul and the Torah.* Vancouver: University of British Columbia Press.

Gathercole, Simon J. 2002. *Where Is Boasting? Early Jewish Soteriology and Paul's Response in Romans 1–5.* Grand Rapids: Eerdmans.

Gaventa, Beverly Roberts. 2003. *Acts.* ANTC. Nashville: Abingdon.

Georgi, Dieter. 1992. *Remembering the Poor: The History of Paul's Collection for Jerusalem.* Nashville: Abingdon (orig. German ed. 1965).

———. 1997. "God Turned Upside Down." In *Paul and Empire: Religion and Power in Roman Imperial Society,* edited by Richard A. Horsley, 148-57. Harrisburg: Trinity Press International.

Hall, Robert G. 1992. "Circumcision." *ABD* 1:1025-31.

Hanson, Anthony Tyrell. 1974. *Studies in Paul's Technique and Theology.* London: SPCK.

Harris, Murray J. 1992. *Jesus as God. The New Testament Use of* Theos *in Reference to Jesus.* Grand Rapids: Baker Book House.

Hays, Richard B. 1980. "Psalm 143 and the Logic of Romans 3." *JBL* 99:107-15.

———. 1985. "'Have We Found Abraham to Be Our Forefather According to the Flesh?' A Reconsideration of Rom 4.1." *NovT* 27:76-98.

———. 1989a. *Echoes of Scripture in the Letters of Paul.* New Haven/London: Yale University Press.

———. 1989b. "'The Righteous One' as Eschatological Deliverer: A Case Study in Paul's Apocalyptic Hermeneutics." In *Apocalyptic and the New Testament: Essays in Honor of J. Louis Martyn,* edited by Joel Marcus and Marion Soards. JSNTSup 24, 122-36. Sheffield: JSOT Press.

———. 1993. "Christ Prays the Psalms: Paul's Use of an Early Christian Exegetical Convention." In *The Future of Christology: Essays in Honor of Leander E. Keck,* edited by Abraham J. Malherbe and Wayne A. Meeks, 122-36. Minneapolis: Fortress.

———. 2002. "Appendix 2: Pistis and Pauline Christology: What Is at Stake?" In Hays, *The Faith of Jesus Christ: The Narrative Substructure of Galatians 3:1–4:11,* second ed., 272-97. Grand Rapids: Eerdmans.

Hennecke, Edgar, and Wilhelm Schneemelcher. 1992. *New Testament Apocrypha.* 2 vols. Rev. ed. by W. Schneemelcher. Cambridge, UK: James Clarke/Louisville: Westminster/John Knox.

Hooker, Morna D. 1960. "Adam in Romans 1." *NTS* 6:297-306.

Horsley, Richard A., ed. 1997. *Paul and Empire: Religion and Power in Roman Imperial Society.* Harrisburg, Penn.: Trinity Press International.

Jervell, Jacob. 1971. "The Letter to Jerusalem." In *The Romans Debate*, edited by Paul J. Donfried, revised and expanded ed. 1991, 57-64. Peabody, Mass.: Hendrickson.

Jewett, Robert. 1982. "Romans as an Ambassadorial Letter." *Interp* 36:5-20.

———. 1985. "The Redaction and Use of an Early Christian Confession in Romans 1.3-4." In *The Living Text: Essays in Honor of Ernest W. Saunders*, edited by Dennis E. Groh and Robert Jewett, 99-122. Lanham/New York/London: University Press of America.

———. 1991. "Following the Argument of Romans." In *The Romans Debate*, edited by Karl P. Donfried, revised and expanded ed. 1991, 265-77. Peabody, Mass.: Hendrickson.

Johnson, E. Elizabeth. 1989. *The Function of Apocalyptic and Wisdom Traditions in Romans 9–11.* SBLDS 109. Atlanta: Scholars Press.

Johnson, E. Elizabeth, and David M. Hay eds. 1997. *Pauline Theology IV: Looking Back, Pressing On.* Atlanta: Scholars Press.

Johnson, Luke Timothy. 1997. *Reading Romans: A Literary and Theological Commentary.* New York: Crossroad Publishing Co.

Joubert, Stephan. 2000. *Paul as Benefactor: Reciprocity, Strategy and Theological Reflection in Paul's Collection.* WUNT 2.124. Tübingen: Mohr Siebeck.

Kallas, James. 1965. "Romans xiii. 1-7: An Interpolation." *NTS* 11:365-74.

Karris, Robert J. 1991. "Romans 14:1–15:13 and the Occasion of Romans." In *The Romans Debate*, edited by Karl P. Donfried, revised and expanded ed. 1991, 65-84. Peabody, Mass.: Hendrickson.

Keck, Leander E. 1965. "The Poor Among the Saints in the New Testament." *ZNW* 56:100-29.

———. 1966. "The Poor Among the Saints in Qumran and Jewish Christianity." *ZNW* 57:54-78.

———. 1978. "The Function of Rom 3:10-18: Observations and Suggestions." In *God's Christ and His People: Studies in Honor of Nils Alstrup Dahl*, edited by Jacob Jervell and Wayne A. Meeks, 141-57. Oslo: Universitetsforlaget.

———. 1979. "The Post-Pauline Interpretation of Jesus' Death in Rom. 5:6-7." In *Theologia Crucis—Signum Crucis: Festschrift für Erich Dinkler*, edited by Carl Andresen and Günter Klein, 237-48. Tübingen: J. C. B. Mohr (Paul Siebeck).

———. 1980. "The Law and 'The Law of Sin and Death' (Romans 8:1-4): Reflections on the Spirit and Ethics in Paul." In *The Divine Helmsman: Studies on God's Control of Human Events, Presented to Lou H. Silberman*, edited by James Crenshaw and Samuel Sandmel, 41-58. New York: KTAV.

———. 1989. "'Jesus' in Romans." *JBL* 108:443-60.

————. 1990a. "Christology, Soteriology, and the Praise of God." In *The Conversation Continues: Studies in Paul and John in Honor of J. Louis Martyn,* edited by Robert T. Fortna and Beverly R. Gaventa, 85-97. Nashville: Abingdon.

————. 1990b. "Romans 15:4: An Interpolation?" In *Faith and History: Essays in Honor of Paul W. Meyer,* edited by John Carroll, Charles Cosgrove, and E. Elizabeth Johnson, 125-36. Atlanta: Scholars Press.

————. 1993. "Paul as Thinker." *Interp* 47:27-38.

————. 1995. "What Makes Romans Tick?" In *Pauline Theology III: Romans,* edited by David M. Hay and E. Elizabeth Johnson, 3-29. Minneapolis: Fortress.

————. 1999. "The Absent Good: The Significance of Rom 7:18a." In *Text und Geschichte: Dieter Lührmann zum 60. Geburtstag.* Marburger Theologische Studien 50, edited by Stefan Maser and Egbert Schlarb, 66-75. Marburg: N.G. Elwert.

————. 2001. "*Pathos* in Romans?" In *Paul and* Pathos, edited by Thomas H. Olbricht and Jerry L. Sumney, 71-96. Symposium Series 16. Atlanta: Scholars Press.

Kennedy, George A. 2001. "The Genres of Rhetoric." In *Handbook of Classical Rhetoric in the Hellenistic Period 330 B.C.–A.D. 400,* edited by Stanley E. Porter, 43-50. Boston/Leiden: Brill Academic Publishers.

Kim, Johann D. 2000. *God, Israel, and the Gentiles: Rhetoric and Situation in Romans 9–11.* SBLDS 176. Atlanta: Society of Biblical Literature.

Klassen, William. 1963. "Coals of Fire: Sign of Repentance or Revenge?" *NTS* 9:337-50.

Klein, Günter. 1969. "Paul's Purpose in Writing the Epistle to the Romans." In *The Romans Debate,* edited by Karl P. Donfried, revised and expanded ed. 1991, 29-43. Peabody, Mass.: Hendrickson.

Knox, John. 1954. "Romans." In *IB* 9:355-668. New York/Nashville: Abingdon.

Lampe, Peter. 1991. "The Roman Christians of Romans 16." In *The Romans Debate,* edited by Karl P. Donfried, revised and expanded ed. 1991, 216-30. Peabody, Mass.: Hendrickson.

————. 2003a. *From Paul to Valentinus: Christians at Rome in the First Two Centuries.* Minneapolis: Fortress.

————. 2003b. "Paul, Patrons, and Clients." In *Paul in the Greco-Roman World,* edited by Paul J. Sampley, 288-523. Harrisburg/London/New York: Trinity Press International.

Lyall, Francis. 1969. "Roman Law in the Writings of Paul—Adoption." *JBL* 88:458-66.

Malherbe, Abraham J. 1983. *Social Aspects of Early Christianity.* 2d enlarged ed. Philadelphia: Fortress.

————. 1986. *Moral Exhortation. A Greco-Roman Sourcebook.* Philadelphia: Fortress.

———. 1989. "*Mē Genoito* in the Diatribe and Paul." In *Paul and the Popular Philosophers*, edited by Abraham J. Malherbe, 25-32. Minneapolis: Fortress.

Manson, T. W. 1962a. "The Gospel According to St. Matthew." In *Studies in the Gospels and Epistles,* edited by Matthew Black, 68-104. Philadelphia: Westminster.

———. 1962b. "St Paul's Letter to the Romans—and Others." In *The Romans Debate*, edited by Karl P. Donfried, revised and expanded ed. 1991, 3-15. Peabody, Mass.: Hendrickson.

Marcus, Joel. 1986. "The Evil Inclination in the Letters of Paul." *IBS* 8:8-21.

———. 1988. "'Let God Arise and End the Reign of Sin!' A Contribution to the Study of Pauline Parenesis." *Bib* 69:386-95.

———. 1989. "The Circumcised and the Uncircumcised in Rome." *NTS* 35:67-81.

Martyn, J. Louis. 1997a. "Romans as One of the Earliest Interpretations of Galatians." In *Theological Issues in the Letters of Paul*, edited by J. Louis Martyn, 37-46. Nashville: Abingdon.

———. 1997b. *Galatians*. AB. New York: Doubleday.

———. 2003. "*Nomos* Plus Genitive Noun in Paul: The History of God's Law." In *Earliest Christianity and Classical Culture: Comparative Studies in Honor of Abraham J. Malherbe*, edited by John Fitzgerald, Thomas H. Olbricht, and L. Michael White, 575-87. Leiden/Boston: Brill Academic Publishers.

Matera, Frank J. 1996. *New Testament Ethics: The Legacies of Jesus and Paul.* Louisville: Westminster/John Knox.

Meeks, Wayne A. 1983. *The First Urban Christians: The Social World of the Apostle Paul.* New Haven: Yale University Press.

———. 1991. "On Trusting an Unpredictable God: A Hermeneutical Meditation on Romans 9–11." In *Faith and History: Essays in Honor of Paul W. Meyer*, edited by John Carroll, Charles Cosgrove, and E. Elizabeth Johnson, 105-24. Atlanta: Scholars Press.

Meyer, Paul W. 1980. "Romans 10:4 and the End of the Law." In *The Divine Helmsman: Studies on God's Control of Human Events, Presented to Lou H. Silberman*, edited by James Crenshaw and Samuel Sandmel, 59-78. New York: KTAV (in Meyer's collected essays, *The Word in This World*, edited by John T. Carroll, 78-94. Louisville: Westminster/John Knox, 2004).

———. 1990. "The Worm at the Core of the Apple: Exegetical Reflections on Romans 7." In *The Conversation Continues: Studies in Paul and John in Honor of J. Louis Martyn*, edited by Robert T. Fortna and Beverly R. Gaventa, 62-84. Nashville: Abingdon (now in Meyer's collected essays, *The Word in This World*, edited by John T. Carroll, 57-77. Louisville: Westminster/John Knox, 2004).

Minear, Paul S. 1991. *The Obedience of Faith: The Purposes of Paul in the Epistle to the Romans*. SBT 2d Ser. Nr. 19. London: SCM.

Mitchell, Margaret M. 1991. *Paul and the Rhetoric of Reconciliation: An Exegetical Investigation of the Language and Composition of 1 Corinthians.* Louisville: Westminster/John Knox.

Moxnes, Halvor. 1988. "Honor, Shame, and the Outside World in Paul's Letter to the Romans." In *The Social World of Formative Christianity and Judaism: Essays in Tribute to Howard Clark Kee*, edited by Jacob Neusner, Peder Borgen, Ernest S. Frerichs, and Richard Horsley, 207-18. Philadelphia: Fortress.

Munck, Johannes. 1967. *Christ and Israel: An Interpretation of Romans 9–11*. Philadelphia: Fortress.

Nanos, Mark D. 1996. *The Mystery of Romans: The Jewish Context of the Letter*. Minneapolis: Fortress.

Nardoni, Enrique. 1993. "The Concept of Charism in Paul." *CBQ* 55:68-80.

Olbricht, Thomas H. 2001. "Pathos as Proof in Greco-Roman Rhetoric." In *Paul and* Pathos, edited by Thomas H. Olbricht and Jerry L. Sumney, 7-22. Symposium Series. Atlanta: Society of Biblical Literature, 2001.

Packer, J. I. 1999. "The 'Wretched Man' Revisited: Another Look at Romans 7:14-25." In *Romans and the People of God: Essays in Honor of Gordon D. Fee on the Occasion of His 65th Birthday,* edited by Sven K. Soderlund and N. T. Wright, 70-81. Grand Rapids: Eerdmans.

Pallis, Alexander. 1920. *To the Romans: A Commentary*. Liverpool: The Liverpool Booksellers' Co., Ltd.

Park, Eung Chun. 2003. *Either Jew or Gentile: Paul's Unfolding Theology of Inclusivity*. Louisville/London: Westminster/John Knox.

Peerbolte, L. J. Lietaert. 2003. *Paul the Missionary*. CBET 34. Leuven: Peeters.

Peterson, Norman B. 1995. "On the Ending(s) to Paul's Letter to Rome." In *The Future of Early Christianity: Essays in Honor of Helmut Koester*, edited by Birger Pearson, 237-47. Minneapolis: Fortress.

Petit, Paul. 1976. *Pax Romana*. Berkeley: University of California Press (orig. French ed. 1967).

Piper, John. 1983. *The Justification of God: An Exegetical and Theological Study of Romans 9:1-23*. Grand Rapids: Baker Book House.

Porter, Stanley E., ed. 2001. *Handbook of Classical Rhetoric in the Hellenistic Period 300 B.C.–A.D. 400*. Boston/Leiden: Brill Academic Publishers.

Price, S. R. F. 1984. *Rituals of Power: The Roman Imperial Cult in Asia Minor*. Cambridge: Cambridge University Press.

Rhyne, C. Thomas. 1981. *Faith Establishes the Law*. SBLDS 55. Chico, Calif.: Scholars Press.

Richardson, Peter. 1969. *Israel in the Apostolic Church*. SNTSMS 10. Cambridge: Cambridge University Press.

Rowe, Galen O. 2001. *"Syle."* In *Handbook of Classical Rhetoric in the Hellenistic Period 330 B.C.–A.D. 400,* edited by Stanley E. Porter, 121-58. Boston/Leiden: Brill Academic Publishers.

Sampley, J. Paul. 1995. "The Weak and the Strong: Paul's Careful and Crafty Rhetorical Strategy in Romans 14:1–15:13." In *The Social World of the First Christians: Essays in Honor of Wayne A. Meeks*, edited by L. Michael White and O. Larry Yarbrough, 40-52. Minneapolis: Fortress.

————., ed. 2003. *Paul in the Greco-Roman World: A Handbook*. Harrisburg/London/New York: Trinity Press International.

Sanday, William, and Arthur C. Headlam. 1895. *The Epistle to the Romans*. ICC. Edinburgh: T. & T. Clark.

Sanders, E. P. 1983. *Paul, the Law, and the Jewish People*. Philadelphia: Fortress.

Sandmel, Samuel. 1956. *Philo's Place in Judaism: A Study of Conceptions of Abraham in Jewish Literature*. Cincinnati: Hebrew Union College Press.

Schoedel, William R. 2000. "Same-Sex Eros: Paul and the Greco-Roman Tradition." In *Homosexuality, Science and the "Plain Sense" of Scripture*, edited by David L. Balch, 43-72. Grand Rapids: Eerdmans.

Scroggs, Robin. 1966. *The Last Adam: A Study in Pauline Anthropology*. Philadelphia: Fortress.

————. 1976. "Paul as Rhetorician: Two Homilies in Romans 9–11." In *Jews, Greeks and Christians: Religious Cultures in Late Antiquity: Essays in Honor of William David Davies*, edited by Robert Hamerton-Kelly and Robin Scroggs, 271-98. Leiden: Brill.

————. 1983. *The New Testament and Homosexuality: Contextual Background for Contemporary Debate*. Philadelphia: Fortress.

Sherwin-White, A. N. 1978. *Roman Society and Roman Law in the New Testament*. Grand Rapids: Baker Book House. (Orig. published in 1963 by Oxford University Press.)

Stendahl, Krister. 1976. *Paul Among Jews and Gentiles*. Philadelphia: Fortress.

Stowers, Stanley Kent. 1994. *A Rereading of Romans: Justice, Jews, and Gentiles*. New Haven and London: Yale University Press.

————. 2003. "Paul and Self-Mastery." In *Paul in the Greco-Roman World: A Handbook*, edited by J. Paul Sampley, 524-50. Harrisburg/London/New York: Trinity Press International.

Suggs, M. Jack. 1967. "'The Word Is Near You': Romans 10:6-10 within the Purpose of the Letter." In *Christian History and Interpretation: Studies Presented to John Knox*, edited by William R. Farmer, C. F. D. Moule, and Richard R. Niebuhr, 289-312. Cambridge: Cambridge University Press.

Thielman, Frank. 1994. *Paul and the Law: A Contextual Approach*. Downers Grove, Ill.: InterVarsity Press.

Thompson, Michael. 1991. *Clothed with Christ: The Example and Teaching of Jesus in Romans 12:1–15:13*. JSNTSup 59. Sheffield: Sheffield Academic Press.

Thurén, Lauri. 2000. *Derhetorizing Paul: A Dynamic Perspective on Pauline Theology and the Law*. Harrisburg: Trinity Press International.

Towner, Philip H. 1999. "Romans 13:1-7 and Paul's Missiological Imperative: A Call to Political Quietism or Transformation?" In *Romans and the People of God: Essays in Honor of Gordon D. Fee on the Occasion of His 65th Birthday*, edited by Sven K. Soderlund and N. T. Wright, 149-69. Grand Rapids: Eerdmans.

Vermes, Geza. 1991. *The Dead Sea Scrolls in English*. Revised extended fourth ed. London: Penguin.

Via, Dan O., Jr. 1990. *Self-Deception and Wholeness in Paul and Matthew.* Minneapolis: Fortress.

Wagner, J. Ross. 1997. "The Christ, Servant of Jew and Gentile: A Fresh Approach to Romans 15:8-9." *JBL* 116:473-85.

———. 2002. *Heralds of the Good News: Isaiah and Paul in Concert in the Letter to the Romans.* Boston/Leiden: Brill Academic Publishers.

Walker, William O., Jr. 2001. *Interpolations in the Pauline Letters.* JSNTSup 213. Sheffield: Sheffield Academic Press.

Watson, Francis. 1986. "The Two Roman Congregations: Romans 14:1–15:13." In *The Romans Debate,* edited by Karl P. Donfried, revised and expanded edition, 1991, 203-15. Peabody, Mass.: Hendrickson.

———. 1997. *Text and Truth: Redefining Biblical Theology.* Grand Rapids: Eerdmans.

Wedderburn, A. J. M. 1973. "The Theological Structure of Romans v. 12." *NTS* 19:339-54.

———. 1988. *The Reasons for Romans.* Edinburgh: T. & T. Clark.

Wengst, Klaus. 1987. *Pax Romana and the Peace of Jesus Christ.* Philadelphia: Fortress.

Wenham, David. 1995. *Paul: Follower of Jesus or Founder of Christianity?* Grand Rapids: Eerdmans.

Westerholm, Stephen. 2001. "Paul and the Law in Romans 9–11." In *Paul and the Mosaic Law,* edited by James D. G. Dunn, 215-38. Grand Rapids: Eerdmans.

Wiefel, Wolfgang. 1970. "The Jewish Community in Ancient Rome and the Origins of Roman Christianity." In *The Romans Debate,* edited by Karl P. Donfried, revised and expanded ed., 1991, 85-101. Peabody, Mass.: Hendrickson.

Williams, Sam K. 1975. *Jesus' Death as Saving Event: The Background and Origin of a Concept.* HDR 2. Missoula, Mont.: Scholars Press.

———. 1980. "The 'Righteousness of God' in Romans." *JBL* 99:241-90.

Winter, Bruce W. 1994. *Seek the Welfare of the City: Christians as Benefactors and Citizens.* Grand Rapids: Eerdmans.

Wright, N. T. 1991. *The Climax of the Covenant: Christ and the Law in Pauline Theology.* Edinburgh: T. & T. Clark.

———. 1995. "Romans and the Theology of Paul." In *Pauline Theology III: Romans,* edited by David M. Hay and E. Elizabeth Johnson, 30-67. Minneapolis: Fortress.

———. 2003. *The Resurrection of the Son of God.* Minneapolis: Fortress.

Wuellner, Wilhelm. 1976. "Paul's Rhetoric of Argumentation in Romans: An Alternative to the Donfried–Karris Debate over Romans." In *The Romans Debate,* edited by Karl P. Donfried, revised and expanded ed. 1991, 128-46. Peabody, Mass.: Hendrickson.

Yoder, John Howard. 1972. *The Politics of Jesus.* Grand Rapids: Eerdmans.

Ziesler, John. 1989. *Paul's Letter to the Romans.* TPINTC. London: SCM/Philadelphia: Trinity Press International.

INDEX